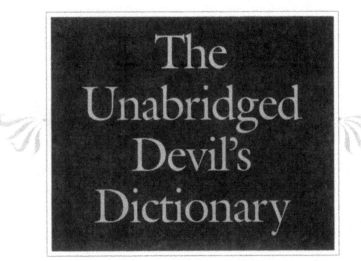

The
Unabridged
Devil's
Dictionary

AMBROSE BIERCE

EDITED BY DAVID E. SCHULTZ & S. T. JOSHI

The Unabridged Devil's Dictionary

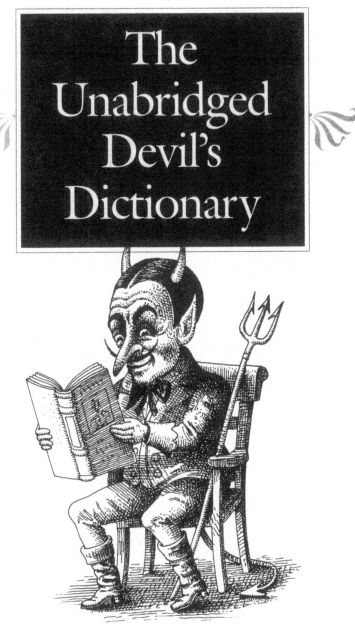

The University of Georgia Press   Athens & London

University of Georgia Press paperback edition, 2002
© 2000 by the University of Georgia Press
Athens, Georgia 30602
All rights reserved
Illustration © Ed Lindlof
Set in Carter & Cone Galliard by G&S Typesetters

Printed Digitally

The Library of Congress has cataloged the hardcover edition
of this book as follows:
Library of Congress Cataloging-in-Publication Data
Bierce, Ambrose, 1842–1914?
The unabridged devil's dictionary / by Ambrose Bierce ;
edited by David E. Schultz and S. T. Joshi.
p.   cm.
Rev. ed. of: Devil's dictionary.
Includes bibliographical references and index.
ISBN 0-8203-2196-6 (alk. paper)
1. English language—Dictionaries—Humor. 2. English
language—Semantics—Humor. 3. Vocabulary—Humor.
I. Schultz, David E., 1952– II. Joshi, S. T., 1958– III. Bierce,
Ambrose, 1842–1914? Devil's dictionary. IV. Title.
PS1097 .D43 2000b
423'.02'07—dc21   99-087396

Paperback ISBN-13: 978-0-8203-2401-2
ISBN-10: 0-8203-2401-9

British Library Cataloging-in-Publication Data available

2017 hardcover reissue ISBN-13:978-0-8203-5278-7

CONTENTS

ACKNOWLEDGMENTS

We conducted most of our research at the Bancroft Library, University of California, Berkeley; Beinecke Rare Book and Manuscript Library, Yale University; Huntington Library and Art Gallery; Los Angeles Public Library; New York Public Library; New York University Library; Princeton University Library; San Francisco Public Library; and O. Meredith Wilson Library, University of Minnesota, Minneapolis. We are grateful to librarians at the Milwaukee (Wisconsin) Public Library; Arizona State University (Tempe); St. Cloud (Minnesota) State University; and New York Public Library for their assistance. Leslie Crabtree and Alan Gullette assisted in obtaining some of the material used in preparing this volume. John D. Beatty, Lawrence I. Berkove, Jonathan Johnson, and Gary Pokorny provided information for some of the annotations.

We are grateful to the Bancroft Library, University of California, Berkeley, for permission to print extracts from "From which to select and prepare additions to 'The Devil's Dictionary' if needed"; and to the Huntington Library and Art Gallery, San Marino, California, for permission to quote extracts from the typesetting copy of *The Devil's Dictionary*.

INTRODUCTION

Any writer of worth, no matter how large or varied his or her literary corpus, typically has a single work that encapsulates precisely his or her worldview and major themes or concerns. That piece may or may not be the writer's very best performance, but it is the one by which his or her essential thought can be most readily identified. Ambrose Bierce's "What I Saw of Shiloh" and "An Occurrence at Owl Creek Bridge" may be his greatest works, but *The Devil's Dictionary* is quintessential Bierce. In fact, his life and career can be summarized in a single sentence:

> Cynic, *n.* A blackguard whose faulty vision sees things as they are, not as they ought to be.

There can be no mistaking that this definition, lodged between "Curse" and "Damn" in the first edition of his celebrated dictionary (nestled somewhat innocuously herein between "Custard" and "Dad"), is Bierce's manifesto; that he defiantly and proudly equates the "blackguard" with himself; and that it is not his vision that is "faulty" but everyone else's. The coda to the definition— "Hence the custom among the Scythians of plucking out a cynic's eyes to improve his vision" —is the purest distillation of his vocation: to sing out the truth, loudly and unflinchingly, no matter the cost. The removal of one's organs of sight merely thwarts one's ability to observe firsthand the misdeeds of one's fellow human beings, who continue to commit the misdeeds. Bierce's mission was to eradicate the misdeeds.

Bierce was not one to write directly of personal matters in his work. In his later years he penned a few autobiographical sketches, mostly about his Civil War days and other select colorful moments, but he wrote no sustained account of his life, which he considered irrelevant to the evaluation of his work. His entire journalistic corpus can be read as a kind of autobiography—not a detailed chronological record of the primary events of his life, for his life was largely dedicated to the solitary work of writing, but instead a record of the life of the mind. Even such terse, unexplicated statements as dictionary definitions speak volumes about the private dimension of Bierce's life.

So wherefore *The Devil's Dictionary?* Its author, ostensibly Ambrose Bierce (1842–1914?), said nothing in private correspondence or in print about his purpose or intent in writing it. It was initially published not as a complete (albeit mock) reference book from which bits were occasionally extracted but as a work in progress in irregular installments published in various magazines and newspapers over a period of thirty years. Bierce's "Devil's Dictionary" made its unheralded debut in 1881 along with "Prattle," his weekly column of miscellaneous commentary, as his first contributions to the San Francisco weekly, the *Wasp.* In those days Bierce's work was published mostly unsigned or pseudonymously, but readers recognized the distinctive work of the former "Town Crier" of the *San Francisco News Letter and California Advertiser* and the "Prattler" of the *Argonaut,* so that a byline would have been little more than a formality.

The Devil's Dictionary may be said ostensibly to be Bierce's work, because one installment declared it instead to be "one of the most useful works that its author, Dr. John Satan, has ever produced."[1] Could anyone but Satan himself be the author of a "devil's dictionary"? Possibly. Fundamentalists and literalists believe God to be the author of the Bible. But just as biblical tradition holds that God did not literally put pen to paper to reveal his thought, instead inspiring certain writers to undertake that task, we find that the "writer who evolves this [devil's] dictionary [is inspired] from an understanding illuminated from Below . . . by the Personage whose title it bears."[2]

The persona Bierce had affected in print since his days as the Town Crier (1868–72)—probably in vehement rebellion against his fundamentalist upbringing—was that of a close partner of Satan, if not Satan himself.[3] For two thirds of his career, Bierce tirelessly affected the persona of a demonic journalist.[4] His first book, the pseudonymously published *The Fiend's Delight* (1873), named for one of Satan's minions, contains a preface that four decades later could have applied to *The Devil's Dictionary:*

The atrocities constituting this "cold collation" of diabolisms are taken mainly from various Californian journals. They are cast in the American language, and liberally enriched with unintelligibility. . . . In the pursuit of my design I think I have killed a good many people in one way and another; but the reader will please to observe that they are not people worth the trouble of leaving alive. Besides, I had the interests of my collaborator to consult. In writing, as in compiling, I have been ably assisted by my scholarly friend Mr. Satan; and to this worthy gentleman must be attributed most of the views herein set forth. While the plan of the work is partly my own, its spirit is wholly his; and this illustrates the ascendancy of the creative over the merely imitative mind. *Palmam qui meruit ferat* — I shall be content with the profit.[5]

The Devil's Dictionary, regardless of whether Satan composed or inspired it, mockingly celebrates humanity's proclivity for willfully bending and distorting language to camouflage less than admirable behavior. The lexicographer professes to have compiled a "compendium of everything that is known up to date of its completion," just as any lexicographer might.[6] But whereas we might expect a dictionary to be a useful reference book that enlightens upon each consultation or an authority by which to interpret the meanings of unknown or unfamiliar words, we are warned that this "devil's dictionary" is likely to produce only gloom.[7] Even the staunchest optimist would be unable to disagree with this assessment, for *The Devil's Dictionary* is an unrelenting catalog of the moral failings of human beings. It abounds with examples of sin and immorality, egomania, hypocrisy, gross stupidity not only of individuals but also of the human race (at least the American species), fraudulence, intolerance, euphemism, phony gentility, hairsplitting about trivial religious matters, outmoded and useless habits and rites, death and funerary practices, the desire for immortality, deception (often of self), and, perhaps most sadly of all, selfishness. Could such a compendium produce anything but gloom in the reader?

H. P. Lovecraft, who had an uncanny ability to synopsize entire literary careers in a few sentences, remarked insightfully of *The Devil's Dictionary*, "That sort of thing wears thin — for when one's cynicism becomes perfect and absolute, there is no longer anything amusing in the stupidity and hypocrisy of the herd. It is all to be expected — what else *could* human nature produce? — so irony annuls itself by means of its own victories! Once utterly disillusioned, we turn to the realistic and unhumorous study of the scene in an objectively scientific light, or else weave new and conscious illusions in the spirit of phantasy."[8] True as this statement may be (some of Bierce is, indeed, best taken in small doses), it oversimplifies, as must all such capsule decrees. Bierce did not seek merely to be ironic. As devil's advocate, his mission was to expose rogues, hypocrites, and fools.

On a superficial level, both Satan and Bierce are opponents of good, but there is one key difference. Bierce was no Boy Scout, but he upheld goodness; what he opposed was the smug, phony brand of goodness espoused by pious hypocrites. When Bierce detected hypocrisy, villainy, and stupidity, he spared no effort to expose and eradicate them and as such may have done more to promote genuinely right behavior than all the pious clerics in California. It was not a matter he approached lightly. Bierce recognized that the religion or moral code claimed in some form or another by virtually the entire Western world for nineteen hundred years had not much improved human behavior. Yet Satan's collaborator was himself an adherent of the teachings of Christ in a highly individualized way. He once confessed:

This is my ultimate and determining test of right— "What, under the circumstances, would Jesus have done?"—the Jesus of the New Testament, not the Jesus of the commentators, theologians, priests and parsons. The test is perhaps not infallible, but it is excellently simple and gives as good practical results as any. I am not a Christian, but so far as I know, the best and truest and sweetest character in literature, next to Buddha, is that of Jesus Christ. He taught nothing new in goodness, for all goodness was ages old before he came; but with an intuition that never failed he applied to life and conduct the entire law of righteousness. He was a moral lightning calculator:[9] to his luminous intelligence the statement of the problem conveyed the solution— he could not hesitate, he seldom erred. That upon his deeds and words was founded a religion which in a debased form persists and even spreads to this day is mere attestation of his marvelous gift: adoration is merely a primitive form of recognition.

It seems a pity that this wonderful man had not a longer life under more complex conditions—conditions more nearly resembling those of the modern world and of the future. One would like to be able to see, through the eyes of his biographers, his genius applied to more and more difficult questions. Yet one can hardly go wrong in inference of his thought and act. In many of the complexities and entanglements of modern affairs it is no easy matter to find an answer off-hand to the question, "What is it right to do?" But put it in another way: "What would Christ have done?" and lo! there is light! Doubt spreads her bat-like wings and is away; the sun of truth springs into the sky, splendoring the path of right and masking that of wrong with a deeper shade.[10]

Compare to this statement his withering definition of "Christian": "One who believes that the New Testament is a divinely inspired book admirably suited to the spiritual needs of his neighbor. One who follows the teachings of Christ in so far as they are not inconsistent with a life of sin";[11] or to the Town Crier's solemnly professed New Year's resolutions for 1871, suitably tempered so as not to place his goals for self-improvement unrealistically beyond reach:

In deference to a time-worn custom, on the first day of the year the *Town Crier* swore to, affixed a revenue stamp upon, and recorded the following document: "I do hereby firmly resolve that during one year from date I will not drink any spirituous, vinous or malt liquors of any kind whatsoever, except in case I may think it would be a good thing to temporarily suspend this pledge. I will not utter a profane word—unless in sport—without having been previously vexed at something. I will make use of no tobacco in any of its forms, unless I think it would be kind of nice. I will steal no more than I have actual use for. I will murder no one that does not offend me, except for his money. I will commit highway robbery upon none but small school children, and then only under the stimulus of present or prospective hunger. I will not bear false witness against my neighbor where nothing is to be made by it. I will be as moral and religious as the law shall compel me to be. I will run away with no man's wife without her full and free consent, and never, no never, so help me heaven! will I take his children along. I won't write any wicked slanders against anybody, unless by refraining I should sacrifice a good joke. I won't whip any cripples, unless they come fooling about me when I am busy; and I will give all my roommates' boots to the poor.[12]

How, then, to change human behavior? Bierce's moral yardstick—doing what Christ would do—informs many of the definitions in his dictionary. Some may feel that Bierce's methods were decidedly un-Christlike, but this is not so. Recall the Christ of the Gospels who tossed the cheating money changers out of the temple (Luke 19:45); who warned, "And why beholdest thou the mote that is in thy brother's eye, but perceivest not the beam that is in thine own eye?" (Luke 6:41); who advised, "And if thine eye offend thee, pluck it out: it is better for thee to enter into the kingdom of God with one eye, than having two eyes to be cast into hell fire" (Mark 9:47). Bierce's method, not entirely unlike Christ's, was not to mince words but to employ them with some exaggeration or hyperbole if necessary. Perhaps only by being utterly outrageous could he demonstrate that the very *opposite* of what was said was to be preferred. For example, Bierce recognized that human behavior is a matter of choice, not circumstance. Yet when he solemnly decrees that the modern religion Theosophy holds that "one life is not long enough for our complete spiritual development; that is, a single lifetime does not suffice for us to become as wise and good as we choose to wish to become," he clearly meant that one lifetime *is* sufficient for any person to become good—if he or she truly desires.[13] Bierce knew well that people are neither fated nor forced to be immoral; they choose to be so, just as others choose not to be. Given more time, even more lifetimes, to change themselves would in all likelihood result in no change at all. Thus, *The Devil's Dictionary* contains definitions of many terms so commonplace as to need no defining—we all know what the words mean, yet when they are held as an enchanted mirror before the human heart, as in the fable Bierce tells at "Looking-glass," we are shocked to find that the reflected image is often not what we *know* we should be seeing. Those content to fool themselves might find Bierce's trenchant definitions unsettling:

Adore, *v.t.* To venerate expectantly.

Close-communion, *n.* The sectarian practice of excluding the Sinners, and several smaller denominations, from the Lord's supper. The supper being commonly a pretty bad one, no great injustice is done.

Forgiveness, *n.* A stratagem to throw an offender off his guard and catch him red-handed in his next offense.

Hospitality, *n.* The virtue which induces us to feed and lodge certain persons who are not in need of food and lodging.

It was not Bierce's intent to imply that these concepts are outmoded or irrelevant, merely that they have become so debased and watered down, so perverted, as to mean the opposite of what they once meant, at least as adduced from his observation of human beings. Adoration stripped of the "expectant" component would become real, true adoration. Hospitality extended to persons other than one's relatives or cronies would be real, true hospitality. It is not Bierce's definitions that are perverted, as is often charged, but the human tendency not only to turn one's head from what was once unacceptable but then to make it acceptable by labeling it with an agreeable term—to define "black" as "white."

The Devil's Dictionary is a mocking and damning assessment of the condition of the human heart. An exhaustive catalog could be prepared of the vocabulary of sin employed in *The Devil's Dictionary,* but let us be content to point out but a few of numerous references to the seven deadly sins:[14]

For Wrath, see	Wrath
Avarice	Mammon, Tenacity
Sloth	Laziness
Pride	Great, Mausoleum, Worship
Lust	Dance, Friar
Envy	Congratulation, Covet, Envy, Illustrious
Gluttony	Abdomen, Christmas, Club, Corned, Feast, Glutton, Soul, Tope

Numerous transgressions subordinate to these most deadly sins are represented as well; in fact, this unique dictionary explores at considerable length the underworld of sin and impenitence.

And yet, as with all great satire, *The Devil's Dictionary* is much more than a witty condemnation of iniquity. One could call it, not unreasonably, a manual for good behavior.[15] Just as C. S. Lewis's *Screwtape Letters* document the devil Screwtape's sage advice to his nephew Wormwood, a neophyte, on how to succeed at deviltry, his very words can also urge the receptive human reader to the exact opposite (and the author's desired) behavior.

Bierce's affinity for cynical lexicography became apparent long before the first installment of "The Devil's Dictionary" appeared in the *Wasp*. One of his very earliest published pieces, the essay "Concerning Tickets," contains a satiric definition of the term "San Francisco lady" (hardly the sort of expression that would be found in a real dictionary), attributed to "Some astute philosopher with a *penchant* for definition."[16] This fledgling bit of lexicography was a bit awkward, but it showed that Bierce could capably turn a phrase. Before long he was writing for a weekly paper, the *San Francisco News Letter and California Advertiser*. It was in the *News Letter* that Bierce explored and then began to hone virtually all his chief media for self-expression: fictional sketches, aphorisms, poems, fables, tall tales, fictitious letters, futuristic commentaries, essays, imaginary dialogues, and, of course, mock dictionary definitions. Perhaps Bierce could not manage longer forms, or perhaps he did not find them conducive to his satiric method. Either way, he excelled at satire in miniature, which was well suited to a journalist who needed steadily to produce great quantities of varied and engaging material.

Bierce took over the *News Letter*'s famous "Town Crier" column in December 1868, and it served as his chief sounding board for the duration of his tenure. The column comprised short, tart, and unflinchingly barbed commentary on doings in San Francisco and on notices culled from papers published around the country. Bierce included only a few definitions in "The Town Crier," tidbits lodged deeply within columns running from 2,500 to nearly 3,000 words. On one occasion, he published a separate item called "Webster Revised" that consisted of four satirical definitions.[17] This unsigned piece is indisputably his, for several of the jokes in it were represented later in *The Devil's Dictionary*. Another piece, " 'News Letter' Aphorisms—By Our Special Philosopher," contained the first of several definitions formed as theoretical situations in which the characters are not expressed by name but merely by letters.[18]

The notion of an entire dictionary of such definitions is broached in an early "Town Crier," where Bierce wrote:

> We have frequent occasion to rebuke our neighbors of the press for their weak attempts to imitate our style, but until yesterday it never entered our head that we should have to take an eminently respectable lexicographer to task for the same amiable weakness. But there is no betting on the undeviating hard sense of anybody, and the lexicographic mind is a merely human affair and will occasionally cut its caper. Observe this, from Webster's latest and biggest: "VICEREGENT, *n*. [L. *vicem regens*, acting in the place of another.] A lieutenant; a vicar; an officer who is deputed by a superior or by proper authority to exercise the powers of another. Kings are sometimes called God's viceregents. *It is to be wished they would always deserve the appellation*."[19] Could

any one but an American humorist ever have conceived the idea of a *Comic Dictionary?*[20] It is mournful to think what a fame Noah Webster might have acquired had his genius not been diverted into a philological channel.[21]

Bierce then largely ignored the dictionary definition as a satiric medium until he returned from his period of journeyman's work in England from 1872 to 1875.

Bierce's last work published in London before he returned to the United States appeared in September 1875. Nothing by him is known to have been published in the United States following his return until the appearance of two items in the *News Letter* for 11 December 1875: a letter attributed to one "Theophilus Smallbeer" and a piece entitled "The Demon's Dictionary." The latter item consisted of forty-eight brief definitions, satiric in nature, beginning with the letter A—"The first letter in every properly constructed alphabet"—and ending with "Accoucheur." Bierce's biographer Carey McWilliams declared that "The Demon's Dictionary" "ran for only a few issues," but no other appearances have been found, and it is unlikely that more than one installment appeared.[22] Although "The Demon's Dictionary" is unsigned and although Bierce included none of its definitions in *The Devil's Dictionary,* it can be ascribed to Bierce based on a fair amount of internal evidence.[23] The most obvious is the definition of "Abatis," which is virtually identical to Bierce's definition of the term in his pseudonymous book, *Cobwebs from an Empty Skull* (1874). However, many other examples show clearly that the similarities between terms in "The Demon's Dictionary" and later definitions of the same words known to be by Bierce are not merely coincidental. Bierce used satiric definitions only sporadically during his tenure as the Prattler at the *Argonaut,* and it was not until 1881, following an unsuccessful stint as general agent for the Black Hills Placer Mining Company in the Dakota Territory, that he unleashed one of his longest running features in his very first appearance in the *Wasp.*

There has been considerable confusion about the actual inception of "The Devil's Dictionary." Biographer Carey McWilliams wrote: "It was in January of that year [1881] that it [the *Wasp*] began to publish the first of his work, part of 'The Devil's Dictionary.' . . . With the first issue of the *Wasp,* he began the publication of this dictionary of wit, beginning with the letter 'P,' and continued down the alphabet until March 5th, 1881, when he started the dictionary all over again, apparently with the thought in mind of rewriting and enlarging the original plan."[24] Ernest J. Hopkins repeats this in his *Enlarged Devil's Dictionary* (1967). The unsigned column to which McWilliams and Hopkins refer, dated 1 January 1881 (two months before Bierce's tenure with the *Wasp* began), is "Wasp's Improved Webster: In Ten-Cent Doses." They claim that Bierce somewhat illogically launched his column, beginning with the letter P—more specifically, with the word "Pluck." It is then supposed that "Wasp's Improved Webster" lasted only six installments through 5 February, ending with the word "Rye,"[25] and that after a month's hiatus, Bierce resumed publishing dictionary definitions beginning on 5 March, now calling the column "The Devil's Dictionary" and restarting at a logical beginning, with words beginning with the letter A.

The simple fact is that "Wasp's Improved Webster" had been running in the *Wasp* since 7 August 1880 (issue no. 210). The appearance of the P through R items in early 1881 was merely part of the ongoing sequence. In a letter to S. O. Howes, an admirer to whom Bierce lent his files of his published work, Bierce wrote: "By the way, please give me the date at which *I* began it ["The Devil's Dictionary"] in the Wasp—at A. Salmi Morse had something like it going when I took the editorship."[26] Thus, Bierce did not inexplicably start his column midway through the letter P, stop, and recommence at A. The work was not his. Bierce resumed exactly where he left off five years before, for the first word he defined under "The Devil's Dictionary" was "Accuracy," a logical successor to "Accoucheur" from "The Demon's Dictionary."

"The Devil's Dictionary" began as many new projects do, with energy and enthusiasm. The column ran for twelve weeks from 5 March until 21 May, the single longest unbroken stretch in its six-year history. The inaugural column contained twenty-four definitions, more than any future installment. As Bierce's duties at the *Wasp* increased, he found himself with less time to devote to "The Devil's Dictionary,"[27] but the column continued, if sporadically, until Bierce left the paper in 1886. Between 1882 and 1884, Bierce published only twenty-one "Devil's Dictionary" columns, fewer than the twenty-five published in all of 1881. There were breaks ranging from fifteen weeks to as long as thirty-two weeks between columns. In one period of fifty-seven weeks, Bierce published only three installments. The column regained some of its initial vitality in 1885, when twenty-seven installments appeared, usually with only one- to three-week separations. But in 1886 the column appeared only six times, and before year's end Bierce had resigned from the *Wasp*, the final definition published being "Lickspittle."

Like all Bierce's other writings, the definitions in "The Devil's Dictionary" encompass a mélange of rhetorical styles, all clearly in the voice of their author. Some are written, albeit tongue-in-cheek, in a serious lexicographical style. Some are homiletic, using the rhetorical language of preachers. Some are written in dialect, some in the owlish manner of scholars and scientists. Others unabashedly stoop to the level of corny puns or one-liners. And some contain pedantic, even schoolmarmish instruction against the sins of grammatical abuse. Most of the definitions are general enough to be timeless, but many are aimed at the local events and personages of Bierce's day. He relentlessly lampooned local politicians, clerics, poetasters, and poseurs. When Bierce eventually compiled a book of his definitions, he simply changed the names of the guilty to those who would be recognized by a broader audience.

The work showcases not only Bierce's considerable erudition but also his ability to feign erudition. The definitions contain numerous literary, biblical, and scientific allusions. Many of the illustrative quotations and poems are clever parodies of well-known writers and their work: Pope, Byron, Tennyson, Gray, Longfellow, Lincoln, Jefferson, and Burns, to name only a few. Bierce also fabricated illustrative stories that sound like genuinely researched history that mocked persistent legends, as seen in the definitions for "Fairy," "Ghoul," "Gnome," and "Reliquary."

For the most part, the definitions appeared in continuous alphabetical sequence, despite lapses in time between columns. Definitions sometimes appeared out of sequence; that is, a definition that logically belonged in a certain column might instead appear in the subsequent installment, as if it were inserted as an afterthought. One particularly drastic exception occurred following the extraordinarily long hiatus of thirty-two weeks between 6 October 1883 and 17 May 1884. The definitions published on 17 and 24 May 1884 should have appeared among those in the four columns prior to 6 October 1883, that is, 23 December 1882 and 17 February, 10 March, and 28 April 1883. The situation is further complicated by the fact that Bierce chose to redefine the words "Elysium," "Embalm," "Envy," "Epicure," "Epigram," "Epitaph," "Esteem," "Ethnology," "Eucalyptus," "Euphemism," and "Excommunication." One might assume that the reason for the long lapses in appearances of "The Devil's Dictionary" between 1883 and 1884 was that Bierce had tired of it, or that he felt his definitions had begun to sag, and that after some time away from them he resumed with new vigor, rewriting definitions with which he was dissatisfied. But this scenario is unlikely, for it seems that Bierce ultimately favored the initial versions of the respective definitions, as nearly all of the rewritten terms were passed over when Bierce compiled the book versions of his dictionary.

When Bierce stopped writing for the *Wasp*, he did not remain unemployed for long. His celebrated tenure with William Randolph Hearst's *San Francisco Examiner* began quietly in February 1887 with some unsigned editorials, but on 27 March "Prattle" reappeared, and since Bierce's addition to the *Examiner* was intended to attract readers, it was published with his byline, as was all his feature writing for Hearst. Bierce steadily filled the editorial page with copy. His weekly "Prattle" was supplemented by installments of fables, essays, reminiscences, poems, "Little Johnny" sketches, and unsigned editorials. Elsewhere in the *Examiner* his fiction began to appear regularly. But it was not until 4 September 1887 that his dictionary definitions resumed, albeit briefly, on the Sunday edition's editorial page as "The Cynic's Dictionary," with the all but invisible tagline "B." As with the transition from "The Demon's Dictionary" to "The Devil's Dictionary," Bierce continued where he had stopped previously at the *Wasp*, resuming with the word "Life," as though loyal followers of his work were eagerly awaiting the next installment, despite a change of publishers, a hiatus between appearances, and even a change in the column's title. But it was nearly eight months before Bierce published another installment on 29 April 1888, and then the column was mysteriously discontinued for more than sixteen years.

Bierce never explained why "The Cynic's Dictionary" resumed so fitfully in the *Examiner* nor why it was so unimaginatively renamed. Although Hearst gave Bierce virtually a free rein with all his other work for the *Examiner*, presumably it was Hearst himself or his editors who censored the title "The Devil's Dictionary," as did the publisher of the first book collection of the definitions. As Bierce later acknowledged to George Sterling, "They (the publishers) won't have 'The Devil's Dictionary.' Here in the East the Devil is a sacred personage (the Fourth Person of the Trinity, as an Irishman might say) and his name must not be taken in vain." [28]

By the time Bierce next resumed "The Cynic's Dictionary" in July 1904, his work had been appearing regularly in the *Examiner* and the *New York American*, a paper Hearst had acquired in 1895, when it was the *New York Journal*. His audience now was much larger than San Francisco alone, and so he needed to make his work less parochial. Perhaps for that reason, along with the column's absence for sixteen long years, Bierce sought to reinaugurate his column properly by beginning with the letter A. In the new "Cynic's Dictionary," Bierce eschewed humorous definitions of obscure words as had appeared in the "The Demon's Dictionary," redefined some words that had been treated nearly thirty years previously, and wrote entirely new definitions. But after two consecutive columns of A definitions, Bierce halted briefly, then unaccountably resumed with the word "Ma," the point at which he had ceased in April 1888. The jarring manner in which Bierce resumed publishing his definitions could not have escaped general notice. George Sterling wrote to Bierce, "Please tell me if in the 'Cynic's Dictionary' you 'jumped' from A to M. Otherwise the 'Examiner' is buncoing me." [29] Bierce explained less than helpfully: "Yes, in The Cynic's Dictionary I did 'jump' from A to M. I had previously done the stuff in various papers as far as M, then lost the beginning. So in resuming I re-did that part (quite differently, of course) in order to have the thing complete if I should want to make a book of it. I guess the Examiner isn't running much of it, nor much of anything of mine." [30] Quite simply, he ended with "Accuse," the word that follows the very first word that appeared in the *Wasp*. Bierce wrote a batch of definitions to account for A words up to the word "Accuracy," thereby replacing with rewritten or new definitions those contained in "The Demon's Dictionary," almost as though he needed to reconstruct the opening pages of his dictionary. [31]

The resumption of "The Cynic's Dictionary" in 1904 appears to have been the result of discussion the previous year among Bierce and his protégés about possible publication of his definitions as a book. Bierce wrote to Herman Scheffauer,

"No, I have not enough 'epigrams and aphorisms' for a book—at least not without going through a mess of other stuff—principally my 'Devil's Dictionary', which I want to keep intact in the hope that some publisher of the future may happen to take a fancy to it. It is a trifle less unwitty than anything else I've written, and more lively than a whole book of *mere* epigrams can be—even a small book."[32] Later he commented,

> I'll bet a pretty penny that not a publisher on this side of the continent will look at the stuff unless I will give it another title. It is ready for compilation, but not compiled. It will consist of definitions (somewhat original) of such words that struck my fancy, regularly arranged as in a real dictionary. Some of the definitions stand alone, some are followed by a few lines of illustration or comment, some run to the length of small essays. Many are in verse or partly in verse—a bit cynical.
>
> I shall compile it next winter and that, doubtless, will be the end o' it. My intention, by the way, is a secret known (now) to you only. Keep it, please.[33]

Bierce's admonition to Scheffauer went unheeded, for in October Sterling wrote to Bierce, "If you'll get your 'Devil's Dictionary' ready I'll try to get it published by next Spring, if you care to have me do so. That title alone would sell anything. Sheff. [*sic*] mentioned it to me in ignorance of your wish to keep it a secret; but I'll not let it go farther."[34] Sterling and Scheffauer had, earlier in 1903, arranged for the publication of Bierce's *Shapes of Clay* through W. E. Wood of San Francisco. Bierce was embarrassed that they had done so, for they published the book at their own expense. He did not wish to see the situation repeated.

Although Bierce had stated that he had abundant material on hand to prepare a book of definitions, he instead resumed publishing, and presumably writing, definitions for "The Cynic's Dictionary." Between July 1904 and January 1905 he published twenty-five installments, running well through the letter P. The reason for renewed activity is not clear, but perhaps it lay in Bierce's growing dissatisfaction with Hearst's editors. To Robert Mackay, editor of the magazine *Success,* Bierce wrote, "Just now I'm making one of my periodical attempts to release my leg from the 'Oregon boot' of yellow journalism. If successful I shall apply a match to every river in the country and bask in the light and heat of a restored public attention."[35] New installments of his dictionary would certainly restore the attention he desired, for as Bierce pointed out, his material was popular (and controversial) enough that it was now being plagiarized and imitated. After the first two weeks, the appearances were not limited to only one per week, as they had been even after he stopped writing for the *Wasp,* and the installments published in San Francisco did not always appear on the same day as or even lag at the same rate behind the appearances in New York. Some columns never appeared in the San Francisco paper. But after January 1905 the column again went into hiatus, now for more than a year. Bierce wrote wistfully to S. O. Howes, "I'm working rather hard these days—at work that is mere pot-boiling; so 'The Cynic's Dictionary,' which you are good enough to care for, has gone out of commission."[36]

Not long thereafter, Bierce wrote to Robert Mackay, "I thank you for your offer to publish 'The Cynic's Dictionary' — or, as it used to be entitled in California, 'The Devil's Dictionary.' There are two objections. First, it is not completed and I cannot now work upon it. (As it is not intended for a comprehensive word-book of the language that is perhaps unimportant—there's plenty for one volume, and another could follow if the first should succeed.) Second, it would not succeed—you would lose money on it. I don't profess to know that; it is what I think."[37] Nevertheless, by 10 November Bierce was writing to Howes that he was "now compiling" *The Cynic's Dictionary* at the request of Doubleday, Page and Company. The nature of the manuscript is not known, but its sources are clear enough. It consists largely of selections from his "Devil's Dictionary" columns from the *Wasp,* as they covered the letters A through L, but it also contains many of the new A definitions of 1904 and the L definitions of 1887 and 1888. Bierce completed his work by mid-January 1906. He did not at that time intend to publish a comprehensive dictionary covering the entire alphabet. He wrote to Howes, "I have all the stuff from 'A' forward . . . though in the manner of publishers they want some alterations made—as if I had not made enough! We may split on that question, or on that of title. I've selected none, finally, and they have suggested an impossible one—'A Few Definitions.' The idea!"[38] The following month he wrote to Howes, "I've supplied Doubleday, Page & Co., with the typescript [*sic*] of 'The Cynic's Dictionary' (the first volume, A–F) and signed a contract for its publication."[39] Ultimately, the book contained definitions through the letter L. By May the book was "a-printing," and Bierce began reading proofs.

Shortly after Bierce submitted the manuscript of his book to Doubleday, "The Cynic's Dictionary" once again resumed publication in the newspapers. Four installments appeared under that title between 22 February and 11 April in the *New York American;* only three of these appeared in the *Examiner.*[40] After another lull, the column resumed from late May at least until mid-July, but now under the title "The Cynic's Word Book" to correspond with the title of the book to be published in October. As Bierce told George Sterling, "I shall have to call it something else, for the publishers tell me there is a 'Cynic's Dictionary' already out. I dare say the author took more than my title—the stuff has been a rich mine for a plagiarist for many a year."[41] The last appearance of Bierce's column ended with the word "Reconciliation."[42] No further installments of Bierce's satiric definitions appeared in the newspapers.

Bierce stated that the reason *The Cynic's Word Book* contained words only through the letter L was that if the book sold well, then a second volume with the balance of the alphabet would be published. But the book did not sell well, as hinted by the brusque statement from a letter to Sterling: "The other half of the 'Devil's Dictionary' is in the fluid state—not even liquid. And so, doubtless, it will remain."[43] Bierce soured on nearly all his current prospective publishing ventures. He could not find publishers for his collection of political satires, *The Fall of the Republic,* which he considered his finest work, or a collection of his Little Johnny sketches. His growing frustration with Hearst's editors caused him more than once to resign, though he was always persuaded to return. Hearst was content to publish Bierce in *Cosmopolitan,* and Bierce attempted to satisfy Hearst by writing for the magazine from 1905 into 1909; but Bierce was unable to deal effectively with the editors and resigned for good in 1909. The only books of Bierce's to be published during this frustrating time were the collection of his journalism, *The Shadow on the Dial,* culled by S. O. Howes from various of Bierce's columns, and the inconsequential *Write It Right.*

In May 1908 Bierce's friend and publisher Walter Neale began to broach the possibility of publishing Bierce's collected works in ten volumes.[44] Bierce was not optimistic about the prospects of such an undertaking, but Neale was willing to take the risk, and by June Bierce had signed a contract. With Bierce's assistance, Neale wrote a thirty-two-page prospectus for the project.[45] The plan initially was to publish two volumes a year. The first six volumes consisted primarily of material that Bierce had previously published or already compiled. The first volume consisted of what Bierce considered to be his finest work—his recollections of his Civil War days and his long political satires—and he wisely chose to publish that material first in the event that the project did not see completion. Subsequent volumes consisted of his two collections of fiction, two volumes of verse, *Fantastic Fables,* and the joint translation with Gustav Adolphe Danziger of *The Monk and the Hangman's Daughter.* The published material was not entirely ready-made, for Bierce extensively revised the organization, content, and text of the books. His selection of *The Devil's Dictionary* as volume 7 bears out his feeling that the book was merely "a trifle less unwitty" than some of his other work.

With *The Devil's Dictionary,* work on the *Collected Works* became more complicated and difficult. For the most part, the book was founded on *The Cynic's Word Book.* Bierce took a copy of that book and marked revisions on the printed pages. His revisions are light, and he did not attempt to restore to their previous state definitions that he had revised to accommodate Doubleday. He excised a few, added some, and moved others to the back half of the manuscript under different headings for balance. Because *The Cynic's Word Book* ended with the letter L, Bierce had to compile the entire remainder of the book. The definitions for the letters L through R derive primarily from his more recent dictionary columns in the *Examiner* (1887–88) and the *American* (1904–06).[46] The thirty-seven pages of the typesetting copy following the revised pages of *The Cynic's Word Book* consist almost entirely of clippings from newspapers, lightly revised. Still, this reached only partly through the letter R, to the word "Reconciliation." The typesetting copy concludes with a seventy-two-page typescript of mostly new, unpublished material. These pages also contain several clippings from Bierce's newspaper work, used to illustrate certain definitions.

It is not known how Bierce had prepared his material for publication in the newspapers, but it appears that he prepared copy somewhat ahead of time, and it was used as necessary to fill space.[47] However, it is unlikely that Bierce had anything prepared beyond the last appearance of "The Cynic's Word Book" in the *American* in 1906, and so he had to compose new definitions for the letters R through Z. There is considerable evidence to show this. In the first place, most of the illustrative verses in the typescript had been previously published in his newspaper columns or separately.[48] Second, many of the late definitions derive from other previously published sources, chiefly from Bierce's editorials from 1903 through 1905. One additional clue to the method in which he prepared *The Devil's Dictionary* is given in an envelope among the Bierce papers at the Bancroft Library that contains fifty clippings labeled "From which to select and prepare additions to 'The Devil's Dictionary' if needed" (see Appendix, "Supplemental Definitions"). These consist of twelve complete definitions from "The Devil's Dictionary" in the *Wasp*, but primarily of extracts of verse or text from Bierce's columns. These latter are not definitions but most likely text to be used to illustrate new definitions. Of the items not from "The Devil's Dictionary," all but nine are labeled as to the definition for which they might be used. The number of items in the envelope originally contained is not known, but it is likely that the envelope yielded some of the definitions added to the book at the proof stage.[49]

Publication of *The Devil's Dictionary* — indeed, the whole of *The Collected Works* — was an arduous undertaking. Bierce continually complained to Neale about the typesetter's work. The published book does contain numerous typographical errors, many of which were never corrected in subsequent editions of the book. A particularly vexing problem for Bierce was getting the word "Hades" to be set correctly in Greek. Despite corrected second proofs, the printed version was still incorrect. The worst defect by far occurred in the printing of the R definitions, which are inexplicably out of order, until one consults the typesetting copy and sees that the clippings for those words are pasted up in exactly the order printed. Despite Bierce's instruction to the typesetter to put all definitions in alphabetical order, regardless of their location in the manuscript, it appears that Bierce and his assistant, Carrie Christiansen, failed to rectify the improper alphabetization of the definitions in the proofs.

The Devil's Dictionary probably achieved even less notice than *The Cynic's Word*

Book. Because *The Collected Works* was sold as a set to subscribers, *The Devil's Dictionary* could not be obtained separately. Reviewers of *The Collected Works* tended wearily to address several books at a time. A brief review of four volumes of *The Collected Works* in the *New York Times* did not even mention that one of the four books under consideration was *The Devil's Dictionary*. In fact, it appears that the reviewer mistakenly thought it a volume of Bierce's "collected epigrams."[50] The reviewer in the *Athenæum* likewise reviewed four volumes at once but devoted considerable space to *The Devil's Dictionary*. Like H. P. Lovecraft, the reviewer noted that "a sameness in the intention tends to tire, especially when it is ill-intention," but this is a bit unfair, as few people read any dictionary cover to cover. The reviewer perceptively observed that "dealing with a wide range of topics as well as a great number of words, it presents a sort of summary index of the author's characteristic views as well as his literary aptitudes and poses. . . . Sometimes irony sophisticated and ponderous is conjoined with fun of a more simple sort. . . . We discover frankness, and the humility of true learning." The reviewer also recognized the antipodal effects that a definition could have on different readers: "Those to whom the term applies ["Jealous" is cited specifically] may find either consolation or rebuke."[51] Bierce seemed underwhelmed when he passed the review along to Walter Neale, writing: "As is my habit in the case of 'The Athenaeum', I submit its final remarks. On the whole, I think that it has treated us pretty decently."[52] Before long, both *The Devil's Dictionary* and its compiler had disappeared from the public eye.

It was not until Albert and Charles Boni reprinted *The Devil's Dictionary* in 1925 and again in 1926, during the first brief Bierce renaissance, that the book began to attract attention. It was the new printings of *The Devil's Dictionary* that caught the eye of not only H. P. Lovecraft's young correspondent but also H. L. Mencken, who wrote that it contains "some of the most gorgeous witticisms in the English language."[53] The Boni brothers brought out two more printings in 1935 and 1936, and many other editions were published by others. In his introduction to the Hill and Wang edition of the dictionary, Carey McWilliams's enthusiastic account of his discovery of Bierce must be typical of the new generation of readers encountering Bierce for the first time in the mid-1920s:

> *The Devil's Dictionary* provides perhaps the best introduction to the man and his work; at least it proved so for me. One day many years ago—I was a freshman in college at the time—I was prowling through the open stacks of the Los Angeles Public Library when I came by chance on the massive Collected Works. Bierce's name meant nothing to me then except that I had seen some references to his writings in Mencken's *Smart Set*. The first volume I pulled down from the shelf was *The Devil's Dictionary*. By the time I found my way to a table, reading all the while, I was "hooked"—nor has time diminished my

enthusiasm for Bierce. Those of Bierce's readers who have "discovered" his writings in much this same fortuitous manner—and I suspect that they constitute a majority—will appreciate that this was quite an experience for me; then as now Bierce is an impressive figure to come upon by chance.[54]

The Devil's Dictionary and its compiler have outlasted and surpassed the cheap, popular imitators of their day and in fact inspired a new host of imitators whose skill sadly does not match their admiration for the master lexicographer. By 1927 H. P. Lovecraft could state authoritatively, as he was inclined to do, "Ambrose Bierce, almost unknown in his own time, has now reached something like general recognition."[55] To be sure, Lovecraft was writing of Bierce's Civil War and weird fiction, but *The Devil's Dictionary* contributes much to that recognition. Many definitions in the dictionary have become standard, and the work is now an American classic. It is hoped that this "unabridged" edition will serve to broaden its appeal.

A NOTE ON THE TEXT

The purpose of *The Unabridged Devil's Dictionary,* as implied by the title, is to present all of Bierce's known satirical definitions. The notion is not new. Ernest J. Hopkins attempted the same in his *Enlarged Devil's Dictionary* (1967), but that edition omitted some definitions and included nearly two hundred that are spurious.

In an age in which books based upon "auctorial intent" are flourishing, *The Unabridged Devil's Dictionary* is something of an anomaly. The works of authors restored to their state of auctorial intent are generally of a piece; they do not sprawl over a period of composition of nearly forty years or consist of many hundreds of discrete components. Bierce's intentions for such a book cannot be known, considering the differing constraints under which he edited the edition of 1911 and its predecessor, *The Cynic's Word Book.* Surely Bierce would not have indiscriminately reprinted every definition he had written over thirty-five years, even without restrictions on space; nor would he have reprinted every definition as initially written, even without restriction on content. In the work at hand, the careful reader will detect unevenness of style and polish, grammatical errors or usages that the older Bierce would have expunged, and perhaps some items that the author, exercising more critical judgment than the editors, would have left unreprinted. Nevertheless, every attempt has been made to adhere closely to Bierce's plan as evidenced in *The Devil's Dictionary.* The restoration of uncollected definitions and the inclusion of select early versions will shed light upon Bierce's compositional and revisory practices.

The Devil's Dictionary (1911) and the typesetting copy for the book are the foundation for this new edition. All definitions from the 1911 edition are included as published with only minor modifications, primarily corrections of typographical errors. They are supplemented with uncollected definitions from the following sources: (1) the single appearance of "The Demon's Dictionary" (1875); (2) installments of "The Devil's Dictionary" from the *Wasp* (1881–86); (3) installments of "The Cynic's Dictionary" (later "The Cynic's Word Book") from the *New York American* (1904–06) and the *San Francisco Examiner* (1887–88; 1904–06); (4) *The Cynic's Word Book* (1906); (5) the typesetting copy for *The Devil's Dictionary;* and (6) a proof for a single definition for which no published appearance has been found. No manuscripts of these items save (5) are known to exist.

Uncollected definitions are included as found with only minor editorial revision to bring them into conformity with Bierce's own practice in preparing *The Devil's Dictionary*. Such revisions include regularizing the abbreviations used for parts of speech, not italicizing the word defined when it appears in verse or text examples, using Bierce's manner of punctuation in all notes of attribution following verse and text, using a uniform style to indicate cross-references, omitting serial commas, and so on. No attempt is made to apply Bierce's later stylistic preferences to his early work, for example, correcting split infinitives, as he always did.

A very few items have been omitted because of duplication, for reasons identified in the notes, but always in adherence to Bierce's wishes. For example, the verses that appeared with the definition "Cackle" in its appearances in the *Wasp* and *The Cynic's Word Book* are not printed here because in *The Devil's Dictionary* Bierce used them with the definition "Vanity"; thus the definition for "Cackle" is restored, but without the verses. In the case of "Aversion," Bierce simply renamed it "Satiety." Thus, the entire definition is not restored at "Aversion."

In cases where Bierce defined words more than once and published the definitions separately over time, the definitions are grouped under a single heading, each labeled with numbers in square brackets (see, for example, "Abatis"); numbers not in brackets are Bierce's own. Definitions that appeared in *The Devil's Dictionary* are preferentially given first; if no definition appeared in the book, multiple definitions of a given word are listed chronologically.

NOTES

1. In "Dictionary" as it appeared in *W* (24 May 1882).

2. In "Immoral" as it appeared in *W* (12 Sept. 1885).

3. AB began his diabolical career as a "printer's devil" for a local newspaper when he was fifteen.

4. He never tired of it. As late as 1891, when AB was writing for the *Examiner*, he published a regular feature in the *Wasp* titled "Social Chatter" as written by "Satanella." He seemed quite eager to have *The Devil's Dictionary* published under his preferred title after suffering more than twenty years with the bland substitute "The Cynic's Dictionary."

5. "Dod Grile," in *FD* (London: John Camden Hotten, [1873]), [7].

6. In "Dictionary" as it appeared in *W* (24 May 1882).

7. See both "Depression" and "Gloom."

8. H. P. Lovecraft to August W. Derleth [late Jan. 1928] (ALS, State Historical Society of Wisconsin). AB ultimately turned to both alternatives.

9. See "Prattle," *W* (15 Sept. 1883): 5.

10. "Religion," *CW* 11. 225–26 (this extract dates to 2 June 1891).

11. In the verses published with this definition in *D,* Christ vehemently asserts that he is no Christian and is insulted to be mistaken for one.

12. "The Town Crier," *NL* (7 Jan. 1871): 9. Note also AB's several "revised" versions of the Ten Commandments (s.v. "Decalogue," for example).

13. See "Theosophy."

14. Considering that the majority of the definitions appeared in the weekly magazine the *Wasp,* it is somewhat ironic that the mnemonic device students were once urged to employ to remember the seven deadly sins was the anagram "wasp leg."

15. Cf. [unsigned,] "A Cynic's Word Book: Some New Definitions," *T.P.'s Weekly,* no. 244 (12 July 1907): 51): "Many of my readers will find amusement and even instruction in 'The Cynic's Word Book.'"

16. "A. Gwinnett," *Californian* 7, no. 32 (Dec. 1867): 8. See Appendix B, item B1, for text. In AB's earliest writings he posed as a philosopher.

17. *NL* (30 Jan. 1869): 3. See Appendix B, item B3.

18. *NL* (24 July 1869): 4. This unsigned item is known to be by AB because it contains material later reprinted in *CW.*

19. Noah Webster (1758–1843), *An American Dictionary of the English Language,* vol. 2 (New York: S. Converse, 1828). AB quotes the text verbatim, although the emphasis is his. He apparently was unaware that this definition was written by Webster himself for the first edition of the dictionary, not by a subsequent reviser.

20. Gustave Flaubert, *Le Dictionnaire des idées reçues,* written between 1850 and 1855; first published in 1913 (translated as *Dictionary of Accepted Ideas* [1954]). The work is more a collection of clichés than a comic lexicon.

21. "The Town Crier," *NL* (14 Aug. 1869): 11.

22. More recently, Roy Morris Jr. has stated that more installments of "The Demon's Dictionary" appeared not only in *NL* but also in *Fu,* but this has not been found to be the case.

23. Possibly because he had no record of this early piece. See p. xix and n. 30.

24. Carey McWilliams, *Ambrose Bierce: A Biography* (New York: Albert & Charles Boni, 1929), 154–55. By "first issue," McWilliams means the first issue containing AB's writing, for the paper had been appearing since 1876.

25. Ernest J. Hopkins included the 189 definitions from these six columns in his *Enlarged Devil's Dictionary* (1967).

26. AB to S. O. Howes, 19 Jan. 1906 (ALS, Huntington Library and Art Gallery). AB's emphasis of the word "I" suggests that Howes may have made the same mistake made by McWilliams and Hopkins—of assuming that Morse's "Webster" definitions were AB's. AB must have lent Howes his bound copies of the *Wasp.* The volume for the first six months

of 1881 contained issues for January through February, when AB was not yet writing for the *Wasp*.

27. From 1883 to 1885, Bierce was writing not only his "Prattle" and other pieces but also the paper's editorial column.

28. AB to George Sterling, 6 May 1906 (ALS, NYPL). AB lived in Washington, D.C., from 1900 onward.

29. George Sterling to AB, 10 Sept. 1904 (ALS, NYPL).

30. AB to George Sterling, 5 Oct. 1904 (TLS, NYPL).

31. AB probably did not repudiate "The Demon's Dictionary" of 1875 but lost it, as suggested in his letter to George Sterling of 5 Oct. 1904. In saying he "re-did" the early A definitions, AB hints that "The Demon's Dictionary" was indeed his, for he redid none of the A work from the *Wasp*.

32. AB to Herman Scheffauer, 12 Sept. 1903 (transcript, Bancroft Library).

33. AB to Herman Scheffauer, 27 Sept. 1903 (transcript, Bancroft Library).

34. George Sterling to AB, 10 Oct. 1903 (ALS, NYPL).

35. AB to Robert Mackay, 25 Apr. 1904 (ALS, Harvard).

36. AB to S. O. Howes, 18 Feb. 1905 (ALS, Huntington Library and Art Gallery).

37. AB to Robert Mackay, 10 Mar. 1905 (ALS, Library of Congress).

38. AB to S. O. Howes, 3 Mar. 1906 (ALS, Huntington Library and Art Gallery).

39. AB to S. O. Howes, 5 Apr. 1906 (ALS, Huntington Library and Art Gallery).

40. Appearances also have been found in the *Los Angeles Examiner,* and it is likely that "The Cynic's Word Book" also appeared in other of Hearst's papers.

41. AB to George Sterling, 6 May 1906 (ALS, NYPL). AB refers to Harry Thompson (1867–?), *The Cynic's Dictionary* (Philadelphia: H. Altemus Co., 1905). Thompson did not plagiarize any of AB's work, but the nature of his definitions occasionally resembles AB's.

42. The dates of the last two columns are unknown. The typesetting copy contains clippings of two installments published sometime after the last appearance that can be dated (*Am,* 11 July 1906).

43. AB to George Sterling, [18 Aug. 1907] (ALS, NYPL).

44. Twelve volumes ultimately were published. Neale had republished *Can Such Things Be?* (1893) in 1903 and *The Monk and the Hangman's Daughter* (1892) in 1907 and later published *Write It Right* (1909), initially intended for but ultimately excluded from *CW.*

45. AB lifted part of the copy from the prospectus for the preface to *D.*

46. Although the column appeared in both *E* and *Am*, AB favored the *Am* appearances in compiling *D.*

47. On several occasions, definitions that should have appeared side by side for maximum effect were separated between two installments, thus weakening the intended jokes.

48. Of forty-three definitions containing verse between "Reconsider" and "Zoölogy," twenty-nine are known to have previously published verse (see "Notes" and "Bibliography"). To be sure, some definitions for which previously published verses have not been found probably contain lines composed specifically for inclusion in *D.*

49. For example, the definitions "Story," "Trial," "Weakness," "Whangdepootenawah," "Zany," and "Zanzibar."

50. [Unsigned,] "Mr. Bierce's Works," *New York Times* (19 Nov. 1911): 730. AB's "Epigrams" take up only a small part of volume 8, which contains the long essay "On with the Dance!" which the reviewer actually addresses, and many short pieces of fiction.

51. [Unsigned review of *CW*], *Athenæum* (16 Sept. 1911): 322.

52. AB to Walter Neale, 10 Oct. 1911 (ALS, University of Virginia).

53. H. L. Mencken, "Ambrose Bierce," in *Prejudices: Sixth Series* (New York: Knopf, 1927), 260. Mencken's article first appeared in the *Chicago Tribune* (1 Mar. 1925).

54. Carey McWilliams, "Introduction," in *The Devil's Dictionary* (New York: Hill and Wang, 1957), vi. Renewed publication of and interest in AB's work in the mid-1920s resulted in the publication of four biographies of AB in 1929, including one by McWilliams.

55. H. P. Lovecraft, "Supernatural Horror in Literature," in *Dagon and Other Macabre Tales* (Sauk City, WI: Arkham House, [1986]), 436.

AB : Ambrose Bierce

Am : *New York American*

Ar : *Argonaut*

AHD : *The American Heritage Dictionary of the English Language* (3rd ed., 1992)

C : *The Cynic's Word Book* (1906)

Co : *Cosmopolitan*

CW : *The Collected Works of Ambrose Bierce* (12 vols., 1909–12)

D : *The Devil's Dictionary* (vol. 7 of *CW*, 1911)

Dx : typesetting copy of *D*

E : *San Francisco Examiner*

FD : *The Fiend's Delight* (1873)

Fi : *Figaro*

Fu : *Fun*

J : *New York Journal*

ND : *Nuggets and Dust* (1873)

NL : *San Francisco News Letter and California Advertiser*

NYPL : New York Public Library

OED : *Oxford English Dictionary* (1933 ed.)

SS : *A Sole Survivor* (1998)

W : *Wasp*

WR : *Write It Right* (1909)

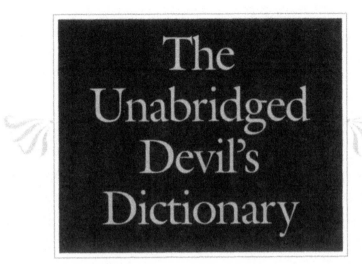

The
Unabridged
Devil's
Dictionary

PREFACE

The Devil's Dictionary was begun in a weekly paper in 1881, and was continued in a desultory way and at long intervals until 1906. In that year a large part of it was published in covers with the title *The Cynic's Word Book,* a name which the author had not the power to reject nor the happiness to approve. To quote the publishers of the present work: "This more reverent title had previously been forced upon him by the religious scruples of the last newspaper in which a part of the work had appeared, with the natural consequence that when it came out in covers the country already had been flooded by its imitators with a score of 'cynic' books— *The Cynic's This, The Cynic's That* and *The Cynic's t'Other.* Most of these books were merely stupid, though some of them added the distinction of silliness. Among them, they brought the word 'cynic' into disfavor so deep that any book bearing it was discredited in advance of publication."

Meantime, too, some of the enterprising humorists of the country had helped themselves to such parts of the work as served their needs, and many of its definitions, anecdotes, phrases and so forth, had become more or less current in popular speech. This explanation is made, not with any pride of priority in trifles, but in simple denial of possible charges of plagiarism, which is no trifle. In merely resuming his own the author hopes to be held guiltless by those to whom the work is addressed—enlightened souls who prefer dry wines to sweet, sense to sentiment, wit to humor and clean English to slang.

A conspicuous, and it is hoped not unpleasant, feature of the book is its abundant illustrative quotations from eminent poets, chief of whom is that learned and ingenious cleric, Father Gassalasca Jape, S.J., whose lines bear his initials. To Father Jape's kindly encouragement and assistance the author of the prose text is greatly indebted.

A. B.

A. The first letter in every properly constructed alphabet. It is the first natural utterance of the human vocal organs, and is variously sounded, according to the pleasure and convenience of the speaker. In logic, A asserts and B denies. Assertions being proverbially untrue, the presumption would be in favor of B's innocence were it not that denials are notoriously false. In grammar, A is called the indefinite article, probably because, denoting a definite number, it is so obviously a numeral adjective.

Abacot, *n.* A cap of state wrought into the shape of two crowns, formerly worn by kings. Very pretty monarchs had it made in the form of three crowns.

Abactor, *n.* One who steals a whole herd of cattle, as distinguished from the inferior actor who steals one animal at a time—a superior stock actor, as it were.

Abacus, *n.* In architecture, the upper part of a column, upon which, in all good architecture, sits the thoughtful stork pondering unutterable things.

Abada, *n.* An African animal having three horns, two on the head and one on the nape of the neck by which to hang up the carcass after the head has been removed. In those varieties that are not hunted by man, this third horn is imperfectly developed or wholly wanting.

Abaddon, *n.* [1.] A certain person who is much in society, but whom one does not meet. A bad one. [2.] The Adversary of Souls, considered under one of his many charming aspects.

Abandon, *v.t.* [1.] To correct an erring friend or admonish a needy one. Of women the word *abandoned* is used in the sense of indiscreet. [2.] To confer the advantage of being rid of you. To recant.

> Thank heaven, I have abandoned the follies of youth for those of age. —*Chauncey Depew.*

Abasement, *n.* A decent and customary mental attitude in the presence of wealth or power. Peculiarly appropriate in an employee when addressing an employer.

Abatis, *n.* [1.] Rubbish in front of a fort, to prevent the rubbish outside from molesting the rubbish inside. [2.] Embarrassing circumstances placed outside a fort in order to augment the coy reluctance of the enemy.

Abattoir, *n.* A place where cattle slaughter kine. It is commonly placed at some distance from the haunts of our species, in order that they who devour the flesh may not be shocked by the sight of the blood.

Abat-voix, *n.* A sounding brass above a tinkling cymbal.

Abba, *n.* A father who has made a vow not to be a husband.

Abbess, *n.* A female father.

Abderian, *adj.* *Abderian laughter* is idle and senseless laughter; so called because Democritus, an idle and senseless philosopher, is said to have been born at Abdera, whence the word was hardly worth importing.

Abdest, *n.* The Mohammedan ceremony of inspiring water through the nose before expiring prayer from the stomach.

Abdication, *n.* [1.] An act whereby a sovereign attests his sense of the high temperature of the throne.

> Poor Isabella's dead, whose abdication
> Set all tongues wagging in the Spanish nation.
> For that performance 'twere unfair to scold her:
> She wisely left a throne too hot to hold her.
> To History she'll be no royal riddle—
> Merely a plain parched pea that jumped the griddle.
>
> G. J.

[2.] The surrender of a crown for a cowl, in order to compile the shin-bones and toe-nails of saints. The voluntary renunciation of that of which one has previously been deprived by force. The giving up of a throne for the purpose of enjoying the discomfiture of a successor. For these several definitions we are indebted to Spanish history.

Abdomen, *n.* [1.] The temple of the god Stomach, in whose worship, with sacrificial rites, all true men engage. From women this ancient faith commands but a stammering assent. They sometimes minister at the altar in a half-hearted and ineffective way, but true reverence for the one deity that men really adore they know not. If woman had a free hand in the world's marketing the race would become graminivorous. [2.] A shrine enclosing the object of man's sincerest devotion.

Abduction, *n.* [1.] In law, a crime; in morals, a punishment. [2.] A species of invitation without persuasion. See KIDNAP.

> "You act as if you were given," said she,
> "To abduction—but pray do not kidnap me."
> "Oh, well," said that bold and impenitent chap,
> "You're the kind of kid I should like to nap."

Abelians, *n.* A religious sect of Africa who practiced the virtues of Abel. They were unfortunate in flourishing contemporaneously with the Cainians, and are now extinct.

Aberration, *n.* Any deviation in another from one's own habit of thought, not sufficient in itself to constitute insanity.

Abet, *v.t.* To encourage in crime, as to aid poverty with pennies.

Abhorrence, *n.* One of the degrees of disapproval due to what is imperfectly understood.

Abide, *v.i.* To treat with merited indifference the landlord's notification that he has let his house to a party willing to pay.

Ability, *n.* [1.] The natural equipment to accomplish some small part of the meaner ambitions distinguishing able men from dead ones. In the last analysis ability is commonly found to consist mainly in a high degree of solemnity. Perhaps, however, this impressive quality is rightly appraised; it is no easy task to be solemn. [2.] That rare quality of mind to which monuments are erected by posterity above the bones of paupers.

Abject, *adj.* Innocent of income; without estate; devoid of good clothing.

Abjectly, *adv.* In the manner of a poor but honest person.

Abjure, *v.t.* To take the preliminary step toward resumption.

Ablative, *adj.* A certain case of Latin nouns. The ablative absolute is an ancient form of grammatical error much admired by modern scholars.

Abnegation, *n.* Renunciation of unprofitable pleasures or painful gains.

Abnormal, *adj.* Not conforming to standard. In matters of thought and conduct, to be independent is to be abnormal, to be abnormal is to be detested. Wherefore the lexicographer adviseth a striving toward a straiter resemblance to the Average Man than he hath to himself. Whoso attaineth thereto shall have peace, the prospect of death and the hope of Hell.

Abominable, *adj.* The quality of another's opinions.

Aborigines, *n.* [1.] Persons of little worth found cumbering the soil of a newly discovered country. They soon cease to cumber; they fertilize. [2.] Considerate persons who will not trouble the lexicographer of the future to describe them.

Abracadabra.

> By *Abracadabra* we signify
> > An infinite number of things.
> 'Tis the answer to What? and How? and Why?
> And Whence? and Whither?—a word whereby
> > The Truth (with the comfort it brings)
> Is open to all who grope in night,
> Crying for Wisdom's holy light.

Whether the word is a verb or a noun
    Is knowledge beyond my reach.
I only know that 'tis handed down
      From sage to sage,
      From age to age—
    An immortal part of speech!

Of an ancient man the tale is told
That he lived to be ten centuries old,
    In a cave on a mountain side.
    (True, he finally died.)
The fame of his wisdom filled the land,
For his head was bald, and you'll understand
    His beard was long and white
    And his eyes uncommonly bright.

Philosophers gathered from far and near
To sit at his feet and hear and hear,
      Though he never was heard
      To utter a word
    But *"Abracadabra, abracadab,*
    Abracada, abracad,
   Abraca, abrac, abra, ab!"
      'Twas all he had,
'Twas all they wanted to hear, and each
Made copious notes of the mystical speech,
      Which they published next—
      A trickle of text
In a meadow of commentary.
    Mighty big books were these,
    In number, as leaves of trees;
In learning, remarkable—very!

      He's dead,
      As I said,
And the books of the sages have perished,
But his wisdom is sacredly cherished.
In *Abracadabra* it solemnly rings,
Like an ancient bell that forever swings.

O, I love to hear

That word make clear

Humanity's General Sense of Things.

Jamrach Holobom.

Abridge, *v.t.* To shorten.

When in the course of human events it becomes necessary for a
people to abridge their king, a decent respect for the opinions of
mankind requires that they should declare the causes which impel them
to the separation. — *Oliver Cromwell.*

Abridgement, *n.* A brief summary of some person's literary work, in which
those parts that tell against the convictions of the abridger are omitted for
want of space.

Abroad, *adj.* At war with savages and idiots. To be a Frenchman abroad is to be
miserable; to be an American abroad is to make others miserable.

Abrupt, *adj.* Sudden, without ceremony, like the arrival of a cannon-shot and
the departure of the soldier whose interests are most affected by it. Dr. Samuel Johnson beautifully said of another author's ideas that they were "concatenated without abruption."

Abruption, *n.* Dr. Johnson said of a certain work that the ideas were "concatenated without abruption." In deference to that great authority we have given
the word a place.

Abscond, *v.i.* [1.] To "move in a mysterious way," commonly with the property
of another.

Spring beckons! All things to the call respond;

The trees are leaving and cashiers abscond.

Phela Orm.

[2.] To be unexpectedly called away to the bedside of a dying relative and
miss the return train.

Absence, *n.* That which "makes the heart grow fonder" — of absence. Absence
of mind is the cerebral condition essential to success in popular preaching.
It is sometimes termed lack of sense.

Absent, *adj.* [1.] Peculiarly exposed to the tooth of detraction; vilified; hope-
lessly in the wrong; superseded in the consideration and affection of another.

To men a man is but a mind. Who cares

What face he carries or what form he wears?

But woman's body is the woman. O,

Stay thou, my sweetheart, and do never go,

But heed the warning words the sage hath said:

A woman absent is a woman dead.

Jogo Tyree.

[2.] Exposed to the attacks of friends and acquaintances; defamed; slandered.

Absentee, *n.* A person with an income who has had the forethought to remove himself from the sphere of exaction.

Absolute, *adj.* [1.] Independent, irresponsible. An absolute monarchy is one in which the sovereign does as he pleases so long as he pleases the assassins. Not many absolute monarchies are left, most of them having been replaced by limited monarchies, where the sovereign's power for evil (and for good) is greatly curtailed, and by republics, which are governed by chance. [2.] In Philosophy existing without reference to anything, and for a purely selfish purpose. *Absolute certainty* is one of the possible degrees of probability. *Absolute monarchy* is a form of government in which the chief power is vested in a gentleman who is near his end.

Abstainer, *n.* A weak person who yields to the temptation of denying himself a pleasure. A total abstainer is one who abstains from everything but abstention, and especially from inactivity in the affairs of others.

> Said a man to a crapulent youth: "I thought
> You a total abstainer, my son."
> "So I am, so I am," said the scapegrace caught —
> "But not, sir, a bigoted one."
>
> *G. J.*

Abstemious, *adj.* Thoughtfully deferential to one's overtaxed capacity.

Abstruseness, *n.* The bait of a bare hook.

Absurdity, *n.* [1.] A statement or belief manifestly inconsistent with one's own opinion. [2.] The argument of an opponent. A belief in which one has not had the misfortune to be instructed.

Abundance, *n.* A means, under Providence, of withholding alms from the destitute.

Abuse, *n.* [1.] The goal of debate. Abuse of power is the exercise of authority in a manner unpleasant to ourselves. [2.] Unanswerable wit.

Academe, *n.* An ancient school where morality and philosophy were taught.

Academy, *n.* (from academe). [1.] A modern school where football is taught. [2.] Originally a grove in which philosophers sought a meaning in nature; now a school in which naturals seek a meaning in philosophy.

Accept, *v.t.* In Courtship to reap the whirlwind after sowing the wind. To accept office is to take with decent reluctance the reward of immodest avidity. To accept a challenge is to become a sincere believer in the sanctity of human life.

Accident, *n.* An inevitable occurrence due to the action of immutable natural laws.

Acclimated, *pp.* Secured against endemic diseases through having died of one.

Accommodate, *v.t.* To oblige; to lay the foundation of future exactions.

Accomplice, *n.* [1.] One associated with another in a crime, having guilty knowledge and complicity, as an attorney who defends a criminal, knowing him guilty. This view of the attorney's position in the matter has not hitherto commanded the assent of attorneys, no one having offered them a fee for assenting. [2.] Your partner in business.

Accord, *n.* Harmony.

Accordion, *n.* An instrument in harmony with the sentiments of an assassin.

Accoucheur, *n.* The devil's purveyor.

Accountability, *n.* The mother of caution.

> "My accountability, bear in mind,"
> Said the Grand Vizier: "Yes, yes,"
> Said the Shah: "I do—'tis the only kind
> Of ability you possess."

> *Joram Tate.*

Accountable, *adj.* Liable to an abatement of pleasure, profit or advantage; exposed to the peril of a penalty.

Accuracy, *n.* A certain uninteresting quality carefully excluded from human statements.

Accuse, *v.t.* To affirm another's guilt or unworth; most commonly as a justification of ourselves for having wronged him.

Accuser, *n.* One's former friend; particularly the person for whom one has performed some friendly service.

Ace, *n.* The one-fourth part of the Hand of Fate.

Aceldama, *n.* A piece of real estate near Jerusalem, in which the broker, Judas Iscariot, invested the money he made by selling short and escaping a corner.

Acephalous, *adj.* In the surprising condition of the Crusader who absently pulled at his forelock some hours after a Saracen scimitar had, unconsciously to him, passed through his neck, as related by de Joinville.

Acerbity, *n.* The quality which distinguishes the disposition of Deacon Fitch from a crabapple.

Ache, *v.i.* To act like the tomb of a cucumber.

Achievement, *n.* The death of endeavor and the birth of disgust.

Acknowledge, *v.t.* To confess. Acknowledgment of one another's faults is the highest duty imposed by our love of truth.

Acorn, *n.* A small nut about which cluster the American patriot's hopes of a navy. It makes tyranny tremble.

Acquaintance, *n.* A person whom we know well enough to borrow from, but not well enough to lend to. A degree of friendship called slight when its object is poor or obscure, and intimate when he is rich or famous.

Acquit, *v.t.* To render judgment in a murder case in San Francisco.

Acrobat, *n.* (Gr. *a,* priv., and Eng. *crow-bait,* a lean creature.) A muscular, well-conditioned fellow. A man who breaks his back to fill his belly.

Acrostic, *n.* A severe trial to the feelings. Commonly inflicted by a fool.

Actor, *n.* One who peddles ready-made emotion, and who, despising us for the qualities upon which he feeds, is by us despised for the unwholesome character of his diet. See STICK.

Actress, *n.* A woman whose good name is commonly tainted from being so much in our mouths.

Actually, *adv.* Perhaps; possibly.

Adage, *n.* [1.] Boned wisdom for weak teeth. [2.] A hoary-headed platitude that is kicked along the centuries until nothing is left of it but its clothes. A "saw" which has worn out its teeth on the human understanding.

Adamant, *n.* A mineral frequently found beneath a corset. Soluble in solicitate of gold.

Adam's Apple, *n.* A protuberance on the throat of a man, thoughtfully provided by Nature to keep the rope in place.

Adder, *n.* A species of snake. So called from its habit of adding funeral outlays to the other expenses of living.

Address, *n.* 1. A formal discourse, usually delivered to a person who has something by a person who wants something that he has. 2. The place at which one receives the delicate attentions of creditors.

Adherent, *n.* A follower who has not yet obtained all that he expects to get.

Adipose, *adj.* Fat, ragged and saucy.

Adjutant, *n.* In military affairs, a bustling officer of inferior rank, whose function it is to divert attention from the commander.

Administration, *n.* An ingenious abstraction in politics, designed to receive the kicks and cuffs due to the premier or president. A man of straw, proof against bad-egging and dead-catting.

Admirability, *n.* My kind of ability, as distinguished from your kind of ability.

Admiral, *n.* That part of a war-ship which does the talking while the figure-head does the thinking.

Admiration, *n.* Our polite recognition of another's resemblance to ourselves.

Admonition, *n.* Gentle reproof, as with a meat-axe. Friendly warning.

> Consigned, by way of admonition,
> His soul forever to perdition.
>
> *Judibras.*

Adolescent, *adj.* Recovering from boyhood.

Adonis, *n.* A comely youth, remembered chiefly for his unkindness to Venus. He has been unjustly censured by those who forget that in his time goddesses were only ten cents a bunch.

Adore, *v.t.* To venerate expectantly.

Advice, *n.* The smallest current coin.

> "The man was in such deep distress,"
> Said Tom, "that I could do no less
> Than give him good advice." Said Jim:
> "If less could have been done for him
> I know you well enough, my son,
> To know that's what you would have done."
>
> *Jebel Jocordy.*

Æsthetics, *n.* The most unpleasant ticks afflicting the race. Worse than wood-ticks.

Affection, *n.* In morals, a sentiment; in medicine, a disease. To a young woman an affection of the heart means love; to a doctor it may mean fatty degeneration. The difference is one of nomenclature merely.

Affectionate, *adj.* Addicted to being a nuisance. The most affectionate creature in the world is a wet dog.

Affianced, *pp.* Fitted with an ankle-ring for the ball-and-chain.

Affirm, *v.t.* To declare with suspicious gravity when one is not compelled to wholly discredit himself with an oath.

Affliction, *n.* An acclimatizing process preparing the soul for another and bitter world.

Afraid, *adj.* Civilly willing that things should be other than they seem.

African, *n.* A nigger that votes our way.

Age, *n.* That period of life in which we compound for the vices that we still cherish by reviling those that we have no longer the enterprise to commit.

Agitator, *n.* A statesman who shakes the fruit trees of his neighbors—to dislodge the worms.

Agony, *n.* A superior degree of bodily disgust. The corresponding mental condition is called "all broke up."

Agrarian, *n.* A politician who carries his real estate under his nails. A son of the soil who, like Æneas, carries his father on his person.

Aim, *n.* The task we set our wishes to.

> "Cheer up! Have you no aim in life?"
> She tenderly inquired.
> "An aim? Well, no, I haven't, wife;
> The fact is—I have fired."
>
> *G. J.*

Air, *n.* A nutritious substance supplied by a bountiful Providence for the fattening of the poor.

Album, *n.* An instrument of torture in which one's lady friends crucify him between two thieves.

Alcohol, *n.* (Arabic *al kohl,* a paint for the eyes.) The essential principle of all such liquids as give a man a black eye.

Alderman, *n.* An ingenious criminal who covers his secret thieving with a pretence of open marauding.

Alien, *n.* An American sovereign in his probationary state.

All, *n.* Every single cent—except what you have kept out for yourself.

Allah, *n.* The Mahometan Supreme Being, as distinguished from the Christian, Jewish, and so forth.

> Allah's good laws I faithfully have kept,
> And ever for the sins of man have wept;
> And sometimes kneeling in the temple I
> Have reverently crossed my hands and slept.
>
> *Junker Barlow.*

Allegiance, *n.*

> This thing Allegiance, as I suppose,
> Is a ring fitted in the subject's nose,
> Whereby that organ is kept rightly pointed
> To smell the sweetness of the Lord's anointed.
>
> *G. J.*

Allegory, *n.* A metaphor in three volumes and a tiger.

Alliance, *n.* In international politics, the union of two thieves who have their hands so deeply inserted in each other's pocket that they cannot separately plunder a third.

Alligator, *n.* The crocodile of America, superior in every detail to the crocodile of the effete monarchies of the Old World. Herodotus says the Indus is, with one exception, the only river that produces crocodiles, but they appear to have gone West and grown up with the other rivers. From the notches on his back the alligator is called a sawrian.

Alone, *adj.* In bad company.

> In contact, lo! the flint and steel,
> By spark and flame, the thought reveal
> That he the metal, she the stone,
> Had cherished secretly alone.
>
> *Booley Fito.*

Altar, *n.* The place whereon the priest formerly raveled out the small intestine of the sacrificial victim for purposes of divination and cooked its flesh for the gods. The word is now seldom used, except with reference to the sacrifice of their liberty and peace by a male and a female fool.

They stood before the altar and supplied
The fire themselves in which their fat was fried.
In vain the sacrifice! — no god will claim
An offering burnt with an unholy flame.

M. P. Nopput.

Amateur, *n.* A public nuisance who mistakes taste for skill, and confounds his ambition with his ability.

Amatory, *adj.* We should blush to murmur it.

Amazon, *n.* One of an ancient race who do not appear to have been much concerned about woman's rights and the equality of the sexes. Their thoughtless habit of twisting the necks of the males has unfortunately resulted in the extinction of their kind.

Ambidextrous, *adj.* Able to pick with equal skill a right-hand pocket or a left.

Ambition, *n.* An overmastering desire to be vilified by enemies while living and made ridiculous by friends when dead.

Ambrosia, *n.* The diet of the gods — the modern peanut.

A Mensa et Thoro. (Latin, "from bed and board.") A term of the divorce courts, but more properly applied to a man who has been kicked out of his hotel.

Amnesty, *n.* The state's magnanimity to those offenders whom it would be too expensive to punish.

Animal, *n.* An organism which, requiring a great number of other animals for its sustenance, illustrates in a marked way the bounty of Providence in preserving the lives of his creatures.

Animalism, *n.* The state and quality of human nature in which we flatter ourselves we resemble "the beasts that perish."

Anoint, *v.t.* To grease a king or other great functionary already sufficiently slippery.

As sovereigns are anointed by the priesthood,
So pigs to lead the populace are greased good.

Judibras.

Antagonist, *n.* The miserable scoundrel who won't let us.

Ante-chamber, *n.* An apartment in which one does penance in advance for the sin of asking for a postoffice.

Antipathy, *n.* The sentiment inspired by one's friend's friend.

Antiquity, *n.* A kind of leather, probably.

Beated and chopped with tanned antiquity.

Shakspeare.

Apathetic, *adj.* Six weeks married.

Aphorism, *n.* Predigested wisdom.

The flabby wine-skin of his brain

Yields to some pathologic strain,
And voids from its unstored abysm
The driblet of an aphorism.

"The Mad Philosopher," 1697.

Apologize, *v.i.* To lay the foundation for a future offence.

Apostate, *n.* A leech who, having penetrated the shell of a turtle only to find that the creature has long been dead, deems it expedient to form a new attachment to a fresh turtle.

Apothecary, *n.* The physician's accomplice, undertaker's benefactor and grave worm's provider.

> When Jove sent blessings to all men that are,
> And Mercury conveyed them in a jar,
> That friend of tricksters introduced by stealth
> Disease for the apothecary's health,
> Whose gratitude impelled him to proclaim:
> "My deadliest drug shall bear my patron's name!"

G. J.

Appeal, *v.t.* In law, to put the dice into the box for another throw.

Appetite, *n.* An instinct thoughtfully implanted by Providence as a solution to the labor question.

Applause, *n.* The echo of a platitude.

Apple, *n.* A fruit, for eating which the first man was justly turned out of Paradise. For, the first apple being a crabapple, the first man was an idiot for eating it.

April Fool, *n.* The March fool with another month added to his folly.

Apron, *n.* A piece of cloth worn in front to keep the clothes from soiling the hands.

> She wore an apron ('tis a thing I loathe),
> A dress beneath—a corset *à la mode.*
> No further seek her merits to disclothe,
> Nor draw her frailties from their dread abode.

Gray.

Arab, *n.* A scourge created in order that the wicked may torture us by mispronouncing his tribal designation. For our sins they call it *Ay*-rab.

Arbitration, *n.* [1.] A modern device for promoting strife by substituting for an original dispute a score of inevitable disagreements as to the manner of submitting it for settlement. [2.] A patent medicine for allaying international heat, designed to supersede the old-school treatment of blood-letting. It makes the unsuccessful party to the dispute hate two or more nations instead of one—to the unspeakable advantage of peace.

Archbishop, *n.* An ecclesiastical dignitary one point holier than a bishop.

> If I were a jolly archbishop,
> On Fridays I'd eat all the fish up—
> Salmon and flounders and smelts;
> On other days everything else.
>
> *Jodo Rem.*

Architect, *n.* One who drafts a plan of your house, and plans a draft of your money.

Ardor, *n.* The quality that distinguishes love without knowledge.

Arena, *n.* In politics, an imaginary rat-pit in which the statesman wrestles with his record.

Argonaut, *n.* An instrument of torture for violently unkinking the small intestine of that religious persecutor, the Pope. (Local.)

Argue, *v.t.* To tentatively consider with the tongue.

Aristocracy, *n.* Government by the best men. (In this sense the word is obsolete; so is that kind of government.) Fellows that wear downy hats and clean shirts—guilty of education and suspected of bank accounts.

Armor, *n.* The kind of clothing worn by a man whose tailor is a blacksmith.

Army, *n.* A class of non-producers who defend the nation by devouring everything likely to tempt an enemy to invade.

Arrayed, *pp.* Drawn up and given an orderly disposition, as a rioter hanged to a lamp-post.

Arrears, *n.* (In deference to the feelings of a large and worthy class of our subscribers and advertisers, the definition of this word is withheld.)

Arrest, *v.t.* Formally to detain one accused of unusualness.

> God made the world in six days and was arrested on the seventh. — *The Unauthorized Version.*

Arrested, *pp.* Caught criming without the money to satisfy the policeman.

Arsenic, *n.* A kind of cosmetic greatly affected by the ladies, whom it greatly affects in turn.

> "Eat arsenic? Yes, all you get,"
> Consenting, he did speak up;
> "'Tis better you should eat it, pet,
> Than put it in my teacup."
>
> *Joel Huck.*

Art, *n.* This word has no definition. Its origin is related as follows by the ingenious Father Gassalasca Jape, S.J.

> One day a wag—what would the wretch be at?—
> Shifted a letter of the cipher RAT,
> And said it was a god's name! Straight arose

Fantastic priests and postulants (with shows,
And mysteries, and mummeries, and hymns,
And disputations dire that lamed their limbs)
To serve his temple and maintain the fires,
Expound the law, manipulate the wires.
Amazed, the populace the rites attend,
Believe whate'er they cannot comprehend,
And, inly edified to learn that two
Half-hairs joined so and so (as Art can do)
Have sweeter values and a grace more fit
Than Nature's hairs that never have been split,
Bring cates and wines for sacrificial feasts,
And sell their garments to support the priests.

Artlessness, *n.* A certain engaging quality to which women attain by long study and severe practice upon the admiring male, who is pleased to fancy it resembles the candid simplicity of his young.

Asbestos, *n.* An incombustible mineral substance which, woven into cloth, was formerly much used for making shrouds for the dead. It is no longer believed that the soul will be permitted to wear the body's cerements, and asbestine shrouds have gone out of fashion.

Asperse, *v.t.* Maliciously to ascribe to another vicious actions which one has not had the temptation and opportunity to commit.

Ass, *n.* A public singer with a good voice but no ear. In Virginia City, Nevada, he is called the Washoe Canary, in Dakota, the Senator, and everywhere the Donkey. The animal is widely and variously celebrated in the literature, art and religion of every age and country; no other so engages and fires the human imagination as this noble vertebrate. Indeed, it is doubted by some (Ramasilus, *lib. II., De Clem.*, and C. Stantatus, *De Temperamente*) if it is not a god; and as such we know it was worshiped by the Etruscans, and, if we may believe Macrobius, by the Cupasians also. Of the only two animals admitted into the Mahometan Paradise along with the souls of men, the ass that carried Balaam is one, the dog of the Seven Sleepers the other. This is no small distinction. From what has been written about this beast might be compiled a library of great splendor and magnitude, rivaling that of the Shakspearean cult, and that which clusters about the Bible. It may be said, generally, that all literature is more or less Asinine.

"Hail, holy Ass!" the quiring angels sing;
"Priest of Unreason, and of Discords King!
Great co-Creator, let Thy glory shine:
God made all else; the Mule, the Mule is thine!"

G. J.

Astrology, *n.* The science of making the dupe see stars. Astrology is by some held in high respect as the precursor of astronomy. Similarly, the night-howling tomcat has a just claim to reverential consideration as precursor to the hurtling bootjack.

Attorney, *n.* A person legally appointed to mismanage one's affairs which one has not himself the skill to rightly mismanage.

Attraction, *n.* The influence which tends to establish neighborly relations among things. There are various kinds of attraction, but the attraction of gravity is the most celebrated. In a woman, however, it is distinctly inferior to the attraction of vivacity.

Auctioneer, *n.* The man who proclaims with a hammer that he has picked a pocket with his tongue.

Auricle, *n.* The outlying provinces of the ear, as distinguished from the interior counties.

> Dogmatic Dan, with more of ears than brain,
> Was laying down the law to Mary Jane.
> "You're famous for your oracles," she said.
> A sudden anger dyed his cheeks with red;
> He seized his hat. "My auricles!" said he—
> "Madam, good-bye; you've seen the last of *me!*"

Austere, *adj.* Having the quality of an antique virgin, or a legislator approached with a bribe by the side that he has been paid to oppose. The care that is taken to guard against confounding this word with "oyster" will be well rewarded.

Australia, *n.* A country lying in the South Sea, whose industrial and commercial development has been unspeakably retarded by an unfortunate dispute among geographers as to whether it is a continent or an island.

Authentic, *adj.* Indubitably true—in somebody's opinion.

> He ne'er discredited authentic news,
> That tended to substantiate his views,
> And never controverted an assertion
> When true, if it was easy of perversion.
> So frank was he that where he was unjust
> He always would confess it when he must.
>
> <div align="right">"<i>The Lawyer</i>," <i>1750.</i></div>

Autocrat, *n.* A dictatorial gentleman with no other restraint upon him than the hand of the assassin. The founder and patron of that great political institution, the dynamite bomb-shell system.

Avaunt, *exc.* The tragic actor's equivalent for "get out!"

Avenge, *v.t.* In modern usage, to take satisfaction for an injury by cheating the inflictor.

Avernus, *n.* The lake by which the ancients entered the infernal regions. The fact that access to the infernal regions was obtained by a lake is believed by the learned Marcus Ansello Scrutator to have suggested the Christian rite of baptism by immersion. This, however, has been shown by Lactantius to be an error.

> *Facilis descensus Averni,*
>> The poet remarks; and the sense
> Of it is that when down-hill I turn I
>> Will get more of punches than pence.
>
> *Jehal Dai Lupe.*

Awkward, *adj.* Charming in the natural and unaffected way of the sylvan damsel, unaccustomed to a train.

> Awkward? you should have seen the pace
>> With which she left her seat,
> And, gliding with peculiar grace,
>> Fell over her own feet.
>
> *Book of Etiquette.*

Baal, *n.* An old deity formerly much worshiped under various names. As Baal he was popular with the Phœnicians; as Belus or Bel he had the honor to be served by the priest Berosus, who wrote the famous account of the Deluge; as Babel he had a tower partly erected to his glory on the Plain of Shinar. From Babel comes our English word "babble." Under whatever name worshiped, Baal is the Sun-god. As Beëlzebub he is the god of flies, which are begotten of the sun's rays on stagnant water. In Physicia Baal is still worshiped as Bolus, and as Belly he is adored and served with abundant sacrifice by the priests of Guttledom.

Babe or Baby, *n.* A misshapen creature of no particular age, sex or condition, chiefly remarkable for the violence of the sympathies and antipathies it excites in others, itself without sentiment or emotion. There have been famous babes; for example, little Moses, from whose adventure in the bulrushes the Egyptian hierophants of seven centuries before doubtless derived their idle tale of the child Osiris being preserved on a floating lotus leaf.

> Ere babes were invented
> The girls were contented.
> Now man is tormented
> Until to buy babes he has squandered
> His money. And so I have pondered
> This thing, and thought maybe
> 'Twere better that Baby
> The First had been eagled or condored.
>
> *Ro Amil.*

Bacchus, *n.* A convenient deity invented by the ancients as an excuse for getting drunk.

> Is public worship, then, a sin,
> That for devotions paid to Bacchus

The lictors dare to run us in,
> And resolutely thump and whack us?

Jorace.

Bachelor, *n.* A man whom women are still sampling.

Back, *n.* That part of your friend which it is your privilege to contemplate in your adversity.

Backbite, *v.t.* To speak of a man as you find him when he can't find you.

Back-slide, *v.i.* To join another communion.

Bacon, *n.* The mummy of a pig embalmed in brine. To "save one's bacon" is to narrowly escape some particular woman, or other peril.

> By heaven forsaken,
> By Justice o'ertaken,
> He saved his bacon
> By cutting a single slice of it;
> For 'twas cut from the throat,
> And we venture to quote
> Death, hell and the grave as the price of it.

S. F. Journal of Commerce.

Bait, *n.* A preparation that renders the hook more palatable. The best kind is beauty.

Bald, *adj.* Destitute of hair from hereditary or accidental causes — never from age.

Balloon, *n.* A contrivance for larding the earth with the fat of fools.

Ballot, *n.* A simple device by which a majority proves to a minority the folly of resistance. Many worthy persons of imperfect thinking apparatus believe that majorities govern through some inherent right; and minorities submit, not because they must, but because they ought.

Bandit, *n.* A person who takes by force from A what A has taken by guile from B.

Bang, *n.* The cry of a gun. That arrangement of a woman's hair which suggests the thought of shooting her; hence the name.

Bang, *v.t.* To admonish, protest or persuade, with a club.

> Tom having taken Jane to be his wife,
> His friends expect of him a better life;
> For still by her example he is led,
> And when she bangs her hair he bangs her head.

Baptism, *n.* A sacred rite of such efficacy that he who finds himself in heaven without having undergone it will be unhappy forever. It is performed with water in two ways — by immersion, or plunging, and by aspersion, or sprinkling.

> But whether the plan of immersion

Is better than simple aspersion
  Let those immersed
  And those aspersed
Decide by the Authorized Version,
And by matching their agues tertian.

G. J.

Barber, *n.* (Lat. *barbarus*, savage, from *barba*, the beard.) A savage whose laceration of your cheek is unobserved in the superior torment of his conversation.

Bard, *n.* A person who makes rhymes. The word is one of the numerous *aliases* under which the poet seeks to veil his identity and escape opprobrium.

Bark, *n.* The song of the dog.

  "My bark is on the wave," all writers quote.
  "Mine too," says the retriever, "is afloat."

Barometer, *n.* An ingenious instrument which indicates what kind of weather we are having.

Barrack, *n.* A house in which soldiers enjoy a portion of that of which it is their business to deprive others.

Barrister, *n.* One of the ten thousand varieties of the genus Lawyer. In England the functions of a barrister are distinct from those of a solicitor. The one advises, the other executes; but the thing advised and the thing executed is the client.

Base, *adj.* The quality of a competitor's motive.

Basilisk, *n.* The cockatrice. A sort of serpent hatched from the egg of a cock. The basilisk had a bad eye, and its glance was fatal. Many infidels deny this creature's existence, but Semprello Aurator saw and handled one that had been blinded by lightning as a punishment for having fatally gazed on a lady of rank whom Jupiter loved. Juno afterward restored the reptile's sight and hid it in a cave. Nothing is so well attested by the ancients as the existence of the basilisk, but the cocks have stopped laying.

Bassinet, *n.* A shrine in which is worshiped "the image of its pa." The word is from the French *berceaunette*, but the "image" is derived Lord knows whence.

Bassoon, *n.* A brazen instrument into which a fool blows out his brains.

Basso-relievo, *n.* (Italian.) Low relief. The relief of a sick vulgarian.

Bastinado, *n.* The act of walking on wood without exertion.

Bath, *n.* A kind of mystic ceremony substituted for religious worship, with what spiritual efficacy has not been determined.

  The man who taketh a steam bath
  He loseth all the skin he hath,
  And, for he's boiled a brilliant red,

Thinketh to cleanliness he's wed,
Forgetting that his lungs he's soiling
With dirty vapors of the boiling.

Richard Gwow.

Battle, *n.* A method of untying with the teeth a political knot that would not yield to the tongue.

Bayonet, *n.* An instrument for pricking the bubble of a nation's conceit.

Bear, *n.* In the stock market, a broker who, having sold short, uses his customers' stocks to break the price.

Beard, *n.* The hair that is commonly cut off by those who justly execrate the absurd Chinese custom of shaving the head.

Beauty, *n.* The power by which a woman charms a lover and terrifies a husband.

Bed, *n.* A rack for the torture of the wicked; a citadel unfortified against remorse.

Bedlam, *n.* A house whose inmates are all poets—"of imagination all compact."

Bed-quilt, *n.* The exterior covering of a bed. Sometimes called Charity.

Befriend, *v.t.* To make an ingrate.

Beg, *v.* To ask for something with an earnestness proportioned to the belief that it will not be given.

Who is that, father?

A mendicant, child,
Haggard, morose, and unaffable—wild!
See how he glares through the bars of his cell!
With Citizen Mendicant all is not well.

Why did they put him there, father?

Because
Obeying his belly he struck at the laws.

His belly?

Oh, well, he was starving, my boy—
A state in which, doubtless, there's little of joy.
No bite had he eaten for days, and his cry
Was "Bread!" ever "Bread!"

What's the matter with pie?

With little to wear, he had nothing to sell;
To beg was unlawful—improper as well.

Why didn't he work?

He would even have done that,
But men said: "Get out!" and the State remarked: "Scat!"
I mention these incidents merely to show
That the vengeance he took was uncommonly low.
Revenge, at the best, is the act of a Sioux,
But for trifles—

Pray what did bad Mendicant do?

Stole two loaves of bread to replenish his lack
And tuck out the belly that clung to his back.

Is that *all* father dear?

There is little to tell:
They sent him to jail, and they'll send him to—well,
The company's better than here we can boast,
And there's—

Bread for the needy, dear father?

Um—toast.
Atka Mip.

Beggar, *n.* [1.] One who has relied on the assistance of his friends. [2.] A pest
  unkindly inflicted upon the suffering rich.
Beggary, *n.* The condition of one who has relied on the co-operation of his
  friends.
Behavior, *n.* Conduct, as determined, not by principle, but by breeding. The
  word seems to be somewhat loosely used in Dr. Jamrach Holobom's translation of the following lines in the *Dies Iræ:*
      Recordare, Jesu pie,
      Quod sum causa tuæ viæ.
      Ne me perdas illa die.

  Pray remember, sacred Savior,
  Whose the thoughtless hand that gave your
  Death-blow. Pardon such behavior.

Belladonna, *n.* In Italian a beautiful lady; in English a deadly poison. A striking
  example of the essential identity of the two tongues.
Benedictines, *n.* An order of monks otherwise known as black friars.
      She thought it a crow, but it turned out to be
      A monk of St. Benedict croaking a text.

"Here's one of an order of cooks," said she —
"Black friars in this world, fried black in the next."

"The Devil on Earth" (*London, 1712*).

Benefactor, *n.* One who makes heavy purchases of ingratitude, without, however, materially affecting the price, which is still within the means of all.

Benevolence, *n.* Subscribing five dollars toward the relief of one's aged grandfather in the alms house, and publishing it in the newspaper.

Bequeath, *v.t.* To generously give to another that which can be no longer denied to *somebody*.

Berenice's Hair, *n.* A constellation (*Coma Berenices*) named in honor of one who sacrificed her hair to save her husband.

> Her locks an ancient lady gave
> Her loving husband's life to save;
> And men — they honored so the dame —
> Upon some stars bestowed her name.
>
> But to our modern married fair,
> Who'd give their lords to save their hair,
> No stellar recognition's given.
> There are not stars enough in heaven.
>
> G. J.

Betray, *v.t.* To make payment for confidence.

Betrothed, *pp.* The condition of a man and woman who, pleasing to one another and objectionable to their friends, are anxious to propitiate society by becoming unendurable to each other.

Biddy, *n.* One of the oppressed of all nations, for whom our forefathers thoughtfully provided an asylum in our kitchens.

Bigamy, *n.* A mistake in taste for which the wisdom of the future will adjudge a punishment called trigamy.

Bigot, *n.* One who is obstinately and zealously attached to an opinion that you do not entertain.

Billet-doux, *n.* In the bright lexicon of Shoddy, a love-letter.

Billingsgate, *n.* The invective of an opponent.

Biography, *n.* The literary tribute that a little man pays to a big one.

Birth, *n.* The first and direst of all disasters. As to the nature of it there appears to be no uniformity. Castor and Pollux were born from the egg. Pallas came out of a skull. Galatea was once a block of stone. Peresilis, who wrote in the tenth century, avers that he grew up out of the ground where a priest had spilled holy water. It is known that Arimaxus was derived from a hole in the earth, made by a stroke of lightning. Leucomedon was the son of a cavern in Mount Ætna, and I have myself seen a man come out of a wine cellar.

Blackguard, *n.* A man whose qualities, prepared for display like a box of berries in a market—the fine ones on top—have been opened on the wrong side. An inverted gentleman.

Blank-verse, *n.* Unrhymed iambic pentameters—the most difficult kind of English verse to write acceptably; a kind, therefore, much affected by those who cannot acceptably write any kind.

Bloodthirsty, *adj.* Addicted to the wanton wasting of blood—which is probably very good to drink.

Blubber, *n.* The part of a whale which is to that creature what beauty is to a woman—the thing for which it is pursued.

> During his past illness a dose of some kind of oil was administered to him by mistake, whereupon one of the ladies of his household began to weep. Some one attempting to comfort her, "Never mind," said the patient; "I've had my oil; let her have her blubber." — *Unpublished Memoirs of the late John B. Felton.*

Blue-stocking, *n.* A woman who for their slight of her personal charms revenges herself upon men by caricaturing science, art, letters or learning.

> "They call me a blue-stocking!" madam exclaimed;
> "Pray why, of all ladies, should I, sir, be named
> From the hue of my stockings, which man never spied?"
> "Nor ever desired to," the villain replied.

Blushing, *n.* A trick formerly in great favor with women, but now fallen into disuse as a lost art, though by laborious practice the modern damsel is still able to achieve it at the risk of being taken in hand and treated for apoplexy.

Body-snatcher, *n.* A robber of grave-worms. One who supplies the young physicians with that with which the old physicians have supplied the undertaker. The hyena.

> "One night," a doctor said, "last fall,
> I and my comrades, four in all,
>   When visiting a graveyard stood
> Within the shadow of a wall.
>
> "While waiting for the moon to sink
> We saw a wild hyena slink
>   About a new-made grave, and then
> Begin to excavate its brink!
>
> "Shocked by the horrid act, we made
> A sally from our ambuscade,
>   And, falling on the unholy beast,
> Dispatched him with a pick and spade."
>
> *Bettel K. Jhones.*

Bologna-sausage, *n.* A dead dog that is better than a living lion, but not to eat.

Bomb, or Bomb-shell, *n.* A besieger's argument in favor of capitulation, skillfully adapted to the understandings of the women and children.

Bondsman, *n.* A fool who, having property of his own, undertakes to become responsible for that entrusted by another to a third.

> Philippe of Orleans wishing to appoint one of his favorites, a dissolute nobleman, to a high office, asked him what security he would be able to give. "I need no bondsmen," he replied, "for I can give you my word of honor." "And pray what may be the value of that?" inquired the amused Regent. "Monsieur, it is worth its weight in gold."

Book-learning, *n.* The dunce's derisive term for all knowledge that transcends his own impenitent ignorance.

Bore, *n.* A person who talks when you wish him to listen.

Botany, *n.* The science of vegetables—those that are not good to eat, as well as those that are. It deals largely with their flowers, which are commonly badly designed, inartistic in color and ill-smelling.

Bottle, *n.* An oracle consulted by Panurge as to whether he should marry. By the ancient Crapuli the bottle was worshiped as a deity, but since the great reformation the Amphoristic religion has prevailed among their descendants—that is to say, the worship of the Little Brown Jug, who, under the name of Juggernaut, is revered also by the Hindoos.

Bottle-nosed, *adj.* Having a nose created in the image of its maker.

Boundary, *n.* In political geography, an imaginary line between two nations, separating the imaginary rights of one from the imaginary rights of the other.

Bounty, *n.* The liberality of one who has much, in permitting one who has nothing to get all that he can.

> A single swallow, it is said, devours ten millions of insects every year. The supplying of these insects I take to be a signal instance of the Creator's bounty in providing for the lives of His creatures. — *Henry Ward Beecher.*

Bow-wow, or Bough-wow, *n.* See PERUVIAN BARK.

Brahma, *n.* He who created the Hindoos, who are preserved by Vishnu and destroyed by Siva—a rather neater division of labor than is found among the deities of some other nations. The Abracadabranese, for example, are created by Sin, maintained by Theft and destroyed by Folly. The priests of Brahma, like those of the Abracadabranese, are holy and learned men who are never naughty.

> O Brahma, thou rare old Divinity,
> First Person of the Hindoo Trinity,
> You sit there so calm and securely,

With feet folded up so demurely—
You're the First Person Singular, surely.

Polydore Smith.

Brain, *n.* An apparatus with which we think that we think. That which distinguishes the man who is content to *be* something from the man who wishes to *do* something. A man of great wealth, or one who has been pitchforked into high station, has commonly such a headful of brain that his neighbors cannot keep their hats on. In our civilization, and under our republican form of government, brain is so highly honored that it is rewarded by exemption from the cares of office.

Brain, *v.t.* To rebuke bluntly, but not pointedly; to dispel a source of error in an opponent.

Brandy, *n.* A cordial composed of one part thunder-and-lightning, one part remorse, two parts bloody murder, one part death-hell-and-the-grave and four parts clarified Satan. Dose, a headful all the time. Brandy is said by Dr. Johnson to be the drink of heroes. Only a hero will venture to drink it.

Bribe, *n.* That which enables a member of the Californian Legislature to live on his pay without any dishonest economies.

Bride, *n.* A woman with a fine prospect of happiness behind her.

Brute, *n.* See HUSBAND.

Buddhism, *n.* A preposterous form of religious error perversely preferred by about three-fourths of the human race. According to the Rev. Dr. Stebbins it is infinitely superior to the religion which he has the honor to expound. Therefore it is.

Caaba, *n.* A large stone presented by the archangel Gabriel to the patriarch Abraham, and preserved at Mecca. The patriarch had perhaps asked the archangel for bread.

Cab, *n.* A tormenting vehicle in which a pirate jolts you through devious ways to the wrong place, where he robs you.

Cabbage, *n.* A familiar kitchen-garden vegetable about as large and wise as a man's head.

The cabbage is so called from Cabagius, a prince who on ascending the throne issued a decree appointing a High Council of Empire consisting of the members of his predecessor's Ministry and the cabbages in the royal garden. When any of his Majesty's measures of state policy miscarried conspicuously it was gravely announced that several members of the High Council had been beheaded, and his murmuring subjects were appeased.

Cabinet, *n.* The principal persons charged with the mismanagement of a government, the charge being commonly well founded.

Cackle, *v.i.* To celebrate the birth of an egg.

Cadet, *n.* A young military gentleman who ten years hence may be shaking the world and cutting the throats of nations, but in the meantime is solicitous about the best method of slitting the colored ear.

Cairn, *n.* A kind of sepulchre which it is no sacrilege to rifle.

This, by the way, is a peculiarity of all ancient tombs, and the learned Dr. Berosus Huggyns (1561) gives it as his opinion that an unknown grave may be plundered without sin in the interest of knowledge as soon as the bones have done "smellynge" — the soul being then all exhaled.

"The holy dead," said he (nor stayed
    His shovel, apprehensive)
"Are not offended by my trade,
    Unless themselves offensive."
He dug — then held his nose and fled,

With penitent misgiving;
They were, indeed, "the wholly dead,"
But their bouquet was living!

Calamity, *n*. A more than commonly plain and unmistakable reminder that the affairs of this life are not of our own ordering. Calamities are of two kinds: misfortune to ourselves, and good fortune to others.

Calliope, *n*. One of the nine Muses, who has had a narrow escape from the dread immortality of having a steam whistle named in her honor. Happily the name is popularly so mispronounced as to defeat the malevolent intent.

Callous, *adj*. Gifted with great fortitude to bear the evils afflicting another.

When Zeno was told that one of his enemies was no more he was observed to be deeply moved. "What!" said one of his disciples, "you weep at the death of an enemy?" "Ah, 'tis true," replied the great Stoic; "but you should see me smile at the death of a friend."

Calumnus, *n*. A graduate of the School for Scandal.

Calvary, *n*. An eminence on Mission street, where James O'Neill died for the sins of Salmi Morse.

Camel, *n*. A quadruped (the *Splaypes humpidorsus*) of great value to the show business. There are two kinds of camels — the camel proper and the camel improper. It is the latter that is always exhibited.

Candidate, *n*. One who by the advice of his friends reluctantly consents to sacrifice his private interests to the public good.

This word comes from the same root as "candid" and "candy," originally signifying white. It was formerly supposed to be an allusion to the Athenian method of selecting a nominee by a white ballot, but later researches of that eminent philologist, Professor Ned Townsend, show that it marks the survival of the political aspirant's custom of giving taffy.

Candy, *n*. 1. A confection composed of terra alba, glucose, flour and premature death. 2. In local commercial usage at Bombay, a weight of 560 pounds — that being about the amount of candy that a Bombegian girl will consume in a day.

Cane, *n*. A convenient article for admonishing the gentle slanderer and the inconsiderate rival.

Cannibal, *n*. A gastronome of the old school who preserves the simple tastes and adheres to the natural diet of the pre-pork period.

Cannon, *n*. An instrument employed in the rectification of national boundaries.

Canonicals, *n*. The motley worn by Jesters of the Court of Heaven.

Canonize, *v.t.* To make a saint out of a dead sinner.

Capital, *n*. The seat of misgovernment. That which provides the fire, the pot, the dinner, the table and the knife and fork for the anarchist; the part of the repast that himself supplies is the disgrace before meat. *Capital punishment,* a penalty regarding the justice and expediency of which many worthy persons — including all the assassins — entertain grave misgivings.

Carmelite, *n.* A mendicant friar of the order of Mount Carmel.

> As Death was a-riding out one day,
> Across Mount Carmel he took his way,
> > Where he met a mendicant monk,
> > Some three or four quarters drunk,
> With a holy leer and a pious grin,
> Ragged and fat and as saucy as sin,
> > Who held out his hands and cried:
> "Give, give in Charity's name, I pray.
> Give in the name of the Church. O give,
> Give that her holy sons may live!"
> > And Death replied,
> > Smiling long and wide:
> "I'll give, holy father, I'll give thee — a ride."
>
> > With a rattle and bang
> > Of his bones, he sprang
> From his famous Pale Horse, with his spear;
> > By the neck and the foot
> > Seized the fellow, and put
> Him astride with his face to the rear.
>
> The Monarch laughed loud with a sound that fell
> Like clods on the coffin's sounding shell:
> "Ho, ho! A beggar on horseback, they say,
> > Will ride to the devil!" — and *thump*
> > Fell the flat of his dart on the rump
> Of the charger, which galloped away.
>
> Faster and faster and faster it flew,
> Till the rocks and the flocks and the trees that grew
> By the road were dim and blended and blue
> > To the wild, wide eyes
> > Of the rider — in size
> Resembling a couple of blackberry pies.
> Death laughed again, as a tomb might laugh
> > At a burial service spoiled,
> > And the mourners' intentions foiled

By the body erecting
Its head and objecting
To further proceedings in its behalf.

Many a year and many a day
Have passed since these events away.
The monk has long been a dusty corse,
And Death has never recovered his horse.
For the friar got hold of its tail,
And steered it within the pale
Of the monastery gray,
Where the beast was stabled and fed
With barley and oil and bread
Till fatter it grew than the fattest friar,
And so in due course was appointed Prior.

G. J.

Carnivorous, *adj.* Addicted to the cruelty of devouring the timorous vegetarian, his heirs and assigns.

Carouse, *v.i.* To celebrate with appropriate ceremonies the birth of a noble headache.

Cartesian, *adj.* Relating to Descartes, a famous philosopher, author of the celebrated dictum, *Cogito ergo sum* —whereby he was pleased to suppose he demonstrated the reality of human existence. The dictum might be improved, however, thus: *Cogito cogito ergo cogito sum* —"I think that I think, therefore I think that I am;" as close an approach to certainty as any philosopher has yet made.

Cat, *n.* A soft, indestructible automaton provided by nature to be kicked when things go wrong in the domestic circle.
This is a dog,
This is a cat.
This is a frog,
This is a rat.
Run, dog, mew, cat.
Jump, frog, gnaw, rat.

Elevenson.

Catechism, *n.* A form of theological riddles in which universal and eternal doubts are resolved by local and fugitive answers.

Caterpillar, *n.* The capitalist of insects before he gets his start in life.

Caviler, *n.* A critic of our own work.

Cemetery, *n.* An isolated suburban spot where mourners match lies, poets write at a target and stone-cutters spell for a wager. The inscriptions following will serve to illustrate the success attained in these Olympian games:

His virtues were so conspicuous that his enemies, unable to overlook them, denied them, and his friends, to whose loose lives they were a rebuke, represented them as vices. They are here commemorated by his family, who shared them.

In the earth we here prepare a
Place to lay our little Clara.

Thomas M. and Mary Frazer.

P.S.—Gabriel will raise her.

Cenotaph, *n.* A tomb from which the body is absent, living elsewhere. The grave whose headstone bore the famous inscription,

Here lies me two children dear,
One in ould Ireland, t'other one here,

was a cenotaph, so far as regarded the "one in ould Ireland."

Censor, *n.* An officer of certain governments, employed to suppress the works of genius. Among the Romans the censor was an inspector of public morals, but the public morals of modern nations will not bear inspection.

Centaur, *n.* One of a race of persons who lived before the division of labor had been carried to such a pitch of differentiation, and who followed the primitive economic maxim, "Every man his own horse." The best of the lot was Chiron, who to the wisdom and virtues of the horse added the fleetness of man. The scripture story of the head of John the Baptist on a charger shows that pagan myths have somewhat sophisticated sacred history.

Cerberus, *n.* The watch-dog of Hades, whose duty it was to guard the entrance—against whom or what does not clearly appear; everybody, sooner or later, had to go there, and nobody wanted to carry off the entrance. Cerberus is known to have had three heads, and some of the poets have credited him with as many as a hundred. Professor Graybill, whose clerky erudition and profound knowledge of Greek give his opinion great weight, has averaged all the estimates, and makes the number twenty-seven—a judgment that would be entirely conclusive if Professor Graybill had known (*a*) something about dogs, and (*b*) something about arithmetic.

Charity, *n.* An amiable quality of the heart which moves us to condone in others the sins and vices to which ourselves are addicted.

Chemise, *n.* Don't know what it means.

Child, *n.* An accident to the occurrence of which all the forces and arrangements of nature are specially devised and accurately adapted.

Childhood, *n.* The period of human life intermediate between the idiocy of infancy and the folly of youth—two removes from the sin of manhood and three from the remorse of age.

Chimpanzee, *n*. A species of pansy cultivated in Africa.

Chinaman, *n*. A working man whose faults are docility, skill, industry, frugality and temperance, and whom we clamor to be forbidden by law to employ; whose labor opens countless avenues of employment to the whites, and cheapens the necessities of life to the poor; to whom the squalor of poverty is imputed as a congenial vice, exciting not compassion but resentment.

> It's very rough to fine a man
> For stoning of a Chinaman.
>
> *Candidate.*

Chiromancer, *n*. A romancer who tells fortunes by hand.

Chivalry, *n*. That wing of the Democratic party that has all the plumes. The other wing raises the wind for the bird to fly.

Chop, *n*. A piece of leather skilfully attached to a bone and administered to the patients at restaurants.

Chorus, *n*. In opera, a band of howling dervishes who terrify the audience while the singers are taking breath.

Christen, *v.t.* To ceremoniously afflict a helpless child with a name.

> This is in christening the only trick:
> The child is wetted so the name will stick.

Christian, *n*. One who believes that the New Testament is a divinely inspired book admirably suited to the spiritual needs of his neighbor. One who follows the teachings of Christ in so far as they are not inconsistent with a life of sin.

> I dreamed I stood upon a hill, and, lo!
> The godly multitudes walked to and fro
> Beneath, in Sabbath garments fitly clad,
> With pious mien, appropriately sad,
> While all the church bells made a solemn din—
> A fire-alarm to those who lived in sin.
> Then saw I gazing thoughtfully below,
> With tranquil face, upon that holy show
> A tall, spare figure in a robe of white,
> Whose eyes diffused a melancholy light.
> "God keep you, stranger," I exclaimed. "You are
> No doubt (your habit shows it) from afar;
> And yet I entertain the hope that you,
> Like these good people, are a Christian too."
> He raised his eyes and with a look so stern
> It made me with a thousand blushes burn
> Replied—his manner with disdain was spiced:
> "What! I a Christian? No, indeed! I'm Christ."
>
> *G. J.*

Christmas, *n.* A day set apart and consecrated to gluttony, drunkenness, maudlin sentiment, gift-taking, public dulness and domestic misbehavior.

> What! not religious? You should see, my pet,
> On every Christmas day how drunk I get!
> O, I'm a Christian—not a pious monk
> Honors the Master with so dead a drunk.

Church, *n.* A place where the parson worships God and the women worship the parson.

Circumlocution, *n.* A literary trick whereby the writer who has nothing to say breaks it gently to the reader.

Circus, *n.* A place where horses, ponies and elephants are permitted to see men, women and children acting the fool.

Clairvoyant, *n.* A person, commonly a woman, who has the power of seeing that which is invisible to her patron—namely, that he is a blockhead.

Clarionet, *n.* An instrument of torture operated by a person with cotton in his ears. There are two instruments that are worse than a clarionet—two clarionets.

Clergyman, *n.* A man who undertakes the management of our spiritual affairs as a method of bettering his temporal ones.

Client, *n.* A person who has made the customary choice between the two methods of being legally robbed.

Clinic, *adj.* Relating to a bed. A *clinical lecture* is a discourse on certain disease, illustrated by exhibiting a patient made suitably sick for the purpose.

Clio, *n.* One of the nine Muses. Clio's function was to preside over history— which she did with great dignity, many of the prominent citizens of Athens occupying seats on the platform, the meetings being addressed by Messrs. Xenophon, Herodotus and other popular speakers.

Clock, *n.* A machine of great moral value to man, allaying his concern for the future by reminding him what a lot of time remains to him.

> A busy man complained one day:
> "I get no time!" "What's that you say?"
> Cried out his friend, a lazy quiz;
> "You have, sir, all the time there is.
> There's plenty, too, and don't you doubt it—
> We're never for an hour without it."
>
> *Purzil Crofe.*

Close-communion, *n.* The sectarian practice of excluding the Sinners, and several smaller denominations, from the Lord's supper. The supper being commonly a pretty bad one, no great injustice is done.

Close-corporation, *n.* The Ring in the Board of Supervisors.

Close-fisted, *adj.* Unduly desirous of keeping that which many meritorious persons wish to obtain.

> "Close-fisted Scotchman!" Johnson cried
>   To thrifty J. Macpherson;
> "See me—I'm ready to divide
>   With any worthy person."
>
> Said Jamie: "That is very true—
>   The boast requires no backing;
> And all are worthy, sir, to you,
>   Who have what you are lacking."
>
> *Anita M. Bobe.*

Clove, *n.* A small spice that lures a man away from his girl between the acts at a theater or the dances at a ball. A man who has the clove-habit will leave a very nice girl to get a very poor clove.

Club, *n.* An association of men for purposes of drunkenness, gluttony, unholy hilarity, murder, sacrilege and the slandering of mothers, wives and sisters.

> For this definition I am indebted to several estimable ladies who have the best means of information, their husbands being members of several clubs.

Cœnobite, *n.* A man who piously shuts himself up to meditate upon the sin of wickedness; and to keep it fresh in his mind joins a brotherhood of awful examples.

> O cœnobite, O cœnobite,
>   Monastical gregarian,
> You differ from the anchorite,
>   That solitudinarian:
> With vollied prayers you wound Old Nick;
> With dropping shots he makes him sick.
>
> *Quincy Giles.*

Colonel, *n.* The most gorgeously appareled man of a regiment.

> "Colonel, the fire
>   Is fierce and dire—
> I fear we sha'n't outlive it.
>   Go take that hill!"
>   "Yes, sir, I will—
> If anybody'll give it."
>
> "O colonel bland,
>   At your command
> How many men, I pray thee?"

"Only my own—
    The foes are prone
At times to disobey me."

Comedy, *n.* A play in which none of our fellow-actors are visibly killed.

Comet, *n.* An excuse for being out late at night and going home drunk in the morning.

Comfort, *n.* A state of mind produced by contemplation of a neighbor's uneasiness.

Commendation, *n.* The tribute that we pay to achievements that resemble, but do not equal, our own.

Commerce, *n.* A kind of transaction in which A plunders from B the goods of C, and for compensation B picks the pocket of D of money belonging to E.

Commit, *v.t.* In law, to hold for trial. In England this is one of the most irregular of verbs, its past participle being *fullied*. The ingenious reader may conjecture why.

    'Tis plain that crime we'll ne'er suppress,
        Nor bate its force a whit,
    While all the magistrates possess
        The power to commit.

Common-law, *n.* The will and pleasure of the judge.

Commonwealth, *n.* An administrative entity operated by an incalculable multitude of political parasites, logically active but fortuitously efficient.

    This commonwealth's capitol's corridors view,
    So thronged with a hungry and indolent crew
    Of clerks, pages, porters and all attachés
    Whom rascals appoint and the populace pays
    That a cat cannot slip through the thicket of shins
    Nor hear its own shriek for the noise of their chins.
    On clerks and on pages, and porters, and all,
    Misfortune attend and disaster befall!
    May life be to them a succession of hurts;
    May fleas by the bushel inhabit their shirts;
    May aches and diseases encamp in their bones,
    Their lungs full of tubercles, bladders of stones;
    May microbes, bacilli, their tissues infest,
    And tapeworms securely their bowels digest;
    May corn-cobs be snared without hope in their hair,
    And frequent impalement their pleasure impair.
    Disturbed be their dreams by the awful discourse
    Of audible sofas sepulchrally hoarse,
    By chairs acrobatic and wavering floors—

The mattress that kicks and the pillow that snores!
Sons of cupidity, cradled in sin!
Your criminal ranks may the death angel thin,
Avenging the friend whom I couldn't work in.

K. Q.

Competitor, *n.* A scoundrel who desires that which *we* desire.

Compliment, *n.* A loan that bears interest.

Compromise, *n.* Such an adjustment of conflicting interests as gives each adversary the satisfaction of thinking he has got what he ought not to have, and is deprived of nothing except what was justly his due.

Compulsion, *n.* The eloquence of power.

Compunction, *n.* (Lat. *con*, against, and *punctum*, a point.) The remorse of an offender who has "kicked against the pricks," as the Scripture hath it.

Concatenate, *v.t.* Linked together like the several instalments of a sausage. Dr. Johnson said of a certain literary work that its various parts were "concatenated without abruption."

> When Jove resolved to make the world
>   He gathered all the matter
> In Chaos that was mixed and whirled
>   In unassorted scatter.
>
> He separated that from this,
>   And tagged on each a label,
> Naming all kinds of substances
>   As far as he was able.
>
> Jove hadn't learning, though, enough
>   To execute his aim, for
> There still remained a lot of stuff
>   He hadn't any name for.
>
> And this (the world completed) lies
>   Without concatenation—
> Unutterable!—and supplies
>   The hash for all creation.

Conceit, *n.* Self-respect in one whom we dislike.

Concert, *n.* An entertainment for the humiliation of Baby by superior howling.

Concession, *n.* A lowering of one's guard to elicit an adversary's ill-considered thrust.

Conciliation, *n.* Same as above.

Conclusive, *adj.* Decisive of the matter in dispute if followed by immediate withdrawal from the debate.

Condole, *v.i.* To show that bereavement is a smaller evil than sympathy.

Condone, *v.t.*

> Condone's a word that means to let
> The sinner think that we forget;
> Thus gaining time to meditate
> How we may best retaliate.
> Just as the cat, affecting sleep,
> Permits the wounded mouse to creep
> Half way to cover, and then vaults
> Upon him with renewed assaults,
> So man to his revenge supplies
> The added terrors of surprise.

Conductor, *n.* The man who punches your ticket and your head.

Confession, *n.* A place where the priest sits to forgive the big sins for the pleasure of hearing about the little ones.

Confidant, Confidante, *n.* One entrusted by A with the secrets of B, confided by *him* to C.

Congratulation, *n.* The civility of envy.

Congregation, *n.* The subjects of an experiment in hypnotism.

Congress, *n.* A body of men who meet to repeal laws.

Conjugal, *adj.* (Lat. *con,* mutual, and *jugum,* a yoke.) Relating to a popular kind of penal servitude—the yoking together of two fools by a parson.

Connoisseur, *n.* A specialist who knows everything about something and nothing about anything else.

> An old wine-bibber having been smashed in a railway collision, some wine was poured upon his lips to revive him. "Pauillac, 1873," he murmured and died.

Conscience, *n.* A morbid condition of the stomach, affecting the gray matter of the brain and producing a mental discord.

> His conscience never did afflict him,
>> Save when he'd badly dined;
> Then like a creditor it kicked him,
>> Behind.
>
> Vainly the parson he consulted
>> How to allay the pain;
> E'en while he prays he's catapulted
>> Again.
>
> Thus failing times without a number,
>> He sought a doctor out,

Who said: "You've eaten a cucumber,
 No doubt."

"Yes, Doctor, but I didn't steal it;
 Then why this dark distress?"
"You mean, my friend, you didn't peel it,
 I guess.

"Woes that defy the world's religions—
 The Spirit's brooding ills—
We scatter, like a flock of pigeons,
 With pills."

Conservative, *n*. A statesman who is enamored of existing evils, as distinguished from the Liberal, who wishes to replace them with others.

Consolation, *n*. The knowledge that a better man is more unfortunate than yourself.

Consul, *n*. In American politics, a person who having failed to secure an office from the people is given one by the Administration on condition that he leave the country.

Consult, *v.t*. To seek another's approval of a course already decided on.

Contempt, *n*. The feeling of a prudent man for an enemy who is too formidable safely to be opposed.

Contributor, *n*. In journalism, a patron of the waste-basket, who keeps the editors supplied with postage stamps which he thoughtfully encloses for the return of his rejected favors.

Controversy, *n*. A battle in which spittle or ink replaces the injurious cannonball and the inconsiderate bayonet.

In controversy with the facile tongue—
That bloodless warfare of the old and young—
So seek your adversary to engage
That on himself he shall exhaust his rage,
And, like a snake that's fastened to the ground,
With his own fangs inflict the fatal wound.
You ask me how this miracle is done?
Adopt his own opinions, one by one,
And taunt him to refute them; in his wrath
He'll sweep them pitilessly from his path.
Advance then gently all you wish to prove,
Each proposition prefaced with, "As you've
So well remarked," or, "As you wisely say,
And I cannot dispute," or, "By the way,

This view of it which, better far expressed,
Runs through your argument." Then leave the rest
To him, secure that he'll perform his trust
And prove your views intelligent and just.

Conmore Apel Brune.

Convent, *n.* A place of retirement for women who wish for leisure to meditate upon the vice of idleness.

Conversation, *n.* A fair for the display of the minor mental commodities, each exhibitor being too intent upon the arrangement of his own wares to observe those of his neighbor.

Cookery, *n.* A household art and practice of making unpalatable that which was already indigestible.

The husband threw a hateful look—
A kind of optic snarl and
Growl—on wifey's cookery book,
By Marion Harland.

"Some of these recipes, I see,
Begin with crosses sable;
The meaning please explain to me
If you are able."

"She thus marks those that she has tried
And finds them nicely fitted
For dinner use," the wife replied,
And hubby's dulness pitied.

"I thought those crosses, now," said he,
With brutal sneer and vicious,
"Erected to the memory
Of men who ate those dishes."

Coquette, *n.* A vain, foolish and stupid girl who after a pretty thorough sampling of oneself prefers another.

Cordiality, *n.* The peculiarly engaging quality of manner toward one who is about to enjoy the distinction of being overreached.

Corkscrew, *n.* The outfit of a gentleman who travels flying light.

Corned, *pp.* Boosy, swipy, soaked, hog drunk, set up. (Very low and vulgar.)
Hell has no fury like a woman corned. — *Hector Stuart.*

Coronation, *n.* The ceremony of investing a sovereign with the outward and visible signs of his divine right to be blown skyhigh with a dynamite bomb.

Coroner, *n.* (Lat. *corona,* a crown; the pronunciation "crowner" is therefore legitimate.) A municipal officer charged with the duty of cutting up the unfortunate to see if they are dead. They always are.

Corporal, *n.* A man who occupies the lowest rung of the military ladder.

> Fiercely the battle raged and, sad to tell,
> Our corporal heroically fell!
> Fame from her height looked down upon the brawl
> And said: "He hadn't very far to fall."
>
> *Giacomo Smith.*

Corporation, *n.* An ingenious device for obtaining individual profit without individual responsibility.

Corpse, *n.* A person who manifests the highest possible degree of indifference that is consistent with a civil regard for the solicitude of others.

Corrupt, *adj.* In politics, holding an office of trust or profit.

Corsair, *n.* A politician of the seas.

Counterfeit, *adj.* Similar in appearance but of a different order of merit.

Country, *n.* The circumurban region inhabited by the quail, the trout, the deer and the armed granger. It is a region of romance, where the golden age still lingers, as in the earth's green prime, when Virgil sang and the gods mingled with men and maidens.

> 'Tis a land of corn and swine,
>> Flowing, too, with bilk and honey.
> City folk go there to dine
> In the land of corn and swine.
> 'Neath his big-tree and his pine
>> Frugal swain rakes in the money.
> 'Tis a land of corn and swine,
>> 'Tis the place to drop your money.
>
> There the crookèd shepherd plays
>> On his pandemonian pipes;
> By a table crowned with baise
> Ev'ry crookèd shepherd plays.
> For the city gent he lays
>> With a poker-deck and swipes.
> There the crookèd shepherd lays
>> For the city gent his pipes.

Couple, *n.* Two of a kind, as two aces, two jacks, two fives, etc. A pair. A popular kind of couple is the Bartlett Pair, named in honor of the inventor, Mr. Bartlett, of the *Bulletin.* It consists of an eight and a seven, with one of the spots of the eight covered by the player's thumb. A Bartlett Pair can be made of a seven and a six in the same way.

Court Fool, *n.* The plaintiff.

Covet, *v.i.* To desire that which the owner wickedly withholds.

> Thou shalt not covet thy friend's wife,
> For she would bring thee naught but strife.
> Nor shalt thou with a wish too fervent
> Covet (unless she's fair) his servant;
> Nor yet his horse, nor ox, nor ass,
> For fear that it should come to pass
> That they—unless you've pasture lands—
> Should eat their heads off on your hands.
> Covet not aught, lest it should lead
> You to commit some thieving deed.
> Supply your wants a better way:
> Buy what you need—and never pay.
>> *Revised Edition.*

Cow, *n.* The business partner of the artesian well.

Coward, *n.* One who in a perilous emergency thinks with his legs.

Cowlick, *n.* A tuft of hair which persists in lying the wrong way. In the case of a married man it usually points toward the side that his wife commonly walks on.

Coyness, *n.* A species of reluctance formerly affected by young women but now abandoned as "bad form."

> "She who hesitates is lost" —
> Of coyness that's the fearful cost.
> So, ladies, lest you should repent,
> Be ready with a quick consent.
>> *Old Play.*

Cradle, *n.* A trough in which the human infant is agitated to keep it sweet.

Craft, *n.* A fool's substitute for brains.

Crapulent, *adj.* As gentlemen wish to be who love their landlords—otherwise barkeepers.

Crayfish, *n.* A small crustacean very much resembling the lobster, but less indigestible.

> In this small fish I take it that human wisdom is admirably figured and symbolized; for whereas the crayfish doth move only backward, and can have only retrospection, seeing naught but the perils already passed, so the wisdom of man doth not enable him to avoid the follies that beset his course, but only to apprehend their nature afterward. — *Sir James Merivale.*

Creditor, *n.* One of a tribe of savages dwelling beyond the Financial Straits and dreaded for their desolating incursions.

Cremation, *n.* The process by which the cold meats of humanity are warmed over.

Cremona, *n.* A high-priced violin made in Connecticut.

Crescent, *n.* The moon in the early stages of its monthly growth, when it is a little too bright for burglars and a little too dark for lovers. An Order founded by Renatus of Anjou is called the Order of the Crescent on account of its membership of lunatics. The services of this Order to San Francisco politics consisted in the establishing of a Grand Perquisition to enforce the Salaric Law.

Crest, *n.* An heraldic device displayed by the American descendants of Sir Crassus Vulgarius, Bearonet, one of the famous retainers of William the Corn-curer.

> Son of ten fathers! would you sport a crest
> To honor one, ignoring all the rest—
> The one who in his life you did disgrace
> By taking on his name without his face?
> *His* crest? The only one he knew, poor fool,
> Adorned the dunce-cap that he wore at school.
> Go paint a dandelion and a rag
> Upon your panels, and then gravely brag
> About their origin—how every panel
> Proves that the founder of your line was Dan'l,
> Who, cast among the lions' growling pack,
> Contemptuously turned on them his back;
> But one presuming brute, tradition teaches,
> Tore with his tooth the seat of Dan'l's breeches.
> 'Twas thus the *dent de lion* and the rag
> Became the arms of that illustrious wag.
> And ever since each male of Dan'l's line,
> Yourself included, as a pious sign
> And token of his Scriptural descent,
> Has worn a rag protruding from a rent.

Cribbage, *n.* A substitute for conversation among those to whom nature has denied ideas. See EUCHRE, PEDRO, SEVEN-UP, ETC.

Critic, *n.* A person who boasts himself hard to please because nobody tries to please him.

> There is a land of pure delight,
>   Beyond the Jordan's flood,
> Where saints, apparelled all in white,
>   Fling back the critic's mud.

And as he legs it through the skies,
 His pelt a sable hue,
He sorrows sore to recognize
 The missiles that he threw.

Orrin Goof.

Cross, *n.* An ancient religious symbol erroneously supposed to owe its significance to the most solemn event in the history of Christianity, but really antedating it by thousands of years. By many it has been believed to be identical with the *crux ansata* of the ancient phallic worship, but it has been traced
even beyond all that we know of that, to the rites of primitive peoples. We
have to-day the White Cross as a symbol of chastity, and the Red Cross as a
badge of benevolent neutrality in war. Having in mind the former, the reverend Father Gassalasca Jape smites the lyre to the effect following:

"Be good, be good!" the sisterhood
 Cry out in holy chorus,
And, to dissuade from sin, parade
 Their various charms before us.

But why, O why, has ne'er an eye
 Seen her of winsome manner
And youthful grace and pretty face
 Flaunting the White Cross banner?

Now where's the need of speech and screed
 To better our behaving?
A simpler plan for saving man
 (But, first, is he worth saving?)

Is, dears, when he declines to flee
 From bad thoughts that beset him,
Ignores the Law as 't were a straw,
 And wants to sin—don't let him.

Cudgel, *n.* A medicine for external application to the head and shoulders of a
fool.

Cui Bono? (Latin.) What good would that do *me?*

Culprit, *n.* The other fellow.

Cunning, *n.* The faculty that distinguishes a weak animal or person from a
strong one. It brings its possessor much mental satisfaction and great material adversity. An Italian proverb says: "The furrier gets the skins of more
foxes than asses."

Cupid, *n.* The so-called god of love. This bastard creation of a barbarous fancy
was no doubt inflicted upon mythology for the sins of its deities. Of all

unbeautiful and inappropriate conceptions this is the most reasonless and offensive. The notion of symbolizing sexual love by a semisexless babe, and comparing the pains of passion to the wounds of an arrow—of introducing this pudgy homunculus into art grossly to materialize the subtle spirit and suggestion of the work—this is eminently worthy of the age that, giving it birth, laid it on the doorstep of posterity.

Cur, *n.* The lowest rank in the hierarchy of dogs.

Curiosity, *n.* An objectionable quality of the female mind. The desire to know whether or not a woman is cursed with curiosity is one of the most active and insatiable passions of the masculine soul.

Curse, *v.t.* Energetically to belabor with a verbal slap-stick. This is an operation which in literature, particularly in the drama, is commonly fatal to the victim. Nevertheless, the liability to a cursing is a risk that cuts but a small figure in fixing the rates of life insurance.

Custard, *n.* A detestable substance produced by a malevolent conspiracy of the hen, the cow and the cook.

Cynic, *n.* A blackguard whose faulty vision sees things as they are, not as they ought to be. Hence the custom among the Scythians of plucking out a cynic's eyes to improve his vision.

Dad, *n.* A father whom his vulgar children do not respect.

Dado, *n.* Anything decorative for which the æsthetes know no better name.

Damn, *v.* A word formerly much used by the Paphlagonians, the meaning of which is lost. By the learned Dr. Dolabelly Gak it is believed to have been a term of satisfaction, implying the highest possible degree of mental tranquillity. Professor Groke, on the contrary, thinks it expressed an emotion of tumultuous delight, because it so frequently occurs in combination with the word *jod* or *god,* meaning "joy." It would be with great diffidence that I should advance an opinion conflicting with that of either of these formidable authorities.

Dance, *v.i.* To leap about to the sound of tittering music, preferably with arms about your neighbor's wife or daughter. There are many kinds of dances, but all those requiring the participation of the two sexes have two characteristics in common: they are conspicuously innocent, and warmly loved by the vicious.

Dandle, *v.t.* To set an unresisting child upon one's knee and jolt its teeth loose in a transport of affection. A grown girl may be similarly outraged, but her teeth being more firmly secure, there can be no object in doing so, and the custom is a mere mechanical survival of a habit acquired by practice on babes and sucklings.

> If you care not for the scandal
> You can hold a girl and dandle
> > Her upon your knee all night;
> But the game's not worth the candle —
> > When 'tis played by candle light.
>
> But whene'er you feel the yearning,
> And the candle isn't burning —
> > Or at least not very bright,

> Then the little game concerning
>> Which I sing is very quite.

Dandy, *n.* One who professes a singularity of opinion with regard to his own merits, accentuating his eccentricity with his clothes.

Danger, *n.*

> A savage beast which, when it sleeps,
>> Man girds at and despises,
> But takes himself away by leaps
>> And bounds when it arises.

>> *Ambat Delaso.*

Daring, *n.* One of the most conspicuous qualities of a man in security.

Darling, *n.* The bore of opposite sex in an early stage of development.

Datary, *n.* A high ecclesiastic official of the Roman Catholic Church, whose important function is to brand the Pope's bulls with the words *Datum Romæ*. He enjoys a princely revenue and the friendship of God.

Dawn, *n.* The time when men of reason go to bed. Certain old men prefer to rise at about that time, taking a cold bath and a long walk with an empty stomach, and otherwise mortifying the flesh. They then point with pride to these practices as the cause of their sturdy health and ripe years; the truth being that they are hearty and old, not because of their habits, but in spite of them. The reason we find only robust persons doing this thing is that it has killed all the others who have tried it.

Day, *n.* A period of twenty-four hours, mostly misspent. This period is divided into two parts, the day proper and the night, or day improper—the former devoted to sins of business, the latter consecrated to the other sort. These two kinds of social activity overlap.

Dead, *adj.*

> Done with the work of breathing; done
> With all the world; the mad race run
> Through to the end; the golden goal
> Attained and found to be a hole!

>> *Squatol Johnes.*

Debauchee, *n.* One who has so earnestly pursued pleasure that he has had the misfortune to overtake it.

Debt, *n.* An ingenious substitute for the chain and whip of the slave-driver.

> As, pent in an aquarium, the troutlet
> Swims round and round his tank to find an outlet,
> Pressing his nose against the glass that holds him,
> Nor ever sees the prison that enfolds him;
> So the poor debtor, seeing naught around him,

Yet feels the narrow limits that impound him,
Grieves at his debt and studies to evade it,
And finds at last he might as well have paid it.

Barlow S. Vode.

Decalogue, *n.* A series of commandments, ten in number—just enough to permit an intelligent selection for observance, but not enough to embarrass the choice. Following is the revised edition of the Decalogue, calculated for this meridian.

Thou shalt no God but me adore:
'Twere too expensive to have more.

No images nor idols make
For Robert Ingersoll to break.

Take not God's name in vain; select
A time when it will have effect.

Work not on Sabbath days at all,
But go to see the teams play ball.

Honor thy parents. That creates
For life insurance lower rates.

Kill not, abet not those who kill;
Thou shalt not pay thy butcher's bill.

Kiss not thy neighbor's wife, unless
Thine own thy neighbor doth caress.

Don't steal; thou'lt never thus compete
Successfully in business. Cheat.

Bear not false witness—that is low—
But "hear 'tis rumored so and so."

Covet thou naught that thou hast not
By hook or crook, or somehow, got.

G. J.

Decanter, *n.* A vessel whose functions are most envied by the human stomach.

Decide, *v.i.* To succumb to the preponderance of one set of influences over another set.

A leaf was riven from a tree,
"I mean to fall to earth," said he.

The west wind, rising, made him veer.
"Eastward," said he, "I now shall steer."

The east wind rose with greater force.
Said he: "'Twere wise to change my course."

With equal power they contend.
He said: "My judgment I suspend."

Down died the winds; the leaf, elate,
Cried: "I've decided to fall straight."

"First thoughts are best?" That's not the moral;
Just choose your own and we'll not quarrel.

Howe'er your choice may chance to fall,
You'll have no hand in it at all.

G. J.

Deer, *n.* The patter of a jackass rabbit in the chaparral, as heard by a city sportsman.

Defame, *v.t.* To lie about another. To tell the truth about another.

Defaulter, *n.* An important officer in a bank, who commonly adds to his regular function the duties of cashier.

Defenceless, *adj.* Unable to attack.

Defendant, *n.* In law, an obliging person who devotes his time and character to preserving property for his lawyer.

Defraud, *v.t.* To impart instruction and experience to the confiding.

Degenerate, *adj.* Less conspicuously admirable than one's ancestors. The contemporaries of Homer were striking examples of degeneracy; it required ten of them to raise a rock or a riot that one of the heroes of the Trojan war could have raised with ease. Homer never tires of sneering at "men who live in these degenerate days," which is perhaps why they suffered him to beg his bread — a marked instance of returning good for evil, by the way, for if they had forbidden him he would certainly have starved.

Degradation, *n.* One of the stages of moral and social progress from private station to political preferment.

Deinotherium, *n.* An extinct pachyderm that flourished when the Pterodactyl was in fashion. The latter was a native of Ireland, its name being pronounced Terry Dactyl or Peter O'Dactyl, as the man pronouncing it may chance to have heard it spoken or seen it printed.

Deiparous, *adj.* Giving birth, or capable of giving birth, to gods.

> The grand Greek women, who could count
> Among their friends the nobs of Mount
>   Olympus, were deiparous;
> Our modern dames, whose godlings fill

The skyward spaces of Nob Hill
   Are only—well, stultiparous.

Dame Nature, though, her issues pools,
For all alike are gods and fools
   Who nectar sip from chalices:
On cold Olympus who would dwell
Are fools, and they are gods as well
   Who live in Nob Hill palaces.

Deist, *n.* One who believes in God, but reserves the right to worship the Devil.

Dejeuner, *n.* The breakfast of an American who has been in Paris. Variously pronounced.

Delegation, *n.* In American politics, an article of merchandise that comes in sets.

Deliberation, *n.* The act of examining one's bread to determine which side it is buttered on.

Deluge, *n.* A notable first experiment in baptism which washed away the sins (and sinners) of the world.

Delusion, *n.* The father of a most respectable family, comprising Enthusiasm, Affection, Self-denial, Faith, Hope, Charity and many other goodly sons and daughters.

   All hail, Delusion! Were it not for thee
   The world turned topsy-turvy we should see;
   For Vice, respectable with cleanly fancies,
   Would fly abandoned Virtue's gross advances.
                       Mumfrey Mappel.

Demagogue, *n.* A political opponent.

Demented, *adj.* The melancholy mental condition of one whose arguments we are unable to answer.

Demi-john, *n.* A den of snakes.

Demise, *n.* The death of an exalted personage.

   Death is but death; we go when claimed—
      To all alike the road is;
   But still the great man's death is named
      "Demise" by living toadies.
   Thus sycophancy strives to level
   The royal highway to the Devil.

Demon, *n.* A man whose cruelties are related in the newspapers. See FIEND IN HUMAN SHAPE.

Demonomania, *n.* A condition of mind in which the patient fondly imagines himself acting under the authority of the devil, and is just too proud for anything.

Demure, *adj.* Grave and modest-mannered, like a particularly unscrupulous woman.

> There was a young maid so demure,
> That she fooled all the men who knew her;
>> But the women they smoked her
>> And took her and choked her
> And chucked her into a sewer.
>> *Milton.*

Dentist, *n.* A prestidigitator who, putting metal into your mouth, pulls coins out of your pocket.

Deny, *v.t.* See HURL BACK THE ALLEGATION.

Dependent, *adj.* Reliant upon another's generosity for the support which you are not in a position to exact from his fears.

Depilatory, *adj.* Having the property of removing hair from the skin—a quality highly developed in the hand of a wife.

Deportment, *n.* An invention of the devil, to assist his followers into good society.

Deposit, *n.* A charitable contribution to the support of a bank.

Depraved, *pp.* The moral condition of a gentleman who holds the opposite opinion.

Depression, *n.* The state of mind produced by a newspaper joke, a nigger minstrel performance, or the contemplation of another's success.

Deputy, *n.* A male relative of an office-holder, or of his bondsman. The deputy is commonly a beautiful young man, with a red necktie and an intricate system of cobwebs extending from his nose to his desk. When accidentally struck by the janitor's broom, he gives off a cloud of dust.

> "Chief Deputy," the Master cried,
> "To-day the books are to be tried
> By experts and accountants who
> Have been commissioned to go through
> Our office here, to see if we
> Have stolen injudiciously.
> Please have the proper entries made,
> The proper balances displayed,
> Conforming to the whole amount
> Of cash on hand—which they will count.
> I've long admired your punctual way—
> Here at the break and close of day,
> Confronting in your chair the crowd
> Of business men, whose voices loud
> And gestures violent you quell

By some mysterious, calm spell—
Some magic lurking in your look
That brings the noisiest to book
And spreads a holy and profound
Tranquillity o'er all around.
So orderly all's done that they
Who came to draw remain to pay.
But now the time demands, at last,
That you employ your genius vast
In energies more active. Rise
And shake the lightnings from your eyes;
Inspire your underlings, and fling
Your spirit into everything!"
The Master's hand here dealt a whack
Upon the Deputy's bent back,
When straightway to the floor there fell
A shrunken globe, a rattling shell
A blackened, withered, eyeless head!
The man had been a twelvemonth dead.

Jamrach Holobom.

Deranged, *pp. or adj.* A condition of mind immediately precedent to the commission of a murder.

Derision, *n.* The ineffectual argument by which a fool imagines he has answered the contempt of the wise.

Descendant, *n.* Any person proceeding from an ancestor in any degree.

    Alas for the days when my baboon ancestral
        In Japanese woods from the lithe limb was pendant,
    Instructing, kind hearted, each babooness vestal
        How best to achieve for herself a descendant.

Oscar Wilde.

Descent, *n.* Going lower. Popularly used to indicate the existing generation is a peg worse than that which fathered it. Thus one Darwin justly discourses upon the superiority of the ancestral baboon in a melancholy essay, called "The Descent of Man."

Desert, *n.* An extensive and fertile tract of land producing heavy wheat and vintage crops in colonization prospectuses.

Desertion, *n.* An aversion to fighting, as exhibited by abandoning an army or a wife.

Deserve, *n.* The quality of being entitled to what somebody else obtains.

Deshabille, *n.* A reception costume for intimate friends varying according to locality, e.g. In Boorioboola-Gha, a streak of red and yellow paint across the thorax. In San Francisco, pearl ear-rings and a smile.

Desiccate, *v.a.* To make dry.

> Now Noble to the pulpit leaps,
> The mighty desiccator,
> The audience profoundly sleeps —
> Slow snores the great creator.
>
> *Shelley.*

Despatches, *n.* A complete account of all the murders, outrages and other disgusting crimes which take place everywhere, disseminated daily by an Associated Press for the amelioration of the world in general.

Destiny, *n.* [1.] A tyrant's authority for crime and a fool's excuse for failure. [2.] A force alleged to control affairs, principally quoted by erring human beings to excuse their failures.

> "'Tis destiny," Sam Barrell cried;
> "Once I had gold of Ophir;
> Now humbled is my former pride,
> And I've become a loafer."
> "Not strange," said Turnbull, passing by,
> "That you with fate should fare ill.
> The destiny that rules you, I
> Have always found in barrel."

Detective, *n.* An official employed by the city and county to detect a crime when one has been committed.

Devil, *n.* The author of all our woes and proprietor of all the good things of this world. He was made by the Almighty, but brought into the world by a woman.

> When Eve stood at the judgment seat,
> And argued for salvation,
> She pleaded at Jehovah's feet,
> In sad extenuation,
> That Satan, who had made them eat,
> Was of His own creation.

> "Not so," and frowned the Master's face,
> "That apple 'twas a sin to
> Indulge in, with no saving grace.
> Atone! You can't begin to.
> I merely turned him loose in space,
> The world, *you* brought him into."
>
> *Ella Wheeler.*

Devotion, *n*. A mild type of mental aberration variously produced; in love, by a surplus of blood; in religion, by chronic dyspepsia.

Dew, *n*. A terrestrial perspiration or night sweat invented to nourish the tender huckleberry and the yearning poet. Slightly dashed with goat's milk and whisky, it is an article much affected by Hibernian temperance lecturers, who are sometimes affected by it, in turn.

Dextrality, *n*. The state of being on the right side. See POLITICIAN.

> You will always find me on the right side, sir; always! I cannot afford to get left! — *Gen. McComb.*

Diagnosis, *n*. A physician's forecast of disease by the patient's pulse and purse.

Diamond, *n*. A worthless stone, too soft to be given to a beggar in place of bread and too small to knock him down with.

Diaphragm, *n*. A muscular partition separating disorders of the chest from disorders of the bowels.

Diary, *n*. A daily record of that part of one's life, which he can relate to himself without blushing.

> Hearst kept a diary wherein were writ
> All that he had of wisdom and of wit.
> So the Recording Angel, when Hearst died,
> Erased all entries of his own and cried:
> "I'll judge you by your diary." Said Hearst:
> "Thank you; 'twill show you I am Saint the First" —
> Straightway producing, jubilant and proud,
> That record from a pocket in his shroud.
> The Angel slowly turned the pages o'er,
> Each stupid line of which he knew before,
> Glooming and gleaming as by turns he hit
> On shallow sentiment and stolen wit;
> Then gravely closed the book and gave it back.
> "My friend, you've wandered from your proper track:
> You'd never be content this side the tomb —
> For big ideas Heaven has little room,
> And Hell's no latitude for making mirth,"
> He said, and kicked the fellow back to earth.
>
> *"The Mad Philosopher."*

Dice, *n*. Small polka-dotted cubes of ivory, constructed like a lawyer to lie on any side, but commonly on the wrong one.

Dictator, *n*. The chief of a nation that prefers the pestilence of despotism to the plague of anarchy.

Dictionary, *n*. A malevolent literary device for cramping the growth of a language and making it hard and inelastic. This dictionary, however, is a most useful work.

Die, *n.* The singular of "dice." We seldom hear the word, because there is a prohibitory proverb, "Never say die." At long intervals, however, some one says: "The die is cast," which is not true, for it is cut. The word is found in an immortal couplet by that eminent poet and domestic economist, Senator Depew:

> A cube of cheese no larger than a die
> May bait the trap to catch a nibbling mie.

Digestion, *n.* The conversion of victuals into virtues. When the process is imperfect, vices are evolved instead—a circumstance from which that wicked writer, Dr. Jeremiah Blenn, infers that the ladies are the greater sufferers from dyspepsia.

Dine, *v.i.* To eat a good dinner in good company, and eat it slow. In dining, as distinguished from mere feeding, the palate and stomach never ask the hand, "What are you giving us?"

Diplomacy, *n.* The patriotic art of lying for one's country.

Director, *n.* An officer of a company or corporation who fondly imagines he is on the inside when they don't assess him.

Disabuse, *v.t.* To present your neighbor with another and better error than the one which he has deemed it advantageous to embrace.

Disannul, *v.t.* Same thing as ANNUL, though you wouldn't think it.

Discreditable, *adj.* In the characteristic and customary manner of a rival.

Discriminate, *v.i.* To note the particulars in which one person or thing is, if possible, more objectionable than another.

Discussion, *n.* A method of confirming others in their errors.

Disease, *n.* Nature's endowment of medical schools. A liberal provision for the maintenance of undertakers. A means of supplying the worthy grave-worm with meat that is not too dry and tough for tunneling and stoping.

Disenchant, *v.t.* To free the soul from the chains of illusion in order that the lash of truth may draw blood at a greater number of points.

> Now Mary Walker disenchants
>   All eyes that on her figure dwell,
> Apparelled in a pair of "pants"
>   That fit not wisely but too well.
> But Mrs. St——w, bewitching thing!
> Charms most where most her trowsers cling.

Dishonesty, *n.* An important element of commercial success, to which the business colleges have not as yet accorded an honorable prominence in the curriculum, but have weakly substituted penmanship.

> Dishonesty is the best policy.—*New Testament: St. Judas Iscariot, IXL., 29.*

Disincorporation, *n.* A popular method of eluding the agile liability and annexing the coy asset.

Disobedience, *n.* The silver lining to the cloud of servitude.

Disobey, *v.t.* To celebrate with an appropriate ceremony the maturity of a command.

> His right to govern me is clear as day,
> My duty manifest to disobey;
> And if that fit observance e'er I shun
> May I and duty be alike undone.
>
> *Israfel Brown.*

Disrepute, *n.* The condition of a philosopher. The condition of a fool. The condition of a candidate.

Dissemble, *v.i.* To put a clean shirt upon the character.

> Let us dissemble. —*Adam.*

Dissyllable, *n.* A word of two syllables. The following words are dissyllables, according to the ancient and honorable usage of all the San Francisco poets: *Fire, hire, tire, flour, hour, sour, scour, chasm, spasm, realm, helm* and slippery *elm.*

Distance, *n.* The only thing that the rich are willing for the poor to call theirs, and keep.

Distillery, *n.* An institution for the facture and dissemination of the scarlet snout. It is to the distillery, also, that we owe that precious inheritance, the talking teetotaler.

Distress, *n.* A disease incurred by exposure to the prosperity of a friend.

Divination, *n.* The art of nosing out the occult. Divination is of as many kinds as there are fruit-bearing varieties of the flowering dunce and the early fool.

Divine, *n.* A bird of pray.

Divorce, *n.* A bugle blast that separates the combatants and makes them fight at long range.

Doctor, *n.* A gentleman who thrives upon disease and dies of health.

Doctrinaire, *n.* One whose doctrine has the demerit of antagonizing your own.

Dog, *n.* A kind of additional or subsidiary Deity designed to catch the overflow and surplus of the world's worship. This Divine Being in some of his smaller and silkier incarnations takes, in the affection of Woman, the place to which there is no human male aspirant. The Dog is a survival—an anachronism. He toils not, neither does he spin, yet Solomon in all his glory never lay upon a door-mat all day long, sun-soaked and fly-fed and fat, while his master worked for the means wherewith to purchase the idle wag of the Solomonic tail, seasoned with a look of tolerant recognition.

Domestic, *n.* A person whom one employs about the house to exercise the functions of master or mistress.

Domestic, *adj.* Appertaining to the household, as a *domestic* husband, one who loafs about the house making love to the female domestics. The domestic husband is commonly what Artemus Ward said the Prince of Wales was— "a good provider." That is to say, he commonly provides good looking kitchen maids.

Dotage, *n.* Imbecility from age, commonly manifested in loquacity. (This word was originally ANECDOTAGE, but those of whom it is the characteristic virtue have not time to speak the entire word; they are too busy talking.)

Dowry, *n.* The worm upon the matrimonial hook in man-fishing.

Dragon, *n.* A leading attraction in the menagerie of the antique imagination. It seems to have escaped.

Dragoon, *n.* A soldier who combines dash and steadiness in so equal measure that he makes his advances on foot and his retreats on horseback.

Dramatist, *n.* One who adapts plays from the French.

Dropsy, *n.* A disease which makes the patient's lease of life a kind of naval engagement.

> Dick, through all his life, had cherished
> An ambition when he perished
> To be drowned in the deep ocean,—
> Not from any foolish notion
> That so damp a death was cheerful,
> But because the wretch was fearful
> That he some day would exhibit
> On the tight-rope of a gibbet;
> Or, escaping that curtailment,
> Die of some distressing ailment,
> Giving up the ghost by inches
> With contortions, twinges, flinches.
> Death at last one day assailed him,
> And with agonies impaled him—
> Pegged him firmly for the slaughter
> Fifteen hundred miles from water!
> Now, his bowels all were topsy
> Turvy with a case of dropsy,
> And his abdomen was bloating,
> And his vitals were a-floating,
> When, between the paroxysmal
> Rush of tides along the dismal
> Channels of his ventilating
> Apparatus—when his lungs were
> Full as barrels, and no bungs were

Handy to reduce the billow,
Richard, strangling on his pillow,
Turned his body, spouted finely
Like a whale, and smiled divinely,
Saying 'twixt convulsions frantic:
"Every man his own Atlantic."

Drowsy, *adj.* Profoundly affected by a play adapted from the French.

Druids, *n.* Priests and ministers of an ancient Celtic religion which did not disdain to employ the humble allurement of human sacrifice. Very little is now known about the Druids and their faith. Pliny says their religion, originating in Britain, spread eastward as far as Persia. Cæsar says those who desired to study its mysteries went to Britain. Cæsar himself went to Britain, but does not appear to have obtained any high preferment in the Druidical Church, although his talent for human sacrifice was considerable.

Druids performed their religious rites in groves, and knew nothing of church mortgages and the season-ticket system of pew rents. They were, in short, heathens and—as they were once complacently catalogued by a distinguished prelate of the Church of England—Dissenters.

Drunk, *adj.* Boozy, fuddled, corned, tipsy, mellow, soaken, full, groggy, tired, top-heavy, glorious, overcome, swipey, elevated, overtaken, screwed, raddled, lushy, nappy, muzzy, maudlin, pious, floppy, loppy, happy, etc.

Duck-bill, *n.* Your account at your restaurant during the canvas-back season.

Duel, *n.* A formal ceremony preliminary to the reconciliation of two enemies. Great skill is necessary to its satisfactory observance; if awkwardly performed the most unexpected and deplorable consequences sometimes ensue. A long time ago a man lost his life in a duel.

That dueling's a gentlemanly vice
    I hold; and wish that it had been my lot
    To live my life out in some favored spot—
Some country where it is considered nice
To split a rival like a fish, or slice
    A husband like a spud, or with a shot
    Bring down a debtor doubled in a knot
And ready to be put upon the ice.
Some miscreants there are, whom I do long
    To shoot, or stab, or some such way reclaim
The scurvy rogues to better lives and manners.
I seem to see them now—a mighty throng.
    It looks as if to challenge *me* they came,
Jauntily marching with brass bands and banners!

Xamba Q. Dar.

Dullard, *n.* A member of the reigning dynasty in letters and life. The Dullards came in with Adam, and being both numerous and sturdy have overrun the habitable world. The secret of their power is their insensibility to blows; tickle them with a bludgeon and they laugh with a platitude. The Dullards came originally from Bœotia, whence they were driven by stress of starvation, their dulness having blighted the crops. For some centuries they infested Philistia, and many of them are called Philistines to this day. In the turbulent times of the Crusades they withdrew thence and gradually overspread all Europe, occupying most of the high places in politics, art, literature, science and theology. Since a detachment of Dullards came over with the Pilgrims in the *Mayflower* and made a favorable report of the country, their increase by birth, immigration and conversion has been rapid and steady. According to the most trustworthy statistics the number of adult Dullards in the United States is but little short of thirty millions, including the statisticians. The intellectual center of the race is somewhere about Peoria, Illinois, but the New England Dullard is the most shockingly moral.

Duty, *n.* That which sternly impels us in the direction of profit, along the line of desire.

> Sir Lavender Portwine, in favor at court,
> Was wroth at his master, who'd kissed Lady Port.
> His anger provoked him to take the king's head,
> But duty prevailed, and he took the king's bread,
>   Instead.
>
>   *G. J.*

Eat, *v.i.* To perform successively (and successfully) the functions of mastication, humectation and deglutition.

"I was in the drawing-room, enjoying my dinner," said Brillat-Savarin, beginning an anecdote. "What!" interrupted Rochebriant; "eating dinner in a drawing-room?" "I must beg you to observe, monsieur," explained the great gastronome, "that I did not say I was eating my dinner, but enjoying it. I had dined an hour before."

Eavesdrop, *v.i.* Secretly to overhear a catalogue of the crimes and vices of another or yourself.

> A lady with one of her ears applied
> To an open keyhole heard, inside,
> Two female gossips in converse free—
> The subject engaging them was she.
> "I think," said one, "and my husband thinks
> That she's a prying, inquisitive minx!"
> As soon as no more of it she could hear
> The lady, indignant, removed her ear.
> "I will not stay," she said, with a pout,
> "To hear my character lied about!"
>
> *Gopete Sherany.*

Eccentricity, *n.* A method of distinction so cheap that fools employ it to accentuate their incapacity.

Economy, *n.* Purchasing the barrel of whisky that you do not need for the price of the cow that you cannot afford.

Edible, *adj.* Good to eat, and wholesome to digest, as a worm to a toad, a toad to a snake, a snake to a pig, a pig to a man and a man to a worm.

Editor, *n.* A person who combines the judicial functions of Minos, Rhadamanthus and Æacus, but is placable with an obolus; a severely virtuous censor, but so charitable withal that he tolerates the virtues of others and the vices of himself; who flings about him the splintering lightning and sturdy thunders of admonition till he resembles a bunch of firecrackers petulantly uttering its mind at the tail of a dog; then straightway murmurs a mild, melodious lay, soft as the cooing of a donkey intoning its prayer to the evening star. Master of mysteries and lord of law, high-pinnacled upon the throne of thought, his face suffused with the dim splendors of the Transfiguration, his legs intertwisted and his tongue a-cheek, the editor spills his will along the paper and cuts it off in lengths to suit. And at intervals from behind the veil of the temple is heard the voice of the foreman demanding three inches of wit and six lines of religious meditation, or bidding him turn off the wisdom and whack up some pathos.

O, the Lord of Law on the Throne of Thought,
    A gilded impostor is he.
Of shreds and patches his robes are wrought,
      His crown is brass,
      Himself an ass,
    And his power is fiddle-dee-dee.
Prankily, crankily prating of naught,
Silly old quilly old Monarch of Thought.
    Public opinion's camp-follower he,
    Thundering, blundering, plundering free.
        Affected,
          Ungracious,
        Suspected,
          Mendacious,
Respected contemporaree!

                              J. H. Bumbleshook.

Education, *n.* That which discloses to the wise and disguises from the foolish their lack of understanding.

Effect, *n.* The second of two phenomena which always occur together in the same order. The first, called a Cause, is said to generate the other—which is no more sensible than it would be for one who has never seen a dog except in the pursuit of a rabbit to declare the rabbit the cause of the dog.

Efferous, Effigiate, Efflagitate, Effodient, Effossion. See some other dictionary.

Ego, *n.* I—the Latin form of the word. The Romans were afflicted with an impediment in their speech, and that was as good a stagger as they could make at it. Kings and editors get a little nearer to the true pronunciation; they say "We."

Egotist, *n.* A person of low taste, more interested in himself than in me.

    Megaceph, chosen to serve the State
    In the halls of legislative debate,
    One day with all his credentials came

To the capitol's door and announced his name.
The doorkeeper looked, with a comical twist
Of the face, at the eminent egotist,
And said: "Go away, for we settle here
All manner of questions, knotty and queer,
And we cannot have, when the speaker demands
To be told how every member stands,
A man who to all things under the sky
Assents by eternally voting 'I'."

Ejection, *n.* An approved remedy for the disease of garrulity. It is also much used in cases of extreme poverty.

Elected, *adj.* Chosen to discharge one duty and a hundred subordinates.

Electioneer, *v.i.* To stand on a platform and scream that Smith is a child of light and Jones a worm of the dust.

Elector, *n.* One who enjoys the sacred privilege of voting for the man of another man's choice.

Electricity, *n.* The power that causes all natural phenomena not known to be caused by something else. It is the same thing as lightning, and its famous attempt to strike Dr. Franklin is one of the most picturesque incidents in that great and good man's career. The memory of Dr. Franklin is justly held in great reverence, particularly in France, where a waxen effigy of him was recently on exhibition, bearing the following touching account of his life and services to science:

"Monsieur Franqulin, inventor of electricity. This illustrious savant, after having made several voyages around the world, died on the Sandwich Islands and was devoured by savages, of whom not a single fragment was ever recovered."

Electricity seems destined to play a most important part in the arts and industries. The question of its economical application to some purposes is still unsettled, but experiment has already proved that it will propel a street car better than a gas jet and give more light than a horse.

Elegy, *n.* A composition in verse, in which, without employing any of the methods of humor, the writer aims to produce in the reader's mind the dampest kind of dejection. The most famous English example begins somewhat like this:

The cur foretells the knell of parting day;
The loafing herd winds slowly o'er the lea;
The wise man homeward plods; I only stay
To fiddle-faddle in a minor key.

Elephant, *n.* A joker of the animal kingdom, having a flexible nose and limited warehouse accommodation for his teeth.

Eleusinian, *adj.* Relating to Eleusis, in Greece, where certain famous rites or "mysteries" were celebrated in honor of Ceres, though that discreet goddess commonly sent her regrets and had an engagement elsewhere. There is a good deal of uncertainty among the moderns as to what these mysteries really were. Some of the old Greek writers, who as small boys sneaked in under the tent, have attempted a description, but without success; the spirit was willing but the language was weak.

Elope, *v.i.* To exchange the perils and inconveniences of a fixed residence for the security and comfort of travel.

Eloquence, *n.* [1.] The art of orally persuading fools that white is the color that it appears to be. It includes the gift of making any color appear white. [2.] A method of convincing fools. The art is commonly presented under the visible aspect of a bald-headed little man gesticulating above a glass of water.

Elysium, *n.* [1.] An imaginary delightful country which the ancients foolishly believed to be inhabited by the spirits of the good. This ridiculous and mischievous fable was swept off the face of the earth by the early Christians—may their souls be happy in Heaven! [2.] The Heaven of the ancients. Nothing could be more ludicrous than this crude conception; instead of golden clouds, harps, crowns and a great white throne, there were fields, groves, streams, flowers and temples. In the ancient Elysium we have a signal example of the inferiority of pagan imagination to Christian knowledge.

Emancipation, *n.* A bondman's change from the tyranny of another to the despotism of himself.

> He was a slave: at word he went and came;
> His iron collar cut him to the bone.
> Then Liberty erased his owner's name,
> Tightened the rivets and inscribed his own.
>
> G. J.

Embalm, *v.t.* [1.] To cheat vegetation by locking up the gases upon which it feeds. By embalming their dead and thereby deranging the natural balance between animal and vegetable life, the Egyptians made their once fertile and populous country barren and incapable of supporting more than a meagre crew. The modern metallic burial casket is a step in the same direction, and many a dead man who ought now to be ornamenting his neighbor's lawn as a tree, or enriching his table as a bunch of radishes, is doomed to a long inutility. We shall get him after awhile if we are spared, but in the meantime the violet and rose are languishing for a nibble at his *gluteus maximus*. [2.] To cure the human bacon. The processes of embalming have been essentially the same in all ages and countries. The following recipe from an ancient papyrus, discovered in the pocket of a mummy in a museum, gives a good general notion of the business:

Remove the decedent's refractory tripes
And glut him with various kinds of swipes
Till the pickle pervades all his tissues and drips
In a delicate odorous dew from the tips
Of his fingers and toes. Then carefully stitch
In a league of linen bedaubed with pitch.
Sign him and seal him and pot him away
To await the dawn of the Judgment Day,
A source—as he tranquilly presses his shelf—
Of joy to his widow and pride to himself.

Embassador, *n.* A minister of high rank maintained by one government at the capital of another to execute the will of his wife.

Ember Days, *n.* Certain days specially set apart for punishing the stomach and the knees. They are so called because on these days the ashes are blown off the embers of our holy religion.

Embezzle, *v.t.* To protect property held in trust from the vicissitudes of a brief tenure and a divided control.

Emergency, *n.* The wise man's opportunity and the fool's Waterloo. A condition of things requiring one to think like a mill-stream, look like an idiot and act like an earthquake.

Emetic, *n.* A substance that causes the stomach to take a sudden and enthusiastic interest in outside affairs.

Emotion, *n.* A prostrating disease caused by a determination of the heart to the head. It is sometimes accompanied by a copious discharge of hydrated chloride of sodium from the eyes.

Emperor, *n.* One ranking next above a king. An ace, as it were.

Empyrean, *n.* The "sky" of an orator.

Encomiast, *n.* A special (but not particular) kind of liar.

Encomium, *n.* A kind of intellectual fog, through which the virtues of its objects are seen magnified many diameters.

Encore, *adv.* (French.) Again. An exclamation intended to procure for the exclaimer more than his money's worth by flattering the exclaimee. When shouted out at a concert it means, "Sing us ''Way down upon the S'wanee Ribber.'"

Encourage, *v.t.* To confirm a fool in a folly that is beginning to hurt him.

Encumbrance, *n.* That which makes property worthless without affecting its title. Another fellow's right to the inside of your pie.

End, *n.* The position farthest removed on either hand from the Interlocutor.

The man was perishing apace
Who played the tambourine:

The seal of death was on his face—
'Twas pallid, for 'twas clean.

"This is the end," the sick man said
    In faint and failing tones.
A moment later he was dead,
    And Tambourine was Bones.

Tinley Roquot.

Endear, *v.t.* To procure for yourself, or bestow upon another, the ability to do a favor.

    The friendship of Crocker I tenderly prize—
    I wear many kinds of his collars.
    He's endeared to my heart by the sacred ties
    Of a thousand accessible dollars.

Rare Ben. Truman.

Enemy, *n.* A designing scoundrel who has done you some service which it is inconvenient to repay. In military affairs, a body of men actuated by the basest motives and pursuing the most iniquitous aim.

English, *n.* A language so haughty and reserved that few writers succeed in getting on terms of familiarity with it.

Enigma, *n.* A *Morning Call* editorial by which the illustrious nation-swayer of that journal bends public opinion to what is conjectured to be his will. It is written with the dried tail of a jackass, dipped in liquid moonshine, and interpreted by the light of possible events in the sweet by-and-by.

Enough, *pro.* All there is in the world if you like it.

    Enough is as good as a feast—for that matter
    Enougher's as good as a feast and the platter.

Arbely C. Strunk.

Entertainment, *n.* Any kind of amusement whose inroads stop short of death by dejection.

Enthusiasm, *n.* A distemper of youth, curable by small doses of repentance in connection with outward applications of experience. Byron, who recovered long enough to call it "entuzy-muzy," had a relapse which carried him off—to Missolonghi.

Entr'acte, *n.* An actor's lucid interval, during which he talks rationally with his keeper—barkeeper.

Envelope, *n.* The coffin of a document; the scabbard of a bill; the husk of a remittance; the bed-gown of a love-letter.

Envy, *n.* [1.] Emulation adapted to the meanest capacity. [2.] The feeling that provokes a preacher to denounce the Adversary.

I curse you, Jack Satan, in horns and in hoof,
  For you're a competing divine,
And the souls you pull into your pit are a proof
  That your pull-pit is bigger than mine.

Eocene, *adj.* First in order of the three great periods into which geologists have divided the age of the world. It was during the Eocene Period that most of the current newspaper jokes were deposited, as is abundantly attested by the affection that Mr. Pickering has for them. They were the companions of his childhood.

Epaulet, *n.* An ornamented badge, serving to distinguish a military officer from the enemy—that is to say, from the officer of lower rank to whom his death would give promotion.

Epicure, *n.* [1.] An opponent of Epicurus, an abstemious philosopher who, holding that pleasure should be the chief aim of man, wasted no time in gratification of the senses. [2.] A person who is overmuch given to pleasures of the table. So called from Epicurus, a philosopher widely celebrated for his abstemious habits, as a condition favorable to the cultivation of intellectual enjoyment.

Epidemic, *n.* A disease having a sociable turn and few prejudices.

Epidermis, *n.* The thin integument which lies immediately outside the skin and immediately inside the dirt.

Epigram, *n.* [1.] A short, sharp saying in prose or verse, frequently characterized by acidity or acerbity and sometimes by wisdom. Following are some of the more notable epigrams of the learned and ingenious Dr. Jamrach Holobom:

> We know better the needs of ourselves than of others. To serve oneself is economy of administration.

> In each human heart are a tiger, a pig, an ass and a nightingale. Diversity of character is due to their unequal activity.

> There are three sexes: males, females and girls.

> Beauty in women and distinction in men are alike in this: they seem to the unthinking a kind of credibility.

> Women in love are less ashamed than men. They have less to be ashamed of.

> While your friend holds you affectionately by both your hands you are safe, for you can watch both his.

[2.] A short, sharp and ingenious thought commonly expressed in verse. The following noble example of the epigram is from the inspired pen of the great Californian poet, Hector A. Stuart.

When God had fashioned this terrestrial frame
And given to each created thing a name,
He saw His hands both empty, and explained:
"I've nothing left." The nothing that remained
Said: "Make me into something light and free."
God heard, and made it into brains for *me!*

[3.] A short sharp saying, commonly in rhyme, characterized by a vivacious acidity of thought calculated to make him of whom it is written wish it had been an epitaph instead.

Once Hector Stuart in his tersest mood
Took up his pencil. "By the holy rood!"
He cried, "I'll write an epigram." He did—
Nay, by the holy *mile* his pencil slid.

Epitaph, *n.* [1.] An inscription on a tomb, showing that virtues acquired by death have a retroactive effect. Following is a touching example:

Here lie the bones of Parson Platt,
Wise, pious, humble and all that,
Who showed us life as all should live it;
Let that be said—and God forgive it!

[2.] A monumental inscription designed to remind the deceased of what he might have been if he had had the will and opportunity. The following epitaphs were copied by a prophet from the headstones of the future:

"Here lies the remains of great Senator Vrooman,
Whose head was as hard as the heart of a woman—
Whose heart was as soft as the head of a hammer.
Dame Fortune advanced him to eminence, d——her!"

"We mourn the loss
Of Senator Cross.
If he'd perished later
Our grief had been greater.
If he never had died
We should always have cried.
As he died and decayed
His corruption was stayed."

"Beneath this mound Charles Crocker now reposes;
Step lightly, strangers—also hold your noses."

"The doctors they tried to hold William Stow back, but
We played at his graveside the sham and the sackbut."

Equal, *adj.* As bad as something else.

Equality, *n.* In politics, an imaginary condition in which skulls are counted, instead of brains, and merit is determined by lot and punished by preferment. Pushed to its logical conclusion, the principle requires rotation in office and in the penitentiary. All men being equally entitled to a vote, are equally entitled to office, and equally subject to conviction.

Erin, *n.* The fountain of American political wisdom and principles of municipal government.

Ermine, *n.* The state, dignity or condition of a judge. The word is formed of the two words, *err* and *mine* — the one suggesting the tendency of a judicial mind, the other expressing, in a general way, the judicial notion of the rightful ownership to property in dispute.

Err, *v.i.* To believe or act in a way contrary to my beliefs and actions.

Erudition, *n.* Dust shaken out of a book into an empty skull.

> So wide his erudition's mighty span,
> He knew Creation's origin and plan
> And only came by accident to grief—
> He thought, poor man, 'twas right to be a thief.
>
> *Romach Pute.*

Esophagus, *n.* That portion of the alimentary canal that lies between pleasure and business.

Esoteric, *adj.* Very particularly abstruse and consummately occult. The ancient philosophies were of two kinds, — *exoteric,* those that the philosophers themselves could partly understand, and *esoteric,* those that nobody could understand. It is the latter that have most profoundly affected modern thought and found greatest acceptance in our time.

Esquire, *n.* Formerly a dignity immediately below that of a knight; now a dignity immediately above that of a felon. In this country the only allowable use of the word is, in its abbreviated form, in the superscriptions of letters: but ignorant and vulgar writers attach it to the names of prominent men as a title of respect. Mr. Frank Pixley, of the *Argonaut,* uses it thus, but with commendable discrimination—he appends it only to the names of the rich.

Essential, *adj.* Pertaining to the *essence,* or that which determines the distinctive character of a thing. Persons who, because they do not know the English language, are driven to the unprofitable vocation of writing for American newspapers, commonly use this word in the sense of *necessary,* as "April rains are essential to June harvests."

Esteem, *n.* [1.] The degree of favorable regard that is due to one who has the power to serve us and has not yet refused. [2.] Payment in full for a benefaction.

Estoppel, *n.* In law, the kind of a stopple with which a man is corked up with his plea inside him.

Ethnology, *n.* [1.] The science that treats of the various tribes of Man, as robbers, thieves, swindlers, dunces, lunatics, idiots and ethnologists. [2.] A science that recognizes the difference between a Chinaman and a Nigger, but is oblivious to the difference between a gentleman and a blackguard.

Etiquette, *n.* A code of social rites, ceremonies and observances, constituting a vulgarian's claim to toleration. The fool's credentials.

> When first Society was founded,
> > It was discovered, as time sped,
> That men of sense and taste abounded,
> > But they were mostly dead.
> While, of the women fitted to adorn
> The social circle, few had yet been born.
>
> Those, then, that met were rather lonely,
> > And scarce could call themselves "our set";
> So they, to swell their numbers only,
> > Invented Etiquette,
> And said: "Such fools as will observe these rules
> May meet us, though they're all the greater fools."
>
> Straightway the fools then fell to study
> > The laws of conduct *à la mode,*
> And though their minds were somewhat muddy
> > They soon had learned the code.
> Then, seeing its authors hadn't, plainly told them
> They'd make Society too hot to hold them.

Eucalyptus, *n.* [1.] A genus of trees remarkable for their abundance of assorted ill smells—including the *Eucalyptus disgustus,* the *E. nasocompressus* and the *E. skunkatus.* [2.] A tree holding, in the vegetable kingdom, the high and honored distinction enjoyed in the animal kingdom by the blue skunk. The variety most in favor is the *E. disgustifolium.* The medicinal value of its foliage is very great—it cures happiness.

Eucharist, *n.* A sacred feast of the religious sect of Theophagi.

> A dispute once unhappily arose among the members of this sect as to what it was that they ate. In this controversy some five hundred thousand have already been slain, and the question is still unsettled.

Euchre, *n.* A game of cards in which the highest cards and the best players are knaves.

Eulogy, *n.* Praise of a person who has either the advantages of wealth and power, or the consideration to be dead.

Euphemism, *n*. [1.] A figure of speech in which the speaker or writer makes his expression a good deal softer than the facts would warrant him in doing; as, for example, in the famous triolet of the Rev. Adiposus Drowze, rector of the Church of St. Sinecure, this Diocese:

Iscariot blundered in selling for thirty,

And all the Jews wondered that Judas had blundered.

By asking a hundred his crime were less dirty.

Iscariot blundered in selling for thirty.

[2.] In rhetoric, a figure by which the severe asperity of truth is mitigated by the use of a softer expression than the facts would warrant—as, to call Mr. Charles Crocker ninety-nine kinds of a knave.

Evanescence, *n*. The quality that so charmingly distinguishes happiness from grief, and enables us to make an immediate comparison between pleasure and pain, for better enjoyment of the former.

Evangelist, *n*. A bearer of good tidings, particularly (in a religious sense) such as assure us of our own salvation and the damnation of our neighbors.

Everlasting, *adj*. Lasting forever. It is with no small diffidence that I venture to offer this brief and elementary definition, for I am not unaware of the existence of a bulky volume by a sometime Bishop of Worcester, entitled, *A Partial Definition of the Word "Everlasting," as Used in the Authorized Version of the Holy Scriptures*. His book was once esteemed of great authority in the Anglican Church, and is still, I understand, studied with pleasure to the mind and profit to the soul.

Evolution, *n*. The process by which the higher organisms are gradually developed from the lower, as Man from the Assisted Immigrant, the Office-Holder from the Ward Boss, the Thief from the Office-Holder, etc.

Exception, *n*. A thing which takes the liberty to differ from other things of its class, as an honest man, a truthful woman, etc. "The exception proves the rule" is an expression constantly upon the lips of the ignorant, who parrot it from one another with never a thought of its absurdity. In the Latin, *"Exceptio probat regulam"* means that the exception *tests* the rule, puts it to the proof, not *confirms* it. The malefactor who drew the meaning from this excellent dictum and substituted a contrary one of his own exerted an evil power which appears to be immortal.

Excess, *n*. In morals, an indulgence that enforces by appropriate penalties the law of moderation.

Hail, high Excess—especially in wine.

To thee in worship do I bend the knee

Who preach abstemiousness unto me—

My skull thy pulpit, as my paunch thy shrine.

Precept on precept, aye, and line on line,
    Could ne'er persuade so sweetly to agree
    With reason as thy touch, exact and free,
Upon my forehead and along my spine.
At thy command eschewing pleasure's cup,
    With the hot grape I warm no more my wit;
    When on thy stool of penitence I sit
I'm quite converted, for I can't get up.
Ungrateful he who afterward would falter
To make new sacrifices at thine altar!

Excommunication, *n.*

[1.] This "excommunication" is a word
In speech ecclesiastical oft heard,
And means the damning, with bell, book and candle,
Some sinner whose opinions are a scandal—
A rite permitting Satan to enslave him
Forever, and forbidding Christ to save him.

Gat Huckle.

[2.] A religious rite whereby a person who has offended a priest is given over to the devil to be eternally damned for the betterment of his soul. In the lesser excommunication, however, the offender is only denied the privilege of putting his God into his stomach.

Excursion, *n.* An expedition of so disagreeable a character that steamboat and railroad fares are compassionately mitigated to the miserable sufferers.

Executioner, *n.* A person who does what he can to abate the ravages of senility and reduce the chances of being drowned.

Executive, *n.* An officer of the Government, whose duty it is to enforce the wishes of the legislative power until such time as the judicial department shall be pleased to pronounce them invalid and of no effect. Following is an extract from an old book entitled, *The Lunarian Astonished* —Pfeiffer & Co., Boston, 1803:

LUNARIAN: Then when your Congress has passed a law it goes directly to the Supreme Court in order that it may at once be known whether it is constitutional?

TERRESTRIAN: O no; it does not require the approval of the Supreme Court until having perhaps been enforced for many years somebody objects to its operation against himself—I mean his client. The President, if he approves it, begins to execute it at once.

LUNARIAN: Ah, the executive power is a part of the legislative. Do your policemen also have to approve the local ordinances that they enforce?

TERRESTRIAN: Not yet—at least not in their character of constables. Generally speaking, though, all laws require the approval of those whom they are intended to restrain.

LUNARIAN: I see. The death warrant is not valid until signed by the murderer.

TERRESTRIAN: My friend, you put it too strongly; we are not so consistent.

LUNARIAN: But this system of maintaining an expensive judicial machinery to pass upon the validity of laws only after they have long been executed, and then only when brought before the court by some private person—does it not cause great confusion?

TERRESTRIAN: It does.

LUNARIAN: Why then should not your laws, previously to being executed, be validated, not by the signature of your President, but by that of the Chief Justice of the Supreme Court?

TERRESTRIAN: There is no precedent for any such course.

LUNARIAN: Precedent. What is that?

TERRESTRIAN: It has been defined by five hundred lawyers in three volumes each. So how can any one know?

Exhort, *v.t.* In religious affairs, to put the conscience of another upon the spit and roast it to a nut-brown discomfort.

Exile, *n.* One who serves his country by residing abroad, yet is not an ambassador.

An English sea-captain being asked if he had read "The Exile of Erin," replied: "No, sir, but I should like to anchor on it." Years afterwards, when he had been hanged as a pirate after a career of unparalleled atrocities, the following memorandum was found in the ship's log that he had kept at the time of his reply:

Aug. 3d, 1842. Made a joke on the ex-Isle of Erin. Coldly received. War with the whole world!

Existence, *n.*

A transient, horrible, fantastic dream,
Wherein is nothing yet all things do seem:
From which we're wakened by a friendly nudge
Of our bedfellow Death, and cry: "O fudge!"

Exonerate, *v.t.* To show that from a series of vices and crimes some particular crime or vice was accidentally omitted.

Expectation, *n.* The state or condition of mind which in the procession of human emotions is preceded by hope and followed by despair.

Expediency, *n.* The father of all the virtues.

Experience, *n*. The wisdom that enables us to recognize as an undesirable old
acquaintance the folly that we have already embraced.

> To one who, journeying through night and fog,
> Is mired neck-deep in an unwholesome bog,
> Experience, like the rising of the dawn,
> Reveals the path that he should not have gone.
>
> *Joel Frad Bink.*

Expostulation, *n*. One of the many methods by which fools prefer to lose their
friends.

Extinction, *n*. The raw material out of which theology created the future state.

Fable, *n.* A brief lie intended to illustrate some important truth.

A statue of Eve and the Apple was accosted by a hippopotamus on a show-bill.

"Give me a bite of your apple," said the hippopotamus, "and see me smile."

"I would," said Eve, making a rough estimate of the probable dimensions of the smile, "but I have promised a bite to the Mammoth Cave, another to the crater of Vesuvius, and a third to the interval between the lowest anthropoid Methodist and the most highly organized wooden Indian. I must be just before I am generous."

This fable teaches that Justice and Generosity do not go hand in hand, the hand of Generosity being commonly thrust into the pocket of Justice.

Fairy, *n.* A creature, variously fashioned and endowed, that formerly inhabited the meadows and forests. It was nocturnal in its habits, and somewhat addicted to dancing and the theft of children. The fairies are now believed by naturalists to be extinct, though a clergyman of the Church of England saw three near Colchester as lately as 1855, while passing through a park after dining with the lord of the manor. The sight greatly staggered him, and he was so affected that his account of it was incoherent. In the year 1807 a troop of fairies visited a wood near Aix and carried off the daughter of a peasant, who had been seen to enter it with a bundle of clothing. The son of a wealthy *bourgeois* disappeared about the same time, but afterward returned. He had seen the abduction and been in pursuit of the fairies. Justinian Gaux, a writer of the fourteenth century, avers that so great is the fairies' power of transformation that he saw one change itself into two opposing armies and fight a battle with great slaughter, and that the next day, after it had resumed its original shape and gone away, there were seven hundred bodies of the slain which the villagers had to bury. He does not say if any of the wounded recovered. In the time of Henry III, of England, a law was made which prescribed the death penalty for "Kyllynge, wowndynge, or mamynge" a fairy, and it was universally respected.

Faith, *n.* Belief without evidence in what is told by one who speaks without knowledge, of things without parallel.

Falsehood, *n.* A truth to which the facts are loosely adjusted to an imperfect conformity.

Family, *n.* A body of individuals living in one household, consisting of male, female, young, servants, dog, cat, dicky-bird, cockroaches, bedbugs and fleas—the "unit" of modern civilized society.

Famous, *adj.* Conspicuously miserable.

> Done to a turn on the iron, behold
>> Him who to be famous aspired.
> Content? Well, his grill has a plating of gold,
>> And his twistings are greatly admired.
>
>> *Hassan Brubuddy.*

Fanatic, *n.* One who overestimates the importance of convictions and undervalues the comfort of an existence free from the impact of addled eggs and dead cats upon the human periphery.

Farce, *n.* A brief drama commonly played after a tragedy for the purpose of deepening the dejection of the critical.

Fashion, *n.* A despot whom the wise ridicule and obey.

> A king there was who lost an eye
>> In some excess of passion;
> And straight his courtiers all did try
>> To follow the new fashion.
>
> Each dropped one eyelid when before
>> The throne he ventured, thinking
> 'Twould please the king. That monarch swore
>> He'd slay them all for winking.
>
> What should they do? They were not hot
>> To hazard such disaster;
> They dared not close an eye—dared not
>> See better than their master.
>
> Seeing them lacrymose and glum,
>> A leech consoled the weepers;
> He spread small rags with liquid gum
>> And covered half their peepers.
>
> The court all wore the stuff, the flame
>> Of royal anger dying.

That's how court-plaster got its name
Unless I'm greatly lying.

Naramy Oof.

Father, *n.* A quarter-master and commissary of subsistence provided by nature for our maintenance in the period before we have learned to live by prey.

Fatigue, *n.* The condition of a philosopher after having considered human wisdom and virtue.

Fault, *n.* One of my offenses, as distinguished from one of yours, the latter being crimes.

Faun, *n.* In Latin mythology, a kind of rural deity. The godhood of the Fauns was pretty nearly a sinecure, their duties consisting mainly in having pointed ears and *liaisons* with the nymphs. There were lady fauns (*fauna*) and these fawned on the satyrs.

Fauna, *n.* A general name for the various beasts infesting any locality exclusive of domestic animals, traveling menageries and Democratic politicians.

Fear, *n.* A sense of the total depravity of the immediate future.

He either fears his fate too much,
Or his deserts are small,
Who dares not put it to the touch—
Who'd rather pass than call.

Earl of Montrose.

Feast, *n.* A festival. A religious celebration usually signalized by gluttony and drunkenness, frequently in honor of some holy person distinguished for abstemiousness. In the Roman Catholic Church feasts are "movable" and "immovable," but the celebrants are uniformly immovable until they are full. In their earliest development these entertainments took the form of feasts for the dead; such were held by the Greeks, under the name *Nemeseia*, by the Aztecs and Peruvians, as in modern times they are popular with the Chinese; though it is believed that the ancient dead, like the modern, were light eaters. Among the many feasts of the Romans was the *Novendiale*, which was held, according to Livy, whenever stones fell from heaven.

Felon, *n.* A person of greater enterprise than discretion, who in embracing an opportunity has formed an unfortunate attachment.

Female, *n.* One of the opposing, or unfair, sex.

The Maker, at Creation's birth,
With living things had stocked the earth.
From elephants to bats and snails,
They all were good, for all were males.
But when the Devil came and saw
He said: "By Thine eternal law
Of growth, maturity, decay,

These all must quickly pass away
And leave untenanted the earth
Unless Thou dost establish birth" —
Then tucked his head beneath his wing
To laugh—he had no sleeve—the thing
With deviltry did so accord,
That he'd suggested to the Lord.
The Master pondered this advice,
Then shook and threw the fateful dice
Wherewith all matters here below
Are ordered, and observed the throw;
Then bent His head in awful state,
Confirming the decree of Fate.
From every part of earth anew
The conscious dust consenting flew,
While rivers from their courses rolled
To make it plastic for the mould.
Enough collected (but no more,
For niggard Nature hoards her store)
He kneaded it to flexile clay,
While Nick unseen threw some away.
And then the various forms He cast,
Gross organs first and finer last;
No one at once evolved, but all
By even touches grew and small
Degrees advanced, till, shade by shade,
To match all living things He'd made
Females, complete in all their parts
Except (His clay gave out) the hearts.
"No matter," Satan cried; "with speed
I'll fetch the very hearts they need" —
So flew away and soon brought back
The number needed, in a sack.
That night earth rang with sounds of strife—
Ten million males each had a wife;
That night sweet Peace her pinions spread
O'er Hell—ten million devils dead!

                                                        G. J.

Ferule, *n.*

A wooden implement designed
To open up the infant mind

And make the pupil understand
The bearings of the thing in hand.

Fib, *n.* A lie that has not cut its teeth. An habitual liar's nearest approach to
truth: the perigee of his eccentric orbit.

When David said: "All men are liars," Dave,
Himself a liar, fibbed like any thief.
Perhaps he thought to weaken disbelief
By proof that even himself was not a slave
To Truth; though I suspect the agèd knave
Had been of all her servitors the chief
Had he but known a fig's reluctant leaf
Is more than e'er she wore on land or wave.
No, David served not Naked Truth when he
Struck that sledge-hammer blow at all his race;
Nor did he hit the nail upon the head:
For reason shows that it could never be,
And the facts contradict him to his face.
Men are not liars all, for some are dead.

Bartle Quinker.

Fickleness, *n.* The iterated satiety of an enterprising affection.

Fiddle, *n.* An instrument to tickle human ears by friction of a horse's tail on the
entrails of a cat.

To Rome said Nero: "If to smoke you turn
I shall not cease to fiddle while you burn."
To Nero Rome replied: "Pray do your worst,
'Tis my excuse that you were fiddling first."

Orm Pludge.

Fidelity, *n.* A virtue peculiar to those who are about to be betrayed.

Fiend, *n.* A being whose existence is invaluable to the newspaper reporters, to
whom, however, it is but just to admit that they commonly censure and
deplore his way of life. To the "fiend in human shape" they exhibit a particular animosity, insensible, it would seem, to the compliment implied by the
assumption of the "form divine." Their condemnation of "the fire-fiend" is
notably tempered by a certain lurid enthusiasm, and the "lunch-fiend" suffers only such disfavor as is provoked by his competition.

Fig-leaf, *n.*

An artist's trick by which the Nude's
Protected from the eyes of prudes,
Which else with their peculiar flame
Might scorch the canvas in its frame,
Or melt the bronze, or burn to lime

The marble, to efface his crime.
For sparks are sometimes seen to dance
Where falls a dame's offended glance,
And little curls of smoke to rise
From fingers veiling virgin eyes.

O prudes I know ye,—once ye made
In Frisco here a fool's tirade
Against some casts from the antique,
Great, naked, natural and Greek,
Whereto ye flocked, a prurient crush,
And diligently tried to blush,
Half strangled in the vain attempt
Till some one (may the wretch be hemped!)
Depressed his lordly length of ear
Your loud lubricity to hear,
Then took his chisel up and dealt
At Art a blow below the belt.
Insulted, crimson with the shame,
Her cheeks aglow, her eyes aflame,
The goddess spread her pinions bright,
Sprang, and the town was left in night!

Since then in vain the painter toils:
His canvas still denies the oils.
In vain with melancholy sighs
His burin the engraver plies;
Lines multiply beneath his hand,
But what they mean none understand.
With stubborn clay and unsubdued,
The sculptor shapes his fancies crude,
Unable to refine the work,
And makes a god look like a Turk.
To marble grown, or metal, still
The monstrous image makes him ill,
Till, crazed with rage, the damaged lot
He breaks, or sells to Irving Scott.

Filial, *adj.* In such a manner as to placate the parental purse.

Finance, *n.* The art or science of managing revenues and resources for the best advantage of the manager. The pronunciation of this word with the i long and the accent on the first syllable is one of America's most precious discoveries and possessions.

Flag, *n.* A colored rag borne above troops and hoisted on forts and ships. It appears to serve the same purpose as certain signs that one sees on vacant lots in London— "Rubbish may be shot here."

Flatter, *v.t.* To impress another with a sense of one's own merit.

> The bungler boasts of his excellence—
>> His hearers yawn and nod;
> The artist flatters his audience—
>> They shout: "He is a god!"

Flesh, *n.* The Second Person of the secular Trinity.

Flint, *n.* A substance much in use as a material for hearts. Its composition is silica, 98.00; oxide of iron, 0.25; alumina, 0.25; water, 1.50. When an editor's heart is made, the water is commonly left out; in a lawyer's more water is added—and frozen.

Flirtation, *n.* A game in which you do not want the other player's stake but stand to lose your own.

Flood, *n.* A superior degree of dampness. Specifically, a great storm described by Berosus and Moses, when, according to the latter's rain-gauge, there was a precipitation of moisture to the depth of one-eighth of a mile in twenty-four hours for forty days. The former did not measure, apparently, for he simply explains (in pretty good Greek) that it rained cats and dogs. The learned author of the cuneiform inscriptions from the Mesopotamian mounds draws a number of carpet-tacks on a brick to signify that it was "quite a smart shower considering the season."

Flop, *v.* Suddenly to change one's opinions and go over to another party. The most notable flop on record was that of Saul of Tarsus, who has been severely criticised as a turn-coat by some of our partisan journals.

Flunkey, *n.* Properly, a servant in livery, the application of the word to a member of a uniformed political club being a monstrous degradation of language and a needless insult to a worthy class of menials.

Flute, *n.* A variously perforated hollow stick intended for the punishment of sin, the minister of retribution being commonly a young man with straw-colored eyes and lean hair.

Fly, *n.* A monster of the air owing allegiance to Beëlzebub. The common house-fly (*Musca maledicta*) is the most widely distributed of the species. It is really this creature that

> with comprehensive view
> Surveys mankind from China to Peru.

In respect to space, he clouds the world, and the sun never sets upon him; in point of time, he is from everlasting to everlasting. Alexander fought him unsuccessfully in Persia; he routed Cæsar in Gaul, worried Magellan in Patagonia and spoiled Greely's enjoyment of his meals at Cape Sabine. He is everywhere and always the same. He roosts impartially upon the summit of Olympus and the bald head of a sleepy deacon. The earth, grown wan with age, renews her youth. Seas usurp the continents and polar ice invades the tropics, extinguishing empires, civilizations and races. Where populous cities stood the jackal slinks across the naked sands or falls by the arrow of the savage, himself hard pressed by the encroaching pioneer. Religions and philosophies perish with the tongues in which they were expounded, and the minstrel joke at last gives way to a successor. Cliffs crumble to dust, the goat's appetite fails him, at last the office-holder dies, but always the house-fly is to hand like a run of salmon. By his illustrious line we are connected with the past and future: he wantoned in the eyebrows of our fathers; he will skate upon the shining pates of our sons. He is the King, the *Chief*, the Boss! I salute him.

Fly-speck, *n.* The prototype of punctuation. It is observed by Garvinus that the systems of punctuation in use by the various literary nations depended originally upon the social habits and general diet of the flies infesting the several countries. These creatures, which have always been distinguished for a neighborly and companionable familiarity with authors, liberally or niggardly embellish the manuscripts in process of growth under the pen, according to their bodily habit, bringing out the sense of the work by a species of interpretation superior to, and independent of, the writer's powers. The "old masters" of literature—that is to say, the early writers whose work is so esteemed by later scribes and critics in the same language—never punctuated at all, but worked right along free-handed, without that abruption of the thought which comes from the use of points. (We observe the same thing in children to-day, whose usage in this particular is a striking and beautiful instance of the law that the infancy of individuals reproduces the methods and stages of development characterizing the infancy of races.) In the work of these primitive scribes all the punctuation is found, by the modern investigator with his optical instruments and chemical tests, to have been inserted by the writers' ingenious and serviceable collaborator, the common house-fly—*Musca maledicta*. In transcribing these ancient MSS, for the purpose of either making the work their own or preserving what they naturally regard as divine revelations, later writers reverently and accurately copy whatever marks they find upon the papyrus or parchment, to the unspeakable enhancement of the lucidity of the thought and value of the work. Writers contemporary with the copyists naturally avail themselves of the obvious advantages of these marks in their own work, and with such assistance as the flies of their own household may be willing to grant, frequently rival and sometimes surpass the older compositions, in respect at least of punctuation, which is no small glory. Fully to understand the important services that flies perform to literature it is only necessary to lay a page of some popular novelist alongside a saucer of cream-and-molasses in a sunny room and observe "how the wit brightens and the style refines" in accurate proportion to the duration of exposure.

Foe, *n.* A person instigated by his wicked nature to deny one's merits or exhibit superior merits of his own.

Fog, *n.* A substance remaining after the last analysis of San Franciscan atmosphere—the sewer-gas, dust, cemetery effluvium, disease germs and other ingredients having been eliminated. Of these, however, dust is the chief; and as Mr. Edmund Yates, by combining the words "smoke" and "fog," gave to the London atmosphere the graphic name of "smog," we, in humble imitation but with inferior felicity, may confer upon our own grumous environment the title of "dog."

Fold, *n.* In the miserable nomenclature of those outlying dark corners of the universe beyond the boundaries of the Pacific Slope, a sheep corral. The wretched barbarians infesting those remote dependencies have also the bad taste to call a band of sheep a "flock" and a sheepherder a "shepherd," besides being linguistically disgusting in a reasonless multitude of other ways. In ecclesiastical affairs, the fold means the church.

> By plain analogy we're told
> Why first the church was called the fold:
> Into the fold the sheep are steered
> There guarded from the wolf and—sheared.

Folly, *n.* That "gift and faculty divine" whose creative and controlling energy inspires Man's mind, guides his actions and adorns his life.

> Folly! although Erasmus praised thee once
>   In a thick volume, and all authors known,
>   If not thy glory yet thy power have shown,
> Deign to take homage from thy son who hunts
> Through all thy maze his brothers, fool and dunce,
>   To mend their lives and to sustain his own,
>   However feebly be his arrows thrown,
> Howe'er each hide the flying weapons blunts.
> All-Father Folly! be it mine to raise,
>   With lusty lung, here on his western strand
>   With all thine offspring thronged from every land,
> Thyself inspiring me, the song of praise.
> And if too weak, I'll hire, to help me bawl,
> Dick Watson Gilder, gravest of us all.

> *Aramis Loto Frope.*

Fool, *n.* A person who pervades the domain of intellectual speculation and diffuses himself through the channels of moral activity. He is omnific, omniform, omnipercipient, omniscient, omnipotent. He it was who invented letters, printing, the railroad, the steamboat, the telegraph, the platitude and the circle of the sciences. He created patriotism and taught the nations war—founded theology, philosophy, law, medicine and Chicago. He established monarchical and republican government. He is from everlasting to everlasting—such as creation's dawn beheld he fooleth now. In the morning of time he sang upon primitive hills, and in the noonday of existence headed the procession of being. His grandmotherly hand has warmly tucked-in the set sun of civilization, and in the twilight he prepares Man's evening meal of milk-and-morality and turns down the covers of the universal grave. And after the rest of us shall have retired for the night of eternal oblivion he will sit up to write a history of human civilization.

Foolhardy, *adj.* Unlucky in the execution of a courageous act.

Footprints, *n.* A pedestrian's impressions of the country. A thief's assertion that he has gone over the ground and is not open to conviction.

> Lives of Oakland girls remind us
>> We can't make our lives as fine,
> Nor departing leave behind us
>> Footprints 21 × 9.
>
> *Longfellow.*

Forbidden, *pp.* Invested with a new and irresistible charm.

Force, *n.*

> "Force is but might," the teacher said—
>> "That definition's just."
> The boy said naught but thought instead,
> Remembering his pounded head:
>> "Force is not might but must!"

Forefinger, *n.* The finger commonly used in pointing out two malefactors.

Foreign, *adj.* Belonging to another and inferior country.

Foreigner, *n.* A villain regarded with various and varying degrees of toleration, according to his conformity to the eternal standard of our conceit and the shifting one of our interests. Among the Romans all foreigners were called barbarians because most of the tribes with which the Romans had acquaintance were bearded. The term was merely descriptive, having nothing of reproach in it: Roman disparagement was generally more frankly expressed with a spear. The descendants of the barbarians—the modern barbers—have seen fit, however, to retort with the saw-toothed razor.

Foreman, *n.* Obsolete: see FOREGENTLEMAN.

Forenoon, *n.* The latter part of the night. Vulgar.

Foreordination, *n.* This looks like an easy word to define, but when I consider that pious and learned theologians have spent long lives in explaining it, and written libraries to explain their explanations; when I remember that nations have been divided and bloody battles caused by the difference between fore-ordination and predestination, and that millions of treasure have been expended in the effort to prove and disprove its compatibility with freedom of the will and the efficacy of prayer, praise and a religious life, — recalling these awful facts in the history of the word, I stand appalled before the mighty problem of its signification, abase my spiritual eyes, fearing to contemplate its portentous magnitude, reverently uncover and humbly refer it to His Eminence Cardinal Gibbons and His Grace Bishop Potter.

Foresight, *n.* That peculiar and valuable faculty that enables a politician always to know that his party is going to succeed — as distinguished from *Retrospect,* which sometimes shows him that it got calamitously beaten.

Forgetfulness, *n.* A gift of God bestowed upon debtors in compensation for their destitution of conscience.

Forgiveness, *n.* A stratagem to throw an offender off his guard and catch him red-handed in his next offense.

Fork, *n.* An instrument used chiefly for the purpose of putting dead animals into the mouth. Formerly the knife was employed for this purpose, and by many worthy persons is still thought to have many advantages over the other tool, which, however, they do not altogether reject, but use to assist in charging the knife. The immunity of these persons from swift and awful death is one of the most striking proofs of God's mercy to those that hate Him.

Forma Pauperis. (Latin.) In the character of a poor person — a method by which a litigant without money for lawyers is considerately permitted to lose his case.

When Adam long ago in Cupid's awful court
    (For Cupid ruled ere Adam was invented)
Sued for Eve's favor, says an ancient law report,
    He stood and pleaded unhabilimented.

"You sue *in forma pauperis,* I see," Eve cried;
    "Actions can't here be that way prosecuted."
So all poor Adam's motions coldly were denied:
    He went away — as he had come — nonsuited.

                                                     G. J.

Fortune-hunter, *n.* A man without wealth whom a rich woman catches and marries within an inch of his life.

Foundling, *n.* A child that has disembarrassed itself of parents unsuitable to its condition and prospects.

Fragment, *n.* In literature, a composition which the author had not the skill to finish.

Frail, *adj*. Infirm; liable to betrayal, as a woman who has made up her mind to sin.

Frankalmoigne, *n*. The tenure by which a religious corporation holds lands on condition of praying for the soul of the donor. In mediæval times many of the wealthiest fraternities obtained their estates in this simple and cheap manner, and once when Henry VIII of England sent an officer to confiscate certain vast possessions which a fraternity of monks held by frankalmoigne, "What!" said the Prior, "would your master stay our benefactor's soul in Purgatory?" "Ay," said the officer, coldly, "an ye will not pray him thence for naught he must e'en roast." "But look you, my son," persisted the good man, "this act hath rank as robbery of God!" "Nay, nay, good father, my master the king doth but deliver Him from the manifold temptations of too great wealth."

Fratricide, *n*. The act of killing a jackass for meat.

Fraud, *n*. The life of commerce, the soul of religion, the bait of courtship and the basis of political power.

Freebooter, *n*. A conqueror in a small way of business, whose annexations lack of the sanctifying merit of magnitude.

Freedman, *n*. A person whose manacles have sunk so deeply into the flesh that they are no longer visible.

Freedom, *n*. Exemption from the stress of authority in a beggarly half dozen of restraint's infinite multitude of methods. A political condition that every nation supposes itself to enjoy in virtual monopoly. Liberty. The distinction between freedom and liberty is not accurately known; naturalists have never been able to find a living specimen of either.

> Freedom, as every schoolboy knows,
>> Once shrieked as Kosciusko fell;
> On every wind, indeed, that blows
>> I hear her yell.
>
> She screams whenever monarchs meet,
>> And parliaments as well,
> To bind the chains about her feet
>> And toll her knell.
>
> And when the sovereign people cast
>> The votes they cannot spell,
> Upon the pestilential blast
>> Her clamors swell.
>
> For all to whom the power's given
>> To sway or to compel,

Among themselves apportion Heaven
And give her Hell.

Blary O'Gary.

Freemasons, *n.* An order with secret rites, grotesque ceremonies and fantastic costumes, which, originating in the reign of Charles II, among working artisans of London, has been joined successively by the dead of past centuries in unbroken retrogression until now it embraces all the generations of man on the hither side of Adam and is drumming up distinguished recruits among the pre-Creational inhabitants of Chaos and the Formless Void. The order was founded at different times by Charlemagne, Julius Cæsar, Cyrus, Solomon, Zoroaster, Confucius, Thothmes and Buddha. Its emblems and symbols have been found in the Catacombs of Paris and Rome, on the stones of the Parthenon and the Chinese Great Wall, among the temples of Karnak and Palmyra and in the Egyptian Pyramids—always by a Freemason.

Free-school, *n.* A nursery of American statesmen, where, by promoting the airy flight of paper wads, they are inducted into the parliamentary mysteries of hurling allegations and spittoons.

Freethinker, *n.* A miscreant who wickedly refuses to look out of a priest's eyes, and persists in looking into them with too searching a glance. Freethinkers were formerly

shot,	burned,	boiled,
racked,	flogged,	cropped,
drowned,	hanged,	disemboweled,
impaled,	beheaded,	skinned.

With the lapse of time our holy religion has fallen into the hands and hearts of merciful and humane expounders, and the poor freethinker's punishment is entrusted to Him who said, "Vengeance is mine, I will repay." Here on earth the misguided culprit is only

threatened,	pursued,	reviled,
avoided,	silenced,	cursed,
insulted,	robbed,	cheated,
harassed,	derided,	slandered.

Free-trade, *n.* The unrestricted interchange of commodities between nations—not, it must be observed, between states or provinces of the same nation. That is an entirely different thing, so we are assured by those who oppose free-trade, although wherein the difference consists is not altogether clear to anybody else. To all but those with the better light it seems that what is sauce for the goose is sauce for any part of the goose, and if a number of states are profited by exclusion of foreign products, each would be benefited (and therefore all prosper) by exclusion of the products of the others. To these benighted persons, too, it appears that if high duties on imports are beneficial, their absolute exclusion by law would be more beneficial; and that the former commercial isolation of Japan and China must have been productive of the happiest results to their logical inhabitants, with the courage of their opinions. What defect the Protectionist sees in that system he has never had the goodness to explain—not even their great chief, the unspeakable scoundrel whose ingenious malevolence invented that peerless villainy, the custom house. See PROTECTION.

Free-will, *n.*

> A chip, in floating down a stream,
> Indulged a gratifying dream:
>
> "All things on earth but only I
> Are bound by stern necessity—
>
> "Are moved this way or that, their course
> Determined by some outer force.
>
> "The helpless boughs upon the trees
> Confess the suasion of the breeze.
>
> "The stone where it was placed remains
> Till loosened by the frost or rains.
>
> "The animals go here and there,
> As circumstances may declare.
>
> "The influence they cannot see
> Is clearly visible to me.
>
> "Yet all believe they're governed still
> By nothing but their sovereign will.
>
> "Deluded fools! I—I alone
> Obey no forces but my own.
>
> "Without or sail or oar, I glide
> At pleasure to the ocean's tide.
>
> "No pow'r shall stay me till I lave
> My body in the salt sea wave."
>
> Just then an eddy's gentle strength,
> By hardly half a finger's length,
>
> His chipship drew aside. Said he:
> "'Tis far indeed to reach the sea."

Now more and more, behold him swerve
Along the eddy's outer curve.

He says: "My joy in swimming's o'er:
I'm half inclined to go ashore."

As still he sweeps along his arc,
He adds: "The day is growing dark,

"But still there's time to reach, no doubt,
The point from which I first set out."

The circle was completed quite.
"Right here," he said. "I'll pass the night."

Nor ever once that chip suspected
That aught but he his course deflected.

Free-will, O mortals, is a dream:
Ye all are chips upon a stream.

Freshman, *n.* A student acquainted with grief.

Friar, *n.* One who fries in the heat of his lust. There are four principal orders of friars—Gray Friars, or Franciscans, White Friars, Dominicans and Augustines. Mendicant friars are those who beg to be taken out of the pan. The most eminent of the whole species was Friar John, whose adventures and services to the Church are related by Rabelais.

Friend, *n.* An investigator upon the slide of whose microscope we live, move and have our being.

Friendless, *adj.* Having no favors to bestow. Destitute of fortune. Addicted to utterance of truth and common sense.

Friendship, *n.* A ship big enough to carry two in fair weather, but only one in foul.

The sea was calm and the sky was blue;
Merrily, merrily sailed we two.
   (High barometer maketh glad.)
On the tipsy ship, with a dreadful shout,
The tempest descended and we fell out.
   (O the walking is nasty bad!)

Armit Huff Bettle.

Frisky, *adj.* In the manner of a giddy thing of forty years, sexed somewhat femalewise and sporting on the downslope of a manless existence.

Frog, *n.* A reptile with edible legs. The first mention of frogs in profane literature is in Homer's narrative of the war between them and the mice. Skeptical persons have doubted Homer's authorship of the work, but the learned, ingenious and industrious Dr. Schliemann has set the question forever at rest by uncovering the bones of the slain frogs. One of the forms of moral suasion by which Pharaoh was besought to favor the Israelites was a plague of frogs, but Pharaoh, who liked them *fricasées,* remarked, with truly oriental stoicism, that he could stand it as long as the frogs and the Jews could; so the programme was changed. The frog is a diligent songster, having a good voice but no ear. The libretto of his favorite opera, as written by Aristophanes, is brief, simple and effective— "brekekex-koäx"; the music is apparently by that eminent composer, Richard Wagner. Horses have a frog in each hoof—a thoughtful provision of nature, enabling them to shine in a hurdle race.

Frontispiece, *n.* A protuberance of the human face, beginning between the eyes and terminating, as a rule, in somebody's business.

Frying-Pan, *n.* One part of the penal apparatus employed in that punitive institution, a woman's kitchen. The frying-pan was invented by Calvin, and by him used in cooking span-long infants that had died without baptism; and observing one day the horrible torment of a tramp who had incautiously pulled a fried babe from the waste-dump and devoured it, it occurred to the great divine to rob death of its terrors by introducing the frying-pan into every household in Geneva. Thence it spread to all corners of the world, and has been of invaluable assistance in the propagation of his sombre faith. The following lines (said to be from the pen of his Grace Bishop Potter) seem to imply that the usefulness of this utensil is not limited to this world; but as the consequences of its employment in this life reach over into the life to come, so also itself may be found on the other side, rewarding its devotees:

Old Nick was summoned to the skies.
　　Said Peter: "Your intentions
Are good, but you lack enterprise
　　Concerning new inventions.

"Now, broiling is an ancient plan
　　Of torment, but I hear it
Reported that the frying-pan
　　Sears best the wicked spirit.

"Go get one—fill it up with fat—
　　Fry sinners brown and good in't."
"I know a trick worth two o' that,"
　　Said Nick— "I'll cook their food in't."

Functionary, *n.* A person entrusted with certain official duties. That great and good man, the late President Buchanan, once unluckily mentioned himself with commendable satisfaction as "an old public functionary." The description fitted him like a skin and he wore it to his grave. When he appeared at the Judgment Seat, and his case was called, the Recording Angel ran his finger down the index to the Book of Doom and read off the name: "James Buchanan, O.P.F." "What does that mean?" inquired the Court. And with that readiness of resource which in life had distinguished it from a garden-slug, that truthful immortal part replied: "Oncommonly phaultless filanthropist." Mr. Buchanan was admitted to a seat in the Upper House.

Funeral, *n.* A pageant whereby we attest our respect for the dead by enriching the undertaker, and strengthen our grief by an expenditure that deepens our groans and doubles our tears.

> The savage dies—they sacrifice a horse
> To bear to happy hunting-grounds the corse.
> Our friends expire—we make the money fly
> In hope their souls will chase it to the sky.
>
> *Jex Wopley.*

Funny, *adj.* Having the quality of exciting merriment, as a *Bulletin* editorial by Dr. Bartlett when he is at his sickest.

> He lay on his deathbed and wrote like mad,
> For his will was good though his cough was bad.
> And his humor ran without ever a hitch,
> Urged by the rowels of Editor Fitch,
> Who took the sheets as they fell from his hand,
> Perused and endeavored to understand.
> The work was complete. "'Tis a merry jest,"
> The writer remarked; "I think it is my best.
> How strange that a man at the point of death
> Should have so much wit with so little breath!"
> Then thoughtfully answered him Editor Fitch,
> As he scratched his head, though it didn't itch:
> "The point of death I can certainly see,
> But that of the joke is concealed from *me*."

Future, *n.* That period of time in which our affairs prosper, our friends are true and our happiness is assured.

Gallows, *n.* A stage for the performance of miracle plays, in which the leading actor is translated to heaven. In this country the gallows is chiefly remarkable for the number of persons who escape it.

> Whether on the gallows high
>> Or where blood flows the reddest,
> The noblest place for man to die—
>> Is where he died the deadest.
>
>> *Old Play.*

Gambler, *n.* A man.

Gambling, *n.* A pastime in which the pleasure consists partly in the consciousness of advantages gained for oneself, but mainly in the contemplation of another's loss.

Gargoyle, *n.* A rain-spout projecting from the eaves of mediæval buildings, commonly fashioned into a grotesque caricature of some personal enemy of the architect or owner of the building. This was especially the case in churches and ecclesiastical structures generally, in which the gargoyles presented a perfect rogues' gallery of local heretics and controversialists. Sometimes when a new dean and chapter were installed the old gargoyles were removed and others substituted having a closer relation to the private animosities of the new incumbents.

Garter, *n.* [1.] An elastic band intended to keep a woman from coming out of her stockings and desolating the country. [2.] An order of merit established by Edward III of England, and conferred upon persons who have distinguished themselves in the royal favor. Other kinds of public service are otherwise rewarded.

> "'Tis Britain's boast that knighthood of the Garter
> Was ne'er conferred upon a cad or carter;
> Well, any thrifty and ambitious flunkey
> Can drive a bargain—few can drive a donkey."

So the proud cynic. Some ensuing dicker
Gave him that pretty bauble for his kicker.

Gas-meter, *n.* The family liar in the basement.

Gastric juice, *n.* A liquid for dissolving oxen and making men of the pulp.

Gawby, *n.* A Hector A. Stuart.

Gawk, *n.* A person of imperfect grace, somewhat overgiven to the vice of falling over his own feet.

Geese, *n.* The plural of "Prohibitionist."

Gender, *n.* The sex of words.

> A masculine wooed a feminine noun,
>   But his courting didn't suit her,
> So he begged a verb his wishes to crown,
> But the verb replied, with a frigid frown:
> "What object have I? I'm neuter."

Genealogy, *n.* An account of one's descent from an ancestor who did not particularly care to trace his own.

Generally, *adv.* Usually, ordinarily, as, Men generally lie, A woman is generally treacherous, etc.

Generous, *adj.* Originally this word meant noble by birth and was rightly applied to a great multitude of persons. It now means noble by nature and is taking a bit of a rest.

Genesis, *n.* The first of the five sacred books written by Moses. The evidence of that great man's authorship of this book and the four others is of the most convincing character: he never disavowed them.

Genius, *n.* That particular disposition of the faculties intellectual which enables one to write poetry like Hector Stuart and prose like Loring Pickering; to draw like Carl Browne and paint like Mr. Swan; to model like the immortal designer of the Cogswell statue or the Lotta fountain; to speak like the great O'Donnell. In a general sense, any degree of mental superiority that enables its possessor to live acceptably upon his admirers, and without blame be unbrokenly drunk.

Gent, *n.* The vulgarian's idea of a gentleman. The male of the genus *Hoodlum*.

Genteel, *adj.* Refined, after the fashion of a gent.

> Observe with care, my son, the distinction I reveal:
> A gentleman is gentle and a gent genteel.
> Heed not the definitions your "Unabridged" presents,
> For dictionary makers are generally gents.
>
> G. J.

Gentleman, *n.* A rare animal sufficiently described in the lines immediately foregoing.

Gentlewoman, *n.* The female of the genus *Gentleman.* The word is obsolete, gentlewomen, for no fault of their own, being now known as "ladies."

> The wretch who first called gentlewomen ladies,
> Being first duly hanged, arrived at Hades
> Where, welcomed by the devils to their den,
> He bowed and said: "Good morning—gentlemen."

Genuflection, *n.* Leg-service. The act of bending the knee to Him who so made it that the posture is unnatural and fatiguing.

Genuine, *adj.* Real, veritable, as, A genuine counterfeit, Genuine hypocrisy, etc.

Geographer, *n.* A chap who can tell you offhand the difference between the outside of the world and the inside.

> Habeam, geographer of wide renown,
> Native of Abu-Keber's ancient town,
> In passing thence along the river Zam
> To the adjacent village of Xelam,
> Bewildered by the multitude of roads,
> Got lost, lived long on migratory toads,
> Then from exposure miserably died,
> And grateful travelers bewailed their guide.
>
> *Henry Haukhorn.*

Geology, *n.* The science of the earth's crust—to which, doubtless, will be added that of its interior whenever a man shall come up garrulous out of a well. The geological formations of the globe already noted are catalogued thus: The Primary, or lower one, consists of rocks, bones of mired mules, gas-pipes, miners' tools, antique statues minus the nose, Spanish doubloons and ancestors. The Secondary is largely made up of red worms and moles. The Tertiary comprises railway tracks, patent pavements, grass, snakes, mouldy boots, beer bottles, tomato cans, intoxicated citizens, garbage, anarchists, snap-dogs and fools.

German, *n.* A veller dot vas mighty broud (und mighty glat) to coom vrom Deutschland, don't it?

Ghost, *n.* The outward and visible sign of an inward fear.

> He saw a ghost.
> It occupied—that dismal thing!—
> The path that he was following.
> Before he'd time to stop and fly,
> An earthquake trifled with the eye
> That saw a ghost.
> He fell as fall the early good;
> Unmoved that awful vision stood.

The stars that danced before his ken
He wildly brushed away, and then
    He saw a post.

Jared Macphester.

Accounting for the uncommon behavior of ghosts, Heine mentions somebody's ingenious theory to the effect that they are as much afraid of us as we of them. Not quite, if I may judge from such tables of comparative speed as I am able to compile from memories of my own experience.

There is one insuperable obstacle to a belief in ghosts. A ghost never comes naked: he appears either in a winding-sheet or "in his habit as he lived." To believe in him, then, is to believe that not only have the dead the power to make themselves visible after there is nothing left of them, but that the same power inheres in textile fabrics. Supposing the products of the loom to have this ability, what object would they have in exercising it? And why does not the apparition of a suit of clothes sometimes walk abroad without a ghost in it? These be riddles of significance. They reach away down and get a convulsive grasp on the very tap-root of this flourishing faith.

Ghoul, *n.* A demon addicted to the reprehensible habit of devouring the dead. The existence of ghouls has been disputed by that class of controversialists who are more concerned to deprive the world of comforting beliefs than to give it anything good in their place. In 1640 Father Secchi saw one in a cemetery near Florence and frightened it away with the sign of the cross. He describes it as gifted with many heads and an uncommon allowance of limbs, and he saw it in more than one place at a time. The good man was coming away from dinner at the time and explains that if he had not been "heavy with eating" he would have seized the demon at all hazards. Atholston relates that a ghoul was caught by some sturdy peasants in a churchyard at Sudbury and ducked in a horsepond. (He appears to think that so distinguished a criminal should have been ducked in a tank of rose-water.) The water turned at once to blood "and so contynues unto ys daye." The pond has since been bled with a ditch. As late as the beginning of the fourteenth century a ghoul was cornered in the crypt of the cathedral at Amiens and the whole population surrounded the place. Twenty armed men with a priest at their head, bearing a crucifix, entered and captured the ghoul, which, thinking to escape by the stratagem, had transformed itself to the semblance of a well-known citizen, but was nevertheless hanged, drawn and quartered in the midst of hideous popular orgies. The citizen whose shape the demon had assumed was so affected by the sinister occurrence that he never again showed himself in Amiens and his fate remains a mystery.

Gimlet, *n.* An instrument somewhat smaller than the man "with an inexhaustible fund of anecdote."

Gipsy, *n.* A person who is willing to tell your fortune for a small portion of it.

Giraffe, *n.* An animal that loves to bathe its fevered brow in the mists of dizzy altitudes, and supplies its own pinnacle for the occasion, whence it overlooks you like a step-ladder.

Gloom, *n.* The mental condition produced by a nigger minstrel, the funny column of a newspaper, a hope in heaven and a devil's dictionary.

Glutton, *n.* A person who escapes the evils of moderation by committing dyspepsia.

Gnome, *n.* In North-European mythology, a dwarfish imp inhabiting the interior parts of the earth and having special custody of mineral treasures. Bjorsen, who died in 1765, says gnomes were common enough in the southern parts of Sweden in his boyhood, and he frequently saw them scampering on the hills in the evening twilight. Ludwig Binkerhoof saw three as recently as 1792, in the Black Forest, and Sneddeker avers that in 1803 they drove a party of miners out of a Silesian mine. Basing our computations upon data supplied by these statements, we find that the gnomes were probably extinct as early as 1764.

Gnostics, *n.* A sect of philosophers who tried to engineer a fusion between the early Christians and the Platonists. The former would not go into the caucus and the combination failed, greatly to the chagrin of the fusion managers.

Gnu, *n.* An animal of South Africa, which in its domesticated state resembles a horse, a buffalo and a stag. In its wild condition it is something like a thunderbolt, an earthquake and a cyclone.

> A hunter from Kew caught a distant view
> Of a peacefully meditative gnu,
> And he said: "I'll pursue, and my hands imbrue
> In its blood at a closer interview."
> But that beast did ensue and the hunter it threw
> O'er the top of a palm that adjacent grew;
> And he said as he flew: "It is well I withdrew
> Ere, losing my temper, I wickedly slew
> That really meritorious gnu."
>
> *Jarn Leffer.*

Gold, *n.* A yellow metal greatly prized for its convenience in the various kinds of robbery known as trade. The word was formerly spelled "God" — the *l* was inserted to distinguish it from the name of another and inferior deity. Gold is the heaviest of all the metals except platinum, and a considerable amount of it will sink a man so much more quickly and deeply than platinum will that the latter is made into lifebelts and used as a lifting power for balloons. *British gold,* an imaginary metal greatly used in the manufacture of American traitors to the patriotic axiom that two and two are five.

Gold-bug, *n.* In political matters, a miscreant who has the wickedness to know that legislation cannot maintain a permanent relation between the values of two metals, even by the luminous device of binding them together in the same coins. A miller who grinds the faces of the poor and takes the whole grist for toll. A hideous monster that disturbs the *Bulletin's* repose by sitting astride Deacon Fitch's stomach, picking the bones of "the debtor class" and blaspheming the dollar of our fathers.

Good, *adj.* Sensible, madam, to the worth of this present writer. Alive, sir, to the advantages of letting him alone.

Goose, *n.* A bird that supplies quills for writing. These, by some occult process of nature, are penetrated and suffused with various degrees of the bird's intellectual energies and emotional character, so that when inked and drawn mechanically across paper by a person called an "author," there results a very fair and accurate transcript of the fowl's thought and feeling. The difference in geese, as discovered by this ingenious method, is considerable: many are found to have only trivial and insignificant powers, but some are seen to be very great geese indeed.

Gordian Knot, *n.* Gordon, the King of Khartoum, had as a fastening to his war-chariot a knot so intricate that neither end of the thong could be seen, and he used to brag about it a good deal. Instructed by an oracle, he declared that anybody attempting to undo it and failing should stand the beer, but anybody succeeding should receive the greatest honor that he had ever conferred—a favor which would turn the unsuccessful competitors pea-green with envy and break them all up: the King would shake him for the drinks. When this decree was promulgated all Gordon's subjects joined the Good Templars, but Alexander Badlam of Macedon hearing about it, started at once for the Soudanese capital. Ushered with great pomp into the harness-room, he took out his pocket-knife and calmly cut the knot, remarking with the ready wit which distinguished him from the humorist of the period: "Get onto that racket, my son." "Shake," replied the monarch with truly oriental exuberance of imagery. They shook, using four dice. The King threw four sixes. "Two small pairs," he explained, with royal unconcern. Alexander dumped the cubes back into the box, blew into it, muttered a few cabalistic words and threw. Five deuces! "In Macedon this is the national game, endeared to the popular heart by seventeen centuries of unbroken success, and I have been through it with a lantern," said he, laconically. Graciously pleased to mark his sense of the performance in words of memorable significance, the monarch exlaimed: "You take the cake," and led the way to the royal sideboard, when, later in the day, Alexander, over three fingers of the same as before, explained with the richness of metaphor which characterizes the speech of men familiar with that barbaric splendor of Eastern courts: "It's a cold day when I get left."

Gorgon, *n.*

> The Gorgon was a maiden bold
> Who turned to stone the Greeks of old
> That looked upon her awful brow.
> We dig them out of ruins now,
> And swear that workmanship so bad
> Proves all the ancient sculptors mad.

Gout, *n.* A physician's name for the rheumatism of a rich patient.

Government, *n.* A modern Chronos who devours his own children. The priest-hood are charged with the duty of preparing them for his tooth.

Governor, *n.* An aspirant to the United States Senate.

Graces, *n.* Three beautiful goddesses, Aglaia, Thalia and Euphrosyne, who at-tended upon Venus, serving without salary. They were at no expense for board and clothing, for they ate nothing to speak of and dressed according to the weather, wearing whatever breeze happened to be blowing.

Grammar, *n.* A system of pitfalls thoughtfully prepared for the feet of the self-made man, along the path by which he advances to distinction.

Grape, *n.*

> Hail noble fruit!—by Homer sung,
>   Anacreon and Khayyam;
> Thy praise is ever on the tongue
>   Of better men than I am.
>
> The lyre my hand has never swept,
>   The song I cannot offer:
> My humbler service pray accept—
>   I'll help to kill the scoffer.
>
> The water-drinkers and the cranks
>   Who load their skins with liquor—
> I'll gladly bare their belly-tanks
>   And tap them with my sticker.
>
> Fill up, fill up, for wisdom cools
>   When e'er we let the wine rest.
> Here's death to Prohibition's fools,
>   And every kind of vine-pest!
>
>   *Jamrach Holobom.*

Grapeshot, *n.* An argument which the future is preparing in answer to the de-mands of American Socialism.

Grass, *n.* All flesh.

> Two monks upon a field of battle
> Observed some lean and hungry cattle.
> Said one: "But little feed is growing
> Where Death so lately has been mowing."
> Replied the other, gravely eying
> The piles of dead about them lying:
> "All flesh is grass—I'm quite confounded
> That cows should starve by hay surrounded."

Grasshopper, *n.* An insect with legs like a couple of step-ladders. The *Gryllus campestris* of Linnæus; the *Yumyum chawbully* of Sarah Winnemucca.

Gratitude, *n.* A sentiment lying midway between a benefit received and a benefit expected.

Grave, *n.* A place in which the dead are laid to await the coming of the medical student.

> Beside a lonely grave I stood—
>   With brambles 'twas encumbered;
> The winds were moaning in the wood,
>   Unheard by him who slumbered,
>
> A rustic standing near, I said:
>   "He cannot hear it blowing!"
> "'Course not," said he: "the feller's dead—
>   He can't hear nowt that's going."
>
> "Too true," I said; "alas, too true—
>   No sound his sense can quicken!"
> "Well, mister, wot is that to you?—
>   The deadster ain't a-kickin'."
>
> I knelt and prayed: "O Father, smile
>   On him, and mercy show him!"
> That countryman looked on the while,
>   And said: "Ye didn't know him."
>
>   *Pobeter Dunk.*

Gravitation, *n.* The tendency of all bodies to approach one another with a strength proportioned to the quantity of matter they contain—the quantity of matter they contain being ascertained by the strength of their tendency to approach one another. This is a lovely and edifying illustration of how science, having made A the proof of B, makes B the proof of A.

Great, *adj.*

> "I'm great," the Lion said — "I reign
> The monarch of the wood and plain!"
>
> The Elephant replied: "I'm great —
> No quadruped can match my weight!"
>
> "I'm great — no animal has half
> So long a neck!" said the Giraffe.
>
> "I'm great," the Kangaroo said — "see
> My femoral muscularity!"
>
> The 'Possum said: "I'm great — behold,
> My tail is lithe and bald and cold!"
>
> An Oyster fried was understood
> To say: "I'm great because I'm good!"
>
> Each reckons greatness to consist
> In that in which he heads the list,
>
> And Vierick thinks he tops his class
> Because he is the greatest ass.

> *Arion Spurl Doke.*

Griffin, *n.* An animal having the body and legs of a beast and the head and wings of a bird. It is now thought to be extinct, though Arsène Marsil saw one as lately as 1783, in the Vosges. Its fossil remains in singular preservation are so frequently found in the ruins of ancient cities that many eminent scientists (including Drs. Harkness and Behr, of the California Academy of Sciences) suppose it to have been generally domesticated. Linnæus, following Pliny, calls it the *Quadrupavis amalgamata mirabilis,* but the learned Professor of Natural History at the Berkeley University ingeniously points out that it belongs to the genus *Aquileo.* Like the mule (*Asinequus obstinatus*) the griffin owed nothing to the Creator: it was the result of an entangling alliance between the eagle and the lion.

Grime, *n.* A peculiar substance widely distributed throughout nature, but found most abundantly on the hands of eminent American statesmen. It is insoluble in public money.

Grip, *n.* Ex-Speaker Parks's manner of fondling the property of the commonwealth.

Groan, *n.* The language in which a Republican Federal officeholder expounds his view of the political situation.

Guardian, *n.* One who undertakes to protect from others what he is not ready to get for himself.

Guillotine, *n.* A machine which makes a Frenchman shrug his shoulders with good reason.

> In his great work on *Divergent Lines of Racial Evolution,* the learned Professor Brayfugle argues from the prevalence of this gesture—the shrug—among Frenchmen, that they are descended from turtles and it is simply a survival of the habit of retracting the head inside the shell. It is with reluctance that I differ with so eminent an authority, but in my judgment (as more elaborately set forth and enforced in my work entitled *Hereditary Emotions*—lib. II, c. XI) the shrug is a poor foundation upon which to build so important a theory, for previously to the Revolution the gesture was unknown. I have not a doubt that it is directly referable to the terror inspired by the guillotine during the period of that instrument's activity.

Guilt, *n.* The condition of one who is known to have committed an indiscretion, as distinguished from the state of him who has covered his tracks.

Guinea, *n.* A coin of twenty-one shillings, formerly minted in Great Britain, and still used as the unit of computation in fees for professional service, bribes and other transactions between gentlemen.

> The bank is but the guinea's camp.—*Burns.*

Guinea-pig, *n.* A small Brazilian animal of the genus *Cavia,* and frequently called the cavy. In the opinion of the President of the California Academy of Sciences it is rather a dog than a pig. He grounds his judgment upon the classical admonition, *Cave canem.*

Gull, *v.t.* To tell the sovereign people that if elected you will not steal.

Gum, *n.* A substance greatly used by young women in place of a contented spirit and religious consolation.

Gunpowder, *n.* An agency employed by civilized nations for the settlement of disputes which might become troublesome if left unadjusted. By most writers the invention of gunpowder is ascribed to the Chinese, but not upon very convincing evidence. Milton says it was invented by the devil to dispel angels with, and this opinion seems to derive some support from the scarcity of angels. Moreover, it has the hearty concurrence of the Hon. James Wilson, Secretary of Agriculture.

> Secretary Wilson became interested in gunpowder through an event that occurred on the Government experimental farm in the District of Columbia. One day, several years ago, a rogue imperfectly reverent of the Secretary's profound attainments and personal character presented him with a sack of gunpowder, representing it as the seed of the *Flashawful flabbergastor,* a Patagonian cereal of great commercial value, admirably adapted to this climate. The good Secretary was instructed to spill it along in a furrow and

afterward inhume it with soil. This he at once proceeded to do, and had made a continuous line of it all the way across a ten-acre field, when he was made to look backward by a shout from the generous donor, who at once dropped a lighted match into the furrow at the starting-point. Contact with the earth had somewhat dampened the powder, but the startled functionary saw himself pursued by a tall moving pillar of fire and smoke in fierce evolution. He stood for a moment paralyzed and speechless, then he recollected an engagement and, dropping all, absented himself thence with such surprising celerity that to the eyes of spectators along the route selected he appeared like a long, dim streak prolonging itself with inconceivable rapidity through seven villages, and audibly refusing to be comforted. "Great Scott! what is that?" cried a surveyor's chainman, shading his eyes and gazing at the fading line of agriculturist which bisected his visible horizon. "That," said the surveyor, carelessly glancing at the phenomenon and again centering his attention upon his instrument, "is the Meridian of Washington."

Gymnast, *n.* A man who puts his brains into his muscles. The word is from the Greek *gumnos,* naked, all the athletic exercises of the Greeks being performed in that shocking condition; but the members of the Olympic Club make a compromise between the requirements of the climate and those of the ladies who attend their exhibitions. They wear their *pajamas.*

Gymnodontes, *n.* Malacopterygian Plectognathes, if you please.

Gymnosophists, *n.* Not sloggers who fought with the naked fist, as Professor Adolph Spreckels of the Olympic Club so learnedly but erroneously contends, but a sect of Hindoo philosophers who found the doctrine of metempsychosis a cheap and serviceable substitute for wearing apparel.

Habeas Corpus, *n.* A writ by which a man may be taken out of jail when confined for the wrong crime.

Habit, *n.* A shackle for the free.

Hades, *n.* The lower world; the residence of departed spirits; the place where the dead live.

Among the ancients the idea of Hades was not synonymous with our Hell, many of the most respectable men of antiquity residing there in a very comfortable kind of way. Indeed, the Elysian Fields themselves were a part of Hades, though they have since been removed to Paris. When the Jacobean version of the New Testament was in process of evolution the pious and learned men engaged in the work insisted by a majority vote on translating the Greek word Ἅιδης as "Hell"; but a conscientious minority member secretly possessed himself of the record and struck out the objectionable word wherever he could find it. At the next meeting, the Bishop of Salisbury, looking over the work, suddenly sprang to his feet and said with considerable excitement: "Gentlemen, somebody has been razing 'Hell' here!" Years afterward the good prelate's death was made sweet by the reflection that he had been the means (under Providence) of making an important, serviceable and immortal addition to the phraseology of the English tongue.

Hag, *n.* An elderly lady whom you do not happen to like; sometimes called, also, a hen, or cat. Old witches, sorceresses, etc., were called hags from the belief that their heads were surrounded by a kind of baleful lumination or nimbus—hag being the popular name of that peculiar electrical light sometimes observed in the hair. At one time hag was not a word of reproach: Drayton speaks of a "beautiful hag, all smiles," much as Shakspeare said, "sweet wench." It would not now be proper to call your sweetheart a hag—that compliment is reserved for the use of her grandchildren.

Halcyon (*Alcedo*), *n.* The kingfisher. *Halcyon days* are days of tranquillity and calm; so called because for a few days in the season of storms, when the kingfisher was rearing its young, the gods used to curb the fury of the elements. So at least, the simple ancient was pleased to believe. It was an abominable superstition, altogether beneath contempt, and not at all comparable to the Christian belief that at midnight on Christmas eve the weather is moderated in deference to the birds and beasts which wake at that hour to worship the Savior.

Half, *n.* One of two equal parts into which a thing may be divided, or considered as divided. In the fourteenth century a heated discussion arose among theologists and philosophers as to whether Omniscience could part an object into three halves; and the pious Father Aldrovinus publicly prayed in the cathedral at Rouen that God would demonstrate the affirmative of the proposition in some signal and unmistakable way, and particularly (if it should please Him) upon the body of that hardy blasphemer, Manutius Procinus, who maintained the negative. Procinus, however, was spared to die of the bite of a viper.

Halo, *n.* Properly, a luminous ring encircling an astronomical body, but not infrequently confounded with "aureola," or "nimbus," a somewhat similar phenomenon worn as a head-dress by divinities and saints. The halo is a purely optical illusion, produced by moisture in the air, in the manner of a rainbow; but the aureola is conferred as a sign of superior sanctity, in the same way as a bishop's mitre, or the Pope's tiara. In the painting of the Nativity, by Szedgkin, a pious artist of Pesth, not only do the Virgin and the Child wear the nimbus, but an ass nibbling hay from the sacred manger is similarly decorated and, to his lasting honor be it said, appears to bear his unaccustomed dignity with a truly saintly grace.

Hammer, *n.* An instrument for smashing the human thumb—a *malleus*, as the Latin hath it. One of the old Frankish kings was called Charles Martel, or Charles the Hammer, because he was a beat.

Hand, *n.* A singular instrument worn at the end of the human arm and commonly thrust into somebody's pocket.

Handkerchief, *n.* A small square of silk or linen, used in various ignoble offices about the face and especially serviceable at funerals to conceal the lack of tears. The handkerchief is of recent invention; our ancestors knew nothing of it and intrusted its duties to the sleeve. Shakspeare's introducing it into the play of "Othello" is an anachronism: Desdemona dried her nose with her skirt, as Dr. Mary Walker and other reformers have done with their coat-tails in our own day—an evidence that revolutions sometimes go backward.

Hangman, *n.* [1.] An officer of the law charged with duties of the highest dignity and utmost gravity, and held in hereditary disesteem by a populace having a criminal ancestry. In some of the American States his functions are now performed by an electrician, as in New Jersey, where executions by electricity have recently been ordered—the first instance known to this lexicographer of anybody questioning the expediency of hanging Jerseymen. [2.] An officer of the law who produces suspended animation.

Happiness, *n*. An agreeable sensation arising from contemplating the misery of another.

Harangue, *n*. A speech by an opponent, who is known as an harangue-outang.

Harbor, *n*. A place where ships taking shelter from storms are exposed to the fury of the customs.

Hardware, *n*. Women's consciences.

Hare, *n*. A quadruped of the genus *Lepus*, of which the principal variety is the jackass rabbit—the *Felis nevadensis*, of Humboldt. The jackass rabbit is sometimes called *Cervus chismori*, in honor of a celebrated sportsman who in moments of excitement commonly swears it is a deer.

Harmonists, *n*. A sect of Protestants, now extinct, who came from Europe in the beginning of the last century and were distinguished for the bitterness of their internal controversies and dissensions.

Hash, *x*. There is no definition for this word—nobody knows what hash is.

Hatchet, *n*. A young axe, known among Indians as a Thomashawk.

> "O bury the hatchet, irascible Red,
> For peace is a blessing," the White Man said.
> The Savage concurred, and that weapon interred,
> With imposing rites, in the White Man's head.
>
> *John Lukkus.*

Hatred, *n*. A sentiment appropriate to the occasion of another's superiority.

Haughty, *adj*. Proud and disdainful, like a waiter.

Hautboy, *n*. The least noisy of boys.

Head, *n*. That portion of the human body which is supposed to be responsible for all the others. It is customary in some countries to remove it, and many have acquired great skill and proficiency in the art. In ancient Japan, especially, this art was carried to a high degree of perfection.

Head-money, *n*. A capitation tax, or poll-tax.

> In ancient times there lived a king
> Whose tax-collectors could not wring
> From all his subjects gold enough
> To make the royal way less rough.
> For pleasure's highway, like the dames
> Whose premises adjoin it, claims
> Perpetual repairing. So
> The tax-collectors in a row
> Appeared before the throne to pray
> Their master to devise some way

To swell the revenue. "So great,"
Said they, "are the demands of state
  A tithe of all that we collect
  Will scarcely meet them. Pray reflect:
How, if one-tenth we must resign,
Can we exist on t'other nine?"
The monarch asked them in reply:
"Has it occurred to you to try
  The advantage of economy?"
"It has," the spokesman said: "we sold
  All of our gay garrotes of gold;
  With plated-ware we now compress
  The necks of those whom we assess.
Plain iron forceps we employ
To mitigate the miser's joy
Who hoards, with greed that never tires,
That which your Majesty requires."
Deep lines of thought were seen to plow
Their way across the royal brow.
"Your state is desperate, no question;
  Pray favor me with a suggestion."
"O King of Men," the spokesman said,
"If you'll impose upon each head
  A tax, the augmented revenue
  We'll cheerfully divide with you."
As flashes of the sun illume
The parted storm-cloud's sullen gloom,
The king smiled grimly. "I decree
That it be so—and, not to be
In generosity outdone,
Declare you, each and every one,
Exempted from the operation
Of this new law of capitation.
But lest the people censure me
Because they're bound and you are free,
'Twere well some clever scheme were laid
By you this poll-tax to evade.
I'll leave you now while you confer
With my most trusted minister."
The monarch from the throne-room walked

And straightway in among them stalked
A silent man, with brow concealed,
Bare-armed—his gleaming axe revealed!

G. J.

Hearer, *n.* A person who finds in the remarks of a public speaker something singularly stimulating to thought about his own affairs.

Hearse, *n.* Death's baby-carriage.

Heart, *n.* An automatic, muscular blood-pump. Figuratively, this useful organ is said to be the seat of emotions and sentiments—a very pretty fancy which, however, is nothing but a survival of a once universal belief. It is now known that the sentiments and emotions reside in the stomach, being evolved from food by chemical action of the gastric fluid. The exact process by which a beefsteak becomes a feeling—tender or not, according to the age of the animal from which it was cut; the successive stages of elaboration through which a caviar sandwich is transmuted to a quaint fancy and reappears as a pungent epigram; the marvelous functional methods of converting a hard-boiled egg into religious contrition, or a cream-puff into a sigh of sensibility—these things have been patiently ascertained by M. Pasteur, and by him expounded with convincing lucidity. (See, also, my monograph, *The Essential Identity of the Spiritual Affections and Certain Intestinal Gases Freed in Digestion* — 4to, 687 pp.) In a scientific work entitled, I believe, *Delectatio Demonorum* (John Camden Hotten, London, 1873) this view of the sentiments receives a striking illustration; and for further light consult Professor Dam's famous treatise on *Love as a Product of Alimentary Maceration.*

Heat, *n.*

Heat, says Professor Tyndall, is a mode
Of motion, but I know not how he's proving
His point; but this I know—hot words bestowed
With skill will set the human fist a-moving,
And where it stops the stars burn free and wild.
Crede expertum —I have seen them, child.

Gorton Swope.

Heathen, *n.* A benighted creature who has the folly to worship something that he can see and feel. According to Professor Howison, of the California State University, Hebrews are heathens.

"The Hebrews are heathens!" says Howison. He's
A Christian philosopher. I'm
A scurril agnostical chap, if you please,
Addicted too much to the crime
Of religious discussion in rhyme.

Though Hebrew and Howison cannot agree
    On a *modus vivendi* —not they!—
Yet Heaven has had the designing of me,
    And I haven't been reared in a way
    To joy in the thick of the fray.

For this of my creed is the soul and the gist,
    And the truth of it I aver:
Who differs from me in his faith is an 'ist,
    An 'ite, an 'ic, or an 'er—
    And I'm down upon him or her!

Let Howison urge with perfunctory chin
    Toleration—that's all very well,
But a roast is "nuts" to his nostril thin,
    And he's running—I know by the smell—
    A secret and personal Hell!

                                        Bissell Gip.

Heaven, *n.* A place where the wicked cease from troubling you with talk of
    their personal affairs, and the good listen with attention while you expound
    your own.

Hebrew, *n.* A male Jew, as distinguished from the Shebrew, an altogether supe-
    rior creation.

Hedgehog, *n.* The cactus of the animal kingdom.

Heigh-ho, *int.* This word is supposed to denote a certain degree of languor,
    mingled with regret. It is frequently seen in literature, but never heard in life.
    By some it is supposed to stand for a yawn, by some, for a sigh. The poets
    use it variously, Joaquin Miller as a war-whoop, Adair Welcker with good
    effect as the love-plaint of the night-blooming tomcat.

Hell, *n.* The residence of the late Dr. Noah Webster, dictionary-maker.

Helpmate, *n.* A wife, or bitter half.

"Now, why is yer wife called a helpmate, Pat?"
        Says the priest. "Since the time 'o yer wooin'
    She's niver assisted in what ye were at—
        For it's naught ye are ever doin'."

"That's true of yer Riverence," Patrick replies,
        And no sign of contrition evinces;
    "But, bedad, it's a fact which the word implies,
        For she helps to mate the expinses!"

                                        Marley Wottel.

Hemp, *n*. A plant from whose fibrous bark is made an article of neckwear which is frequently put on after public speaking in the open air and prevents the wearer from taking cold.

Hermit, *n*. A person whose vices and follies are not sociable.

Hers, *pro*. His.

Hesitation, *n*.

> You've heard, my dear, "the woman's lost
>> Who hesitates." Then stand
> Not foolishly to count the cost,
>> But kiss me on demand.

Hibernate, *v.i.* To pass the winter season in domestic seclusion. There have been many singular popular notions about the hibernation of various animals. Many believe that the bear hibernates during the whole winter and subsists by mechanically sucking its paws. It is admitted that it comes out of its retirement in the spring so lean that it has to try twice before it can cast a shadow. Three or four centuries ago, in England, no fact was better attested than that swallows passed the winter months in the mud at the bottoms of the brooks, clinging together in globular masses. They have apparently been compelled to give up the custom on account of the foulness of the brooks. Sotus Escobius discovered in Central Asia a whole nation of people who hibernate. By some investigators, the fasting of Lent is supposed to have been originally a modified form of hibernation, to which the Church gave a religious significance; but this view was strenuously opposed by that eminent authority, Bishop Kip, who did not wish any honors denied to the memory of the Founder of his family.

Hippogriff, *n*. An animal (now extinct) which was half horse and half griffin. The griffin was itself a compound creature, half lion and half eagle. The hippogriff was actually, therefore, only one-quarter eagle, which is two dollars and fifty cents in gold. The study of zoölogy is full of surprises.

Hireling, *n*. A mercenary wretch who serves another person for wages, as distinguished from the respectable functionary who receives a salary.

Historian, *n*. A broad-gauge gossip.

History, *n*. An account mostly false, of events mostly unimportant, which are brought about by rulers mostly knaves, and soldiers mostly fools.

> Of Roman history, great Niebuhr's shown
> 'Tis nine-tenths lying. Faith, I wish 'twere known,
> Ere we accept great Niebuhr as a guide,
> Wherein he blundered and how much he lied.
>> *Salder Bupp.*

Hog, *n*. A bird remarkable for the catholicity of its appetite and serving to illustrate that of ours. Among the Mahometans and Jews, the hog is not in favor as an article of diet, but is respected for the delicacy of its habits, the beauty of its plumage and the melody of its voice. It is chiefly as a songster that the fowl is esteemed; a cage of him in full chorus has been known to draw tears from two persons at once. The scientific name of this dicky-bird is *Porcus rockefelleri*. Mr. Rockefeller did not discover the hog, but it is considered his by right of resemblance.

Home, *n.* The place of last resort—open all night.

Homesick, *adj.* Dead broke abroad.

Homicide, *n.* The slaying of one human being by another. There are four kinds of homicide: felonious, excusable, justifiable and praiseworthy, but it makes no great difference to the person slain whether he fell by one kind or another—the classification is for advantage of the lawyers.

Homiletics, *n.* The science of adapting sermons to the spiritual needs, capacities and conditions of the congregation.

> So skilled the parson was in homiletics
> That all his moral purges and emetics
> To medicine the spirit were compounded
> With a most just discrimination founded
> Upon a rigorous examination
> Of tongue and pulse and heart and respiration.
> Then, having diagnosed each one's condition,
> His scriptural specifics this physician
> Administered—his pills so efficacious
> And pukes of disposition so vivacious
> That souls afflicted with ten kinds of Adam
> Were convalescent ere they knew they had 'em.
> But Slander's tongue—itself all coated—uttered
> Her bilious mind and scandalously muttered
> That in the case of patients having money
> The pills were sugar and the pukes were honey.
> > *Biography of Bishop Potter.*

Homœopathist, *n.* The humorist of the medical profession.

Homœopathy, *n.* [1.] A school of medicine midway between Allopathy and Christian Science. To the last both the others are distinctly inferior, for Christian Science will cure imaginary diseases, and they can not. [2.] A theory and practice of medicine which aims to cure the diseases of fools. As it does not cure them, and does sometimes kill the fools, it is ridiculed by the thoughtless, but commended by the wise.

Homoiousian, *n.* In ecclesiastical history one who without having committed actual crime believes that the Son is not exactly the same as the Father. An Arian by another name, smelling as sweet.

Honest, *adj.* Afflicted with an impediment in his dealing.

Honorable, *adj.* [1.] Afflicted with an impediment in one's reach. In legislative bodies it is customary to mention all members as honorable; as, "the honorable gentleman is a scurvy cur." [2.] Holding or having held a certain office in the public service—a title of courtesy, as "the Honorable Snatchgobble Bilque, Member of Congress."

Hope, *n.* Desire and expectation rolled into one.

> Delicious Hope! when naught to man is left—
> Of fortune destitute, of friends bereft;
> When even his dog deserts him, and his goat
> With tranquil disaffection chews his coat
> While yet it hangs upon his back; then thou,
> The star far-flaming on thine angel brow,
> Descendest, radiant, from the skies to hint
> The promise of a clerkship in the Mint.
>
> *Fogarty Weffing.*

Hornet, *n.* A red-hot meteor of many tons weight, which sometimes hits a fellow unexpectedly between the eyes and knocks him silly. It is represented symbolically, as an insect with a bald head and an influential tail, but the man who has incurred a hornet shot out of a clear sky is not satisfied with that kind of representation, and avers with feeling that an instantaneous photograph of a hornet in flight would tell a different story.

Horrid, *adj.* In English, hideous, frightful, appalling. In Youngwomanese, mildly objectionable.

> There was a pretty girl.
> In the terror and the whirl
> Of the tempest of her passion she was torrid!
> But when moderately moved
> By what she disapproved
> She said, with gentle censure, it was horrid.

Horse, *n.* The founder and conservator of civilization.

> What should we do without the steed—
> The good strong steed, the friendly steed?
> He bore us from barbaric night
> Up the steep slope and into light—
> He served the purpose of our need.
>
> All honor to the noble horse—
> The friendly horse, the faithful horse!
> His saddle is Dominion's seat—

They say in France he's good to eat.
I'll back him—yea, I will indorse!

Hospital, *n.* A place where the sick generally obtain two kinds of treatment— medical by the doctor and inhuman by the superintendent.

Hospitality, *n.* The virtue which induces us to feed and lodge certain persons who are not in need of food and lodging.

Host, *n.* In popular usage, a man who in consideration of your weekly payments permits you to call yourself his guest.

Hostility, *n.* A peculiarly sharp and specially applied sense of the earth's over-population. Hostility is classed as active and passive; as (respectively) the feeling of a woman for her female friends, and that which she entertains for all the rest of her sex.

Houri, *n.* A comely female inhabiting the Mohammedan Paradise to make things cheery for the good Mussulman, whose belief in her existence marks a noble discontent with his earthly spouse, whom he denies a soul. By that good lady the Houris are said to be held in deficient esteem.

House, *n.* A hollow edifice erected for the habitation of man, rat, mouse, beetle, cockroach, fly, mosquito, flea, bacillus and microbe. *House of Correction,* a place of reward for political and personal service, and for the detention of offenders and appropriations. *House of God,* a building with a steeple and a mortgage on it. *House-dog,* a pestilent beast kept on domestic premises to insult persons passing by and appal the hardy visitor. *House-maid,* a youngerly person of the opposing sex employed to be variously disagreeable and ingeniously unclean in the station in which it has pleased God to place her.

Houseless, *adj.* Having paid all taxes on household goods.

Hovel, *n.* The fruit of a flower called the Palace.

> Twaddle had a hovel,
>   Twiddle had a palace;
> Twaddle said: "I'll grovel
>   Or he'll think I bear him malice" —
> A sentiment as novel
>   As a castor on a chalice.
>
> Down upon the middle
>   Of his legs fell Twaddle
> And astonished Mr. Twiddle,
>   Who began to lift his noddle,
> Feed upon the fiddle-
>   Faddle flummery, unswaddle
> A new-born self-sufficiency and think himself a model.

G. J.

Hug, *v. very a.* To —— to —— What the devil does it mean, anyhow?

Humanitarian, *n.* A person who believes the Savior was human and himself is divine. In Californian journalism, the word means an Eastern man who favors Chinese immigration, but Humaniac would seem to be the better name.

Humanity, *n.* The human race, collectively, exclusive of the anthropoid poets.

Humorist, *n.* A plague that would have softened down the hoar austerity of Pharaoh's heart and persuaded him to dismiss Israel with his best wishes, cat-quick.

> Lo! the poor humorist, whose tortured mind
> Sees jokes in crowds, though still to gloom inclined—
> Whose simple appetite, untaught to stray,
> His brains, renewed by night, consumes by day.
> He thinks, admitted to an equal sty,
> A graceful hog would bear his company.
>
> *Alexander Poke.*

Hun, *n.* The Scythian ancestor of the current Hungarian. He wasn't a nice man and his descendant has inherited him.

Hunger, *n.* A peculiar disease afflicting all classes of mankind and commonly treated by dieting. It is observed that those who live in fine houses have it the lightest. This information is useful to chronic sufferers.

Hunt, *v.a.* To get after, with horse, dog or gun.

> O I love to hunt the tiger bold,
>   With shouting loud and free,
> In jungles where the sands of gold
>   Border the black Gangee.
>
> But when the tiger turns about
>   And takes to hunting me,
> That's not so fine—I'd rather shout
>   As hunter than huntee.
>
> The "pleasures of the chase" depend
>   On this, as you'll agree:
> When I and tiger in speed contend,
>   If I'm ahead or he.
>
> It's a solemn sight for a Christian soul
>   The angry game to see
> Urging the hunter to hunt his hole
>   With a sad celeritee.

Hurricane, *n.* An atmospheric demonstration once very common but now generally abandoned for the tornado and cyclone. The hurricane is still in popular use in the West Indies and is preferred by certain old-fashioned sea-captains. It is also used in the construction of the upper decks of steamboats, but generally speaking, the hurricane's usefulness has outlasted it.

Hurry, *n*. The dispatch of bunglers.

Husband, *n*. One who, having dined, is charged with the care of the plate.

Hybrid, *n*. A pooled issue.

Hydra, *n*. A kind of animal that the ancients catalogued under many heads.

Hyena, *n*. A beast held in reverence by some oriental nations from its habit of frequenting at night the burial-places of the dead. But the medical student does that.

Hygeia, *n*. In Grecian mythology the goddess of health—the only one of the goddesses whom it was healthy to have anything to do with.

Hypochondriasis, *n*. Depression of one's own spirits.

> Some heaps of trash upon a vacant lot
> Where long the village rubbish had been shot
> Displayed a sign among the stuff and stumps—
> "Hypochondriasis." It meant The Dumps.
>
> *Bogul S. Purvy.*

Hypocrite, *n*. One who, professing virtues that he does not respect, secures the advantage of seeming to be what he despises.

I is the first letter of the alphabet, the first word of the language, the first thought of the mind, the first object of affection. In grammar it is a pronoun of the first person and singular number. Its plural is said to be *We*, but how there can be more than one myself is doubtless clearer to the grammarians than it is to the author of this incomparable dictionary. Conception of two myselves is difficult, but fine. The frank yet graceful use of "I" distinguishes a good writer from a bad; the latter carries it with the manner of a thief trying to cloak his loot.

Ichor, *n.* A fluid that serves the gods and goddesses in place of blood.

> Fair Venus, speared by Diomed,
> Restrained the raging chief and said:
> "Behold, rash mortal, whom you've bled—
> Your soul's stained white with ichorshed!"

> *Mary Doke.*

Ichthyologist, *n.* A Jo. Redding.

Iconoclast, *n.* A breaker of idols, the worshipers whereof are imperfectly gratified by the performance, and most strenuously protest that he unbuildeth but doth not reëdify, that he pulleth down but pileth not up. For the poor things would have other idols in place of those he thwacketh upon the mazzard and dispelleth. But the iconoclast saith: "Ye shall have none at all, for ye need them not; and if the rebuilder fooleth round hereabout, behold I will depress the head of him and sit thereon till he squawk it."

Idiot, *n.* A member of a large and powerful tribe whose influence in human affairs has always been dominant and controlling. The Idiot's activity is not confined to any special field of thought or action, but "pervades and regulates the whole." He has the last word in everything; his decision is unappealable. He sets the fashions of opinion and taste, dictates the limitations of speech and circumscribes conduct with a dead-line.

Idleness, *n.* A model farm where the devil experiments with seeds of new sins and promotes the growth of staple vices.

Idol, *n*. An image representing symbolically some object of worship. That the image is itself worshiped is probably not true of any people in the world, though some idols are ugly enough to be divine. The honors paid to idols are justly deprecated by the true believer, for he knows that nothing with a head can be omniscient, nothing with a hand omnipotent and nothing with a body omnipresent. No deity could fill any of our requirements if handicapped with existence.

Idolator, *n*. One who professes a religon which we do not believe, with a symbolism different from our own. A person who thinks more of an image on a pedestal than of an image on a coin.

Ignis Fatuus, *n*. Love.

Ignoramus, *n*. A person unacquainted with certain kinds of knowledge familiar to yourself, and having certain other kinds that you know nothing about.

> Dumble was an ignoramus,
> Mumble was for learning famous.
> Mumble said one day to Dumble:
> "Ignorance should be more humble.
> Not a spark have you of knowledge
> That was got in any college."
> Dumble said to Mumble: "Truly
> You're self-satisfied unduly.
> Of things in college I'm denied
> A knowledge—you of all beside."
>
> *Borelli.*

Illuminati, *n*. A sect of Spanish heretics of the latter part of the sixteenth century; so called because they were light weights—*cunctationes illuminati*.

Illustrious, *adj*. Suitably placed for the shafts of malice, envy and detraction.

Imagination, *n*. A warehouse of facts, with poet and liar in joint ownership.

Imbecility, *n*. A kind of divine inspiration, or sacred fire, affecting censorious critics of this dictionary.

Immaculate, *adj*. Not as yet spotted by the police.

Immigrant, *n*. An unenlightened person who thinks one country better than another.

Immodest, *adj*. Having a strong sense of one's own merit, coupled with a feeble conception of worth in others.

> There was once a man in Ispahan
>   Ever and ever so long ago,
> And he had a head, the phrenologists said,
>   That fitted him for a show.

For his modesty's bump was so large a lump
    (Nature, they said, had taken a freak)
That its summit stood far above the wood
    Of his hair, like a mountain peak.

So modest a man in all Ispahan,
    Over and over again they swore—
So humble and meek, you would vainly seek;
    None ever was found before.

Meantime the hump of that awful bump
    Into the heavens contrived to get
To so great a height that they called the wight
    The man with the minaret.

There wasn't a man in all Ispahan
    Prouder, or louder in praise of his chump:
With a tireless tongue and a brazen lung
    He bragged of that beautiful bump

Till the Shah in a rage sent a trusty page
    Bearing a sack and a bow-string too,
And that gentle child explained as he smiled:
    "A little present for you."

The saddest man in all Ispahan,
    Sniffed at the gift, yet accepted the same.
"If I'd lived," said he, "my humility
    Had given me deathless fame!"

                          Sukker Uffro.

Immolation, *n.* Killing, as a sacrificial act.
    The butcher knocks his victim on the head—
    That's slaughter, for 'tis man who's to be fed;
    The priest downs his, before the gods to set it,
    That's immolation—pray do not forget it.
    If I have made the difference distinct
    My fingers to some purpose I have inked;
    But there I stop—you'll have to ask the priest
    Why gods who love the meat can't kill the beast.
    Perhaps he'll give your question recognition,
    Perhaps condemn your spirit to perdition.

Immoral, *adj.* Inexpedient. Whatever in the long run and with regard to the greater number of instances men find to be generally inexpedient comes to be considered wrong, wicked, immoral. If man's notions of right and wrong have any other basis than this of expediency; if they originated, or could have originated, in any other way; if actions have in themselves a moral character apart from, and nowise dependent on, their consequences—then all philosophy is a lie and reason a disorder of the mind.

Immortality, *n.*

> A toy which people cry for,
> And on their knees apply for,
> Dispute, contend and lie for,
> > And if allowed
> > Would be right proud
> Eternally to die for.

> > > *G. J.*

Impale, *v.t.* In popular usage to pierce with any weapon which remains fixed in the wound. This, however, is inaccurate; to impale is, properly, to put to death by thrusting an upright sharp stake into the body, the victim being left in a sitting posture. This was a common mode of punishment among many of the nations of antiquity, and is still in high favor in China and other parts of Asia. Down to the beginning of the fifteenth century it was widely employed in "churching" heretics and schismatics. Wolecraft calls it the "stoole of repentynge," and among the common people it was jocularly known as "riding the one legged horse." Ludwig Salzmann informs us that in Thibet impalement is considered the most appropriate punishment for crimes against religion; and although in China it is sometimes awarded for secular offences, it is most frequently adjudged in cases of sacrilege. To the person in actual experience of impalement it must be a matter of minor importance by what kind of civil or religious dissent he was made acquainted with its discomforts; but doubtless he would feel a certain satisfaction if able to contemplate himself in the character of a weather-cock on the spire of the True Church.

Impartial, *adj.* Unable to perceive any promise of personal advantage from espousing either side of a controversy or adopting either of two conflicting opinions.

Impeccable, *adj.* Not liable to detection.

Impenitence, *n.* A state of mind intermediate in point of time between sin and punishment.

Imperialist, *n.* A political thinker to whom neither a kingdom nor a republic offers the hope of political preferment or other substantial advantage.

Impiety, *n.* Your irreverence toward my deity.

Implacable, *adj.* Not to be appeased without a large sum of money.

Importer, *n.* One of a class of miscreants whose business receives from tariff legislation "the protection which vultures give to lambs."

Imposition, *n.* The act of blessing or consecrating by the laying on of hands—a ceremony common to many ecclesiastical systems, but performed with the frankest sincerity by the sect known as Thieves.

> "Lo! by the laying on of hands,"
>> Say parson, priest and dervise,
> "We consecrate your cash and lands
>> To ecclesiastic service.
> No doubt you'll swear till all is blue
> At such an imposition. Do."
>
> *Pollo Doncas.*

Impostor, *n.* A rival aspirant to public honors.

Improbability, *n.*

> His tale he told with a solemn face
> And a tender, melancholy grace.
>> Improbable 'twas, no doubt,
>> When you came to think it out,
>> But the fascinated crowd
>> Their deep surprise avowed
> And all with a single voice averred
> 'Twas the most amazing thing they'd heard—
> All save one who spake never a word,
>> But sat as mum
>> As if deaf and dumb,
> Serene, indifferent and unstirred.
>> Then all the others turned to him
>> And scrutinized him limb from limb—
>> Scanned him alive;
>> But he seemed to thrive
>> And tranquiler grow each minute,
>> As if there were nothing in it.
> "What! what!" cried one, "are you not amazed
> At what our friend has told?" He raised
> Soberly then his eyes and gazed
>> In a natural way
>> And proceeded to say,
> As he crossed his feet on the mantel-shelf:
> "O no—not at all; I'm a liar myself."

Impromptu, *adv.* Off hand—said of verses that are written without confusing the legs and protruding the tongue. F'rexample.

Bulbous bangs enormous roared
    And swamping pickled he,
Through beetling barbarous restored
    Fuliginous and free;
For bellicose arbitrament
He on his nether ear had went!

Impropriety, *n.* Next to vulgarity, the highest conceivable degree of sin.

    His wife was so improper
        In her fun
    He thought it best to stop her
        With a gun,
    And blowing her to Limbo
        Then, said he:
   "I hate all kinds of impro-
    Prietee."

Improvidence, *n.* Provision for the needs of to-day from the revenues of to-morrow.

Improvisator, (Italian, *improvisatore.*) *n.* A chap who is happier at making verses than his auditors are in hearing them.

Imprudence, *n.* A peculiar charm attaching to certain actions, adding a new delight to such as are sinful and somewhat mitigating the wearisome character of those that are good.

Impudence, *n.* The stunted and deformed illegitimate offspring of audacity and vulgarity.

Impunity, *n.* Wealth.

Inadmissible, *adj.* Not competent to be considered. Said of certain kinds of testimony which juries are supposed to be unfit to be entrusted with, and which judges, therefore, rule out, even of proceedings before themselves alone. Hearsay evidence is inadmissible because the person quoted was unsworn and is not before the court for examination; yet most momentous actions, military, political, commercial and of every other kind, are daily undertaken on hearsay evidence. There is no religion in the world that has any other basis than hearsay evidence. Revelation is hearsay evidence; that the Scriptures are the word of God we have only the testimony of men long dead whose identity is not clearly established and who are not known to have been sworn in any sense. Under the rules of evidence as they now exist in this country, no single assertion in the Bible has in its support any evidence admissible in a court of law. It cannot be proved that the battle of Blenheim ever was fought, that there was such a person as Julius Cæsar, such an empire as Assyria.

But as records of courts of justice are admissible, it can easily be proved that powerful and malevolent magicians once existed and were a scourge to mankind. The evidence (including confession) upon which certain women were convicted of witchcraft and executed was without a flaw; it is still unimpeachable. The judges' decisions based on it were sound in logic and in law. Nothing in any existing court was ever more thoroughly proved than the charges of witchcraft and sorcery for which so many suffered death. If there were no witches, human testimony and human reason are alike destitute of value.

Inalterable, *adj.* Incapable of being changed; for example, a ten-dollar piece in a company of wits.

Inappropriateness, *n.* Holding divine service during a dog-fight in a church.

Inauspicious, *adj.* Not lousy with it in the crop.

The author of this dictionary feels it his duty to explain to the Eastern reader that the appalling phrase immediately foregoing is not of his own invention, and that he employs it here, with reluctance, in order to be clearly understood in the mining camps of this state, where "English as she is spoke" on the Atlantic seaboard is altogether unintelligible. The author begs to assure his Eastern readers that the phrase in question means nothing very disagreeable; it may be translated thus: "Not showing much free gold in the outcroppings." Let us now proceed.

Inauspiciously, *adv.* In an unpromising manner, the auspices being unfavorable. Among the Romans it was customary before undertaking any important action or enterprise to obtain from the augurs, or state prophets, some hint of its probable outcome; and one of their favorite and most trustworthy modes of divination consisted in observing the flight of birds—the omens thence derived being called *auspices*. Newspaper reporters and certain miscreant lexicographers have decided that the word—always in the plural—shall mean "patronage" or "management"; as, "The festivities were under the auspices of the Ancient and Honorable Order of Body-Snatchers"; or, "The hilarities were auspicated by the Knights of Hunger."

> A Roman slave appeared one day
> Before the Augur. "Tell me, pray,
> If—" here the Augur, smiling, made
> A checking gesture and displayed
> His open palm, which plainly itched,
> For visibly its surface twitched.
> A *denarius* (the Latin nickel)
> Successfully allayed the tickle,
> And then the slave proceeded: "Please
> Inform me whether Fate decrees

Success or failure in what I
To-night (if it be dark) shall try.
Its nature? Never mind—I think
'Tis writ on this"—and with a wink
Which darkened half the earth, he drew
Another denarius to view,
Its shining face attentive scanned,
Then slipped it into the good man's hand,
Who with great gravity said: "Wait
While I retire to question Fate."
That holy person then withdrew
His sacred clay and, passing through
The temple's rearward gate, cried "Shoo!"
Waving his robe of office. Straight
Each sacred peacock and its mate
(Maintained for Juno's favor) fled
With clamor from the trees o'erhead,
Where they were perching for the night.
The temple's roof received their flight,
For thither they would always go,
When danger threatened them below.
Back to the slave the Augur went:
"My son, forecasting the event
By flight of birds, I must confess
The auspices deny success."
That slave retired, a sadder man,
Abandoning his secret plan—
Which was (as well the crafty seer
Had from the first divined) to clear
The wall and fraudulently seize
On Juno's poultry in the trees.

G. J.

Incatenation, *n.* The act of linking together, or the state of being joined in a series.

It was an ancient butcher man,
    His merchandise displaying,
And eke an academian
    Before the meat-stall straying.

"O butcher, though 'tis naught to me
    Who may as rogues be rated,

Thy sausages, 'tis plain to see,
  Are all incatenated."

"Now, scholar, cap and gown shall not
  Protect thee from the whacking
I'll give to thee, for thou, God wot,
  Giv'st me a scurril blacking."

Then rose the wrathful butcher man
  And drave the scholar from him,
And shouted as that caitiff ran:
  "I'll *cat* the cuss, dud gom him!"

Incense, *n.* In religious affairs, an argument addressed to the nose.

Incivism, *n.* A crime which consists in not wearing a handle.

"He's no good citizen!" the crowd
  Of politicians cries aloud.

"How so?" says one.

            "Because—why, curse
The man! while we deplete his purse
Some air contentedly he hums,
Or twiddles his incivic thumbs."

"What more could you desire?"

              "The whelp!
We want him to stand in and help."

"*Two* crowds contend, his purse to twist
Away—pray which should he assist?"

"It matters not whose hand unsacks
His shekels, for we all go snacks."

Income, *n.* The natural and rational gauge and measure of respectability, the commonly accepted standards being artificial, arbitrary and fallacious; for, as "Sir Sycophas Chrysolater" in the play has justly remarked, "the true use and function of property (in whatsoever it consisteth—coins, or land, or houses, or merchant-stuff, or anything which may be named as holden of right to one's own subservience) as also of honors, titles, preferments and place, and all favor and acquaintance of persons of quality or ableness, are but to get money. Hence it followeth that all things are truly to be rated as of worth in measure of their serviceableness to that end; and their possessors should take rank in agreement thereto, neither the lord of an unproducing manor, howsoever broad and ancient, nor he who bears an unremunerate dignity, nor yet the pauper favorite of a king, being esteemed of level excellency with him whose riches are of daily accretion; and hardly should they whose wealth is barren claim and rightly take more honor than the poor and unworthy."

Incompatibility, *n.* In matrimony a similarity of tastes, particularly the taste for domination. Incompatibility may, however, consist of a meek-eyed matron living just around the corner. It has even been known to wear a moustache.

Incompossible, *adj.* Unable to exist if something else exists. Two things are incompossible when the world of being has scope enough for one of them, but not enough for both—as Walt Whitman's poetry and God's mercy to man. Incompossibility, it will be seen, is only incompatibility let loose. Instead of such low language as "Go heel yourself—I mean to kill you on sight," the words, "Sir, we are incompossible," would convey an equally significant intimation and in stately courtesy are altogether superior.

Incomprehensibility, *n.* One of the principal attributes of Deity and the poet Welcker.

Inconsiderate, *adj.* Imperfectly attentive to the welfare, happiness, comfort or desires of others; as cholera, small-pox, the rattlesnake and the satirical newspaper.

Inconsolable, *adj.* Very recently bereft.

    "I'm inconsolable," she said;

    "My lord and heart alike are dead.

    As Lazarus came forth from night,

    By love restored in death's despite,

    O may love's miracle impart

    New life and light to my poor—heart."

Inconstancy, *n.* See WOMAN.

Inconstant, *adj.* See MAN.

Incorporation, *n.* The act of uniting several persons into one fiction called a corporation, in order that they may be no longer responsible for their actions. A, B and C are a corporation. A robs, B steals and C (it is necessary that there be one gentleman in the concern) cheats. It is a plundering, thieving, swindling corporation. But A, B and C, who have jointly determined and severally executed every crime of the corporation, are blameless. It is wrong to mention them by name when censuring their acts as a corporation, but right when praising. Incorporation is somewhat like the ring of Gyges: it bestows the blessing of invisibility—comfortable to knaves. The scoundrel who invented incorporation is dead—he has disincorporated.

Incubate, *v.i.* To lie, sit or press upon. In popular usage, to hatch young fowls out of eggs, even by artificial means; though Professor George Bayley prefers to call this latter process "machining 'em out."

> Said a hen to a wit: "You can't deny
> We're very similar, you and I,
> In one, at least, of our useful labors."
> "The devil we are!" replied the wit.
> "O yes: we're both accustomed to sit—
> I on my eggs and you on your neighbors."

Incubus, *n.* One of a race of highly improper demons who, though probably not wholly extinct, may be said to have seen their best nights. For a complete account of *incubi* and *succubi,* including *incubæ* and *succubæ,* see the *Liber Demonorum* of Protassus (Paris, 1328), which contains much curious information that would be out of place in a dictionary intended as a text-book for the public schools.

Victor Hugo relates that in the Channel Islands Satan himself—tempted more than elsewhere by the beauty of the women, doubtless—sometimes plays at *incubus,* greatly to the inconvenience and alarm of the good dames who wish to be loyal to their marriage vows, generally speaking. A certain lady applied to the parish priest to learn how they might, in the dark, distinguish the hardy intruder from their husbands. The holy man said they must feel his brow for horns; but Hugo is ungallant enough to hint a doubt of the efficacy of the test.

Incumbent, *n.* A person of the liveliest interest to the outcumbents.

Indecision, *n.* The chief element of success; "for whereas," saith Sir Thomas Brewbold, "there is but one way to do nothing and divers ways to do something, whereof, to a surety, only one is the right way, it followeth that he who from indecision standeth still hath not so many chances of going astray as he who pusheth forwards" —a most clear and satisfactory exposition on the matter.

"Your prompt decision to attack," said General Grant on a certain occasion to General Gordon Granger, "was admirable; you had but five minutes to make up your mind in."

"Yes, sir," answered the victorious subordinate, "it is a great thing to know exactly what to do in an emergency. When in doubt whether to attack or retreat I never hesitate a moment—I toss up a copper."

"Do you mean to say that's what you did this time?"

"Yes, General; but for Heaven's sake don't reprimand me: I disobeyed the coin."

Indian, *n.*

> Columbus sailing out of Spain,
> Across old Neptune's wide domain,
> Came, joyous, to an unknown land
> And lightly leaped upon the strand,

Confronting there a painted cuss
In puris naturalibus —
An aboriginal and rude
But stately occidental dude.

"My friend, you are discovered," cried
Columb.

       "Not much," the man replied;
"'Tis you, my hearty, who are found,
For I'm upon my native ground,
While you, by wave and tempest tossed,
Until you landed here, were lost."

"Well, well," said Chris., "we'll not dispute
Of that, for either way will suit.
You're chief, no doubt, of all this isle."
And the man answered:
          "I should smile."

"So be it. Henceforth you shall reign
As vassal to the King of Spain,
An Indian cazique no more,
But Viceroy of San Salvador."

"You make me tired," the native said;
"Get off the roof—go soak your head.
Your ignorance (upon my life
A man could cut it with a knife,
So dense it is) surpasses all
In daisiness except your gall,
And that's the worst I ever saw.
Now hear me fiddle on my jaw:
I'm not an Injun—I'm a pup
Of Caribs from the grass roots up,
And this is not San Salvador,
But Anacanguango."

      More,
No doubt, the fellow would have said,
But Christofer cut off his head,
Which, feathered well on every lock,
Seemed, as it flew, a shuttlecock.

Indifferent, *adj.* Imperfectly sensible to distinctions among things.

> "You tiresome man!" cried Indolentio's wife,
> "You've grown indifferent to all in life."
> "Indifferent?" he drawled with a slow smile;
> "I would be, dear, but it is not worth while."
>
> *Apuleius M. Gokul.*

Indigestion, *n.* A disease which the patient and his friends frequently mistake for deep religious conviction and concern for the salvation of mankind. As the simple Red Man of the western wild put it, with, it must be confessed, a certain force: "Plenty well, no pray; big bellyache, heap God."

Indiscretion, *n.* The guilt of woman.

Inexpedient, *adj.* Not calculated to advance one's interests.

Infallible, *adj.* Not liable to error; dead-sure—as Frank Pixley, when speaking *ex cathartica.*

Infancy, *n.* The period of our lives when, according to Wordsworth, "Heaven lies about us." The world begins lying about us pretty soon afterward.

Inferiæ, *n.* (Latin.) Among the Greeks and Romans, sacrifices for propitiation of the *Dii Manes,* or souls of the dead heroes; for the pious ancients could not invent enough gods to satisfy their spiritual needs, and had to have a number of makeshift deities, or, as a sailor might say, jury-gods, which they made out of the most unpromising materials. It was while sacrificing a bullock to the spirit of Agamemnon that Laiaides, a priest of Aulis, was favored with an audience of that illustrious warrior's shade, who prophetically recounted to him the birth of Christ and the triumph of Christianity, giving him also a rapid but tolerably complete review of events down to the reign of Saint Louis. The narrative ended abruptly at that point, owing to the inconsiderate crowing of a cock, which compelled the ghosted King of Men to scamper back to Hades. There is a fine mediæval flavor to this story, and as it has not been traced back further than Père Brateille, a pious but obscure writer at the court of St. Louis, we shall probably not err on the side of presumption in considering it apocryphal, though Monsignor Capel's judgment of the matter might be different; and to that I bow—wow.

Infidel, *n.* In New York, one who does not believe in the Christian religion; in Constantinople, one who does. (See GIAOUR.) A kind of scoundrel imperfectly reverent of, and niggardly contributory to, divines, ecclesiastics, popes, parsons, canons, monks, mollahs, voodoos, presbyters, hierophants, prelates, obeah-men, abbés, nuns, missionaries, exhorters, deacons, friars, hadjis, high-priests, muezzins, brahmins, medicine-men, confessors, eminences, elders, primates, prebendaries, pilgrims, prophets, imaums, beneficiaries, clerks, vicars-choral, archbishops, bishops, abbots, priors, preachers, padres, abbotesses, caloyers, palmers, curates, patriarchs, bonzes, santons, beadsmen, canonesses, residentiaries, diocesans, deans, subdeans, rural deans, abdals, charm-sellers, archdeacons, hierarchs, class-leaders, incumbents, capitulars, sheiks, talapoins, postulants, scribes, gooroos, precentors, beadles, fakeers, sextons, reverences, revivalists, cœnobites, perpetual curates, chaplains, mudjoes, readers, novices, vicars, pastors, rabbis, ulemas, lamas, sacristans, vergers, dervises, lectors, church wardens, cardinals, prioresses, suffragans, acolytes, rectors, curés, sophis, muftis and pumpums.

Influence, *n.* In politics, a visionary *quo* given in exchange for a substantial *quid.*

Infralapsarian, *n.* One who ventures to believe that Adam need not have sinned unless he had a mind to—in opposition to the Supralapsarians, who hold that that luckless person's fall was decreed from the beginning. Infralapsarians are sometimes called Sublapsarians without material effect upon the importance and lucidity of their views about Adam.

> Two theologues once, as they wended their way
> To chapel, engaged in colloquial fray—
> An earnest logomachy, bitter as gall,
> Concerning poor Adam and what made him fall.
> "'Twas Predestination," cried one—"for the Lord
> Decreed he should fall of his own accord."
> "Not so—'twas Free-will," the other maintained,
> "Which led him to choose what the Lord had ordained."
> So fierce and so fiery grew the debate
> That nothing but bloodshed their dudgeon could sate;
> So off flew their cassocks and caps to the ground
> And, moved by the spirit, their hands went round.
> Ere either had proved his theology right
> By winning, or even beginning, the fight,
> A gray old professor of Latin came by,
> A staff in his hand and a scowl in his eye,
> And learning the cause of their quarrel (for still
> As they clumsily sparred they disputed with skill
> Of foreordinational freedom of will)
> Cried: "Sirrahs! this reasonless warfare compose:
> Atwixt ye's no difference worthy of blows.
> The sects ye belong to—I'm ready to swear
> Ye wrongly interpret the names that they bear.
> *You* —Infralapsarian son of a clown!—
> Should only contend that Adam slipped down;
> While *you* —you Supralapsarian pup!—
> Should nothing aver but that Adam slipped up."

It's all the same whether up or down
You slip on a peel of banana brown.
Even Adam analyzed not his blunder,
But thought he had slipped on a peal of thunder!

G. J.

Ingrate, *n.* One who receives a benefit from another, or is otherwise an object of charity.

> "All men are ingrates," sneered the cynic. "Nay,"
> The good philanthropist replied;
> "I did great service to a man one day
> Who never since has cursed me to repay,
> Nor vilified."

> "Ho!" cried the cynic, "lead me to him straight—
> With veneration I am overcome,
> And fain would have his blessing." "Sad your fate—
> He cannot bless you, for I grieve to state
> The man is dumb."

Ariel Selp.

Ingratitude, *n.* A form of self-respect that is not inconsistent with acceptance of favors.

Inhumanity, *n.* One of the signal and characteristic qualities of humanity.

Injury, *n.* An offence next in degree of enormity to a slight.

Injustice, *n.* A burden which of all those that we load upon others and carry ourselves is lightest in the hands and heaviest upon the back.

Ink, *n.* A villainous compound of tannogallate of iron, gum-arabic and water, chiefly used to facilitate the infection of idiocy and promote intellectual crime. The properties of ink are peculiar and contradictory: it may be used to make reputations and unmake them; to blacken them and to make them white; but it is most generally and acceptably employed as a mortar to bind together the stones in an edifice of fame, and as a whitewash to conceal afterward the rascal quality of the material. There are men called journalists who have established ink baths which some persons pay money to get into, others to get out of. Not infrequently it occurs that a person who has paid to get in pays twice as much to get out.

In'ards, *n.* The stomach, heart, soul and other bowels. Many eminent investigators do not class the soul as an in'ard, but that acute observer and renowned authority, Dr. Gunsaulus, is persuaded that the mysterious organ known as the spleen is nothing less than our immortal part. To the contrary, Professor Garrett P. Serviss holds that man's soul is that prolongation of his spinal marrow which forms the pith of his no tail; and for demonstration of his faith points confidently to the fact that tailed animals have no souls. Concerning these two theories, it is best to suspend judgment by believing both.

Innate, *adj.* Natural, inherent—as innate ideas, that is to say, ideas that we are born with, having had them previously imparted to us. The doctrine of innate ideas is one of the most admirable faiths of philosophy, being itself an innate idea and therefore inaccessible to disproof, though Locke foolishly supposed himself to have given it "a black eye." Among innate ideas may be mentioned the belief in one's ability to conduct a newspaper, in the greatness of one's country, in the superiority of one's civilization, in the importance of one's personal affairs and in the interesting nature of one's diseases.

Innocence, *n.* The state or condition of a criminal whose counsel has fixed the jury.

> "My client, gentlemen," the lawyer cried,
>   "Is innocent as any babe unborn—
> As spotless as the snows upon the side
>   Of giant Blanc or skyward Matterhorn.
>
> "What! *he* steal hogs—this honorable youth?
>   A thought so monstrous makes the angels weep!
> When that vile felony was wrought, in truth,
>   My client was in jail for stealing sheep."

Inquisition, *n.* An ecclesiastical court for the discouragement of error by mitigating the prevalence and ameliorating the comfort of the erring.

Insane, *adj.* Addicted to the conviction that others are insane.

Insanity, *n.* A glossy and gorgeous intellectual fabric, of which sanity is the seamy side. The nature of insanity is not clearly known except by those who know everything. Amongst Western nations it is commonly regarded as a disorder, but Oriental peoples consider it an inspiration. The Mohammedan venerates the same lunatic whom the Christian would put into a strait-jacket or chain to a post. As the poet hath said:

> Unto the Sun, with deep salaams,
> The Parsee spreads his morning palms
> (A beacon blazing on a height
> Warms-o'er his piety by night).
> The Moslem deprecates the deed,
> Cuts off the head that holds the creed
> Then reverently goes to grass,
> Muttering thanks to Balaam's Ass
> For faith and learning to refute
> Idolatry so dissolute.
> But should a maniac dash by,

With straws in beard and hands on high,
To him (through whom to Madamkind
The Holy Prophet speaks his mind)
Our true believer lifts his eyes
Devoutly and his prayer applies;
But next to Solyman the Great
Reveres the idiot's sacred state.

Inscription, *n*. Something written on another thing. Inscriptions are of many kinds, but mostly memorial, intended to commemorate the fame of some illustrious person and hand down to distant ages the record of his services and virtues. To this class of inscriptions belongs the name of John Smith, penciled on the Washington monument. Following are examples of memorial inscriptions on tombstones: (See EPITAPH.)

"In the sky my soul is found,
And my body in the ground.
By and by my body'll rise
To my spirit in the skies,
Soaring up to Heaven's gate.
    1878."

"Sacred to the memory of Jeremiah Tree. Cut down May 9th, 1862, aged 27 yrs. 4 mos. and 12 ds. Indigenous."

"Affliction sore long time she boar,
    Phisicians was in vain,
Till Deth released the dear deceased
    And left her a remain.
Gone to join Ananias in the regions of bliss."

"The clay that rests beneath this stone
As Silas Wood was widely known.
Now, lying here, I ask what good
It was to let me be S. Wood.
O Man, let not ambition trouble you,
Is the advice of Silas W."

"Richard Haymon, of Heaven. Fell to Earth Jan. 20, 1807, and had the dust brushed off him Oct. 3, 1874."

Insectivora, *n*.
"See," cries the chorus of admiring preachers,
"How Providence provides for all His creatures!"

"His care," the gnat said, "even the insects follows:
For us He has provided wrens and swallows."

Sempen Railey.

Insolvent, *adj.* Destitute of property to pay just debts. Destitution of the will to pay them is not insolvency; it is commercial sagacity.

Inspiration, *n.* Literally, the act of breathing into, as a prophet is inspired by the Spirit, and a flute by an enemy of mankind.

"Ho-ho!" said the Scribe as he brandished his quill,
"I'm full of an inspiration!"
Said the blown-up Bladder: "I too have a fill,"
And he swelled with great elation.
Then that writer he sneered: "My friend, your own
Is nothing but just inflation."
And that orb replied in a mocking tone:
"And yours is but dilatation."
So they came to blows, and the Bladder blew
With a forceful sibilation,
And that Scribe's remarks as he skyward flew
Were unfit for publication.

Insurance, *n.* An ingenious modern game of chance in which the player is permitted to enjoy the comfortable conviction that he is beating the man who keeps the table.

INSURANCE AGENT: My dear sir, that is a fine house—pray let me insure it.

HOUSE OWNER: With pleasure. Please make the annual premium so low that by the time when, according to the tables of your actuary, it will probably be destroyed by fire I will have paid you considerably less than the face of the policy.

INSURANCE AGENT: O dear, no—we could not afford to do that. We must fix the premium so that you will have paid more.

HOUSE OWNER: How, then, can *I* afford *that*?

INSURANCE AGENT: Why, your house may burn down at any time. There was Smith's house, for example, which—

HOUSE OWNER: Spare me—there were Brown's house, on the contrary, and Jones's house, and Robinson's house, which—

INSURANCE AGENT: Spare *me!*

HOUSE OWNER: Let us understand each other. You want me to pay you money on the supposition that something will occur previously to the time set by yourself for its occurrence. In other words, you expect me to bet that my house will not last so long as you say that it will probably last.

INSURANCE AGENT: But if your house burns without insurance it will be a total loss.

HOUSE OWNER: Beg your pardon—by your own actuary's tables I shall probably have saved, when it burns, all the premiums I would otherwise have paid to you—amounting to more than the face of the policy they would have bought. But suppose it to burn, uninsured, before the time upon which your figures are based. If I could not afford that, how could you if it were insured?

INSURANCE AGENT: O, we should make ourselves whole from our luckier ventures with other clients. Virtually, they pay your loss.

HOUSE OWNER: And virtually, then, don't I help to pay their losses? Are not their houses as likely as mine to burn before they have paid you as much as you must pay them? The case stands this way: you expect to take more money from your clients than you pay to them, do you not?

INSURANCE AGENT: Certainly; if we did not—

HOUSE OWNER: I would not trust you with my money. Very well then. If it is *certain,* with reference to the whole body of your clients, that they lose money on you it is *probable,* with reference to any one of them, that *he* will. It is these individual probabilities that make the aggregate certainty.

INSURANCE AGENT: I will not deny it—but look at the figures in this pamph—

HOUSE OWNER: Heaven forbid!

INSURANCE AGENT: You spoke of saving the premiums which you would otherwise pay to me. Will you not be more likely to squander them? We offer you an incentive to thrift.

HOUSE OWNER: The willingness of A to take care of B's money is not peculiar to insurance, but as a charitable institution you command esteem. Deign to accept its expression from a Deserving Object.

Insurrection, *n.* An unsuccessful revolution. Disaffection's failure to substitute misrule for bad government.

Intellectual, *adj.* Employed on the *Bulletin,* in the department of Art, Literature and Agriculture; residing in Boston; near-sighted.

Intelligent, *adj.* In politics, having a vote—in journalism, taking the paper; holding the same opinion as oneself; rich; veneered by the Chautauqua Society.

Sourissa was intelligent—
She worshiped only brain.
Dudeus was so swell a gent
He looked with high disdain
On intellect. He said: "If you
Were nicely stupid I would woo."

> Sourissa, contumelius,
>> Induced him with a kick
> To revolute cartwheelious
>> Until the man was sick.
> Contemplative of his gyrade,
> "Nobody axled you," she sayd.

Intemperance, *n.* A monster which, attacking all, overcomes the weaklings and results in the survival of the fightest.

Intention, *n.* The mind's sense of the prevalence of one set of influences over another set; an effect whose cause is the imminence, immediate or remote, of the performance of an involuntary act.

Interim, *n.* A period of time, considered with reference to two dates or events which it falls between; as, "Byron died in the first half of the nineteenth century, Hugo in the second half. In the interim Adair Welcker arose." A famous decree of Charles V of Germany, designed to reconcile the Catholic and Protestant churches and make Frank Pixley impossible.

Interlocutor, *n.* The barometrical center of depression at a minstrel show.

Interpreter, *n.* One who enables two persons of different languages to understand each other by repeating to each what it would have been to the interpreter's advantage for the other to have said.

Interregnum, *n.* The period during which a monarchical country is governed by a warm spot on the cushion of the throne. The experiment of letting the spot grow cold has commonly been attended by most unhappy results from the zeal of many worthy persons to make it warm again.

Interview, *n.* In journalism, a confessional where vulgar impudence bends an ear to the follies of vanity and ambition.

Intimacy, *n.* A relation into which fools are providentially drawn for their mutual destruction.

> Two Seidlitz powders, one in blue
> And one in white, together drew,
> And having each a pleasant sense
> Of t'other powder's excellence,
> Forsook their jackets for the snug
> Enjoyment of a common mug.
> So close their intimacy grew
> One paper would have held the two.
> To confidences straight they fell,
> Less anxious each to hear than tell;
> Then each remorsefully confessed
> To all the virtues he possessed,
> Acknowledging he had them in

So high degree it was a sin.
The more they said, the more they felt
Their spirits with emotion melt,
Till tears of sentiment expressed
Their feelings. Then they effervesced!

So Nature executes her feats
Of wrath on friends and sympathetes
The good old rule who won't apply,
That you are you and I am I.

Intoxication, *n.* A spiritual condition that goeth before the next morning.

Intractable, *adj.* Stubbornly unwilling to adopt a course from which nothing can divert ourselves.

Introduction, *n.* A social ceremony invented by the devil for the gratification of his servants and the plaguing of his enemies. The introduction attains its most malevolent development in this century, being, indeed, closely related to our political system. Every American being the equal of every other American, it follows that everybody has the right to know everybody else, which implies the right to introduce without request or permission. The Declaration of Independence should have read thus:

> "We hold these truths to be self-evident: that all men are created
> equal; that they are endowed by their Creator with certain inalienable
> rights; that among these are life, and the right to make that of
> another miserable by thrusting upon him an incalculable quantity of
> acquaintances; liberty, particularly the liberty to introduce persons to
> one another without first ascertaining if they are not already acquainted
> as enemies; and the pursuit of another's happiness with a running pack
> of strangers."

Intruder, *n.* A person who should not be too hastily kicked out—he may be a reporter.

Inundation, *n.* A flood. The greatest inundation of which we have any account was the Noachian deluge described by Moses, Berosus and an Assyrian chronicler translated by the late Mr. George Smith. Inundations are caused variously, but this one was due to a long spell of wet weather—forty days and forty nights, Moses says. So much water fell in that period that it covered every mountain on the earth, some of which—the highest being near where Noah lived—have an elevation above the sea-level of 30,000 feet. Our heaviest rains are at the rate of about six inches in twenty-four hours—a fall of two feet would strangle one who should attempt to walk abroad in it. But Noah's rain fell at the rate of 750 feet per twenty-four hours, or 31½ feet per hour. It was quite a rain.

Invasion, *n.* The patriot's most approved method of attesting his love of his country.

Inventor, *n.* A person who makes an ingenious arrangement of wheels, levers and springs, and believes it civilization.

Irreligion, *n.* The principal one of the great faiths of the world.

Isthmus, *n.* A canal site. A cemetery for capital.

Itch, *n.* The patriotism of a Scotchman.

Ivory, *n.* A substance kindly provided by nature for making billiard balls. It is usually harvested from the mouths of elephants.

J is a consonant in English, but some nations use it as a vowel—than which nothing could be more absurd. Its original form, which has been but slightly modified, was that of the tail of a subdued dog, and it was not a letter but a character, standing for a Latin verb, *jacere,* "to throw," because when a stone is thrown at a dog the dog's tail assumes that shape. This is the origin of the letter, as expounded by the renowned Dr. Jocolpus Bumer, of the University of Belgrade, who established his conclusions on the subject in a work of three quarto volumes and committed suicide on being reminded that the j in the Roman alphabet had originally no curl.

Jacob's-ladder, *n.* A ladder which Jacob saw in a dream, reaching from earth to heaven, with angels ascending and descending. Seeing that angels have wings, the purpose of this ladder is so imperfectly apparent that many learned commentators had contended that it was not a real ladder, but only a ray of glory. One cannot help thinking it rather hard on Jacob that he should be required to dream with logical realism.

Jealous, *adj.* Unduly concerned about the preservation of that which can be lost only if not worth keeping.

Jealousy, *n.* The seamy side of love.

Jester, *n.* An officer formerly attached to a king's household, whose business it was to amuse the court by ludicrous actions and utterances, the absurdity being attested by his motley costume. The king himself being attired with dignity, it took the world some centuries to discover that his own conduct and decrees were sufficiently ridiculous for the amusement not only of his court but of all mankind. The jester was commonly called a fool, but the poets and romancers have ever delighted to represent him as a singularly wise and witty person. In the circus of to-day the melancholy ghost of the court fool effects the dejection of humbler audiences with the same jests wherewith in life he gloomed the marble hall, panged the patrician sense of humor and tapped the tank of royal tears.

The widow-queen of Portugal
    Had an audacious jester
Who entered the confessional
    Disguised, and there confessed her.

"Father," she said, "thine ear bend down—
    My sins are more than scarlet:
I love my fool—blaspheming clown,
    And common, base-born varlet."

"Daughter," the mimic priest replied,
    "That sin, indeed, is awful:
The church's pardon is denied
    To love that is unlawful.

"But since thy stubborn heart will be
    For him forever pleading,
Thou'dst better make him, by decree,
    A man of birth and breeding."

She made the fool a duke, in hope
    With Heaven's taboo to palter;
Then told a priest, who told the Pope,
    Who damned her from the altar!

Barel Dort.

Jews-harp, *n.* An unmusical instrument, played by holding it fast with the teeth and trying to brush it away with the finger.

Jockey, *n.* A person whose business it is to ride and throw races.

Joss-sticks, *n.* Small sticks burned by the Chinese in their pagan tomfoolery, in imitation of certain sacred rites of our holy religion.

Jove, *n.* A mythical being whom the Greeks and Romans ridiculously supposed to be the supreme ruler of the universe—unacquainted as they were with our holy religion.

Joy, *n.* An emotion variously excited, but in its highest degree arising from the contemplation of grief in another.

Judge, *n.* A person who is always interfering in disputes in which he has no personal interest. An official whose functions, as a great legal luminary recently informed a body of local law-students, very closely resemble those of God. The latter, however, is not afraid to punish Chris. Buckley for contempt, and the former has attained no great distinction as the hero of popular oaths.

Jurisprudence, *n.* The kind of prudence that keeps one inside the law.

Jury, *n.* A number of persons appointed by a court to assist the attorneys in preventing law from degenerating into justice.

> Against all law and evidence,
> > The prisoner was acquitted.
> The judge exclaimed: "Is common sense
> > To jurors not permitted?"
>
> The prisoner's counsel rose and bowed:
> > "Your Honor, why this fury?
> By law the judge is not allowed
> > To sit upon the jury."

Justice, *n.* A commodity which in a more or less adulterated condition the State sells to the citizen as a reward for his allegiance, taxes and personal service.

Jute, *n.* A plant grown in India, the fruit of which supplies a nutritious diet to the directors of our State prison.

K is a consonant that we get from the Greeks, but it can be traced away back beyond them to the Cerathians, a small commercial nation inhabiting the peninsula of Smero. In their tongue it was called *Klatch,* which means "destroyed." The form of the letter was originally precisely that of our H, but the erudite Dr. Snedeker explains that it was altered to its present shape to commemorate the destruction of the great temple of Jarute by an earthquake, *circa* 730 B.C. This building was famous for the two lofty columns of its portico, one of which was broken in half by the catastrophe, the other remaining intact. As the earlier form of the letter is supposed to have been suggested by these pillars, so, it is thought by the great antiquary, its later was adopted as a simple and natural—not to say touching—means of keeping the calamity ever in the national memory. It is not known if the name of the letter was altered as an additional mnemonic, or if the name was always *Klatch* and the destruction one of nature's puns. As each theory seems probable enough, I see no objection to believing both—and Dr. Snedeker arrayed himself on that side of the question.

Kangaroo, *n.* An unconventional kind of animal which in shape is farther than any other from being the square of its base. It is assisted in jumping by its tail (which makes very good soup) and when it has happened to alight on the surprised Australian it is usually observable that his skin is unbuttoned from the neck downward and he carries his bowels in his arms.

Keep, *v.t.*

> He willed away his whole estate,
>> And then in death he fell asleep,
> Murmuring: "Well, at any rate,
>> My name unblemished I shall keep."
> But when upon the tomb 'twas wrought
> Whose was it?—for the dead keep naught.
>> *Durang Gophel Arn.*

Kill, *v.t.* To create a vacancy without nominating a successor.

Kilt, *n.* A costume sometimes worn by Scotchmen in America and Americans in Scotland.

Kindness, *n.* A brief preface to ten volumes of exaction.

Kine, *n.* Cows.

> If kine is the plural of cow,
>> And the plural of sow is swine,
> Then pumpkins may hang from a vow,
>> And coronets rest upon brine.

King, *n.* A male person commonly known in America as a "crowned head," although he never wears a crown and has usually no head to speak of.

> A king, in times long, long gone by,
>> Said to his lazy jester:
> "If I were you and you were I
> My moments merrily would fly—
>> No care nor grief to pester."

> "The reason, Sire, that you would thrive,"
>> The fool said—"if you'll hear it—
> Is that of all the fools alive
> Who own you for their sovereign, I've
>> The most forgiving spirit."

Oogum Bem.

King's Evil, *n.* A malady that was formerly cured by the touch of the sovereign, but has now to be treated by the physicians. Thus "the most pious Edward" of England used to lay his royal hand upon his ailing subjects and make them whole—

>> a crowd of wretched souls
> That stay his cure: their malady convinces
> The great essay of art; but at his touch,
> Such sanctity hath Heaven given his hand,
> They presently amend,

as the "Doctor" in *Macbeth* hath it. This useful property of the royal hand could, it appears, be transmitted along with other crown properties; for according to "Malcolm,"

>> 'tis spoken,
> To the succeeding royalty he leaves
> The healing benediction.

But the gift somewhere dropped out of the line of succession: the later sovereigns of England have not been tactual healers, and the disease once honored with the name "king's evil" now bears the humbler one of "scrofula," from *scrofa*, a sow. The date and author of the following epigram are known only to the author of this dictionary, but it is old enough to show that the jest about Scotland's national disorder is not a thing of yesterday.

Yᵉ Kynge his evill in me laye,
Wh. he of Scottlande charmed awaye.
He layde his hand on mine and sayd:
"Be gone!" Yᵉ ill no longer stayd.
But O yᵉ wofull plyght in wh.
I'm now y-pight: I have yᵉ itche!

The superstition that maladies can be cured by royal taction is dead, but like many a departed conviction it has left a monument of custom to keep its memory green. The practice of forming in line and shaking the President's hand had no other origin, and when that great dignitary bestows his healing salutation on

strangely visited people,
All swoln and ulcerous, pitiful to the eye,
The mere despair of surgery,

he and his patients are handing along an extinguished torch which once was kindled at the altar-fire of a faith long held by all classes of men. It is a beautiful and edifying "survival" — one which brings the sainted past close home to our "business and bosoms."

Kiss, *n.* A word invented by the poets as a rhyme for "bliss." It is supposed to signify, in a general way, some kind of rite or ceremony appertaining to a good understanding; but the manner of its performance is unknown to this lexicographer.

Kleptomaniac, *n.* A rich thief.

Knight, *n.*

Once a warrior gentle of birth,
Then a person of civic worth,
Now a fellow to move our mirth.
Warrior, person and fellow—no more:
We must knight our dogs to get any lower.
Brave Knights Kennelers then shall be,
Noble Knights of the Golden Flea,
Knights of the Order of St. Steboy,
Knights of St. Gorge and Sir Knights Jawy.
God speed the day when this knighting fad
Shall go to the dogs and the dogs go mad.

Koran, *n.* A book which the Mohammedans foolishly believe to have been written by divine inspiration, but which Christians know to be a wicked imposture, contradictory to the Holy Scriptures.

Krishna, *n.* A form under which the pretended god Vishnu became incarnate. A very likely story indeed.

Labor, *n.* One of the processes by which A acquires property for B.

Lace, *n.* A delicate and costly textile fabric with which the female soul is netted like a fish.

Lacteal Fluid, *n.* (*Reporterese.*) Milk.

Lady, *n.* A vulgarian's name for a woman. A Lieutenant-Governor of California and Warden of the State Prison once reported the number of prisoners under his care as "931 males and 27 ladies."

Land, *n.* A part of the earth's surface, considered as property. The theory that land is property subject to private ownership and control is the foundation of modern society, and is eminently worthy of the superstructure. Carried to its logical conclusion, it means that some have the right to prevent others from living; for the right to own implies the right exclusively to occupy; and in fact laws of trespass are enacted wherever property in land is recognized. It follows that if the whole area of *terra firma* is owned by A, B and C, there will be no place for D, E, F and G to be born, or, born as trespassers, to exist.

> A life on the ocean wave,
> A home on the rolling deep,
> For the spark that nature gave
> I have there the right to keep.
>
> They give me the cat-o'-nine
> Whenever I go ashore.
> Then ho! for the flashing brine—
> I'm a natural commodore!
>
> *Dodle.*

Language, *n.* The music with which we charm the serpents guarding another's treasure.

Laocoön, *n.* A famous piece of antique sculpture representing a priest of that name and his two sons in the folds of two enormous serpents. The skill and diligence with which the old man and lads support the serpents and keep them up to their work have been justly regarded as one of the noblest artistic illustrations of the mastery of human intelligence over brute inertia.

Lap, *n.* One of the most important organs of the female system—an admirable provision of nature for the repose of infancy, but chiefly useful in rural festivities to support plates of cold chicken and heads of adult males. The male of our species has a rudimentary lap, imperfectly developed and in no way contributing to the animal's substantial welfare.

Lapidate, *v.t.* To rebuke with stones. St. Stephen, for example, was lapidated like a Chinaman.

> Lamented St. Steve,
> What Christian can grieve
> For the way that you came to your death?
> For the monument fair
> Of memorial stones
> Was reared in the air
> O'er your honored bones
> Ere yet you'd relinquished your breath.
> No doubt as your soul exhaled
> You were thanked by resolution;
> For the builders' design had failed
> Except for *your* execution.

Last, *n.* A shoemaker's implement, named by a frowning Providence as opportunity to the maker of puns.

> Ah, punster, would my lot were cast,
> Where the cobbler is unknown,
> So that I might forget his last
> And hear your own.
>
> *Gargo Repsky.*

Latitudinarian, *n.* In Theology, a miscreant who does his thinking at home instead of putting it out. He is regarded by the priesthood and clergy with the same aversion that a barber feels for the man who shaves himself.

Laughter, *n.* An interior convulsion, producing a distortion of the features and accompanied by inarticulate noises. It is infectious and, though intermittent, incurable. Liability to attacks of laughter is one of the characteristics distinguishing man from the animals—these being not only inaccessible to the provocation of his example, but impregnable to the microbes having original jurisdiction in bestowal of the disease. Whether laughter could be imparted to animals by inoculation from the human patient is a question that has not been answered by experimentation. Dr. Meir Witchell holds that the infectious character of laughter is due to the instantaneous fermentation of *sputa* diffused in a spray. From this peculiarity he names the disorder *Convulsio spargens.*

Laureate, *adj.* Crowned with leaves of the laurel. In England the Poet Laureate is an officer of the sovereign's court, acting as dancing skeleton at every royal feast and singing-mute at every royal funeral. Of all incumbents of that high office, Robert Southey had the most notable knack at drugging the Samson of public joy and cutting his hair to the quick; and he had an artistic color-sense which enabled him so to blacken a public grief as to give it the aspect of a national crime.

Laurel, *n.* The *laurus,* a vegetable dedicated to Apollo, and formerly defoliated to wreathe the brows of victors and such poets as had influence at court. (*Vide supra.*)

Law, *n.*

> Once Law was sitting on the bench,
>> And Mercy knelt a-weeping.
> "Clear out!" he cried, "disordered wench!
>> Nor come before me creeping.
> Upon your knees if you appear,
>> 'Tis plain you have no standing here."
>
> Then Justice came. His Honor cried:
>> "*Your* status? — devil seize you!"
> "*Amica curiæ,*" she replied —
>> "Friend of the court, so please you."
> "Begone!" he shouted — "there's the door —
>> I never saw your face before!"
>
>> G. J.

Lawful, *adj.* Compatible with the will of a judge having jurisdiction.

Lawyer, *n.* One skilled in circumvention of the law.

Lay-figure, *n.* The number which represents a hen's periodical output of eggs.

Laziness, *n.* Unwarranted repose of manner in a person of low degree.

Lead, *n.* A heavy blue-gray metal much used in giving stability to light lovers — particularly to those who love not wisely but other men's wives. Lead is also of great service as a counterpoise to an argument of such weight that it turns the scale of debate the wrong way. An interesting fact in the chemistry of international controversy is that at the point of contact of two patriotisms lead is precipitated in great quantities.

> Hail, holy Lead! — of human feuds the great
>> And universal arbiter; endowed
>> With penetration to pierce any cloud
> Fogging the field of controversial hate,

And with a swift, inevitable, straight,
    Searching precision find the unavowed
    But vital point. Thy judgment, when allowed
By the chirurgeon, settles the debate.
O useful metal!—were it not for thee
    We'd grapple one another's ears alway:
But when we hear thee buzzing like a bee
    We, like old Muhlenberg, "care not to stay."
And when the quick have run away like pullets
Jack Satan smelts the dead to make new bullets.

League, *n.* A union of two or more parties, factions or associations for promoting some purpose, commonly nefarious.

Learning, *n.* [1.] The kind of ignorance distinguishing the studious. [2.] The kind of ignorance affected by (and affecting) civilized races, as distinguished from *Ignorance,* the sort of learning incurred by savages. See NONSENSE.

Leatherhead, *n.* Dr. Bartlett, of the *Bulletin.*

Lecturer, *n.* One with his hand in your pocket, his tongue in your ear and his faith in your patience.

Legacy, *n.* A gift from one who is legging it out of this vale of tears.

Legislator, *n.* A person who goes to the capital of his country to increase his own; one who makes laws and money.

Leisure, *n.* Lucid intervals in a disordered life.

    THE JUDGE:
You lazy dog! all industry you shirk
As 'twere a crime—why don't you go to work?

    THE TOUGH CITIZEN:
I'm always planning to, but, may it please your
Honor, I do never get the leisure.

Leonine, *adj.* Unlike a menagerie lion. *Leonine verses* are those in which a word in the middle of a line rhymes with a word at the end, as in this famous passage from Bella Peeler Silcox:

The electric light invades the dunnest deep of Hades.
Cries Pluto, 'twixt his snores: "O tempora! O mores!"

It should be explained that Mrs. Silcox does not undertake to teach pronunciation of the Greek and Latin tongues. Leonine verses are so called in honor of a poet named Leo, whom prosodists appear to find a pleasure in believing to have been the first to discover that a rhyming couplet could be run into a single line.

Leptocephalidans, *n.* Authors of other dictionaries.

Lethe, *n.* An infernal river whose waters caused those who drank them to forget all they knew; whereas the drinker of Spring Valley forgets nothing but the Third Commandment and the pious precepts of a sainted mother.

Lettuce, *n.* An herb of the genus *Lactuca,* "Wherewith," says that pious gastronome, Hengist Pelly, "God has been pleased to reward the good and punish the wicked. For by his inner light the righteous man has discerned a manner of compounding for it a dressing to the appetency whereof a multitude of gustible condiments conspire, being reconciled and ameliorated with profusion of oil, the entire comestible making glad the heart of the godly and causing his face to shine. But the person of spiritual unworth is successfully tempted of the Adversary to eat of lettuce with destitution of oil, mustard, egg, salt and garlic, and with a rascal bath of vinegar polluted with sugar. Wherefore the person of spiritual unworth suffers an intestinal pang of strange complexity and raises the song."

Leveler, *n.* The kind of political and social reformer who is more concerned to bring others down to his plane than to lift himself to theirs.

Leviathan, *n.* An enormous aquatic animal mentioned by Job. Some suppose it to have been the whale, but that distinguished ichthyologer, Dr. Jordan, of Stanford University, maintains with considerable heat that it was a species of gigantic Tadpole (*Thaddeus polandensis*) or Polliwig—*Maria pseudo-hirsuta.* For an exhaustive description and history of the Tadpole consult the famous monograph of Jane Porter, *Thaddeus of Warsaw.*

Levite, *n.* A descendant of Levi, from whose posterity the Lord ordained all the Jewish priests—an instance of nepotism deserving of the severest censure, as incompatible with free institutions and the principle of civil and religious equality.

Lexicographer, *n.* A pestilent fellow who, under the pretense of recording some particular stage in the development of a language, does what he can to arrest its growth, stiffen its flexibility and mechanize its methods. For your lexicographer, having written his dictionary, comes to be considered "as one having authority," whereas his function is only to make a record, not to give a law. The natural servility of the human understanding having invested him with judicial power, surrenders its right of reason and submits itself to a chronicle as if it were a statute. Let the dictionary (for example) mark a good word as "obsolete" or "obsolescent" and few men thereafter venture to use it, whatever their need of it and however desirable its restoration to favor—whereby the process of impoverishment is accelerated and speech decays. On the contrary, the bold and discerning writer who, recognizing the truth that language must grow by innovation if it grow at all, makes new words and uses the old in an unfamiliar sense, has no following and is tartly reminded that "it isn't in the dictionary"—although down to the time of the first lexicographer (Heaven forgive him!) no author ever had used a word that *was* in the dictionary. In the golden prime and high noon of English speech; when from the lips of the great Elizabethans fell words that made their own meaning and carried it in their very sound; when a Shakspeare and a Bacon were possible, and the language now rapidly perishing at one end and slowly renewed at the other was in vigorous growth and hardy preservation—sweeter than honey and stronger than a lion—the lexicographer was a person unknown, the dictionary a creation which his Creator had not created him to create.

> God said: "Let Spirit perish into Form,"
> And lexicographers arose, a swarm!
> Thought fled and left her clothing, which they took,
> And catalogued each garment in a book.
> Now, from her leafy covert when she cries:
> "Give me my clothes and I'll return," they rise
> And scan the list, and say without compassion:
> "Excuse us—they are mostly out of fashion."
>
> Sigismund Smith.

Liar, *n.* A lawyer with a roving commission.

Libelous, *adj.* In the nature of an unprivileged excommunication.

Libertarian, *n.* One who is compelled by the evidence to believe in free-will, and whose will is therefore free to reject that doctrine.

Libertine, *n.* Literally a freedman; hence, one who is in bondage to his passions.

Liberty, *n.* One of Imagination's most precious possessions.

> The rising People, hot and out of breath,
> Roared round the palace: "Liberty or death!"
> "If death will do," the King said, "let me reign;
> You'll have, I'm sure, no reason to complain."
>
> Martha Braymance.

Lickspittle, *n.* A useful functionary, not infrequently found editing a newspaper. In his character of editor he is closely allied to the blackmailer by the tie of occasional identity; for in truth the lickspittle is only the blackmailer under another aspect, although the latter is frequently found as an independent species. Lickspittling is more detestable than blackmailing, precisely as the business of a confidence man is more detestable than that of a highway robber; and the parallel maintains itself throughout, for whereas few robbers will cheat, every sneak will plunder if he dare.

Life, *n.* A spiritual pickle preserving the body from decay. We live in daily apprehension of its loss; yet when lost it is not missed. The question, "Is life worth living?" has been much discussed; particularly by those who think it is not, many of whom have written at great length in support of their view and by careful observance of the laws of health enjoyed for long terms of years the honors of successful controversy.

"Life's not worth living, and that's the truth,"
Carelessly caroled the golden youth.
In manhood still he maintained that view
And held it more strongly the older he grew.
When kicked by a jackass at eighty-three,
"Go fetch me a surgeon at once!" cried he.

Han Soper.

Lighthouse, *n.* A tall building on the seashore in which the government maintains a lamp and the friend of a politician.

Limb, *n.* The branch of a tree or the leg of an American woman.

'Twas a pair of boots that the lady bought,
    And the salesman laced them tight
    To a very remarkable height—
Higher, indeed, than I think he ought—
    Higher than *can* be right.
For the Bible declares—but never mind:
    It is hardly fit
To censure freely and fault to find
With others for sins that I'm not inclined
    Myself to commit.
Each has his weakness, and though my own
    Is freedom from every sin,
    It still were unfair to pitch in,
Discharging the first censorious stone.
Besides, the truth compels me to say,
The boots in question were *made* that way.
As he drew the lace she made a grimace,
    And blushingly said to him:
"This boot, I'm sure, is too high to endure,
It hurts my—hurts my—limb."
The salesman smiled in a manner mild,
Like an artless, undesigning child;
Then, checking himself, to his face he gave
A look as sorrowful as the grave,
    Though he didn't care two figs
For her pains and throes,
As he stroked her toes,
Remarking with speech and manner just

Befitting his calling: "Madam, I trust
That it doesn't hurt your twigs."

B. Percival Doke.

Linen, *n.* "A kind of cloth the making of which, when made of hemp, entails a great waste of hemp." —*Calcraft the Hangman.*

Linguist, *n.* A person more learned in the languages of others than wise in his own.

Literally, *adv.* Figuratively, as: "The pond was literally full of fish"; "The ground was literally alive with snakes," etc.

Literature, *n.* The collective body of the writings of all mankind, excepting Hubert Howe Bancroft and Adair Welcker. Theirs are Illiterature.

Litigant, *n.* A person about to give up his skin for the hope of retaining his bones.

Litigation, *n.* A machine which you go into as a pig and come out of as a sausage.

Liver, *n.* A large red organ thoughtfully provided by nature to be bilious with. The sentiments and emotions which every literary anatomist now knows to haunt the heart were anciently believed to infest the liver; and even Gascoygne, speaking of the emotional side of human nature, calls it "our hepaticall parte." It was at one time considered the seat of life; hence its name — liver, the thing we live with. The liver is heaven's best gift to the goose; without it that bird would be unable to supply us with the Strasbourg *pâté.*

LL.D. Letters indicating the degree *Legumptionorum Doctor,* one learned in laws, gifted with legal gumption. Some suspicion is cast upon this derivation by the fact that the title was formerly *££.d.,* and conferred only upon gentlemen distinguished for their wealth. At the date of this writing Columbia University is considering the expediency of making another degree for clergymen, in place of the old D.D. — *Damnator Diaboli.* The new honor will be known as *Sanctorum Custos,* and written $$.¢. The name of the Rev. John Satan has been suggested as a suitable recipient by a lover of consistency, who points out that Professor Harry Thurston Peck has long enjoyed the advantage of a degree.

Lock-and-key, *n.* The distinguishing device of civilization and enlightenment.

Lodger, *n.* A less popular name for the Second Person of that delectable newspaper Trinity, the Roomer, the Bedder and the Mealer.

Logic, *n.* The art of thinking and reasoning in strict accordance with the limitations and incapacities of the human misunderstanding. The basis of logic is the syllogism, consisting of a major and a minor premise and a conclusion — thus:

Major Premise: Sixty men can do a piece of work sixty times as quickly as one man.

Minor Premise: One man can dig a post-hole in sixty seconds; therefore —
Conclusion: Sixty men can dig a post-hole in one second.

This may be called the syllogism arithmetical, in which, by combining logic and mathematics, we obtain a double certainty and are twice blessed.

Logomachy, *n.* A war in which the weapons are words and the wounds punctures in the swim-bladder of self-esteem — a kind of contest in which, the vanquished being unconscious of defeat, the victor is denied the reward of success.

> 'Tis said by divers of the scholar-men
> That poor Salmasius died of Milton's pen.
> Alas! we cannot know if this is true,
> For reading Milton's wit we perish too.

Loke, *n.* A malevolent deity of the Scandinavian mythology, described in the *Edda* as a serpent embracing the world. This is the greatest snake story on record and is now generally disbelieved.

Longanimity, *n.* The disposition to endure injury with meek forbearance while maturing a plan of revenge.

Longevity, *n.* Uncommon extension of the fear of death.

Looking-glass, *n.* A vitreous plane upon which to display a fleeting show for man's disillusion given.

The King of Manchuria had a magic looking-glass, whereon whoso looked saw, not his own image, but only that of the king. A certain courtier who had long enjoyed the king's favor and was thereby enriched beyond any other subject of the realm, said to the king: "Give me, I pray, thy wonderful mirror, so that when absent out of thine august presence I may yet do homage before thy visible shadow, prostrating myself night and morning in the glory of thy benign countenance, as which nothing has so divine splendor, O Noonday Sun of the Universe!"

Pleased with the speech, the king commanded that the mirror be conveyed to the courtier's palace; but after, having gone thither without apprisal, he found it in an apartment where was naught but idle lumber. And the mirror was dimmed with dust and overlaced with cobwebs. This so angered him that he fisted it hard, shattering the glass, and was sorely hurt. Enraged all the more by this mischance, he commanded that the ungrateful courtier be thrown into prison, and that the glass be repaired and taken back to his own palace; and this was done. But when the king looked again on the mirror he saw not his image as before, but only the figure of a crowned ass, having a bloody bandage on one of its hinder hooves — as the artificers and all who had looked upon it had before discerned but feared to report. Taught wisdom and charity, the king restored his courtier to liberty, had the mirror set into the back of the throne and reigned many years with justice and humility; and one day when he fell asleep in death while on the throne, the whole court saw in the mirror the luminous figure of an angel, which remains to this day.

Loquacity, *n.* A disorder which renders the sufferer unable to curb his tongue when you wish to talk.

Lord, *n.* In American society, an English tourist above the state of a costermonger, as, Lord 'Aberdasher, Lord Hartisan and so forth. The traveling Briton of lesser degree is addressed as "Sir," as, Sir 'Arry Donkiboi, of 'Amstead 'Eath. The word "Lord" is sometimes used, also, as a title of the Supreme Being; but this is thought to be rather flattery than true reverence.

> Miss Sallie Ann Splurge, of her own accord,
> Wedded a wandering English lord—
> Wedded and took him to dwell with her "paw,"
> A parent who throve by the practice of Draw.
> Lord Cadde I don't hesitate here to declare
> Unworthy the father-in-legal care
> Of that elderly sport, notwithstanding the truth
> That Cadde had renounced all the follies of youth;
> For, sad to relate, he'd arrived at the stage
> Of existence that's marked by the vices of age.
> Among them, cupidity caused him to urge
> Repeated demands on the pocket of Splurge,
> Till, wrecked in his fortune, that gentleman saw
> Inadequate aid in the practice of Draw,
> And took, as a means of augmenting his pelf,
> To the business of being a lord himself.
> His neat-fitting garments he wilfully shed
> And sacked himself strangely in checks instead;
> Denuded his chin, but retained at each ear
> A whisker that looked like a blasted career.
> He painted his neck an incarnadine hue
> Each morning and varnished it all that he knew.
> The moony monocular set in his eye
> Appeared to be scanning the Sweet Bye-and-Bye.
> His head was enroofed with a billycock hat,
> And his low-necked shoes were aduncous and flat.
> In speech he eschewed his American ways,
> Denying his nose to the use of his A's
> And dulling their edge till the delicate sense
> Of a babe at their temper could take no offence.
> His H's—'twas most inexpressibly sweet,

The patter they made as they fell at his feet!
Re-outfitted thus, Mr. Splurge without fear
Began as Lord Splurge his recouping career.
Alas, the Divinity shaping his end
Entertained other views and decided to send
His lordship in horror, despair and dismay
From the land of the nobleman's natural prey.
For, smit with his Old World ways, Lady Cadde
Fell—suffering Cæsar!—in love with her dad!

G. J.

Lore, *n.* Learning—particularly that sort which is not derived from a regular course of instruction but comes of the reading of occult books, or by nature. This latter is commonly designated as folk-lore and embraces popular myths and superstitions. In Baring-Gould's *Curious Myths of the Middle Ages* the reader will find many of these traced backward, through various peoples on converging lines, toward a common origin in remote antiquity. Among these are the fables of "Teddy the Giant Killer," "The Sleeping John Sharp Williams," "Little Red Riding Hood and the Sugar Trust," "Beauty and the Brisbane," "The Seven Aldermen of Ephesus," "Rip Van Fairbanks" and so forth. The fable which Goethe so affectingly relates under the title of "The Erl-King" was known two thousand years ago in Greece as "The Demos and the Infant Industry." One of the most general and ancient of these myths is that Arabian tale of "Ali Baba and the Forty Rockefellers."

Loss, *n.* Privation of that which we had, or had not. Thus, in the latter sense, it is said of a defeated candidate that he "lost his election"; and of that eminent man, the poet Gilder, that he has "lost his mind." It is in the former and more legitimate sense, that the word is used in the famous epitaph:

Here Huntington's ashes long have lain
Whose loss is our own eternal gain,
For while he exercised all his powers
Whatever he gained, the loss was ours.

Love, *n.* A temporary insanity curable by marriage or by removal of the patient from the influences under which he incurred the disorder. This disease, like *caries* and many other ailments, is prevalent only among civilized races living under artificial conditions; barbarous nations breathing pure air and eating simple food enjoy immunity from its ravages. It is sometimes fatal, but more frequently to the physician than to the patient.

Low-bred, *adj.* "Raised" instead of brought up.

Luminary, *n.* One who throws light upon a subject; as an editor by not writing about it.

Lunarian, *n.* An inhabitant of the moon, as distinguished from Lunatic, one whom the moon inhabits. The Lunarians have been described by Lucian, Locke and other observers, but without much agreement. For example, Bragellos avers their anatomical identity with Man, but Professor Newcomb says they are more like the hill tribes of Vermont.

Lurch, *n*. A place of deposit in which the feeble and incompetent are left, where they have a good time reading our esteemed contemporaries.

Lyre, *n*. An ancient instrument of torture. The word is now used in a figurative sense to denote the poetic faculty, as in the following fiery lines of our great poet, Ella Wheeler Wilcox:

> I sit astride Parnassus with my lyre,
> And pick with care the disobedient wire.
> That stupid shepherd lolling on his crook
> With deaf attention scarcely deigns to look.
> I bide my time, and it shall come at length,
> When, with a Titan's energy and strength,
> I'll grab a fistful of the strings, and O,
> The world shall suffer when I let them go!
>
> *Farquharson Harris.*

Ma, *n.* Mother, in the language of children. Contraction of mommer.

Macaroni, *n.* An Italian food made in the form of a slender, hollow tube. It consists of two parts—the tubing and the hole, the latter being the part that digests.

Mace, *n.* A staff of office signifying authority. Its form, that of a heavy club, indicates its original purpose and use in dissuading from dissent.

Machination, *n.* The method employed by one's opponents in baffling one's open and honorable efforts to do the right thing.

> So plain the advantages of machination
> It constitutes a moral obligation,
> And honest wolves who think upon't with loathing
> Feel bound to don the sheep's deceptive clothing.
> So prospers still the diplomatic art,
> And Satan bows, with hand upon his heart.
>
> *R. S. K.*

Macrobian, *n.* One forgotten of the gods and living to a great age. History is abundantly supplied with examples, from Methuselah to Old Parr, but some notable instances of longevity are less well known. A Calabrian peasant named Coloni, born in 1753, lived so long that he had what he considered a glimpse of the dawn of universal peace. Scanavius relates that he knew an archbishop who was so old that he could remember a time when he did not deserve hanging. In 1566 a linen draper of Bristol, England, declared that he had lived five hundred years, and that in all that time he had never told a lie. There are instances of longevity (*macrobiosis*) in our own country. Senator Chauncey Depew is old enough to know better. The editor of *The American*, a newspaper in New York City, has a memory that goes back to the time when he was a rascal, but not to the fact. The President of the United States was born so long ago that many of the friends of his youth have risen to high political and military preferment without the assistance of personal merit. The verses following were written by a macrobian:

When I was young the world was fair
And amiable and sunny.
A brightness was in all the air,
In all the waters, honey.
The jokes were fine and funny,
The statesmen honest in their views,
And in their lives, as well,
And when you heard a bit of news
'Twas true enough to tell.
Men were not ranting, shouting, reeking,
Nor women "generally speaking."

The Summer then was long indeed:
It lasted one whole season!
The sparkling Winter gave no heed
When ordered by Unreason
To bring the early peas on.
Now, where the dickens is the sense
In calling that a year
Which does no more than just commence
Before the end is near?
When I was young the year extended
From month to month until it ended.

I know not why the world has changed
To something dark and dreary,
And everything is now arranged
To make a fellow weary.
The Weather Man—I fear he
Has much to do with it, for, sure,
The air is not the same:
It chokes you when it is impure,
When pure it makes you lame.
With windows closed you are asthmatic;
Open, neuralgic or sciatic.

Well, I suppose this new régime
Of dun degeneration
Seems eviler than it would seem
To a better observation,
And has for compensation
Some blessings in a deep disguise

Which mortal sight has failed
To pierce, although to angels' eyes
They're visibly unveiled.
If Age is such a boon, good land!
He's costumed by a master hand!

Venable Strigg.

Mad, *adj.* Affected with a high degree of intellectual independence; not conforming to standards of thought, speech and action derived by the conformants from study of themselves; at odds with the majority; in short, unusual. It is noteworthy that persons are pronounced mad by officials destitute of evidence that themselves are sane. For illustration, this present (and illustrious) lexicographer is no firmer in the faith of his own sanity than is any inmate of any madhouse in the land; yet for aught he knows to the contrary, instead of the lofty occupation that seems to him to be engaging his powers he may really be beating his hands against the window bars of an asylum and declaring himself Noah Webster, to the innocent delight of many thoughtless spectators.

Magdalene, *n.* An inhabitant of Magdala. Popularly, a woman found out. This definition of the word has the authority of ignorance, Mary of Magdala being another person than the penitent woman mentioned by St. Luke. It has also the official sanction of the governments of Great Britain and the United States. In England the word is pronounced Maudlin, whence maudlin, adjective, unpleasantly sentimental. With their Maudlin for Magdalene, and their Bedlam for Bethlehem, the English may justly boast themselves the greatest of revisers.

Magic, *n.* An art of converting superstition into coin. There are other arts serving the same high purpose, but the discreet lexicographer does not name them.

Magistrate, *n.* A judicial officer of limited jurisdiction and unbounded incapacity.

Magnet, *n.* Something acted upon by magnetism.

Magnetism, *n.* Something acting upon a magnet.

The two definitions immediately foregoing are condensed from the works of one thousand eminent scientists, who have illuminated the subject with a great white light, to the inexpressible advancement of human knowledge.

Magnificent, *adj.* Having a grandeur or splendor superior to that to which the spectator is accustomed, as the ears of an ass, to a rabbit, or the glory of a glowworm, to a maggot.

Magnitude, *n.* Size. Magnitude being purely relative, nothing is large and nothing small. If everything in the universe were increased in bulk one thousand diameters nothing would be any larger than it was before, but if one thing remained unchanged all the others would be larger than they had been. To an understanding familiar with the relativity of magnitude and distance the spaces and masses of the astronomer would be no more impressive than those of the microscopist. For anything we know to the contrary, the visible universe may be a small part of an atom, with its component ions, floating in the life-fluid (luminiferous ether) of some animal. Possibly the wee creatures peopling the corpuscles of our own blood are overcome with the proper emotion when contemplating the unthinkable distance from one of these to another.

Magpie, *n.* A bird whose thievish disposition suggested to some one that it might be taught to talk.

Maiden, *n.* A young person of the unfair sex addicted to clewless conduct and views that madden to crime. The genus has a wide geographical distribution, being found wherever sought and deplored wherever found. The maiden is not altogether unpleasing to the eye, nor (without her piano and her views) insupportable to the ear, though in respect to comeliness distinctly inferior to the rainbow, and, with regard to the part of her that is audible, beaten out of the field by the canary—which, also, is more portable.

> A lovelorn maiden she sat and sang—
> This quaint, sweet song sang she:
> "It's O for a youth with a football bang
> And a muscle fair to see!
> The Captain he
> Of a team to be!
> On the gridiron he shall shine,
> A monarch by right divine,
> And never to roast on it—me!"

Opaline Jones.

Majesty, *n.* The state and title of a king. Regarded with a just contempt by the Most Eminent Grand Masters, Grand Chancellors, Great Incohonees and Imperial Potentates of the ancient and honorable orders of republican America.

Male, *n.* A member of the unconsidered, or negligible sex. The male of the human race is commonly known (to the female) as Mere Man. The genus has two varieties: good providers and bad providers.

Malefactor, *n.* The chief factor in the progress of the human race.

Malthusian, *adj.* Pertaining to Malthus and his doctrines. Malthus believed in artificially limiting population, but found that it could not be done by talking. One of the most practical exponents of the Malthusian idea was Herod of Judea, though all the famous soldiers have been of the same way of thinking.

Malthusiasm, *n.* An animated acceptance of the doctrines of Malthus.

Mammalia, *n.pl.* A family of vertebrate animals whose females in a state of nature suckle their young, but when civilized and enlightened put them out to nurse, or use the bottle.

Mammon, *n.* The god of the world's leading religion. The chief temple is in the holy city of New York.

> He swore that all other religions were gammon,
> And wore out his knees in the worship of Mammon.
>
> *Jared Oopf.*

Man, *n.* An animal so lost in rapturous contemplation of what he thinks he is as to overlook what he indubitably ought to be. His chief occupation is extermination of other animals and his own species, which, however, multiplies with such insistent rapidity as to infest the whole habitable earth and Canada.

> When the world was young and Man was new,
>   And everything was pleasant,
> Distinctions Nature never drew
>   'Mongst kings and priest and peasant.
>   We're not that way at present,
> Save here in this Republic, where
>   We have that old régime,
> For all are kings, however bare
>   Their backs, howe'er extreme
> Their hunger. And, indeed, each has a voice
> To accept the tyrant of his party's choice.
>
> A citizen who would not vote,
>   And, therefore, was detested,
> Was one day with a tarry coat
>   (With feathers backed and breasted)
>   By patriots invested.
> "It is your duty," cried the crowd,
>   "Your ballot true to cast
> For the man o' your choice." He humbly bowed,
>   And explained his wicked past:
> "That's what I very gladly would have done,
> Dear patriots, but he has never run."
>
> *Apperton Doke.*

Manes, *n.* The immortal parts of dead Greeks and Romans. They were in a state of dull discomfort until the bodies from which they had exhaled were buried and burned; and they seem not to have been particularly happy afterward.

Manicheism, *n.* The ancient Persian doctrine of an incessant warfare between Good and Evil. When Good gave up the fight the Persians joined the victorious Opposition.

Manna, *n.* A food miraculously given to the Israelites in the wilderness. When it was no longer supplied to them they settled down and tilled the soil, fertilizing it, as a rule, with the bodies of the original occupants.

March, *n.* A tide in the affairs of an army swayed by the attraction of loot.

Marriage, *n.* The state or condition of a community consisting of a master, a mistress and two slaves, making in all, two.

Martyr, *n.* [1.] One who moves along the line of least reluctance to a desired death. [2.] One who submits to death rather than do something more disagreeable to him. The distinction between martyrdom and mere assassination is not always clear to the victim.

Marvellous, *adj.* Not understood.

Material, *adj.* Having an actual existence, as distinguished from an imaginary one. Important.

> Material things I know, or feel, or see;
> All else is immaterial to me.
>
> *Jamrach Holobom.*

Mausoleum, *n.* The final and funniest folly of the rich.

Mayonnaise, *n.* One of the sauces which serve the French in place of a state religion.

Me, *pro.* The objectionable case of I. The personal pronoun in English has three cases, the dominative, the objectionable and the oppressive. Each is all three.

Meander, *v.i.* To proceed sinuously and aimlessly. The word is the ancient name of a river about one hundred and fifty miles south of Troy, which turned and twisted in the effort to get out of hearing when the Greeks and Trojans boasted of their prowess.

Medal, *n.* A small metal disk given as a reward for virtues, attainments or services more or less authentic.

> It is related of Bismarck, who had been awarded a medal for gallantly rescuing a drowning person, that, being asked the meaning of the medal, he replied: "I save lives sometimes." And sometimes he didn't.

Mediate, *v.i.* To butt in.

Medicine, *n.* A stone flung down the Bowery to kill a dog in Broadway.

Meekness, *n.* Uncommon patience in planning a revenge that is worth while.

> M is for Moses,
> Who slew the Egyptian.
> As sweet as a rose is
> The meekness of Moses.

No monument shows his
    Post-mortem inscription,
But M is for Moses
    Who slew the Egyptian.

The Biographical Alphabet.

Meerschaum, *n.* (Literally, seafoam, and by many erroneously supposed to be made of it.) A fine white clay, which for convenience in coloring it brown is made into tobacco pipes and smoked by the workmen engaged in that industry. The purpose of coloring it has not been disclosed by the manufacturers.

    There was a youth (you've heard before,
        This woful tale, may be),
    Who bought a meerschaum pipe and swore
        That color it would he!

    He shut himself from the world away,
        Nor any soul he saw.
    He smoked by night, he smoked by day,
        As hard as he could draw.

    His dog died moaning in the wrath
        Of winds that blew aloof;
    The weeds were in the gravel path,
        The owl was on the roof.

    "He's gone afar, he'll come no more,"
        The neighbors sadly say.
    And so they batter in the door
        To take his goods away.

    Dead, pipe in mouth, the youngster lay,
        Nut-brown in face and limb.
    "That pipe's a lovely white," they say,
        "But it has colored him!"

    The moral there's small need to sing—
        'Tis plain as day to you:
    Don't play your game on any thing
        That is a gamester too.

Martin Bulstrode.

Mendacious, *adj.* Addicted to rhetoric.

Merchant, *n.* One engaged in a commercial pursuit. A commercial pursuit is one in which the thing pursued is a dollar.

Mercy, *n.* An attribute beloved of detected offenders.

Mesmerism, *n.* Hypnotism before it wore good clothes, kept a carriage and asked Incredulity to dinner.

Metropolis, *n.* A stronghold of provincialism.

Millennium, *n.* The period of a thousand years when the lid is to be screwed down, with all reformers on the under side.

Mind, *n.* A mysterious form of matter secreted by the brain. Its chief activity consists in the endeavor to ascertain its own nature, the futility of the attempt being due to the fact that it has nothing but itself to know itself with. From the Latin *mens,* a fact unknown to that honest shoe-seller, who, observing that his learned competitor over the way had displayed the motto *"Mens conscia recti,"* emblazoned his own shop front with the words "Men's, women's and children's conscia recti."

Mine, *adj.* Belonging to me if I can hold or seize it.

Minister, *n.* An agent of a higher power with a lower responsibility. In diplomacy an officer sent into a foreign country as the visible embodiment of his sovereign's hostility. His principal qualification is a degree of plausible inveracity next below that of an ambassador.

Minor, *adj.* Less objectionable.

Minstrel, *n.* Formerly a poet, singer or musician; now a nigger with a color less than skin deep and a humor more than flesh and blood can bear.

Miracle, *n.* An act or event out of the order of nature and unaccountable, as beating a normal hand of four kings and an ace with four aces and a king.

Miscreant, *n.* A person of the highest degree of unworth. Etymologically, the word means unbeliever, and its present signification may be regarded as theology's noblest contribution to the development of our language.

Misdemeanor, *n.* An infraction of the law having less dignity than a felony and constituting no claim to admittance into the best criminal society.

> By misdemeanors he essayed to climb
> Into the aristocracy of crime.
> O, woe was him!—with manner chill and grand
> "Captains of industry" refused his hand,
> "Kings of finance" denied him recognition
> And "railway magnates" jeered his low condition.
> He robbed a bank to make himself respected.
> They still rebuffed him, for he was detected.
>
> *S. V. Hanipur.*

Misericorde, *n.* A dagger which in mediæval warfare was used by the foot soldier to remind an unhorsed knight that he was mortal.

Misfortune, *n.* The kind of fortune that never misses.

Miss, *n.* A title with which we brand unmarried women to indicate that they are in the market. Miss, Missis (Mrs.) and Mister (Mr.) are the three most distinctly disagreeable words in the language, in sound and sense. Two are corruptions of Mistress, the other of Master. In the general abolition of social titles in this our country they miraculously escaped to plague us. If we must have them let us be consistent and give one to the unmarried man. I venture to suggest Mush, abbreviated to Mh.

Molecule, *n.* The ultimate, indivisible unit of matter. It is distinguished from the corpuscle, also the ultimate, indivisible unit of matter, by a closer resemblance to the atom, also the ultimate, indivisible unit of matter. Three great scientific theories of the structure of the universe are the molecular, the corpuscular and the atomic. A fourth affirms, with Haeckel, the condensation or precipitation of matter from ether—whose existence is proved by the condensation or precipitation. The present trend of scientific thought is toward the theory of ions. The ion differs from the molecule, the corpuscle and the atom in that it is an ion. A fifth theory is held by idiots, but it is doubtful if they know any more about the matter than the others.

Monad, *n.* The ultimate, indivisible unit of matter. (See MOLECULE.) According to Leibnitz, as nearly as he seems willing to be understood, the monad has body without bulk, and mind without manifestation—Leibnitz knows him by the innate power of considering. He has founded upon him a theory of the universe, which the creature bears without resentment, for the monad is a gentleman. Small as he is, the monad contains all the powers and possibilities needful to his evolution into a German philosopher of the first class—altogether a very capable little fellow. He is not to be confounded with the microbe, or bacillus; by its inability to discern him, a good microscope shows him to be of an entirely distinct species.

Monarch, *n.* A person engaged in reigning. Formerly the monarch ruled, as the derivation of the word attests, and as many subjects have had occasion to learn. In Russia and the Orient the monarch has still a considerable influence in public affairs and in the disposition of the human head, but in western Europe political administration is mostly entrusted to his ministers, he being somewhat preoccupied with reflections relating to the status of his own head.

Monarchical Government, *n.* Government.

Monday, *n.* In Christian countries, the day after the baseball game.

Money, *n.* A blessing that is of no advantage to us excepting when we part with it. An evidence of culture and a passport to polite society. Supportable property.

Monkey, *n.* An arboreal animal which makes itself at home in genealogical trees.

Monogenist, *n.* One who worships at the shrine of his ancestral cell.

Monologue, *n.* The activity of a tongue that has no ears.

Monometallist, *n.* A financial doctrinaire in 1896; in 1904 a purveyor of "crow" to the masses.

Monosyllabic, *adj.* Composed of words of one syllable, for literary babes who never tire of testifying their delight in the vapid compound by appropriate googoogling. The words are commonly Saxon—that is to say, words of a barbarous people destitute of ideas and incapable of any but the most elementary sentiments and emotions.

> The man who writes in Saxon
> Is the man to use an ax on.
>
> *Judibras.*

Monsignor, *n.* A high ecclesiastical title, of which the Founder of our religion overlooked the advantages.

Monument, *n.* A structure intended to commemorate something which either needs no commemoration or cannot be commemorated.

> The bones of Agamemnon are a show,
> And ruined is his royal monument,

but Agamemnon's fame suffers no diminution in consequence. The monument custom has its *reductiones ad absurdum* in monuments "to the unknown dead"—that is to say, monuments to perpetuate the memory of those who have left no memory.

Moral, *adj.* Conforming to a local and mutable standard of right. Having the quality of general expediency.

> It is sayd there be a raunge of mountaynes in the Easte, on one syde of the which certayn conducts are immorall, yet on the other syde they are holden in good esteeme; wherebye the mountayneer is much conveenyenced, for it is given to him to goe downe eyther way and act as it shall suite his moode, withouten offence. — *Gooke's Meditations.*

More, *adj.* The comparative degree of too much.

Morganatic, *adj.* Pertaining to a kind of marriage between a man of exalted rank and a woman of low degree by which the wife gets nothing but a husband, and not much of a husband. From Morgan (J. P.), a king of finance, by a transaction with whom nobody gets anything at all.

Mormon, *n.* A follower of Joseph Smith, who received from an angel a revelation inscribed on brass plates and afterward revised and enlarged by his successor in the prophethood. While still an inoffensive people the Mormons were bitterly persecuted, their prophet assassinated, their homes burned and themselves driven into the desert, where they prospered, practiced polygamy and themselves took a hand in the game of persecution.

> They say the Mormons are liars. They say that Joseph Smith did *not* receive from the hands of an angel the written revelation that we obey. Let them prove it! — *Brigham Young, Prophet and Logician.*

Morning, *n.* The end of night and dawn of dejection. The morning was discovered by a Chaldean astronomer, who, finding his observation of the stars unaccountably interrupted, diligently sought the cause and found it. After several centuries of disputation, morning was generally accepted by the scientific as a reasonable cause of the interruption and a constantly recurrent natural phenomenon.

Morrow, *n.* The day of good deeds and a reformed life. The beginning of happiness. (See TO-MORROW—when we get to it.)

Mortality, *n.* The part of immortality that we know about.

Mosaic, *n.* A kind of inlaid work. From Moses, who when little was inlaid in a basket among the bulrushes.

Mosquito, *n.* The spore of insomnia, as distinguished from Conscience, the bacillus of the same disease. Indigenous to New Jersey, where the marshes in which they multiply are known as meadows and the mosquitoes themselves are affirmed by the natives to be larks.

"I am the master of all things!" Man cried.

"Then, pray, what am I?" the Mosquito replied.

Motion, *n.* A property, condition or state of matter. The existence and possibility of motion is denied by many philosophers, who point out that a thing cannot move where it is and cannot move where it is not. Others, with Galileo, say: "And yet it moves." It is not the province of the lexicographer to decide.

How charming is divine Philosophy! — *Milton.*

Motive, *n.* A mental wolf in moral wool.

Mouse, *n.* An animal which strews its path with fainting women. As in Rome Christians were thrown to the lions, so centuries earlier in Otumwee, the most ancient and famous city of the world, female heretics were thrown to the mice. Jakak-Zotp, the historian, the only Otumwump whose writings have descended to us, says that these martyrs met their death with little dignity and much exertion. He even attempts to exculpate the mice (such is the malice of bigotry) by declaring that the unfortunate women perished, some from exhaustion, some of broken necks from falling over their own feet and some from lack of restoratives. The mice, he avers, enjoyed the pleasures of the chase with composure. But if "Roman history is nine-tenths lying," we can hardly expect a smaller proportion of that rhetorical figure in the annals of a people capable of so incredible cruelty to lovely woman; for a hard heart has a false tongue.

Mousquetaire, *n.* A long glove covering a part of the arm. Worn in New Jersey. But "mousquetaire" is a mighty poor way to spell muskeeter.

Mouth, *n.* In man, the gateway to the soul; in woman, the outlet of the heart.

Mugwump, *n.* In politics one afflicted with self-respect and addicted to the vice of independence. A term of contempt.

Mulatto, *n.* A child of two races, ashamed of both.

Mule, *n.* Creation's afterthought; an animal that Adam did not name.

Multitude, *n.* A crowd; the source of political wisdom and virtue. In a republic, the object of the statesman's adoration. "In a multitude of consellors there is wisdom," saith the proverb. If many men of equal individual wisdom are wiser than any one of them, it must be that they acquire the excess of wisdom by the mere act of getting together. Whence comes it? Obviously from nowhere—as well say that a range of mountains is higher than the single mountains composing it. A multitude is as wise as its wisest member if it obey him; if not, it is no wiser than its most foolish.

Mummy, *n.* An ancient Egyptian, formerly in universal use among modern civilized nations as medicine, and now engaged in supplying art with an excellent pigment. He is handy, too, in museums in gratifying the vulgar curiosity that serves to distinguish man from the lower animals.

> By means of the Mummy, mankind, it is said,
> Attests to the gods its respect for the dead.
> We plunder his tomb, be he sinner or saint,
> Distil him for physic and grind him for paint,
> Exhibit for money his poor, shrunken frame,
> And with levity flock to the scene of the shame.
> O, tell me, ye gods, for the use of my rhyme:
> For respecting the dead what's the limit of time?
>
> *Scopas Brune.*

Mustang, *n.* An indocile horse of the western plains. In English society, the American wife of an English nobleman.

Myrmidon, *n.* A follower of Achilles—particularly when he didn't lead.

Mythology, *n.* The body of a primitive people's beliefs concerning its origin, early history, heroes, deities and so forth, as distinguished from the true accounts which it invents later.

Namby-pamby, *adj.* Having the quality of magazine poetry. (See FLUMMERY.)

Nectar, *n.* A drink served at banquets of the Olympian deities. The secret of its preparation is lost, but the modern Kentuckians believe that they come pretty near to a knowledge of its chief ingredient.

> Juno drank a cup of nectar,
> But the draught did not affect her.
> Juno drank a cup of rye—
> Then she bade herself good-bye.
>
> J. G.

Negro, *n.* The *pièce de résistance* in the American political problem. Representing him by the letter *n*, the Republicans begin to build their equation thus: "Let n = the white man." This, however, appears to give an unsatisfactory solution.

Neighbor, *n.* One whom we are commanded to love as ourselves, and who does all he knows how to make us disobedient.

Nepotism, *n.* Appointing your grandmother to office for the good of the party.

Newtonian, *adj.* Pertaining to a philosophy of the universe invented by Newton, who discovered that an apple will fall to the ground, but was unable to say why. His successors and disciples have advanced so far as to be able to say when.

Nihilist, *n.* A Russian who denies the existence of anything but Tolstoi. The leader of the school is Tolstoi.

Nirvana, *n.* In the Buddhist religion, a state of pleasurable annihilation awarded to the wise, particularly to those wise enough to understand it.

Nobleman, *n.* Nature's provision for wealthy American maids ambitious to incur social distinction and suffer high life.

Noise, *n.* A stench in the ear. Undomesticated music. The chief product and authenticating sign of civilization.

Nominate, *v.* To designate for the heaviest political assessment. To put forward a suitable person to incur the mudgobbing and deadcatting of the opposition.

Nominee, *n.* A modest gentleman shrinking from the distinction of private life and diligently seeking the honorable obscurity of public office.

Non-combatant, *n.* A dead Quaker.

Nonsense, *n.* The objections that are urged against this excellent dictionary.

Nose, *n.* The extreme outpost of the face. From the circumstance that great conquerors have great noses, Getius, whose writings antedate the age of humor, calls the nose the organ of quell. It has been observed that one's nose is never so happy as when thrust into the affairs of another, from which some physiologists have drawn the inference that the nose is devoid of the sense of smell.

> There's a man with a Nose,
> And wherever he goes
> The people run from him and shout:
> "No cotton have we
> For our ears if so be
> He blow that interminous snout!"

> So the lawyers applied
> For injunction. "Denied,"
> Said the Judge: "The defendant prefixion,
> Whate'er it portend,
> Appears to transcend
> The bounds of this court's jurisdiction."

> *Arpad Singiny.*

Notoriety, *n.* The fame of one's competitor for public honors. The kind of renown most accessible and acceptable to mediocrity. A Jacob's-ladder leading to the vaudeville stage, with angels ascending and descending.

Noumenon, *n.* That which exists, as distinguished from that which merely seems to exist, the latter being a phenomenon. The noumenon is a bit difficult to locate; it can be apprehended only by a process of reasoning—which is a phenomenon. Nevertheless, the discovery and exposition of noumena offer a rich field for what Lewes calls "the endless variety and excitement of philosophic thought." Hurrah (therefore) for the noumenon!

Novel, *n.* A short story padded. A species of composition bearing the same relation to literature that the panorama bears to art. As it is too long to be read at a sitting the impressions made by its successive parts are successively effaced, as in the panorama. Unity, totality of effect, is impossible; for besides the few pages last read all that is carried in mind is the mere plot of what has gone before. To the romance the novel is what photography is to painting.

Its distinguishing principle, probability, corresponds to the literal actuality of the photograph and puts it distinctly into the category of reporting; whereas the free wing of the romancer enables him to mount to such altitudes of imagination as he may be fitted to attain; and the first three essentials of the literary art are imagination, imagination and imagination. The art of writing novels, such as it was, is long dead everywhere except in Russia, where it is new. Peace to its ashes—some of which have a large sale.

November, *n.* The eleventh twelfth of a weariness.

Nudity, *n.* That quality in art which is most painful to the prurient.

Oath, *n.* In law, a solemn appeal to the Deity, made binding upon the conscience by a penalty for perjury.

Oblivion, *n.* The state or condition in which the wicked cease from struggling and the dreary are at rest. Fame's eternal dumping ground. Cold storage for high hopes. A place where ambitious authors meet their works without pride and their betters without envy. A dormitory without an alarm clock.

Observatory, *n.* A place where astronomers conjecture away the guesses of their predecessors.

Obsessed, *pp.* Vexed by an evil spirit, like the Gadarene swine and other critics. Obsession was once more common than it is now. Arasthus tells of a peasant who was occupied by a different devil for every day in the week, and on Sundays by two. They were frequently seen, always walking in his shadow, when he had one, but were finally driven away by the village notary, a holy man; but they took the peasant with them, for he vanished utterly. A devil thrown out of a woman by the Archbishop of Rheims ran through the streets, pursued by a hundred persons, until the open country was reached, where by a leap higher than a church spire he escaped into a bird. A chaplain in Cromwell's army exorcised a soldier's obsessing devil by throwing the soldier into the water, when the devil came to the surface. The soldier, unfortunately, did not.

Obsolete, *adj.* No longer used by the timid. Said chiefly of words. A word which some lexicographer has marked obsolete is ever thereafter an object of dread and loathing to the fool writer, but if it is a good word and has no exact modern equivalent equally good, it is good enough for the good writer. Indeed, a writer's attitude toward "obsolete" words is as true a measure of his literary ability as anything except the character of his work. A dictionary of obsolete and obsolescent words would not only be singularly rich in strong and sweet parts of speech; it would add large possessions to the vocabulary of every competent writer who might not happen to be a competent reader.

Obstinacy, *n.* Perverted firmness. Persistence in the objectionable. Constancy to the opposite view. Another's indirect affirmation of one's fallibility.

Obstinate, *adj.* Inaccessible to the truth as it is manifest in the splendor and stress of our advocacy.

The popular type and exponent of obstinacy is the mule, a most intelligent animal.

Occasional, *adj.* Afflicting us with greater or less frequency. That, however, is not the sense in which the word is used in the phrase "occasional verses," which are verses written for an "occasion," such as an anniversary, a celebration or other event. True, they afflict us a little worse than other sorts of verse, but their name has no reference to irregular recurrence.

Occident, *n.* The part of the world lying west (or east) of the Orient. It is largely inhabited by Christians, a powerful subtribe of the Hypocrites, whose principal industries are murder and cheating, which they are pleased to call "war" and "commerce." These, also, are the principal industries of the Orient.

Occult, *adj.* Knowable to those only who think it worth knowing.

Ocean, *n.* A body of water occupying about two-thirds of a world made for man—who has no gills.

Offensive, *adj.* Generating disagreeable emotions or sensations, as the advance of an army against its enemy.

"Were the enemy's tactics offensive?" the king asked. "I should say so!" replied the unsuccessful general. "The blackguard wouldn't come out of his works!"

Old, *adj.* In that stage of usefulness which is not inconsistent with general inefficiency, as an *old man.* Discredited by lapse of time and offensive to the popular taste, as an *old book.*

"Old books? The devil take them!" Goby said.

"Fresh every day must be my books and bread."

Nature herself approves the Goby rule

And gives us every moment a fresh fool.

Harley Shum.

Oleaginous, *adj.* Oily, smooth, sleek.

Disraeli once described the manner of Bishop Wilberforce as "unctuous, oleaginous, saponaceous." And the good prelate was ever afterward known as Soapy Sam. For every man there is something in the vocabulary that would stick to him like a second skin. His enemies have only to find it.

Olympian, *adj.* Relating to a mountain in Thessaly, once inhabited by gods, now a repository of yellowing newspapers, beer bottles and mutilated sardine cans, attesting the presence of the tourist and his appetite.

His name the smirking tourist scrawls
Upon Minerva's temple walls,
Where thundered once Olympian Zeus,
And marks his appetite's abuse.

Averil Joop.

Omen, *n.* A sign that something will happen if nothing happens.

Omnipresent, *adj.* Everywhere at once. That the power of omnipresence, or ubiquity, is denied to mortals was known as early as the time of Sir Boyle Roche, who in a speech in Parliament said: "A man cannot be in two places at once unless he is a bird."

Once, *adv.* Enough.

Opera, *n.* A play representing life in another world, whose inhabitants have no speech but song, no motions but gestures and no postures but attitudes. All acting is simulation, and the word *simulation* is from *simia,* an ape; but in opera the actor takes for his model *Simia audibilis* (or *Pithecanthropos stentor*)—the ape that howls.

The actor apes a man—at least in shape;
The opera performer apes an ape.

Opiate, *n.* An unlocked door in the prison of Identity. It leads into the jail yard.

Opportunity, *n.* A favorable occasion for grasping a disappointment.

Oppose, *v.* To assist with obstructions and objections.

How lonely he who thinks to vex
With badinage the Solemn Sex!
Of levity, Mere Man, beware;
None but the Grave deserve the Unfair.

Percy P. Orminder.

Opposition, *n.* In politics the party that prevents the Government from running amuck by hamstringing it.

The King of Ghargaroo, who had been abroad to study the science of government, appointed one hundred of his fattest subjects as members of a parliament to make laws for the collection of revenue. Forty of these he named the Party of Opposition and had his Prime Minister carefully instruct them in their duty of opposing every royal measure. Nevertheless, the first one that was submitted passed unanimously. Greatly displeased, the King vetoed it, informing the Opposition that if they did that again they would pay for their obstinacy with their heads. The entire forty promptly disemboweled themselves.

"What shall we do now?" the King asked. "Liberal institutions cannot be maintained without a party of Opposition."

"Splendor of the universe," replied the Prime Minister, "it is true these dogs of darkness have no longer their credentials, but all is not lost. Leave the matter to this worm of the dust."

So the Minister had the bodies of his Majesty's Opposition embalmed and stuffed with straw, put back into the seats of power and nailed there. Forty votes were recorded against every bill and the nation prospered. But one day a bill imposing a tax on warts was defeated—the members of the Government party had not been nailed to their seats! This so enraged the King that the Prime Minister was put to death, the parliament was dissolved with a battery of artillery, and government of the people, by the people, for the people perished from Ghargaroo.

Optimism, *n.* The doctrine, or belief, that everything is beautiful, including what is ugly, everything good, especially the bad, and everything right that is wrong. It is held with greatest tenacity by those most accustomed to the mischance of falling into adversity, and is most acceptably expounded with the grin that apes a smile. Being a blind faith, it is inaccessible to the light of disproof—an intellectual disorder, yielding to no treatment but death. It is hereditary, but fortunately not contagious.

Optimist, *n.* A proponent of the doctrine that black is white.

A pessimist applied to God for relief.

"Ah, you wish me to restore your hope and cheerfulness," said God.

"No," replied the petitioner, "I wish you to create something that would justify them."

"The world is all created," said God, "but you have overlooked something—the mortality of the optimist."

Oratory, *n.* A conspiracy between speech and action to cheat the understanding. A tyranny tempered by stenography.

Ordinary, *adj.* Common; customary. In the Southwestern States of the Union this word is pronounced ornery and means ugly—a striking testimony to the prevalence of the disagreeable.

Orphan, *n.* A living person whom death has deprived of the power of filial ingratitude—a privation appealing with a particular eloquence to all that is sympathetic in human nature. When young the orphan is commonly sent to an asylum, where by careful cultivation of its rudimentary sense of locality it is taught to know its place. It is then instructed in the arts of dependence and servitude and eventually turned loose to prey upon the world as a bootblack or scullery maid.

Orthodox, *n.* An ox wearing the popular religious yoke.

Orthography, *n.* The science of spelling by the eye instead of the ear. Advocated with more heat than light by the outmates of every asylum for the insane. They have had to concede a few things since the time of Chaucer, but are none the less hot in defence of those to be conceded hereafter.

A spelling reformer indicted
For fudge was before the court cicted.
   The judge said: "Enough—
   His candle we'll snough,
And his sepulchre shall not be whicted."

Ostrich, *n.* A large bird to which (for its sins, doubtless) nature has denied that hinder toe in which so many pious naturalists have seen a conspicuous evidence of design. The absence of a good working pair of wings is no defect, for, as has been ingeniously pointed out, the ostrich does not fly.

Otherwise, *adv.* No better.

Outcome, *n.* A particular type of disappointment. By the kind of intelligence that sees in an exception a proof of the rule the wisdom of an act is judged by the outcome, the result. This is immortal nonsense; the wisdom of an act is to be judged by the light that the doer had when he performed it.

Outdo, *v.t.* To make an enemy.

Out-of-doors, *n.* That part of one's environment upon which no government has been able to collect taxes. Chiefly useful to inspire poets.

I climbed to the top of a mountain one day
   To see the sun setting in glory,
And I thought, as I looked at his vanishing ray,
   Of a perfectly splendid story.

'Twas about an old man and the ass he bestrode
   Till the strength of the beast was o'ertested;
Then the man would carry him miles on the road
   Till Neddy was pretty well rested.

The moon rising solemnly over the crest
   Of the hills to the east of my station
Displayed her broad disk to the darkening west
   Like a visible new creation.

And I thought of a joke (and I laughed till I cried)
   Of an idle young woman who tarried
About a church-door for a look at the bride,
   Although 'twas herself that was married.

To poets all Nature is pregnant with grand
   Ideas—with thought and emotion.
I pity the dunces who don't understand
   The speech of earth, heaven and ocean.

                      Stromboli Smith.

Outrage, *n.* Any disagreeable act, considered from the viewpoint of the victim of it. A denial of immunity.

Outsider, *n.* A person austerely censorious of that which he is unable to do or become. In commerce and finance, a member of the Army of Provision.

Ovation, *n.* In ancient Rome, a definite, formal pageant in honor of one who had been disserviceable to the enemies of the nation. A lesser "triumph." In modern English the word is improperly used to signify any loose and spontaneous expression of popular homage to the hero of the hour and place.

"I had an ovation!" the actor man said,
But I thought it uncommonly queer,
That people and critics by him had been led
By the ear.

The Latin lexicon makes his absurd
Assertion as plain as a peg;
In "ovum" we find the true root of the word.
It means egg.

Dudley Spink.

Overcharge, *v.* To ask a higher price that you can get.

Overdose, *n.* A fatal dose of medicine when administered by any other than the physician.

Overeat, *v.* To dine.

Hail, Gastronome, Apostle of Excess,
Well skilled to overeat without distress!
Thy great invention, the unfatal feast,
Shows Man's superiority to Beast.

John Boop.

Overwork, *n.* A dangerous disorder affecting high public functionaries who want to go fishing.

Owe, *v.* To have (and to hold) a debt. The word formerly signified not indebtedness, but possession; it meant "own," and in the minds of debtors there is still a good deal of confusion between assets and liabilities.

Oyster, *n.* A slimy, gobby shellfish which civilization gives men the hardihood to eat without removing its entrails! The shells are sometimes given to the poor.

Pagan, *n*. A benighted person who prefers home-made deities and indigenous religious rites.

Pain, *n*. An uncomfortable frame of mind that may have a physical basis in something that is being done to the body, or may be purely mental, caused by the good fortune of another.

Painting, *n*. The art of protecting flat surfaces from the weather and exposing them to the critic.

Formerly, painting and sculpture were combined in the same work: the ancients painted their statues. The only present alliance between the two arts is that the modern painter chisels his patrons.

Palace, *n*. A fine and costly residence, particularly that of a great official. The residence of a high dignitary of the Christian Church is called a palace; that of the Founder of his religion was known as a field, or wayside. There is progress.

Palm, *n*. A species of tree having several varieties, of which the familiar "itching palm" (*Palma hominis*) is most widely distributed and sedulously cultivated. This noble vegetable exudes a kind of invisible gum, which may be detected by applying to the bark a piece of gold or silver. The metal will adhere with remarkable tenacity. The fruit of the itching palm is so bitter and unsatisfying that a considerable percentage of it is sometimes given away in what are known as "benefactions."

Palmistry, *n*. The 947th method (according to Mimbleshaw's classification) of obtaining money by false pretences. It consists in "reading character" in the wrinkles made by closing the hand. The pretence is not altogether false; character can really be read very accurately in this way, for the wrinkles in every hand submitted plainly spell the word "dupe." The imposture consists in not reading it aloud.

Pandemonium, *n*. Literally, the Place of All the Demons. Most of them have escaped into politics and finance, and the place is now used as a lecture hall by the Audible Reformer. When disturbed by his voice the ancient echoes clamor appropriate responses most gratifying to his pride of distinction.

Pantaloons, *n.* A nether habiliment of the adult civilized male. The garment is tubular and unprovided with hinges at the points of flexion. Supposed to have been invented by a humorist. Called "trousers" by the enlightened and "pants" by the unworthy.

Pantheism, *n.* The doctrine that everything is God, in contradistinction to the doctrine that God is everything.

Pantomime, *n.* A play in which the story is told without violence to the language. The least disagreeable form of dramatic action.

Pardon, *v.* To remit a penalty and restore to a life of crime. To add to the lure of crime the temptation of ingratitude.

Parricide, *n.* A filial *coup de grâce* whereby one is released from the lingering torments of paternity.

Partisan, *n.* An adherent without sense.

Passport, *n.* A document treacherously inflicted upon a citizen going abroad, exposing him as an alien and pointing him out for special reprobation and outrage.

Past, *n.* That part of Eternity with some small fraction of which we have a slight and regrettable acquaintance. A moving line called the Present parts it from an imaginary period known as the Future. These two grand divisions of Eternity, of which the one is continually effacing the other, are entirely unlike. The one is dark with sorrow and disappointment, the other bright with prosperity and joy. The Past is the region of sobs, the Future is the realm of song. In the one crouches Memory, clad in sackcloth and ashes, mumbling penitential prayer; in the sunshine of the other Hope flies with a free wing, beckoning to temples of success and bowers of ease. Yet the Past is the Future of yesterday, the Future is the Past of to-morrow. They are one—the knowledge and the dream.

Pastime, *n.* A device for promoting dejection. Gentle exercise for intellectual debility.

Patience, *n.* A minor form of despair, disguised as a virtue.

Patriot, *n.* One to whom the interests of a part seem superior to those of the whole. The dupe of statesmen and the tool of conquerors.

Patriotism, *n.* Combustible rubbish ready to the torch of any one ambitious to illuminate his name.

In Dr. Johnson's famous dictionary patriotism is defined as the last resort of a scoundrel. With all due respect to an enlightened but inferior lexicographer I beg to submit that it is the first.

Peace, *n.* In international affairs, a period of cheating between two periods of fighting.

O, what's the loud uproar assailing
   Mine ears without cease?
'Tis the voice of the hopeful, all-hailing
   The horrors of peace.

Ah, Peace Universal; they woo it—
   Would marry it, too.
If only they knew how to do it
   'Twere easy to do.

They're working by night and by day
   On their problem, like moles.
Have mercy, O Heaven, I pray,
   On their meddlesome souls!

Ro Amil.

Pedestrian, *n.* The variable (and audible) part of the roadway for an automobile.

Pedigree, *n.* The known part of the route from an arboreal ancestor with a swim bladder to an urban descendant with a cigarette.

Penitent, *adj.* Undergoing or awaiting punishment.

Perdition, *n.* The loss of one's soul; also the place in which it can be found.

Perfection, *n.* An imaginary state or quality distinguished from the actual by an element known as excellence; an attribute of the critic.

    The editor of an English magazine having received a letter pointing out the erroneous nature of his views and style, and signed "Perfection," promptly wrote at the foot of the letter: "I don't agree with you," and mailed it to Matthew Arnold.

Pericardium, *n.* A sack of membrane covering a multitude of sins.

Peripatetic, *adj.* Walking about. Relating to the philosophy of Aristotle, who, while expounding it, moved from place to place in order to avoid his pupils' objections. A needless precaution—they knew no more of the matter than he.

Peroration, *n.* The explosion of an oratorical rocket. It dazzles, but to an observer having the wrong kind of nose its most conspicuous peculiarity is the smell of the several kinds of powder used in preparing it.

Perseverance, *n.* A lowly virtue whereby mediocrity achieves an inglorious success.

   "Persevere, persevere!" cry the homilists all,
   Themselves, day and night, persevering to bawl.
   "Remember the fable of tortoise and hare—
   The one at the goal while the other is—where?"
   Why, back there in Dreamland, renewing his lease
   Of life, all his muscles preserving the peace,

The goal and the rival forgotten alike,
And the long fatigue of the needless hike.
His spirit a-squat in the grass and the dew
Of the dogless Land beyond the Stew,
He sleeps, like a saint in a holy place,
A winner of all that is good in a race.

Sukker Uffro.

Persuasion, *n.* A species of hypnotism in which the oral suggestion takes the hindering form of argument or appeal.

In the legislative body of the future, votes will be won, as now, by hypnotic suggestion, but there will be no darkening of counsel and impeding of the public business by debate; opposition will be stared into assent.

Pessimism, *n.* A philosophy forced upon the convictions of the observer by the disheartening prevalence of the optimist with his scarecrow hope and his unsightly smile.

Pettifogger, *n.* A competing or opposing lawyer.

Philanthropist, *n.* A rich (and usually bald) old gentleman who has trained himself to grin while his conscience is picking his pocket.

Philistine, *n.* One whose mind is the creature of its environment, following the fashion in thought, feeling and sentiment. He is sometimes learned, frequently prosperous, commonly clean and always solemn.

Philosophy, *n.* A route of many roads leading from nowhere to nothing.

Phœnix, *n.* The classical prototype of the modern "small hot bird."

Phonograph, *n.* An irritating toy that restores life to dead noises.

Photograph, *n.* A picture painted by the sun without instruction in art. It is a little better than the work of an Apache, but not quite so good as that of a Cheyenne.

Phrenology, *n.* The science of picking the pocket through the scalp. It consists in locating and exploiting the organ that one is a dupe with.

Physician, *n.* One upon whom we set our hopes when ill and our dogs when well.

Physiognomy, *n.* The art of determining the character of another by the resemblances and differences between his face and our own, which is the standard of excellence.

"There is no art," says Shakspeare, foolish man,
    "To read the mind's construction in the face."
The physiognomists his portrait scan,
    And say: "How little wisdom here we trace!
He knew his face disclosed his mind and heart,
So, in his own defence, denied our art."

Lavatar Shunk.

Piano, *n.* A parlor utensil for subduing the impenitent visitor. It is operated by depressing the keys of the machine and the spirits of the audience.

Pianoforte (abbreviated to Piano), *n.* An instrument thoughtfully provided by American husbands and fathers for their wives and daughters, in observance of Bulwer's dictum that "the best way to keep the dear creatures from playing the devil is to encourage them in playing the fool."

Pickaback, *adv.* In the manner of a traveling railroad magnate.

Pickaninny, *n.* The young of the *Procyanthropos*, or *Americanus dominans*. It is small, black and charged with political fatalities.

Picture, *n.* A representation in two dimensions of something wearisome in three.

> "Behold great Daubert's picture here on view—
> Taken from Life." If that description's true,
> Grant, heavenly Powers, that I be taken, too.
>
> *Jali Hane.*

Pie, *n.* An advance agent of the reaper whose name is Indigestion.

> Cold pie was highly esteemed by the remains. — *The Rev. Dr. Mucker, in a Funeral Sermon Over a British Nobleman.*

> Cold pie is a detestable
> American comestible.
> That's why I'm done—or undone—
> So far from that dear London.
> *From the Headstone of a British Nobleman, in Kalamazoo.*

Piety, *n.* Reverence for the Supreme Being, based upon His supposed resemblance to man.

> The pig is taught by sermons and epistles
> To think the God of Swine has snout and bristles.
>
> *Judibras.*

Pig, *n.* An animal (*Porcus omnivorus*) closely allied to the human race by the splendor and vivacity of its appetite, which, however, is inferior in scope, for it sticks at pig.

Pigmy, *n.* One of a tribe of very small men found by ancient travelers in many parts of the world, but by modern in Central Africa only. The Pigmies are so called to distinguish them from the bulkier Caucasians—who are Hogmies.

Pilgrim, *n.* A traveler that is taken seriously. A Pilgrim Father was one who, leaving Europe in 1620 because not permitted to sing psalms through his nose, followed it to Massachusetts, where he could personate God according to the dictates of his conscience.

Pillage, *v.* To carry on business candidly.

Pillory, *n.* A mechanical device for inflicting personal distinction—prototype of the modern newspaper conducted by persons of austere virtues and blameless lives.

Piracy, *n.* Commerce without its folly-swaddles, just as God made it.

Pitiful, *adj.* The state of an enemy or opponent after an imaginary encounter with oneself.

Pity, *n.* A failing sense of exemption, inspired by contrast.

Plagiarism, *n.* A literary coincidence compounded of a discreditable priority and an honorable subsequence.

Plagiarize, *v.* To take the thought or style of another writer whom one has never, never read.

Plague, *n.* In ancient times a general punishment of the innocent for admonition of their ruler, as in the familiar instance of Pharaoh the Immune. The plague as we of to-day have the happiness to know it is merely Nature's fortuitous manifestation of her purposeless objectionableness.

Plan, *v.t.* To bother about the best method of accomplishing an accidental result.

Platitude, *n.* The fundamental element and special glory of popular literature. A thought that snores in words that smoke. The wisdom of a million fools in the diction of a dullard. A fossil sentiment in artificial rock. A moral without the fable. All that is mortal of a departed truth. A demi-tasse of milk-and-morality. The Pope's-nose of a featherless peacock. A jelly-fish withering on the shore of the sea of thought. The cackle surviving the egg. A desiccated epigram.

Platonic, *adj.* Pertaining to the philosophy of Socrates. *Platonic love* is a fool's name for the affection between a disability and a frost.

Platter, *n.* A senseless thing that holds food without eating it.

> She uttered her mind, without ceasing:
> And this is the thought that it carried.
> "I fear that your love is decreasing.
> How is it, dear, now that we're married?"
>
> Replied that aciduous sinner,
> Fatigued of her reasonless chatter:
> "When a fellow has eaten his dinner
> He doesn't make love to the platter."
>
> *Belijah H. Bimbee.*

Plaudits, *n.* Coins with which the populace pays those who tickle and devour it.

Please, *v.* To lay the foundation for a superstructure of imposition.

Pleasure, *n.* [1.] The least hateful form of dejection. [2.] An emotion engendered by something advantageous to one's self or disastrous to others. In the plural this word signifies those mostly artificial aids to melancholy that deepen the general gloom of existence with a particular dejection.

Plebeian, *n.* An ancient Roman who in the blood of his country stained nothing but his hands. Distinguished from the Patrician, who was a saturated solution.

Plebiscite, *n.* A popular vote to ascertain the will of the sovereign.

Plenipotentiary, *adj.* Having full power. A *Minister Plenipotentiary* is a diplomatist possessing absolute authority on condition that he never exert it.

Pleonasm, *n.* An army of words escorting a corporal of thought.

Plow, *n.* An implement that cries aloud for hands accustomed to the pen.

Plunder, *v.* To take the property of another without observing the decent and customary reticences of theft. To effect a change of ownership with the candid concomitance of a brass band. To wrest the wealth of A from B and leave C lamenting a vanished opportunity.

Plutarchy, *n.* Government by those who are wise in personal property and good in real estate.

Plutocracy, *n.* A republican form of government deriving its powers from the conceit of the governed—in thinking they govern.

Pocket, *n.* The cradle of motive and the grave of conscience. In woman this organ is lacking; so she acts without motive, and her conscience, denied burial, remains ever alive, confessing the sins of others.

Poetry, *n.* A form of expression peculiar to the Land beyond the Magazines.

Poker, *n.* A game said to be played with cards for some purpose to this lexicographer unknown.

Polecat, *n.* A small European animal that is kind enough to lend its name to the American tongue as a euphemism for that of the native skunk, than which it is esteemed more genteel. Like the skunk, however, it makes music for the deaf when kicked.

Police, *n.* An armed force for protection and participation.

Polite, *adj.* Skilled in the art and practice of dissimulation.

Politeness, *n.* The most acceptable hypocrisy.

Politician, *n.* An eel in the fundamental mud upon which the superstructure of organized society is reared. When he wriggles he mistakes the agitation of his tail for the trembling of the edifice. As compared with the statesman, he suffers the disadvantage of being alive.

Politics, *n.* A strife of interests masquerading as a contest of principles. The conduct of public affairs for private advantage.

Polygamy, *n.* A house of atonement, or expiatory chapel, fitted with several stools of repentance, as distinguished from monogamy, which has but one.

Populist, *n.* A fossil patriot of the early agricultural period, found in the old red soapstone underlying Kansas; characterized by an uncommon spread of ear, which some naturalists contend gave him the power of flight, though Professors Morse and Whitney, pursuing independent lines of thought, have ingeniously pointed out that had he possessed it he would have gone else-where. In the picturesque speech of his period, some fragments of which have come down to us, he was known as "The Matter with Kansas."

Port, *n*. A place where ships taking shelter from storms are shattered by customs officers.

Portable, *adj*. Exposed to a mutable ownership through vicissitudes of pos-session.

> His light estate, if neither he did make it
> Nor yet its former guardian forsake it,
> Is portable improperty, I take it.
>
> *Worgum Slupsky.*

Portion, *n*. A part—in the loose locution of the letterless unworthy. "Part" means a fraction or piece of the whole, but "portion" means a share and implies an allotment. By reverent observance of this distinction great public disaster may be averted.

Portuguese, *n.pl*. A species of geese indigenous to Portugal. They are mostly without feathers and imperfectly edible, even when stuffed with garlic.

Positive, *adj*. Mistaken at the top of one's voice.

Positivism, *n*. A philosophy that denies our knowledge of the Real and affirms our ignorance of the Apparent. Its longest exponent is Comte, its broadest Mill and its thickest Spencer.

Possession, *n*. An advantage that accrues to A by denial of the right of B to take the property of C.

Posterity, *n*. An appellate court which reverses the judgment of a popular au-thor's contemporaries, the appellant being his obscure competitor.

Potable, *n*. Suitable for drinking. Water is said to be potable; indeed, some de-clare it our natural beverage, although even they find it palatable only when suffering from the recurrent disorder known as thirst, for which it is a medi-cine. Upon nothing has so great and diligent ingenuity been brought to bear in all ages and in all countries, except the most uncivilized, as upon the in-vention of substitutes for water. To hold that this general aversion to that liquid has no basis in the preservative instinct of the race is to be unscien-tific—and without science we are as the snakes and toads.

Poverty, *n*. A file provided for the teeth of the rats of reform. The number of plans for its abolition equals that of the reformers who suffer from it, plus that of the philosophers who know nothing about it. Its victims are distin-guished by possession of all the virtues and by their faith in leaders seeking to conduct them into a prosperity where they believe these to be unknown.

Practically, *adv*. The literary sloven's word for "virtually."

Pray, *v*. To ask that the laws of the universe be annulled in behalf of a single petitioner confessedly unworthy.

Pre-Adamite, *n*. One of an experimental and apparently unsatisfactory race that antedated Creation and lived under conditions not easily conceived. Melsius believed them to have inhabited "the Void" and to have been something intermediate between fishes and birds. Little is known of them beyond the fact that they supplied Cain with a wife and theologians with a controversy.

Precedent, *n*. In Law, a previous decision, rule or practice which, in the absence of a definite statute, has whatever force and authority a Judge may choose to give it, thereby greatly simplifying his task of doing as he pleases. As there are precedents for everything, he has only to ignore those that make against his interest and accentuate those in the line of his desire. Invention of the precedent elevates the trial-at-law from the low estate of a fortuitous ordeal to the noble attitude of a dirigible arbitrament.

Precipitate, *adj*. Anteprandial.

> Precipitate in all, this sinner
> Took action first, and then his dinner.
>
> *Judibras.*

Predestination, *n*. The doctrine that all things occur according to programme. This doctrine should not be confused with that of foreordination, which means that all things are programmed, but does not affirm their occurrence, that being only an implication from other doctrines by which this is entailed. The difference is great enough to have deluged Christendom with ink, to say nothing of the gore. With the distinction of the two doctrines kept well in mind, and a reverent belief in both, one may hope to escape perdition if spared.

Predicament, *n*. The wage of consistency.

Predict, *v.t.* To relate an event that has not occurred, is not occurring and will not occur.

Predilection, *n*. The preparatory stage of disillusion.

Pre-existence, *n*. An unnoted factor in creation.

Preference, *n*. A sentiment, or frame of mind, induced by the erroneous belief that one thing is better than another.

> An ancient philosopher, expounding his conviction that life is no better than death, was asked by a disciple why, then, he did not die. "Because," he replied, "death is no better than life." It is longer.

Prehistoric, *adj*. Belonging to an early period and a museum. Antedating the art and practice of perpetuating falsehood.

> He lived in a period prehistoric,
> When all was absurd and phantasmagoric.
> Born later, when Clio, celestial recorder,
> Set down great events in succession and order,

He surely had seen nothing droll or fortuitous
In anything here but the lies that she threw at us.
Orpheus Bowen.

Prejudice, *n.* A vagrant opinion without visible means of support.

Prelate, *n.* A church officer having a superior degree of holiness and a fat preferment. One of Heaven's aristocracy. A gentleman of God.

Prerogative, *n.* A sovereign's right to do wrong.

Presbyterian, *n.* One who holds the conviction that the governing authorities of the Church should be called presbyters.

Prescription, *n.* A physician's guess at what will best prolong the situation with least harm to the patient.

Present, *n.* [1.] That part of eternity dividing the domain of disappointment from the realm of hope. [2.] Something given in expectation of something better. To-day's payment for to-morrow's service.

Presentable, *adj.* Hideously appareled after the manner of the time and place.

In Boorioboola-Gha a man is presentable on occasions of ceremony if he have his abdomen painted a bright blue and wear a cow's tail; in New York he may, if it please him, omit the paint, but after sunset he must wear two tails made of the wool of a sheep and dyed black.

Presentiment, *n.* Consciousness of a brief immunity from something disagreeable.

Stunning events cast their shadows before. — *Scampbell.*

Preside, *v.* To guide the action of a deliberative body to a desirable result. In Journalese, to perform upon a musical instrument; as, "He presided at the piccolo."

The Headliner, holding the copy in hand,
Read with a solemn face:
"The music was very uncommonly grand —
The best that was ever provided,
For our townsman Brown presided
At the organ with skill and grace."
The Headliner discontinued to read,
And, spreading the paper down
On the desk, he dashed in at the top of the screed:
"Great playing by President Brown."
Orpheus Bowen.

Presidency, *n.* The greased pig in the field game of American politics.

President, *n.* The leading figure in a small group of men of whom — and of whom only — it is positively known that immense numbers of their countrymen did not want any of them for President.

If that's an honor surely 'tis a greater
To have been a simple and undamned spectator.
Behold in me a man of mark and note
Whom no elector e'er denied a vote!—
An undiscredited, unhooted gent
Who might, for all we know, be President
By acclamation. Cheer, ye varlets, cheer—
I'm passing with a wide and open ear!

Jonathan Fomry.

Pretty, *adj.* Vain, conceited, as "a pretty girl." Tiresome, as "a pretty picture."

Prevaricator, *n.* A liar in the caterpillar state.

Price, *n.* Value, plus a reasonable sum for the wear and tear of conscience in demanding it.

Primate, *n.* The head of a church, especially a State church supported by involuntary contributions. The Primate of England is the Archbishop of Canterbury, an amiable old gentleman, who occupies Lambeth Palace when living and Westminster Abbey when dead. He is commonly dead.

Prison, *n.* A place of punishments and rewards. The poet assures us that—
"Stone walls do not a prison make,"
but a combination of the stone wall, the political parasite and the moral instructor is no garden of sweets.

Private, *n.* A military gentleman with a field-marshal's baton in his knapsack and an impediment in his hope.

Proboscis, *n.* The rudimentary organ of an elephant which serves him in place of the knife-and-fork that Evolution has as yet denied him. For purposes of humor it is popularly called a trunk.

Asked how he knew that an elephant was going on a journey, the illustrious Jo. Miller cast a reproachful look upon his tormentor, and answered, absently: "When it is ajar," and threw himself from a high promontory into the sea. Thus perished in his pride the most famous humorist of antiquity, leaving to mankind a heritage of woe! No successor worthy of the title has appeared, though Mr. Edward Bok, of *The Ladies' Home Journal,* is much respected for the purity and sweetness of his personal character.

Projectile, *n.* The final arbiter in international disputes. Formerly these disputes were settled by physical contact of the disputants, with such simple arguments as the rudimentary logic of the times could supply—the sword, the spear and so forth. With the growth of prudence in military affairs the projectile came more and more into favor, and is now held in high esteem by the most courageous. Its capital defect is that it requires personal attendance at the point of propulsion.

Promise, *n.* A form of incantation to conjure up a hope that is to be exorcised later by inattention.

Promote, *v.* In financial affairs, to contribute to the development of a transfer company—one that transfers money from the pocket of the investor to that of the promoter.

Proof, *n.* Evidence having a shade more of plausibility than of unlikelihood. The testimony of two credible witnesses as opposed to that of only one.

Proof-reader, *n.* A malefactor who atones for making your writing nonsense by permitting the compositor to make it unintelligible.

Property, *n.* Any material thing, having no particular value, that may be held by A against the cupidity of B. Whatever gratifies the passion for possession in one and disappoints it in all others. The object of man's brief rapacity and long indifference.

Prophecy, *n.* The art and practice of selling one's credibility for future delivery.

Prospect, *n.* An outlook, usually forbidding. An expectation, usually forbidden.

> Blow, blow, ye spicy breezes—
>> O'er Ceylon blow your breath,
> Where every prospect pleases,
>> Save only that of death.
>
> *Bishop Sheber.*

Providential, *adj.* Unexpectedly and conspicuously beneficial to the person so describing it.

Prude, *n.* A bawd hiding behind the back of her demeanor.

Public, *n.* The negligible factor in problems of legislation.

Publish, *n.* In literary affairs, to become the fundamental element in a cone of critics.

Push, *n.* One of the two things mainly conducive to success, especially in politics. The other is Pull.

Pyrrhonism, *n.* An ancient philosophy, named for its inventor. It consisted of an absolute disbelief in everything but Pyrrhonism. Its modern professors have added that.

Queen, *n.* A woman by whom the realm is ruled when there is a king, and through whom it is ruled when there is not.

Quill, *n.* An implement of torture yielded by a goose and commonly wielded by an ass. This use of the quill is now obsolete, but its modern equivalent, the steel pen, is wielded by the same everlasting Presence.

Quiver, *n.* A portable sheath in which the ancient statesman and the aboriginal lawyer carried their lighter arguments.

> He extracted from his quiver,
>> Did the controversial Roman,
> An argument well fitted
> To the question as submitted,
> Then addressed it to the liver,
>> Of the unpersuaded foeman.

Oglum P. Boomp.

Quixotic, *adj.* Absurdly chivalric, like Don Quixote. An insight into the beauty and excellence of this incomparable adjective is unhappily denied to him who has the misfortune to know that the gentleman's name is pronounced Ke-ho-tay.

> When ignorance from out our lives can banish
> Philology, 'tis folly to know Spanish.

Juan Smith.

Quorum, *n.* A sufficient number of members of a deliberative body to have their own way and their own way of having it. In the United States Senate a quorum consists of the chairman of the Committee on Finance and a messenger from the White House; in the House of Representatives, of the Speaker and the devil.

Quotation, *n.* The act of repeating erroneously the words of another. The words erroneously repeated.

> Intent on making his quotation truer,
> He sought the page infallible of Brewer,

Then made a solemn vow that he would be
Condemned eternally. Ah, me, ah, me!

Stumpo Gaker.

Quotient, *n.* A number showing how many times a sum of money belonging to
one person is contained in the pocket of another—usually about as many
times as it can be got there.

Rabble, *n.* In a republic, those who exercise a supreme authority tempered by fraudulent elections. The rabble is like the sacred Simurgh, of Arabian fable—omnipotent on condition that it do nothing. (The word is Aristocratese, and has no exact equivalent in our tongue, but means, as nearly as may be, "soaring swine.")

Rack, *n.* An argumentative implement formerly much used in persuading devotees of a false faith to embrace the living truth. As a call to the unconverted the rack never had any particular efficacy, and is now held in light popular esteem.

Radical, *n.* A miscreant who would forestall the future by discrediting the past and abolishing the present.

Radicalism, *n.* The conservatism of to-morrow injected into the affairs of to-day.

Radium, *n.* A mineral that gives off heat and stimulates the organ that a scientist is a fool with.

Rags, *n.* The uniform of the poor, serving to distinguish these creatures from their creators.

Railroad, *n.* The chief of many mechanical devices enabling us to get away from where we are to where we are no better off. For this purpose the railroad is held in highest favor by the optimist, for it permits him to make the transit with great expedition.

Ramshackle, *adj.* Pertaining to a certain order of architecture, otherwise known as the Normal American. Most of the public buildings of the United States are of the Ramshackle order, though some of our earlier architects preferred the Ironic. Recent additions to the White House in Washington are Theo-Doric, the ecclesiastic order of the Dorians. They are exceedingly fine and cost one hundred dollars a brick.

Rank, *n.* Relative elevation in the scale of human worth.

> He held at court a rank so high
> That other noblemen asked why.

"Because," 'twas answered, "others lack
His skill to scratch the royal back."

Aramis Jukes.

Ransom, *n.* The purchase of that which neither belongs to the seller, nor can belong to the buyer. The most unprofitable of investments.

Rapacity, *n.* Providence without industry. The thrift of power.

Rarebit, *n.* A Welsh rabbit, in the speech of the humorless, who point out that it is not a rabbit. To whom it may be solemnly explained that the comestible known as toad-in-a-hole is really not a toad, and that *riz-de-veau à la financière* is not the smile of a calf prepared after the recipe of a she banker.

Rascal, *n.* A fool considered under another aspect.

Rascality, *n.* Stupidity militant. The activity of a clouded intellect.

Rash, *adj.* Insensible to the value of our advice.

"Now lay your bet with mine, nor let
These gamblers take your cash."
"Nay, this child makes no bet." "Great snakes!
How can you be so rash?"

Bootle P. Gish.

Rational, *adj.* Devoid of all delusions save those of observation, experience and reflection.

Rattlesnake, *n.* Our prostrate brother, *Homo ventrambulans.*

Razor, *n.* An instrument used by the Caucasian to enhance his beauty, by the Mongolian to make a guy of himself and by the Afro-American to affirm his worth.

Reach, *n.* The radius of action of the human hand. The area within which it is possible (and customary) to gratify directly the propensity to provide.

This is a truth, as old as the hills,
That life and experience teach:
The poor man suffers that keenest of ills,
An impediment in his reach.

G. J.

Read, *v.* To get the sense of something written, if it has any. Commonly, it has not.

Reading, *n.* The general body of what one reads. In our country it consists, as a rule, of Indiana novels, short stories in "dialect" and humor in slang.

We know by one's reading
His learning and breeding;
By what draws his laughter
We know his Hereafter.
Read nothing, laugh never—
The Sphinx was less clever!

Jupiter Muke.

Realism, *n*. The art of depicting nature as it is seen by toads. The charm suffusing a landscape painted by a mole, or a story written by a measuring-worm.

Reality, *n*. The dream of a mad philosopher. That which would remain in the cupel if one should assay a phantom. The nucleus of a vacuum.

Really, *adv*. Apparently.

Rear, *n*. In American military matters, that exposed part of the army that is nearest to Congress.

Reason, *v.i.* To weigh probabilities in the scales of desire.

Reason, *n*. Propensitate of prejudice.

Reasonable, *adj*. Accessible to the infection of our own opinions. Hospitable to persuasion, dissuasion and evasion.

Rebel, *n*. A proponent of a new misrule who has failed to establish it.

Recollect, *v*. To recall with additions something not previously known.

Reconciliation, *n*. A suspension of hostilities. An armed truce for the purpose of digging up the dead.

Reconsider, *v*. To seek a justification for a decision already made.

Recount, *n*. In American politics, another throw of the dice, accorded to the player against whom they are loaded.

Recreation, *n*. A particular kind of dejection to relieve a general fatigue.

Recruit, *n*. A person distinguishable from a civilian by his uniform and from a soldier by his gait.

> Fresh from the farm or factory or street,
> His marching, in pursuit or in retreat,
> > Were an impressive martial spectacle
> Except for two impediments—his feet.
>
> Thompson Johnson.

Rector, *n*. In the Church of England, the Third Person of the parochial Trinity, the Curate and the Vicar being the other two.

Redemption, *n*. Deliverance of sinners from the penalty of their sin, through their murder of the deity against whom they sinned. The doctrine of Redemption is the fundamental mystery of our holy religion, and whoso believeth in it shall not perish, but have everlasting life in which to try to understand it.

> We must awake Man's spirit from its sin,
> > And take some special measure for redeeming it;
> Though hard indeed the task to get it in
> > Among the angels any way but teaming it,
> > Or purify it otherwise than steaming it.
> I'm awkward at Redemption—a beginner:
> My method is to crucify the sinner.
>
> Golgo Brone.

Redress, *n.* Reparation without satisfaction.

Among the Anglo-Saxons a subject conceiving himself wronged by the king was permitted, on proving his injury, to beat a brazen image of the royal offender with a switch that was afterward applied to his own naked back. The latter rite was performed by the public hangman, and it assured moderation in the plaintiff's choice of a switch.

Red-skin, *n.* A North American Indian, whose skin is not red—at least not on the outside.

Redundant, *adj.* Superfluous; needless; *de trop.*

The Sultan said: "There's evidence abundant
To prove this unbelieving dog redundant."
To whom the Grand Vizier, with mien impressive,
Replied: "His head, at least, appears excessive."
Habeeb Suleiman.

Mr. Debs is a redundant citizen.—*Theodore Roosevelt.*

Referendum, *n.* A law for submission of proposed legislation to a popular vote to learn the nonsensus of public opinion.

Reflection, *n.* An action of the mind whereby we obtain a clearer view of our relation to the things of yesterday and are able to avoid the perils that we shall not again encounter.

Reform, *n.* A thing that mostly satisfies reformers opposed to reformation.

Refuge, *n.* Anything assuring protection to one in peril. Moses and Joshua provided six cities of refuge—Bezer, Golan, Ramoth, Kadesh, Schekem and Hebron—to which one who had taken life inadvertently could flee when hunted by relatives of the deceased. This admirable expedient supplied him with wholesome exercise and enabled them to enjoy the pleasures of the chase; whereby the soul of the dead man was appropriately honored by observations akin to the funeral games of early Greece.

Refusal, *n.* Denial of something desired; as an elderly maiden's hand in marriage, to a rich and handsome suitor; a valuable franchise to a rich corporation, by an alderman; absolution to an impenitent king, by a priest and so forth. Refusals are graded in a descending scale of finality thus: the refusal absolute, the refusal conditional, the refusal tentative and the refusal feminine. The last is called by some casuists the refusal assentive.

Regalia, *n.* Distinguishing insignia, jewels and costume of such ancient and honorable orders as Knights of Adam; Visionaries of Detectable Bosh; the Ancient Order of Modern Troglodytes; the League of Holy Humbug; the Golden Phalanx of Phalangers; the Genteel Society of Expurgated Hoodlums; the Mystic Alliances of Gorgeous Regalians; Knights and Ladies of the Yellow Dog; the Oriental Order of Sons of the West; the Blatherhood of Insufferable Stuff; Warriors of the Long Bow; Guardians of the Great

Horn Spoon; the Band of Brutes; the Impenitent Order of Wife-Beaters; the Sublime Legion of Flamboyant Conspicuants; Worshipers at the Electroplated Shrine; Shining Inaccessibles; Fee-Faw-Fummers of the Inimitable Grip; Jannissaries of the Broad-Blown Peacock; Plumed Increscencies of the Magic Temple; the Grand Cabal of Able-Bodied Sedentarians; Associated Deities of the Butter Trade; the Garden of Galoots; the Affectionate Fraternity of Men Similarly Warted; the Flashing Astonishers; Ladies of Horror; Coöperative Association for Breaking into the Spotlight; Dukes of Eden; Disciples Militant of the Hidden Faith; Knights-Champions of the Domestic Dog; the Holy Gregarians; the Resolute Optimists; the Ancient Sodality of Inhospitable Hogs; Associated Sovereigns of Mendacity; Dukes-Guardian of the Mystic Cess-Pool; the Society for Prevention of Prevalence; Kings of Drink; Polite Federation of Gents-Consequential; the Mysterious Order of the Undecipherable Scroll; Uniformed Rank of Lousy Cats; Monarchs of Worth and Hunger; Sons of the South Star; Prelates of the Tub-and-Sword.

Religion, *n.* A daughter of Hope and Fear, explaining to Ignorance the nature of the Unknowable.

"What is your religion, my son?" inquired the Archbishop of Rheims.

"Pardon, monseigneur," replied Rochebriant; "I am ashamed of it."

"Then why do you not become an atheist?"

"Impossible! I should be ashamed of atheism."

"In that case, monsieur, you should join the Protestants."

Reliquary, *n.* A receptacle for such sacred objects as pieces of the true cross, short-ribs of the saints, the ears of Balaam's ass, the lung of the cock that called Peter to repentance and so forth. Reliquaries are commonly of metal, and provided with a lock to prevent the contents from coming out and performing miracles at unseasonable times. A feather from the wing of the Angel of the Annunciation once escaped during a sermon in Saint Peter's and so tickled the noses of the congregation that they woke and sneezed with great vehemence three times each. It is related in the *Gesta Sanctorum* that a sacristan in the Canterbury cathedral surprised the head of Saint Dennis in the library. Reprimanded by its stern custodian, it explained that it was seeking a body of doctrine. This unseemly levity so enraged the diocesan that the offender was publicly anathematized, thrown into the Stour and replaced by another head of Saint Dennis, brought from Rome.

Renown, *n.* A degree of distinction between notoriety and fame—a little more supportable than the one and a little more intolerable than the other. Sometimes it is conferred by an unfriendly and inconsiderate hand.

I touched the harp in every key,
But found no heeding ear;

And then Ithuriel touched me
    With a revealing spear.

Not all my genius, great as 'tis,
    Could urge me out of night.
I felt the faint appulse of his,
    And leapt into the light!

W. J. Candleton.

Reparation, *n.* Satisfaction that is made for a wrong and deducted from the satisfaction felt in committing it.

Repartee, *n.* Prudent insult in retort. Practiced by gentlemen with a constitutional aversion to violence, but a strong disposition to offend. In a war of words, the tactics of the North American Indian.

Repentance, *n.* The faithful attendant and follower of Punishment. It is usually manifest in a degree of reformation that is not inconsistent with continuity of sin.

Desirous to avoid the pains of Hell,
You will repent and join the Church, Parnell?
How needless!—Nick will keep you off the coals
And add you to the woes of other souls.

Jomater Abemy.

Replica, *n.* A reproduction of a work of art, by the artist that made the original. It is so called to distinguish it from a "copy," which is made by another artist. When the two are made with equal skill the replica is the more valuable, for it is supposed to be more beautiful than it looks.

Report, *n.* A rumor. The sound of a firearm.

"Why did you not march to my relief, sir?" said General Ewell to the commander of one of his divisions. "Did you not hear the report of my guns?"

"Well, yes, General, I did hear that report, but I did not believe it."

Reporter, *n.* A writer who guesses his way to the truth and dispels it with a tempest of words.

"More dear than all my bosom knows, O thou
Whose 'lips are sealed' and will not disavow!"
So sang the blithe reporter-man as grew
Beneath his hand the leg-long "interview."

Barson Maith.

Repose, *v.i.* To cease from troubling.

Representative, *n.* In national politics, a member of the Lower House in this world, and without discernible hope of promotion in the next.

Reprobation, *n.* In theology, the state of a luckless mortal prenatally damned.

The doctrine of reprobation was taught by Calvin, whose joy in it was somewhat marred by the sad sincerity of his conviction that although some are foredoomed to perdition, others are predestined to salvation.

Republic, *n.* A nation in which, the thing governing and the thing governed being the same, there is only a permitted authority to enforce an optional obedience. In a republic the foundation of public order is the ever lessening habit of submission inherited from ancestors who, being truly governed, submitted because they had to. There are as many kinds of republics as there are gradations between the despotism whence they came and the anarchy whither they lead.

Requiem, *n.* A mass for the dead which the minor poets assure us the winds sing o'er the graves of their favorites. Sometimes, by way of providing a varied entertainment, they sing a dirge.

Resident, *adj.* Unable to leave.

Resign, *v.t.* To renounce an honor for an advantage. To renounce an advantage for a greater advantage.

> 'Twas rumored Leonard Wood had signed
>> A true renunciation
> Of title, rank and every kind
>> Of military station—
>> Each honorable station.
>
> By his example fired—inclined
>> To noble emulation,
> The country humbly was resigned
>> To Leonard's resignation—
>> His Christian resignation.

Politian Greame.

Resolute, *adj.* Obstinate in a course that we approve.

Respectability, *n.* The offspring of a *liaison* between a bald head and a bank account.

Respirator, *n.* An apparatus fitted over the nose and mouth of an inhabitant of London, whereby to filter the visible universe in its passage to the lungs.

Respite, *n.* A suspension of hostilities against a sentenced assassin, to enable the Executive to determine whether the murder may not have been done by the prosecuting attorney. Any break in the continuity of a disagreeable expectation.

> Altgeld upon his incandescent bed
> Lay, an attendant demon at his head.
>
> "O cruel cook, pray grant me some relief—
> Some respite from the roast, however brief.

"Remember how on earth I pardoned all
Your friends in Illinois when held in thrall."

"Unhappy soul! for that alone you squirm
O'er fire unquenched, a never-dying worm.

"Yet, for I pity your uneasy state,
Your doom I'll mollify and pains abate.

"Naught, for a season, shall your comfort mar,
Not even the memory of who you are."

Throughout eternal space dread silence fell;
Heaven trembled as Compassion entered Hell.

"As long, sweet demon, let my respite be
As, governing down here, I'd respite thee."

"As long, poor soul, as any of the pack
You thrust from jail consumed in getting back."

A genial chill affected Altgeld's hide
While they were turning him on t'other side.
                              Joel Spate Woop.

Resplendent, *adj.* Like a simple American citizen beduking himself in his lodge,
    or affirming his consequence in the Scheme of Things as an elemental unit
    of a parade.

>   The Knights of Dominion were so resplendent in their velvet-and-
>   gold that their masters would hardly have known them. — *"Chronicles
>   of the Classes."*

Respond, *v.i.* To make answer, or disclose otherwise a consciousness of having
    inspired an interest in what Herbert Spencer calls "external coexistences,"
    as Satan "squat like a toad" at the ear of Eve, responded to the touch of
    the angel's spear. To respond in damages is to contribute to the mainte-
    nance of the plaintiff's attorney and, incidentally, to the gratification of the
    plaintiff.

Responsibility, *n.* A detachable burden easily shifted to the shoulders of God,
    Fate, Fortune, Luck or one's neighbor. In the days of astrology it was cus-
    tomary to unload it upon a star.

>   Alas, things ain't what we should see
>   If Eve had let that apple be;
>   And many a feller which had ought
>   To set with monarchses of thought,
>   Or play some rosy little game

With battle-chaps on fields of fame,
Is downed by his unlucky star,
And hollers: "Peanuts!—here you are!"

"The Sturdy Beggar."

Restitution, *n.* The founding or endowing of universities and public libraries by
gift or bequest.

Restitutor, *n.* Benefactor; philanthropist.

Retaliation, *n.* The natural rock upon which is reared the Temple of Law.

Retribution, *n.* A rain of fire-and-brimstone that falls alike upon the just and
such of the unjust as have not procured shelter by evicting them.

> In the lines following, addressed to an Emperor in exile by Father Gas-
> salasca Jape, the reverend poet appears to hint his sense of the imprudence
> of turning about to face Retribution when it is taking exercise:

What, what! Dom Pedro, you desire to go
  Back to Brazil to end your days in quiet?
Why, what assurance have you 'twould be so?
  'Tis not so long since you were in a riot,
And your dear subjects showed a will to fly at
Your throat and shake you like a rat. You know
That empires are ungrateful; are you certain
Republics are less handy to get hurt in?

Reveille, *n.* A signal to sleeping soldiers to dream of battlefields no more, but
get up and have their blue noses counted. In the American army it is ingeniously called "rev-e-lee," and to that pronunciation our countrymen have
pledged their lives, their misfortunes and their sacred dishonor.

Revelation, *n.* A famous book in which St. John the Divine concealed all that he
knew. The revealing is done by the commentators, who know nothing.

Reverence, *n.* The spiritual attitude of a man to a god and a dog to a man.

Review, *v.t.*

To set your wisdom (holding not a doubt of it,
  Although in truth there's neither bone nor skin to it)
At work upon a book, and so read out of it
The qualities that you have first read into it.

Revolution, *n.* In politics, an abrupt change in the form of misgovernment. Specifically, in American history, the substitution of the rule of an Administration for that of a Ministry, whereby the welfare and happiness of the people
were advanced a full half-inch. Revolutions are usually accompanied by a
considerable effusion of blood, but are accounted worth it—this appraisement being made by beneficiaries whose blood had not the mischance to be
shed. The French revolution is of incalculable value to the Socialist of to-

day; when he pulls the string actuating its bones its gestures are inexpressibly terrifying to gory tyrants suspected of fomenting law and order.

Rhadomancer, *n.* One who uses a divining-rod in prospecting for precious metals in the pocket of a fool.

Ribaldry, *n.* Censorious language by another concerning oneself.

Ribroaster, *n.* Censorious language by oneself concerning another. The word is of classical refinement, and is even said to have been used in a fable by Georgius Coadjutor, one of the most fastidious writers of the fifteenth century—commonly, indeed, regarded as the founder of the Fastidiotic School.

Rice-water, *n.* A mystic beverage secretly used by our most popular novelists and poets to regulate the imagination and narcotize the conscience. It is said to be rich in both obtundite and lethargine, and is brewed in a midnight fog by a fat witch of the Dismal Swamp.

Rich, *adj.* Holding in trust and subject to an accounting the property of the indolent, the incompetent, the unthrifty, the envious and the luckless. That is the view that prevails in the underworld, where the Brotherhood of Man finds its most logical development and candid advocacy. To denizens of the midworld the word means good and wise.

Riches, *n.*

A gift from Heaven signifying, "This is my beloved son, in whom I am well pleased." —*John D. Rockefeller.*

The reward of toil and virtue. —*J. P. Morgan.*

The savings of many in the hands of one. —*Eugene Debs.*

To these excellent definitions the inspired lexicographer feels that he can add nothing of value.

Ridicule, *n.* Words designed to show that the person of whom they are uttered is devoid of the dignity of character distinguishing him who utters them. It may be graphic, mimetic or merely rident. Shaftesbury is quoted as having pronounced it the test of truth—a ridiculous assertion, for many a solemn fallacy has undergone centuries of ridicule with no abatement of its popular acceptance. What, for example, has been more valorously derided than the doctrine of Infant Respectability?

Right, *n.* Legitimate authority to be, to do or to have; as the right to be a king, the right to do one's neighbor, the right to have measles and the like. The first of these rights was once universally believed to be derived directly from the will of God; and this is still sometimes affirmed *in partibus infidelium* outside the enlightened realms of Democracy; as in the well-known lines of Sir Abednego Bink, following:

By what right, then, do royal rulers rule?

Whose is the sanction of their state and pow'r?

He surely were as stubborn as a mule
　　Who, God unwilling, could maintain an hour
His uninvited session on the throne, or air
His pride securely in the Presidential chair.

　　Whatever is is so by Right Divine;
　　　　Whate'er occurs, God wills it so. Good land!
　　It were a wondrous thing if His design
　　　　A fool could baffle or a rogue withstand!
　　If so, then God, I say (intending no offence)
　　Is guilty of contributory negligence.

Righteousness, *n.* A sturdy virtue that was once found among the Pantidoodles inhabiting the lower part of the peninsula of Oque. Some feeble attempts were made by returned missionaries to introduce it into several European countries, but it appears to have been imperfectly expounded. An example of this faulty exposition is found in the only extant sermon of the pious Bishop Rowley, a characteristic passage from which is here given:

"Now righteousness consisteth not merely in a holy state of mind, nor yet in performance of religious rites and obedience to the letter of the law. It is not enough that one be pious and just: one must see to it that others also are in the same state; and to this end compulsion is a proper means. Forasmuch as my injustice may work ill to another, so by his injustice may evil be wrought upon still another, the which it is as manifestly my duty to estop as to forestall mine own tort. Wherefore if I would be righteous I am bound to restrain my neighbor, by force if needful, in all those injurious enterprises from which, through a better disposition and by the help of Heaven, I do myself refrain."

Rime, *n.* Agreeing sounds in the terminals of verse, mostly bad. The verses themselves, as distinguished from prose, mostly dull. Usually (and wickedly) spelled "rhyme."

Rimer, *n.* A poet regarded with indifference or disesteem.

The rimer quenches his unheeded fires,
The sound surceases and the sense expires.
Then the domestic dog, to east and west,
Expounds the passions burning in his breast.
The rising moon o'er that enchanted land
Pauses to hear and yearns to understand.

Mowbray Myles.

Riot, *n.* A popular entertainment given to the military by innocent bystanders.

R.I.P. A careless abbreviation of *requiescat in pace,* attesting an indolent goodwill

to the dead. According to the learned Dr. Drigge, however, the letters originally meant nothing more than *reductus in pulvis*.

Rite, *n*. A religious or semi-religious ceremony fixed by law, precept or custom,
with the essential oil of sincerity carefully squeezed out of it.

Ritualism, *n*. A Dutch Garden of God where He may walk in rectilinear freedom, keeping off the grass.

Road, *n*. A strip of land along which one may pass from where it is too tiresome
to be to where it is futile to go.

> All roads, howsoe'er they diverge, lead to Rome,
> Whence, thank the good Lord, at least one leads back home.
>> *Borey the Bald.*

Robber, *n*. A candid man of affairs.

It is related of Voltaire that one night he and some traveling companions
lodged at a wayside inn. The surroundings were suggestive, and after supper
they agreed to tell robber stories in turn. When Voltaire's turn came he said:
"Once there was a Farmer-General of the Revenues." Saying nothing more,
he was encouraged to continue. "That," he said, "is the story."

Romance, *n*. Fiction that owes no allegiance to the God of Things as They Are.
In the novel the writer's thought is tethered to probability, as a domestic
horse to the hitching-post, but in romance it ranges at will over the entire
region of the imagination—free, lawless, immune to bit and rein. Your novelist is a poor creature, as Carlyle might say—a mere reporter. He may invent
his characters and plot, but he must not imagine anything taking place that
might not occur, albeit his entire narrative is candidly a lie. Why he imposes
this hard condition on himself, and "drags at each remove a lengthening
chain" of his own forging he can explain in ten thick volumes without illuminating by so much as a candle's ray the black profound of his own ignorance of the matter. There are great novels, for great writers have "laid waste
their powers" to write them, but it remains true that far and away the most
fascinating fiction that we have is "The Thousand and One Nights."

Rope, *n*. An obsolescent appliance for reminding assassins that they too are
mortal. It is put about the neck and remains in place one's whole life long.
It has been largely superseded by a more complex electrical device worn
upon another part of the person; and this is rapidly giving place to an apparatus known as the preachment.

Rostrum, *n*. In Latin, the beak of a bird or the prow of a ship. In America, a
place from which a candidate for office energetically expounds the wisdom,
virtue and power of the rabble.

Roundhead, *n*. A member of the Parliamentarian party in the English civil war—
so called from his habit of wearing his hair short, whereas his enemy, the

Cavalier, wore his long. There were other points of difference between them, but the fashion in hair was the fundamental cause of quarrel. The Cavaliers were royalists because the king, an indolent fellow, found it more convenient to let his hair grow than to wash his neck. This the Roundheads, who were mostly barbers and soap-boilers, deemed an injury to trade, and the royal neck was therefore the object of their particular indignation. Descendants of the belligerents now wear their hair all alike, but the fires of animosity enkindled in that ancient strife smoulder to this day beneath the snows of British civility.

Rubbish, *n.* Worthless matter, such as the religions, philosophies, literatures, arts and sciences of the tribes infesting the regions lying due south from Boreaplas.

Ruin, *v.* To destroy. Specifically, to destroy a maid's belief in the virtue of maids.

Rum, *n.* Generically, fiery liquors that produce madness in total abstainers.

Rumor, *n.* A favorite weapon of the assassins of character.

> Sharp, irresistible by mail or shield,
> By guard unparried as by flight unstayed,
> O serviceable Rumor, let me wield
> Against my enemy no other blade.
> His be the terror of a foe unseen,
> His the inutile hand upon the hilt,
> And mine the deadly tongue, long, slender, keen,
> Hinting a rumor of some ancient guilt.
> So shall I slay the wretch without a blow,
> Spare me to celebrate his overthrow,
> And nurse my valor for another foe.
>
> *Joel Buxter.*

Russian, *n.* A person with a Caucasian body and a Mongolian soul. A Tartar Emetic.

Sabbath, *n.* A weekly festival having its origin in the fact that God made the world in six days and was arrested on the seventh. Among the Jews observance of the day was enforced by a Commandment of which this is the Christian version: "Remember the seventh day to make thy neighbor keep it wholly." To the Creator it seemed fit and expedient that the Sabbath should be the last day of the week, but the Early Fathers of the Church held other views. So great is the sanctity of the day that even where the Lord holds a doubtful and precarious jurisdiction over those who go down to (and down into) the sea it is reverently recognized, as is manifest in the following deepwater version of the Fourth Commandment:

Six days shalt thou labor and do all thou art able,
And on the seventh holystone the deck and scrape the cable.

Decks are no longer holystoned, but the cable still supplies the captain with opportunity to attest a pious respect for the divine ordinance.

Sacerdotalist, *n.* One who holds the belief that a clergyman is a priest. Denial of this momentous doctrine is the hardiest challenge that is now flung into the teeth of the Episcopalian church by the Neo-Dictionarians.

Sacrament, *n.* A solemn religious ceremony to which several degrees of authority and significance are attached. Rome has seven sacraments, but the Protestant churches, being less prosperous, feel that they can afford only two, and these of inferior sanctity. Some of the smaller sects have no sacraments at all—for which mean economy they will indubitably be damned.

Sacred, *adj.* Dedicated to some religious purpose; having a divine character; inspiring solemn thoughts or emotions; as, the Dalai Lama of Thibet; the Moogum of M'bwango; the temple of Apes in Ceylon; the Cow in India; the Crocodile, the Cat and the Onion of ancient Egypt; the Mufti of Moosh; the hair of the dog that bit Noah, etc.

All things are either sacred or profane.
The former to ecclesiasts bring gain;
The latter to the devil appertain.

Dumbo Omohundro.

Safety-clutch, *n.* A mechanical device acting automatically to prevent the fall of
an elevator, or cage, in case of an accident to the hoisting apparatus.

> Once I seen a human ruin
> In an elevator-well,
> And his members was bestrewin'
> All the place where he had fell.
>
> And I says, apostrophisin'
> That uncommon woful wreck:
> "Your position's so surprisin'
> That I tremble for your neck!"
>
> Then that ruin, smilin' sadly
> And impressive, up and spoke:
> "Well, I wouldn't tremble badly,
> For it's been a fortnight broke."
>
> Then, for further comprehension
> Of his attitude, he begs
> I will focus my attention
> On his various arms and legs—
>
> How they all are contumacious;
> Where they each, respective, lie;
> How one trotter proves ungracious,
> T'other one an *alibi.*
>
> These particulars is mentioned
> For to show his dismal state,
> Which I wasn't first intentioned
> To specifical relate.
>
> None is worser to be dreaded
> That I ever have heard tell
> Than the gent's who there was spreaded
> In that elevator-well.
>
> Now this tale is allegoric—
> It is figurative all,
> For the well is metaphoric
> And the feller didn't fall.
>
> I opine it isn't moral
> For a writer-man to cheat,

And despise to wear a laurel
    As was gotten by deceit.

For 'tis Politics intended
    By the elevator, mind,
It will boost a person splendid
    If his talent is the kind.

Col. Bryan had the talent
    (For the busted man is him)
And it shot him up right gallant
    Till his head begun to swim.

Then the rope it broke above him
    And he painful come to earth
Where there's nobody to love him
    For his detrimented worth.

Though he's livin' none would know him,
    Or at leastwise not as such.
Moral of this woful poem:
    Frequent oil your safety-clutch.

Porfer Poog.

Saint, *n.* A dead sinner revised and edited.

The Duchess of Orleans relates that the irreverent old calumniator, Marshal Villeroi, who in his youth had known St. Francis de Sales, said, on hearing him called saint: "I am delighted to hear that Monsieur de Sales is a saint. He was fond of saying indelicate things, and used to cheat at cards. In other respects he was a perfect gentleman, though a fool."

Salacity, *n.* A certain literary quality frequently observed in popular novels, especially in those written by women and young girls, who give it another name and think that in introducing it they are occupying a neglected field of letters and reaping an overlooked harvest. If they have the misfortune to live long enough they are tormented with a desire to burn their sheaves.

Salamander, *n.* Originally a reptile inhabiting fire; later, an anthropomorphous immortal, but still a pyrophile. Salamanders are now believed to be extinct, the last one of which we have an account having been seen in Carcassonne by the Abbé Belloc, who exorcised it with a bucket of holy water.

Sandlotter, *n.* A vertebrate mammal holding the political views of Denis Kearney, a notorious demagogue of San Francisco, whose audiences gathered in the open spaces (sandlots) of the town. True to the traditions of his species, this leader of the proletariat was finally bought off by his law-and-order enemies, living prosperously silent and dying impenitently rich. But before his treason he imposed upon California a constitution that was a confection of sin in a diction of solecisms. The similarity between the words "sandlotter" and "sans-culotte" is problematically significant, but indubitably suggestive.

Sarcophagus, *n.* Among the Greeks a coffin which, being made of a certain kind of carnivorous stone, had the peculiar property of devouring the body placed in it. The sarcophagus known to modern obsequiographers is commonly a product of the carpenter's art.

Satan, *n.* One of the Creator's lamentable mistakes, repented in sashcloth and axes. Being instated as an archangel, Satan made himself multifariously objectionable and was finally expelled from Heaven. Half-way in his descent he paused, bent his head in thought a moment and at last went back. "There is one favor that I should like to ask," said he.

"Name it."

"Man, I understand, is about to be created. He will need laws."

"What, wretch! you his appointed adversary, charged from the dawn of eternity with hatred of his soul—you ask for the right to make his laws?"

"Pardon; what I have to ask is that he be permitted to make them himself."

It was so ordered.

Satiety, *n.* The feeling that one has for the plate after he has eaten its contents, madam.

Satire, *n.* An obsolete kind of literary composition in which the vices and follies of the author's enemies were expounded with imperfect tenderness. In this country satire never had more than a sickly and uncertain existence, for the soul of it is wit, wherein we are dolefully deficient, the humor that we mistake for it, like all humor, being tolerant and sympathetic. Moreover, although Americans are "endowed by their Creator" with abundant vice and folly, it is not generally known that these are reprehensible qualities, wherefore the satirist is popularly regarded as a sour-spirited knave, and his every victim's outcry for codefendants evokes a national assent.

> Hail Satire! be thy praises ever sung
> In the dead language of a mummy's tongue,
> For thou thyself art dead, and damned as well—
> Thy spirit (usefully employed) in Hell.
> Had it been such as consecrates the Bible
> Thou hadst not perished by the law of libel.
>
> *Barney Stims.*

Satyr, *n.* One of the few characters of the Grecian mythology accorded recognition in the Hebrew. (Leviticus, xvii, 7.) The satyr was at first a member of the dissolute community acknowledging a loose allegiance to Dionysus, but underwent many transformations and improvements. Not infrequently he is confounded with the faun, a later and decenter creation of the Romans, who was less like a man and more like a goat.

Sauce, *n.* The one infallible sign of civilization and enlightenment. A people with no sauces has one thousand vices; a people with one sauce has only nine hundred and ninety-nine. For every sauce invented and accepted a vice is renounced and forgiven.

Saw, *n.* A trite popular saying, or proverb. (Figurative and colloquial.) So called because it makes its way into a wooden head. Following are examples of old saws fitted with new teeth.

> A penny saved is a penny to squander.
>
> A man is known by the company that he organizes.
>
> A bad workman quarrels with the man who calls him that.
>
> A bird in the hand is worth what it will bring.
>
> Better late than before anybody has invited you.
>
> Example is better than following it.
>
> Half a loaf is better than a whole one if there is much else.
>
> Think twice before you speak to a friend in need.
>
> What is worth doing is worth the trouble of asking somebody to do it.
>
> Least said is soonest disavowed.
>
> He laughs best who laughs least.
>
> Speak of the Devil and he will hear about it.
>
> Of two evils choose to be the least.
>
> Strike while your employer has a big contract.
>
> Where there's a will there's a won't.

Scarabæus, *n.* The sacred beetle of the ancient Egyptians, allied to our familiar "tumble-bug." It was supposed to symbolize immortality, the fact that God knew why giving it its peculiar sanctity. Its habit of incubating its eggs in a ball of ordure may also have commended it to the favor of the priesthood, and may some day assure it an equal reverence among ourselves. True, the American beetle is an inferior beetle, but the American priest is an inferior priest.

Scarabee, *n.* The same as scarabæus.

> He fell by his own hand
> Beneath the great oak tree.

He'd traveled in a foreign land.
He tried to make her understand
The dance that's called the Saraband,
    But he called it Scarabee.
He had called it so through an afternoon,
    And she, the light of his harem if so might be,
    Had smiled and said naught. O the body was fair to see,
All frosted there in the shine o' the moon —
    Dead for a Scarabee
And a recollection that came too late.
    O Fate!
They buried him where he lay,
He sleeps awaiting the Day,
    In state,
And two Possible Puns, moon-eyed and wan,
Gloom over the grave and then move on.
    Dead for a Scarabee!

Fernando Tapple.

Scarification, *n.* A form of penance practiced by the mediæval pious. The rite was performed, sometimes with a knife, sometimes with a hot iron, but always, says Arsenius Asceticus, acceptably if the penitent spared himself no pain nor harmless disfigurement. Scarification, with other crude penances, has now been superseded by benefaction. The founding of a library or endowment of a university is said to yield to the penitent a sharper and more lasting pain than is conferred by the knife or iron, and is therefore a surer means of grace. There are, however, two grave objections to it as a penitential method: the good that it does and the taint of justice.

Scepter, *n.* A king's staff of office, the sign and symbol of his authority. It was originally a mace with which the sovereign admonished his jester and vetoed ministerial measures by breaking the bones of their proponents.

Scimitar, *n.* A curved sword of exceeding keenness, in the conduct of which certain Orientals attain a surprising proficiency, as the incident here related will serve to show. The account is translated from the Japanese by Shusi Itama, a famous writer of the thirteenth century.

When the great Gichi-Kuktai was Mikado he condemned to decapitation Jijiji Ri, a high officer of the Court. Soon after the hour appointed for performance of the rite what was his Majesty's surprise to see calmly approaching the throne the man who should have been at that time ten minutes dead!

"Seventeen hundred impossible dragons!" shouted the enraged

monarch. "Did I not sentence you to stand in the market-place and have your head struck off by the public executioner at three o'clock? And is it not now 3 : 10?"

"Son of a thousand illustrious deities," answered the condemned minister, "all that you say is so true that the truth is a lie in comparison. But your heavenly Majesty's sunny and vitalizing wishes have been pestilently disregarded. With joy I ran and placed my unworthy body in the market-place. The executioner appeared with his bare scimitar, ostentatiously whirled it in air, and then, tapping me lightly upon the neck, strode away, pelted by the populace, with whom I was ever a favorite. I am come to pray for justice upon his own dishonorable and treasonous head."

"To what regiment of executioners does the black-boweled caitiff belong?" asked the Mikado.

"To the gallant Ninety-eight Hundred and Thirty-seventh—I know the man. His name is Sakko-Samshi."

"Let him be brought before me," said the Mikado to an attendant, and a half-hour later the culprit stood in the Presence.

"Thou bastard son of a three-legged hunchback without thumbs!" roared the sovereign— "why didst thou but lightly tap the neck that it should have been thy pleasure to sever?"

"Lord of Cranes and Cherry Blooms," replied the executioner, unmoved, "command him to blow his nose with his fingers."

Being commanded, Jijiji Ri laid hold of his nose and trumpeted like an elephant, all expecting to see the severed head flung violently from him. Nothing occurred: the performance prospered peacefully to the close, without incident.

All eyes were now turned on the executioner, who had grown as white as the snows on the summit of Fujiama. His legs trembled and his breath came in gasps of terror.

"Several kinds of spike-tailed brass lions!" he cried; "I am a ruined and disgraced swordsman! I struck the villain feebly because in flourishing the scimitar I had accidentally passed it through my own neck! Father of the Moon, I resign my office."

So saying, he grasped his top-knot, lifted off his head and advancing to the throne laid it humbly at the Mikado's feet.

Scrap-book, *n.* A book that is commonly edited by a fool. Many persons of some small distinction compile scrap-books containing whatever they happen to read about themselves or employ others to collect. One of these egotists was addressed in the lines following, by Agamemnon Melancthon Peters:

Dear Frank, that scrap-book where you boast
    You keep a record true
Of every kind of peppered roast
    That's made of you;

Wherein you paste the printed gibes
    That revel round your name,
Thinking the laughter of the scribes
    Attests your fame;

Where all the pictures you arrange
    That comic pencils trace—
Your funny figure and your strange
    Semitic face—

Pray lend it me. Wit I have not,
    Nor art, but there I'll list
The daily drubbings you'd have got
    Had God a fist.

Scribbler, *n.* A professional writer whose views are antagonistic to one's own.

Scriptures, *n.* The sacred books of our holy religion, as distinguished from the false and profane writings on which all other faiths are based.

Seal, *n.* A mark impressed upon certain kinds of documents to attest their authenticity and authority. Sometimes it is stamped upon wax, and attached to the paper, sometimes into the paper itself. Sealing, in this sense, is a survival of an ancient custom of inscribing important papers with cabalistic words or signs to give them a magical efficacy independent of the authority that they represent. In the British Museum are preserved many ancient papers, mostly of a sacerdotal character, validated by necromantic pentagrams and other devices, frequently initial letters of words to conjure with; and in many instances these are attached in the same way that seals are appended now. As nearly every reasonless and apparently meaningless custom, rite or observance of modern times had origin in some remote utility, it is pleasing to note an example of ancient nonsense evolving in the process of ages into something really useful. Our word "sincere" is derived from *sine cero,* without wax, but the learned are not in agreement as to whether this refers to the absence of the cabalistic signs, or to that of the wax with which letters were formerly closed from public scrutiny. Either view of the matter will serve one in immediate need of an hypothesis. The initials L. S., commonly appended to signatures of legal documents, mean *locum sigillis,* the place of the seal, although the seal is no longer used—an admirable example of conservatism distinguishing Man from the beasts that perish. The words *locum sigillis* are humbly suggested as a suitable motto for the Pribyloff Islands whenever they shall take their place as a sovereign State of the American Union.

Seine, *n.* A kind of net for effecting an involuntary change of environment. For fish it is made strong and coarse, but women are more easily taken with a singularly delicate fabric weighted with small, cut stones.

> The devil casting a seine of lace,
>   (With precious stones 'twas weighted)
> Drew it into the landing place
>   And its contents calculated.
>
> All souls of women were in that sack—
>   A draft miraculous, precious!
> But ere he could throw it across his back
>   They'd all escaped through the meshes.
>
> *Baruch de Loppis.*

Self-esteem, *n.* An erroneous appraisement.

Self-evident, *adj.* Evident to one's self and to nobody else.

Selfish, *adj.* Devoid of consideration for the selfishness of others.

Senate, *n.* A body of elderly gentlemen charged with high duties and misdemeanors.

Serial, *n.* A literary work, usually a story that is not true, creeping through several issues of a newspaper or magazine. Frequently appended to each instalment is a "synopsis of preceding chapters" for those who have not read them, but a direr need is a synopsis of succeeding chapters for those who do not intend to read *them*. A synopsis of the entire work would be still better.

The late James F. Bowman was writing a serial tale for a weekly paper in collaboration with a genius whose name has not come down to us. They wrote, not jointly but alternately, Bowman supplying the instalment for one week, his friend for the next, and so on, world without end, they hoped. Unfortunately they quarreled, and one Monday morning when Bowman read the paper to prepare himself for his task, he found his work cut out for him in a way to surprise and pain him. His collaborator had embarked every character of the narrative on a ship and sunk them all in the deepest part of the Atlantic.

Severalty, *n.* Separateness, as, lands in severalty, *i.e.,* lands held individually, not in joint ownership. Certain tribes of Indians are believed now to be sufficiently civilized to have in severalty the lands that they have hitherto held as tribal organizations, and could not sell to the Whites for waxen beads and potato whisky.

Lo! the poor Indian whose unsuited mind
Saw death before, hell and the grave behind;
Whom thrifty settlers ne'er besought to stay—
His small belongings their appointed prey;
Whom Dispossession, with alluring wile,
Persuaded elsewhere every little while!
His fire unquenched and his undying worm
By "land in severalty" (charming term!)
Are cooled and killed, respectively, at last,
And he to his new holding anchored fast!

Sheriff, *n.* In America the chief executive office of a county, whose most characteristic duties, in some of the Western and Southern States, are the catching
and hanging of rogues.

John Elmer Pettibone Cajee
(I write of him with little glee)
Was just as bad as he could be.

'Twas frequently remarked: "I swon!
The sun has never looked upon
So bad a man as Neighbor John."

A sinner through and through, he had
This added fault: it made him mad
To know another man was bad.

In such a case he thought it right
To rise at any hour of night
And quench that wicked person's light.

Despite the town's entreaties, he
Would hale him to the nearest tree
And leave him swinging wide and free.

Or sometimes, if the humor came,
A luckless wight's reluctant frame
Was given to the cheerful flame.

While it was turning nice and brown,
All unconcerned John met the frown
Of that austere and righteous town.

"How sad," his neighbors said, "that he
So scornful of the law should be—
An anar c, h, i, s, t."

(That is the way that they preferred
   To utter the abhorrent word,
   So strong the aversion that it stirred.)

"Resolved," they said, continuing,
"That Badman John must cease this thing
   Of having his unlawful fling.

"Now, by these sacred relics" —here
   Each man had out a souvenir
   Got at a lynching yesteryear—

"By these we swear he shall forsake
   His ways, nor cause our hearts to ache
   By sins of rope and torch and stake.

"We'll tie his red right hand until
   He'll have small freedom to fulfil
   The mandates of his lawless will."

So, in convention then and there,
   They named him Sheriff. The affair
   Was opened, it is said, with prayer.

                  J. Milton Sloluck.

Siren, *n.* One of several musical prodigies famous for a vain attempt to dissuade Odysseus from a life on the ocean wave. Figuratively, any lady of splendid promise, dissembled purpose and disappointing performance.

Slang, *n.* The grunt of the human hog (*Pignoramus intolerabilis*) with an audible memory. The speech of one who utters with his tongue what he thinks with his ear, and feels the pride of a creator in accomplishing the feat of a parrot. A means (under Providence) of setting up as a wit without a capital of sense.

Smithareen, *n.* A fragment, a decomponent part, a remain. The word is used variously, but in the following verses on a noted female reformer who opposed bicycle-riding by women because it "led them to the devil" it is seen at its best:

   The wheels go round without a sound—
      The maidens hold high revel;
   In sinful mood, insanely gay,
   True spinsters spin adown the way
      From duty to the devil!
   They laugh, they sing, and—ting-a-ling!
      Their bells go all the morning;

Their lanterns bright bestar the night
    Pedestrians a-warning.
With lifted hands Miss Charlotte stands,
    Good-Lording and O-mying,
Her rheumatism forgotten quite,
    Her fat with anger frying.
She blocks the path that leads to wrath,
    Jack Satan's power defying.

The wheels go round without a sound,
    The lights burn red and blue and green.
What's this that's found upon the ground?
    Poor Charlotte Smith's a smithareen!

John William Yope.

Sophistry, *n.* The controversial method of an opponent, distinguished from one's own by superior insincerity and fooling. This method is that of the later Sophists, a Grecian sect of philosophers who began by teaching wisdom, prudence, science, art and, in brief, whatever men ought to know, but lost themselves in a maze of quibbles and a fog of words.

His bad opponent's "facts" he sweeps away,
And drags his sophistry to light of day;
Then swears they're pushed to madness who resort
To falsehood of so desperate a sort.
Not so; like sods upon a dead man's breast,
He lies most lightly who the least is pressed.

Polydore Smith.

Sorcery, *n.* The ancient prototype and forerunner of political influence. It was, however, deemed less respectable and sometimes was punished by torture and death. Augustine Nicholas relates that a poor peasant who had been accused of sorcery was put to the torture to compel a confession. After enduring a few gentle agonies the suffering simpleton admitted his guilt, but naïvely asked his tormentors if it were not possible to be a sorcerer without knowing it.

Soul, *n.* A spiritual entity concerning which there hath been brave disputation. Plato held that those souls which in a previous state of existence (antedating Athens) had obtained the clearest glimpses of eternal truth entered into the bodies of persons who became philosophers. Plato himself was a philosopher. The souls that had least contemplated divine truth animated the bodies of usurpers and despots. Dionysius I, who had threatened to decapitate the broad-browed philosopher, was a usurper and despot. Plato, doubtless, was not the first to construct a system of philosophy that could be quoted against his enemies; certainly he was not the last.

"Concerning the nature of the soul," saith the renowned author of *Diversiones Sanctorum,* "there hath been hardly more argument than that of its place in the body. Mine own belief is that the soul hath her seat in the abdomen—in which faith we may discern and interpret a truth hitherto unintelligible, namely that the glutton is of all men most devout. He is said in the Scripture to 'make a god of his belly'—why, then, should he not be pious, having ever his Deity with him to freshen his faith? Who so well as he can know the might and majesty that he shrines? Truly and soberly, the soul and the stomach are one Divine Entity; and such was the belief of Promasius, who nevertheless erred in denying it immortality. He had observed that its visible and material substance failed and decayed with the rest of the body after death, but of its immaterial essence he knew nothing. This is what we call the Appetite, and it survives the wreck and reek of mortality, to be rewarded or punished in another world, according to what it hath demanded in the flesh. The Appetite whose coarse clamoring was for the unwholesome viands of the general market and the public refectory shall be cast into eternal famine, whilst that which firmly though civilly insisted on ortolans, caviare, terrapin, anchovies, *pâtés de foie gras* and all such Christian comestibles shall flesh its spiritual tooth in the souls of them forever and ever, and wreak its divine thirst upon the immortal parts of the rarest and richest wines ever quaffed here below. Such is my religious faith, though I grieve to confess that neither His Holiness the Pope nor His Grace the Archbishop of Canterbury (whom I equally and profoundly revere) will assent to its dissemination."

Spooker, *n.* A writer whose imagination concerns itself with supernatural phenomena, especially the doings of spooks. One of the most illustrious spookers of our time is Mr. William D. Howells, who introduces a well-credentialed reader to as respectable and mannerly a company of spooks as one could wish to meet. To the terror that invests the chairman of a district school board, the Howells ghost adds something of the mystery enveloping a farmer from another township.

Story, *n.* A narrative, commonly untrue. The truth of the stories here following has, however, not been successfully impeached.

One evening Mr. Rudolph Block, of New York, found himself seated at dinner alongside Mr. Percival Pollard, the distinguished critic.

"Mr. Pollard," said he, "my book, *The Biography of a Dead Cow,* is published anonymously, but you can hardly be ignorant of its authorship. Yet in reviewing it you speak of it as the work of the Idiot of the Century. Do you think that fair criticism?"

"I am very sorry, sir," replied the critic, amiably, "but it did not occur to me that you really might not wish the public to know who wrote it."

Mr. W. C. Morrow, who used to live in San Jose, California, was addicted to writing ghost stories which made the reader feel as if a stream of lizards, fresh from the ice, were streaking it up his back and hiding in his hair. San Jose was at that time believed to be haunted by the visible spirit of a noted bandit named Vasquez, who had been hanged there. The town was not very well lighted, and it is putting it mildly to say that San Jose was reluctant to be out o' nights. One particularly dark night two gentlemen were abroad in the loneliest spot within the city limits, talking loudly to keep up their courage, when they came upon Mr. J. J. Owen, a well-known journalist.

"Why, Owen," said one, "what brings you here on such a night as this? You told me that this is one of Vasquez' favorite haunts! And you are a believer. Aren't you afraid to be out?"

"My dear fellow," the journalist replied with a drear autumnal cadence in his speech, like the moan of a leaf-laden wind, "I am afraid to be in. I have one of Will Morrow's stories in my pocket and I don't dare to go where there is light enough to read it."

Rear-Admiral Schley and Representative Charles F. Joy were standing near the Peace Monument, in Washington, discussing the question, Is success a failure? Mr. Joy suddenly broke off in the middle of an eloquent sentence, exclaiming: "Hello! I've heard that band before. Santlemann's, I think."

"I don't hear any band," said Schley.

"Come to think, I don't either," said Joy; "but I see General Miles coming down the avenue, and that pageant always affects me in the same way as a brass band. One has to scrutinize one's impressions pretty closely, or one will mistake their origin."

While the Admiral was digesting this hasty meal of philosophy General Miles passed in review, a spectacle of impressive dignity. When the tail of the seeming procession had passed and the two observers had recovered from the transient blindness caused by its effulgence—

"He seems to be enjoying himself," said the Admiral.

"There is nothing," assented Joy, thoughtfully, "that he enjoys one-half so well."

The illustrious statesman, Champ Clark, once lived about a mile from the village of Jebigue, in Missouri. One day he rode into town on a favorite mule, and, hitching the beast on the sunny side of a street, in front of a saloon, he went inside in his character of teetotaler, to apprise the barkeeper that wine is a mocker. It was a dreadfully hot day. Pretty soon a neighbor came in and seeing Clark, said:

"Champ, it is not right to leave that mule out there in the sun. He'll roast, sure!—he was smoking as I passed him."

"O, he's all right," said Clark, lightly; "he's an inveterate smoker."

The neighbor took a lemonade, but shook his head and repeated that it was not right.

He was a conspirator. There had been a fire the night before: a stable just around the corner had burned and a number of horses had put on their immortality, among them a young colt, which was roasted to a rich nutbrown. Some of the boys had turned Mr. Clark's mule loose and substituted the mortal part of the colt. Presently another man entered the saloon.

"For mercy's sake!" he said, taking it with sugar, "do remove that mule, barkeeper: it smells."

"Yes," interposed Clark, "that animal has the best nose in Missouri. But if he doesn't mind, you shouldn't."

In the course of human events Mr. Clark went out, and there, apparently, lay the incinerated and shrunken remains of his charger. The boys did not have any fun out of Mr. Clark, who looked at the body and, with the non-committal expression to which he owes so much of his political preferment, went away. But walking home late that night he saw his mule standing silent and solemn by the wayside in the misty moonlight. Mentioning the name of Helen Blazes with uncommon emphasis, Mr. Clark took the back track as hard as ever he could hook it, and passed the night in town.

General H. H. Wotherspoon, president of the Army War College, has a pet rib-nosed baboon, an animal of uncommon intelligence but imperfectly beautiful. Returning to his apartment one evening, the General was surprised and pained to find Adam (for so the creature is named, the general being a Darwinian) sitting up for him and wearing his master's best uniform coat, epaulettes and all.

"You confounded remote ancestor!" thundered the great strategist, "what do you mean by being out of bed after taps?—and with my coat on!"

Adam rose and with a reproachful look got down on all fours in the manner of his kind and, scuffling across the room to a table, returned with a visiting-card: General Barry had called and, judging by an empty champagne bottle and several cigar-stumps, had been hospitably entertained while waiting. The general apologized to his faithful progenitor and retired. The next day he met General Barry, who said:

"Spoon, old man, when leaving you last evening I forgot to ask you about those excellent cigars. Where did you get them?"

General Wotherspoon did not deign to reply, but walked away.

"Pardon me, please," said Barry, moving after him; "I was joking of course. Why, I knew it was not you before I had been in the room fifteen minutes."

Success, *n.* The one unpardonable sin against one's fellows. In literature, and particularly in poetry, the elements of success are exceedingly simple, and are admirably set forth in the following lines by the reverend Father Gassalasca Jape, entitled, for some mysterious reason, "John A. Joyce."

> The bard who would prosper must carry a book,
>> Do his thinking in prose and wear
> A crimson cravat, a far-away look
>> And a head of hexameter hair.
> Be thin in your thought and your body'll be fat;
> If you wear your hair long you needn't your hat.

Suffrage, *n.* Expression of opinion by means of a ballot. The right of suffrage (which is held to be both a privilege and a duty) means, as commonly interpreted, the right to vote for the man of another man's choice, and is highly prized. Refusal to do so has the bad name of "incivism." The incivilian, however, cannot be properly arraigned for his crime, for there is no legitimate accuser. If the accuser is himself guilty he has no standing in the court of opinion; if not, he profits by the crime, for A's abstention from voting gives greater weight to the vote of B. By female suffrage is meant the right of a woman to vote as some man tells her to. It is based on female responsibility, which is somewhat limited. The woman most eager to jump out of her petticoat to assert her rights is first to jump back into it when threatened with a switching for misusing them.

Sycophant, *n.* One who approaches Greatness on his belly so that he may not be commanded to turn and be kicked. He is sometimes an editor.

> As the lean leech, its victim found, is pleased
> To fix itself upon a part diseased
> Till, its black hide distended with bad blood,
> It drops to die of surfeit in the mud,
> So the base sycophant with joy descries
> His neighbor's weak spot and his mouth applies,
> Gorges and prospers like the leech, although,
> Unlike that reptile, he will not let go.
> Gelasma, if it paid you to devote
> Your talent to the service of a goat,
> Showing by forceful logic that its beard
> Is more than Aaron's fit to be revered;

If to the task of honoring its smell
Profit had prompted you, and love as well,
The world would benefit at last by you
And wealthy malefactors weep anew—
Your favor for a moment's space denied
And to the nobler object turned aside.
Is't not enough that thrifty millionaires
Who loot in freight and spoliate in fares,
Or, cursed with consciences that bid them fly
To safer villainies of darker dye,
Forswearing robbery and fain, instead,
To steal (they call it "cornering") our bread
May see you groveling their boots to lick
And begging for the favor of a kick?
Still must you follow to the bitter end
Your sycophantic disposition's trend,
And in your eagerness to please the rich
Hunt hungry sinners to their final ditch?
In Morgan's praise you smite the sounding wire,
And sing hosannas to great Havemeyer!
What's Satan done that him you should eschew?
He too is reeking rich—deducting *you*.

Syllogism, *n.* A logical formula consisting of a major and a minor assumption and an inconsequent. (See LOGIC.)

Sylph, *n.* An immaterial but visible being that inhabited the air when the air was an element and before it was fatally polluted by factory smoke, sewer gas and similar products of civilization. Sylphs were allied to gnomes, nymphs and salamanders, which dwelt, respectively, in earth, water and fire, all now insalubrious. Sylphs, like fowls of the air, were male and female, to no purpose, apparently, for if they had progeny they must have nested in inaccessible places, none of the chicks having ever been seen.

Symbol, *n.* Something that is supposed to typify or stand for something else. Many symbols are mere "survivals"—things which having no longer any utility continue to exist because we have inherited the tendency to make them; as funereal urns carved on memorial monuments. They were once real urns holding the ashes of the dead. We cannot stop making them, but we can give them a name that conceals our helplessness.

Symbolic, *adj.* Pertaining to symbols and the use and interpretation of symbols.
They say 'tis conscience feels compunction;
I hold that that's the stomach's function,

For of the sinner I have noted
That when he's sinned he's somewhat bloated,
Or ill some other ghastly fashion
Within that bowel of compassion.
True, I believe the only sinner
Is he that eats a shabby dinner.
You know how Adam with good reason,
For eating apples out of season,
Was "cursed." But that is all symbolic:
The truth is, Adam had the colic.

G. J.

T, the twentieth letter of the English alphabet, was by the Greeks absurdly called *tau*. In the alphabet whence ours comes it had the form of the rude cork-screw of the period, and when it stood alone (which was more than the Phœnicians could always do) signified *Tallegal*, translated by the learned Dr. Brownrigg, "tanglefoot."

Table d'Hôte, *n.* A caterer's thrifty concession to the universal passion for irresponsibility.

> Old Paunchinello, freshly wed,
> Took Madam P. to table,
> And there deliriously fed
> As fast as he was able.
>
> "I dote upon good grub," he cried,
> Intent upon its throatage.
> "Ah, yes," said the neglected bride,
> "You're in your *table d'hôtage.*"
>
> *Associated Poets.*

Tail, *n.* The part of an animal's spine that has transcended its natural limitations to set up an independent existence in a world of its own. Excepting in its fœtal state, Man is without a tail, a privation of which he attests an hereditary and uneasy consciousness by the coat-skirt of the male and the train of the female, and by a marked tendency to ornament that part of his attire where the tail should be, and indubitably once was. This tendency is most observable in the female of the species, in whom the ancestral sense is strong and persistent. The tailed men described by Lord Monboddo are now generally regarded as a product of an imagination unusually susceptible to influences generated in the golden age of our pithecan past.

Take, *v.t.* To acquire, frequently by force but preferably by stealth.

Talk, *v.t.* To commit an indiscretion without temptation, from an impulse without purpose.

Tariff, *n.* A scale of taxes on imports, designed to protect the domestic producer against the greed of his consumer.

> The Enemy of Human Souls
> Sat grieving at the cost of coals;
> For Hell had been annexed of late,
> And was a sovereign Southern State.

> "It were no more than right," said he,
> "That I should get my fuel free.
> The duty, neither just nor wise,
> Compels me to economize—
> Whereby my broilers, every one,
> Are execrably underdone.
> What would they have?—although I yearn
> To do them nicely to a turn,
> I can't afford an honest heat.
> This tariff makes even devils cheat!
> I'm ruined, and my humble trade
> All rascals may at will invade:
> Beneath my nose the public press
> Outdoes me in sulphureousness;
> The bar ingeniously applies
> To my undoing my own lies;
> My medicines the doctors use
> (Albeit vainly) to refuse
> To me my fair and rightful prey
> And keep their own in shape to pay;
> The preachers by example teach
> What, scorning to perform, I preach;
> And statesmen, aping me, all make
> More promises than they can break.
> Against such competition I
> Lift up a disregarded cry.
> Since all ignore my just complaint,
> By Hokey-Pokey! I'll turn saint!"

> Now, the Republicans, who all
> Are saints, began at once to bawl
> Against *his* competition; so
> There was a devil of a go!
> They locked horns with him, tête-à-tête
> In acrimonious debate,

Till Democrats, forlorn and lone,
Had hopes of coming by their own.
That evil to avert, in haste
The two belligerents embraced;
But since 'twere wicked to relax
A tittle of the Sacred Tax,
'Twas finally agreed to grant
The bold Insurgent-protestant
A bounty on each soul that fell
Into his ineffectual Hell.

Edam Smith.

Technicality, *n.* In an English court a man named Home was tried for slander in having accused his neighbor of murder. His exact words were: "Sir Thomas Holt hath taken a cleaver and stricken his cook upon the head, so that one side of the head fell upon one shoulder and the other side upon the other shoulder." The defendant was acquitted by instruction of the court, the learned judges holding that the words did not charge murder, for they did not affirm the death of the cook, that being only an inference.

Tedium, *n.* Ennui, the state or condition of one that is bored. Many fanciful derivations of the word have been affirmed, but so high an authority as Father Jape says that it comes from a very obvious source—the first words of the ancient Latin hymn *Te Deum Laudamus.* In this apparently natural derivation there is something that saddens.

Teetotaler, *n.* One who abstains from strong drink, sometimes totally, sometimes tolerably totally.

Telephone, *n.* An invention of the devil which abrogates some of the advantages of making a disagreeable person keep his distance.

Telescope, *n.* A device having a relation to the eye similar to that of the telephone to the ear, enabling distant objects to plague us with a multitude of needless details. Luckily it is unprovided with a bell summoning us to the sacrifice.

Tenacity, *n.* A certain quality of the human hand in its relation to the coin of the realm. It attains its highest development in the hand of authority and is considered a serviceable equipment for a career in politics. The following illustrative lines were written of a Californian gentleman in high political preferment, who has passed to his accounting:

Of such tenacity his grip
That nothing from his hand can slip.
Well-buttered eels you may o'erwhelm
In tubs of liquid slippery-elm
In vain—from his detaining pinch

They cannot struggle half an inch!
'Tis lucky that he so is planned
That breath he draws not with his hand,
For if he did, so great his greed
He'd draw his last with eager speed.
Nay, that were well, you say. Not so
He'd draw but never let it go!

Theosophy, *n.* An ancient faith having all the certitude of religion and all the mystery of science. The modern Theosophist holds, with the Buddhists, that we live an incalculable number of times on this earth, in as many several bodies, because one life is not long enough for our complete spiritual development; that is, a single lifetime does not suffice for us to become as wise and good as we choose to wish to become. To be absolutely wise and good—that is perfection; and the Theosophist is so keen-sighted as to have observed that everything desirous of improvement eventually attains perfection. Less competent observers are disposed to except cats, which seem neither wiser nor better than they were last year. The greatest and fattest of recent Theosophists was the late Madame Blavatsky, who had no cat.

Tights, *n.* An habiliment of the stage designed to reinforce the general acclamation of the press agent with a particular publicity. Public attention was once somewhat diverted from this garment to Miss Lillian Russell's refusal to wear it, and many were the conjectures as to her motive, the guess of Miss Pauline Hall showing a high order of ingenuity and sustained reflection. It was Miss Hall's belief that nature had not endowed Miss Russell with beautiful legs. This theory was impossible of acceptance by the male understanding, but the conception of a faulty female leg was of so prodigious originality as to rank among the most brilliant feats of philosophical speculation! It is strange that in all the controversy regarding Miss Russell's aversion to tights no one seems to have thought to ascribe it to what was known among the ancients as "modesty." The nature of that sentiment is now imperfectly understood, and possibly incapable of exposition with the vocabulary that remains to us. The study of lost arts has, however, been recently revived and some of the arts themselves recovered. This is an epoch of *renaissances,* and there is ground for hope that the primitive "blush" may be dragged from its hiding-place amongst the tombs of antiquity and hissed on to the stage.

Tomb, *n.* The House of Indifference. Tombs are now by common consent invested with a certain sanctity, but when they have been long tenanted it is considered no sin to break them open and rifle them, the famous Egyptologist, Dr. Huggyns, explaining that a tomb may be innocently "glened" as soon as its occupant is done "smellynge," the soul being then all exhaled.

This reasonable view is now generally accepted by archæologists, whereby the noble science of Curiosity has been greatly dignified.

Tope, *v.* To tipple, booze, swill, soak, guzzle, lush, bib or swig. In the individual, toping is regarded with disesteem, but toping nations are in the forefront of civilization and power. When pitted against the hard-drinking Christians the abstemious Mahometans go down like grass before the scythe. In India one hundred thousand beef-eating and brandy-and-soda-guzzling Britons hold in subjection two hundred and fifty million vegetarian abstainers of the same Aryan race. With what an easy grace the whisky-loving American pushed the temperate Spaniard out of his possessions! From the time when the Berserkers ravaged all the coasts of western Europe and lay drunk in every conquered port it has been the same way: everywhere the nations that drink too much are observed to fight rather well and not too righteously. Wherefore the estimable old ladies who abolished the canteen from the American army may justly boast of having materially augmented the nation's military power.

Tortoise, *n.* A creature thoughtfully created to supply occasion for the following lines by the illustrious Ambat Delaso:

TO MY PET TORTOISE
My friend, you are not graceful—not at all;
Your gait's between a stagger and a sprawl.

Nor are you beautiful: your head's a snake's
To look at, and I do not doubt it aches.

As to your feet, they'd make an angel weep.
'Tis true you take them in whene'er you sleep.

No, you're not pretty, but you have, I own,
A certain firmness—mostly you're backbone.

Firmness and strength (you have a giant's thews)
Are virtues that the great know how to use—

I wish that they did not; yet, on the whole,
You lack—excuse my mentioning it—Soul.

So, to be candid, unreserved and true,
I'd rather you were I than I were you.

Perhaps, however, in a time to be,
When Man's extinct, a better world may see

Your progeny in power and control,
Due to the genesis and growth of Soul.

So I salute you as a reptile grand
Predestined to regenerate the land.

Father of Possibilities, O deign
To accept the homage of a dying reign!

In the far region of the unforeknown
I dream a tortoise upon every throne.

I see an Emperor his head withdraw
Into his carapace for fear of Law;

A King who carries something else than fat,
Howe'er acceptably he carries that;

A President not strenuously bent
On punishment of audible dissent—

Who never shot (it were a vain attack)
An armed or unarmed tortoise in the back;

Subjects and citizens that feel no need
To make the March of Mind a wild stampede;

All progress slow, contemplative, sedate,
And "Take your time" the word, in Church and State.

O Tortoise, 'tis a happy, happy dream,
My glorious testudinous régime!

I wish in Eden you'd brought this about
By slouching in and chasing Adam out.

Tree, *n.* A tall vegetable intended by nature to serve as a penal apparatus, though through a miscarriage of justice most trees bear only a negligible fruit, or none at all. When naturally fruited, the tree is a beneficent agency of civilization and an important factor in public morals. In the stern West and the sensitive South its fruit (white and black respectively), though not eaten, is agreeable to the public taste and, though not exported, profitable to the general welfare. That the legitimate relation of the tree to justice was no discovery of Judge Lynch (who, indeed, conceded it no primacy over the lamppost and the bridge-girder) is made plain by the following passage from Morryster, who antedated him by two centuries:

> While in yᵗ londe I was carried to see yᵉ Ghogo tree, whereof I had hearde moch talk; but sayynge yᵗ I saw naught remarkabyll in it, yᵉ hed manne of yᵉ villayge where it grewe made answer as followeth:

"Yᵉ tree is not nowe in fruite, but in his seasonne you shall see dependynge fr. his braunches all soch as have affroynted yᵉ King his Majesty."

And I was furder tolde yᵗ yᵉ worde "Ghogo" sygnifyeth in yʳ tong yᵉ same as "rapscal" in our owne. — *Trauvells in yᵉ Easte.*

Trial, *n.* A formal inquiry designed to prove and put upon record the blameless characters of judges, advocates and jurors. In order to effect this purpose it is necessary to supply a contrast in the person of one who is called the defendant, the prisoner or the accused. If the contrast is made sufficiently clear this person is made to undergo such an affliction as will give the virtuous gentlemen a comfortable sense of their immunity, added to that of their worth. In our day the accused is usually a human being, or a socialist, but in mediæval times, animals, fishes, reptiles and insects were brought to trial. A beast that had taken human life, or practiced sorcery, was duly arrested, tried and, if condemned, put to death by the public executioner. Insects ravaging grain fields, orchards or vineyards were cited to appeal by counsel before a civil tribunal, and after testimony, argument and condemnation, if they continued *in contumaciam* the matter was taken to a high ecclesiastical court, where they were solemnly excommunicated and anathematized. In a street of Toledo, some pigs that had wickedly run between the viceroy's legs, upsetting him, were arrested on a warrant, tried and punished. In Naples an ass was condemned to be burned at the stake, but the sentence appears not to have been executed. D'Addosio relates from the court records many trials of pigs, bulls, horses, cocks, dogs, goats, etc., greatly, it is believed, to the betterment of their conduct and morals. In 1451 a suit was brought against the leeches infesting some ponds about Berne, and the Bishop of Lausanne, instructed by the faculty of Heidelberg University, directed that some of "the aquatic worms" be brought before the local magistracy. This was done and the leeches, both present and absent, were ordered to leave the places that they had infested within three days on pain of incurring "the malediction of God." In the voluminous records of this *cause célèbre* nothing is found to show whether the offenders braved the punishment, or departed forthwith out of that inhospitable jurisdiction.

Trichinosis, *n.* The pig's reply to proponents of porcophagy.

Moses Mendelssohn having fallen ill sent for a Christian physician, who at once diagnosed the philosopher's disorder as trichinosis, but tactfully gave it another name. "You need an immediate change of diet," he said; "you must eat six ounces of pork every other day."

"Pork?" shrieked the patient—"pork? Nothing shall induce me to touch it!"

"Do you mean that?" the doctor gravely asked.

"I swear it!"

"Good!—then I will undertake to cure you."

Trinity, *n*. In the multiplex theism of certain Christian churches, three entirely distinct deities consistent with only one. Subordinate deities of the polytheistic faith, such as devils and angels, are not dowered with the power of combination, and must urge individually their claims to adoration and propitiation. The Trinity is one of the most sublime mysteries of our holy religion. In rejecting it because it is incomprehensible, Unitarians betray their inadequate sense of theological fundamentals. In religion we believe only what we do not understand, except in the instance of an intelligible doctrine that contradicts an incomprehensible one. In that case we believe the former as a part of the latter.

Troglodyte, *n*. Specifically, a cave-dweller of the paleolithic period, after the Tree and before the Flat. A famous community of troglodytes dwelt with David in the Cave of Adullam. The colony consisted of "every one that was in distress, and every one that was in debt, and every one that was discontented"—in brief, all the Socialists of Judah.

Truce, *n*. Friendship.

Trust, *n*. In American politics, a large corporation composed in greater part of thrifty working men, widows of small means, orphans in the care of guardians and the courts, with many similar malefactors and public enemies.

Truth, *n*. An ingenious compound of desirability and appearance. Discovery of truth is the sole purpose of philosophy, which is the most ancient occupation of the human mind and has a fair prospect of existing with increasing activity to the end of time.

Truthful, *adj*. Dumb and illiterate.

Turkey, *n*. A large bird whose flesh when eaten on certain religious anniversaries has the peculiar property of attesting piety and gratitude. Incidentally, it is pretty good eating.

Twice, *adv*. Once too often.

Type, *n*. Pestilent bits of metal suspected of destroying civilization and enlightenment, despite their obvious agency in this incomparable dictionary.

Tzetze (or Tsetse) Fly, *n*. An African insect (*Glossina morsitans*) whose bite is commonly regarded as nature's most efficacious remedy for insomnia, though some patients prefer that of the American novelist (*Mendax interminabilis*).

Ubiquity, *n.* The gift or power of being in all places at one time, but not in all places at all times, which is omnipresence, an attribute of God and the luminiferous ether only. This important distinction between ubiquity and omnipresence was not clear to the mediæval Church and there was much bloodshed about it. Certain Lutherans, who affirmed the presence everywhere of Christ's body, were known as Ubiquitarians. For this error they were doubtless damned, for Christ's body is present only in the eucharist, though that sacrament may be performed in more than one place simultaneously. In recent times ubiquity has not always been understood—not even by Sir Boyle Roche, for example, who held that a man cannot be in two places at once unless he is a bird.

Ugliness, *n.* A gift of the gods to certain women, entailing virtue without humility.

Ultimatum, *n.* In diplomacy, a last demand before resorting to concessions.

Having received an ultimatum from Austria, the Turkish Ministry met to consider it.

"O servant of the Prophet," said the Sheik of the Imperial Chibouk to the Mamoosh of the Invincible Army, "how many unconquerable soldiers have we in arms?"

"Upholder of the Faith," that dignitary replied after examining his memoranda, "they are in numbers as the leaves of the forest!"

"And how many impenetrable battleships strike terror to the hearts of all Christian swine?" he asked the Imaum of the Ever Victorious Navy.

"Uncle of the Full Moon," was the reply, "deign to know that they are as the waves of the ocean, the sands of the desert and the stars of Heaven!"

For eight hours the broad brow of the Sheik of the Imperial Chibouk was corrugated with evidences of deep thought: he was calculating the chances of war. Then, "Sons of angels," he said, "the die is cast! I shall suggest to the Ulema of the Imperial Ear that he advise inaction. In the name of Allah, the council is adjourned."

Un-American, *adj*. Wicked, intolerable, heathenish.

Unction, *n*. An oiling, or greasing. The rite of extreme unction consists in touching with oil consecrated by a bishop several parts of the body of one engaged in dying. Marbury relates that after the rite had been administered to a certain wicked English nobleman it was discovered that the oil had not been properly consecrated and no other could be obtained. When informed of this the sick man said in anger: "Then I'll be damned if I die!"

"My son," said the priest, "this is what we fear."

Understanding, *n*. A cerebral secretion that enables one having it to know a house from a horse by the roof on the house. Its nature and laws have been exhaustively expounded by Locke, who rode a house, and Kant, who lived in a horse.

> His understanding was so keen
> That all things which he'd felt, heard, seen,
> He could interpret without fail
> If he was in or out of jail.
> He wrote at Inspiration's call
> Deep disquisitions on them all,
> Then, pent at last in an asylum,
> Performed the service to compile 'em.
> So great a writer, all men swore,
> They never had not read before.
>
> *Jorrock Wormley.*

Unitarian, *n*. One who denies the divinity of a Trinitarian.

Universalist, *n*. One who foregoes the advantage of a Hell for persons of another faith.

Urbanity, *n*. The kind of civility that urban observers ascribe to dwellers in all cities but New York. Its commonest expression is heard in the words, "I beg your pardon," and it is not inconsistent with disregard of the rights of others.

> The owner of a powder mill
> Was musing on a distant hill—
>   Something his mind foreboded—
> When from the cloudless sky there fell
> A deviled human kidney! Well,
>   The man's mill had exploded.
> His hat he lifted from his head;
> "I beg your pardon, sir," he said;
>   "I didn't know 'twas loaded."
>
> *Swatkin.*

Usage, *n.* The First Person of the literary Trinity, the Second and Third being Custom and Conventionality. Imbued with a decent reverence for this Holy Triad an industrious writer may hope to produce books that will live as long as the fashion.

Uxoriousness, *n.* A perverted affection that has strayed to one's own wife.

Valor, *n*. A soldierly compound of vanity, duty and the gambler's hope.

"Why have you halted?" roared the commander of a division at Chickamauga, who had ordered a charge; "move forward, sir, at once."

"General," said the commander of the delinquent brigade, "I am persuaded that any further display of valor by my troops will bring them into collision with the enemy."

Vanity, *n*. The tribute of a fool to the worth of the nearest ass.

> They say that hens do cackle loudest when
> > There's nothing vital in the eggs they've laid;
> > And there are hens, professing to have made
> A study of mankind, who say that men
> Whose business 'tis to drive the tongue or pen
> > Make the most clamorous fanfaronade
> > O'er their most worthless work; and I'm afraid
> They're not entirely different from the hen.
> Lo! the drum-major in his coat of gold,
> > His blazing breeches and high-towering cap—
> Imperiously pompous, grandly bold,
> > Grim, resolute, an awe-inspiring chap!
> Who'd think this gorgeous creature's only virtue
> Is that in battle he will never hurt you?
>
> > > > *Hannibal Hunsiker.*

Virtues, *n.pl.* Certain abstentions.

Vituperation, *n*. Satire, as understood by dunces and all such as suffer from an impediment in their wit.

Vote, *n*. The instrument and symbol of a freeman's power to make a fool of himself and a wreck of his country.

W (double U) has, of all the letters in our alphabet, the only cumbrous name, the names of the others being monosyllabic. This advantage of the Roman alphabet over the Grecian is the more valued after audibly spelling out some simple Greek word, like ἐπιχοριαμβικός. Still, it is now thought by the learned that other agencies than the difference of the two alphabets may have been concerned in the decline of "the glory that was Greece" and the rise of "the grandeur that was Rome." There can be no doubt, however, that by simplifying the name of W (calling it "wow," for example) our civilization could be, if not promoted, at least better endured.

Wall Street, *n*. A symbol of sin for every devil to rebuke. That Wall Street is a den of thieves is a belief that serves every unsuccessful thief in place of a hope in Heaven. Even the great and good Andrew Carnegie has made his profession of faith in the matter.

> Carnegie the dauntless has uttered his call
> To battle: "The brokers are parasites all!"
> Carnegie, Carnegie, you'll never prevail;
> Keep the wind of your slogan to belly your sail,
> Go back to your isle of perpetual brume,
> Silence your pibroch, doff tartan and plume:
> Ben Lomond is calling his son from the fray —
> Fly, fly from the region of Wall Street away!
> While still you're possessed of a single baubee
> (I wish it were pledged to endowment of me)
> 'Twere wise to retreat from the wars of finance
> Lest its value decline ere your credit advance.
> For a man 'twixt a king of finance and the sea,
> Carnegie, Carnegie, your tongue is too free!
>
> *Anonymus Bink.*

War, *n*. A by-product of the arts of peace. The most menacing political condition is a period of international amity. The student of history who has not been taught to expect the unexpected may justly boast himself inaccessible to the light. "In time of peace prepare for war" has a deeper meaning than is commonly discerned; it means, not merely that all things earthly have an end — that change is the one immutable and eternal law — but that the soil of peace is thickly sown with the seeds of war and singularly suited to their germination and growth. It was when Kubla Khan had decreed his "stately pleasure dome" — when, that is to say, there were peace and fat feasting in Xanadu — that he

> heard from afar
> Ancestral voices prophesying war.

One of the greatest of poets, Coleridge was one of the wisest of men, and it was not for nothing that he read us this parable. Let us have a little less of "hands across the sea," and a little more of that elemental distrust that is the security of nations. War loves to come like a thief in the night; professions of eternal amity provide the night.

Washingtonian, *n.* A Potomac tribesman who exchanged the privilege of governing himself for the advantage of good government. In justice to him it should be said that he did not want to.

> They took away his vote and gave instead
> The right, when he had earned, to *eat* his bread.
> In vain — he clamors for his "boss," poor soul,
> To come again and part him from his roll.
>
> *Offenbach Stutz.*

Weaknesses, *n.pl.* Certain primal powers of Tyrant Woman wherewith she holds dominion over the male of her species, binding him to the service of her will and paralyzing his rebellious energies.

Weather, *n.* The climate of an hour. A permanent topic of conversation among persons whom it does not interest, but who have inherited the tendency to chatter about it from naked arboreal ancestors whom it keenly concerned. The setting up of official weather bureaus and their maintenance in mendacity prove that even governments are accessible to suasion by the rude forefathers of the jungle.

> Once I dipt into the future far as human eye could see,
> And I saw the Chief Forecaster, dead as any one can be —
> Dead and damned and shut in Hades as a liar from his birth,
> With a record of unreason seldom paralleled on earth.
> While I looked he reared him solemnly, that incandescent youth,
> From the coals that he'd preferred to the advantages of truth.
> He cast his eyes about him and above him; then he wrote
> On a slab of thin asbestos what I venture here to quote —

For I read it in the rose-light of the everlasting glow:

"Cloudy; variable winds, with local showers; cooler; snow."

Halcyon Jones.

Wedding, *n.* A ceremony at which two persons undertake to become one, one undertakes to become nothing, and nothing undertakes to become supportable.

Werewolf, *n.* A wolf that was once, or is sometimes, a man. All werewolves are of evil disposition, having assumed a bestial form to gratify a bestial appetite, but some, transformed by sorcery, are as humane as is consistent with an acquired taste for human flesh.

Some Bavarian peasants having caught a wolf one evening, tied it to a post by the tail and went to bed. The next morning nothing was there! Greatly perplexed, they consulted the local priest, who told them that their captive was undoubtedly a werewolf and had resumed its human form during the night. "The next time that you take a wolf," the good man said, "see that you chain it by the leg, and in the morning you will find a Lutheran."

Whangdepootenawah, *n.* In the Ojibwa tongue, disaster; an unexpected affliction that strikes hard.

Should you ask me whence this laughter,
Whence this audible big-smiling,
With its labial extension,
With its maxillar distortion
And its diaphragmic rhythmus
Like the billowing of an ocean,
Like the shaking of a carpet,
I should answer, I should tell you:
From the great deeps of the spirit,
From the unplummeted abysmus
Of the soul this laughter welleth
As the fountain, the gug-guggle,
Like the river from the cañon,
To entoken and give warning
That my present mood is sunny.
Should you ask me further question —
Why the great deeps of the spirit,
Why the unplummeted abysmus
Of the soul extrudes this laughter,
This all audible big-smiling,
I should answer, I should tell you
With a white heart, tumpitumpy,

With a true tongue, honest Injun:
William Bryan, he has Caught It,
Caught the Whangdepootenawah!

Is't the sandhill crane, the shankank,
Standing in the marsh, the kneedeep,
Standing silent in the kneedeep
With his wing-tips crossed behind him
And his neck close-reefed before him,
With his bill, his william, buried
In the down upon his bosom,
With his head retracted inly,
While his shoulders overlook it?
Does the sandhill crane, the shankank,
Shiver grayly in the north wind,
Wishing he had died when little,
As the sparrow, the chipchip, does?
No 'tis not the shankank standing,
Standing in the gray and dismal
Marsh, the gray and dismal kneedeep.
No, 'tis peerless William Bryan
Realizing that he's Caught It,
Caught the Whangdepootenawah!

Wheat, *n*. A cereal from which a tolerably good whisky can with some difficulty be made, and which is used also for bread. The French are said to eat more bread *per capita* of population than any other people, which is natural, for only they know how to make the stuff palatable.

White, *adj*. and *n*. Black.

Widow, *n*. A pathetic figure that the Christian world has agreed to take humorously, although Christ's tenderness toward widows was one of the most marked features of his character.

Wine, *n*. Fermented grape-juice known to the Women's Christian Union as "liquor," sometimes as "rum." Wine, madam, is God's next best gift to man.

Wit, *n*. The salt with which the American humorist spoils his intellectual cookery by leaving it out.

Witch, *n*. 1. An ugly and repulsive old woman, in a wicked league with the devil. 2. A beautiful and attractive young woman, in wickedness a league beyond the devil.

Witticism, *n*. A sharp and clever remark, usually quoted, and seldom noted; what the Philistine is pleased to call a "joke."

Woman, *n.* An animal usually living in the vicinity of Man, and having a rudimentary susceptibility to domestication. It is credited by many of the elder zoölogists with a certain vestigial docility acquired in a former state of seclusion, but naturalists of the postsusananthony period, having no knowledge of the seclusion, deny the virtue and declare that such as creation's dawn beheld, it roareth now. The species is the most widely distributed of all beasts of prey, infesting all habitable parts of the globe, from Greenland's spicy mountains to India's moral strand. The popular name (wolf-man) is incorrect, for the creature is of the cat kind. The woman is lithe and graceful in its movements, especially the American variety (*Felis pugnans*), is omnivorous and can be taught not to talk. — *Balthasar Pober.*

Worms'-meat, *n.* The finished product of which we are the raw material. The contents of the Taj Mahal, the Tombeau Napoleon and the Grantarium. Worms'-meat is usually outlasted by the structure that houses it, but "this too must pass away." Probably the silliest work in which a human being can engage is construction of a tomb for himself. The solemn purpose cannot dignify, but only accentuates by contrast the foreknown futility.

> Ambitious fool! so mad to be a show!
> How profitless the labor you bestow
>   Upon a dwelling whose magnificence
> The tenant neither can admire nor know.
>
> Build deep, build high, build massive as you can,
> The wanton grass-roots will defeat the plan
>   By shouldering asunder all the stones
> In what to you would be a moment's span.
>
> Time to the dead so all unreckoned flies
> That when your marble is all dust, arise,
>   If wakened, stretch your limbs and yawn —
> You'll think you scarcely can have closed your eyes.
>
> What though of all man's works your tomb alone
> Should stand till Time himself be overthrown?
>   Would it advantage you to dwell therein
> Forever as a stain upon a stone?
>
>   *Joel Huck.*

Worship, *n.* Homo Creator's testimony to the sound construction and fine finish of Deus Creatus. A popular form of abjection, having an element of pride.

Wrath, *n.* Anger of a superior quality and degree, appropriate to exalted characters and momentous occasions; as, "the wrath of God," "the day of wrath," etc. Amongst the ancients the wrath of kings was deemed sacred, for it could usually command the agency of some god for its fit manifestation, as could also that of a priest. The Greeks before Troy were so harried by Apollo that they jumped out of the frying-pan of the wrath of Chryses into the fire of the wrath of Achilles, though Agamemnon, the sole offender, was neither fried nor roasted. A similar noted immunity was that of David when he incurred the wrath of Yahveh by numbering his people, seventy thousand of whom paid the penalty with their lives. God is now Love, and a director of the census performs his work without apprehension of disaster.

X in our alphabet being a needless letter has an added invincibility to the attacks of the spelling reformers, and like them, will doubtless last as long as the language. X is the sacred symbol of ten dollars, and in such words as Xmas, Xn, etc., stands for Christ, not, as is popularly supposed, because it represents a cross, but because the corresponding letter in the Greek alphabet is the initial of his name— Χριστός. If it represented a cross it would stand for St. Andrew, who "testified" upon one of that shape. In the algebra of psychology *x* stands for Woman's mind. Words beginning with X are Grecian and will not be defined in this standard English dictionary.

Yankee, *n.* In Europe, an American. In the Northern States of our Union, a New Englander. In the Southern States the word is unknown. (See DAMYANK.)

Year, *n.* A period of three hundred and sixty-five disappointments.

Yesterday, *n.* The infancy of youth, the youth of manhood, the entire past of age.

> But yesterday I should have thought me blest
> To stand high-pinnacled upon the peak
> Of middle life and look adown the bleak
> And unfamiliar foreslope to the West,
> Where solemn shadows all the land invest
> And stilly voices, half-remembered, speak
> Unfinished prophecy, and witch-fires freak
> The haunted twilight of the Dark of Rest.
> Yea, yesterday my soul was all aflame
> To stay the shadow on the dial's face
> At manhood's noonmark! Now, in God His name
> I chide aloud the little interspace
> Disparting me from Certitude, and fain
> Would know the dream and vision ne'er again.
>
> *Baruch Arnegriff.*

It is said that in his last illness the poet Arnegriff was attended at different times by seven doctors.

Yoke, *n.* An implement, madam, to whose Latin name, *jugum,* we owe one of the most illuminating words in our language—a word that defines the matrimonial situation with precision, point and poignancy. A thousand apologies for withholding it.

Youth, *n.* The Period of Possibility, when Archimedes finds a fulcrum, Cassandra has a following and seven cities compete for the honor of endowing a living Homer.

Youth is the true Saturnian Reign, the Golden Age on earth again, when figs are grown on thistles, and pigs betailed with whistles and, wearing silken bristles, live ever in clover, and cows fly over, delivering milk at every door, and Justice never is heard to snore, and every assassin is made a ghost and, howling, is cast into Baltimost! — *Polydore Smith.*

Zany, *n.* A popular character in old Italian plays, who imitated with ludicrous incompetence the *buffone,* or clown, and was therefore the ape of an ape; for the clown himself imitated the serious characters of the play. The zany was progenitor to the specialist in humor, as we to-day have the unhappiness to know him. In the zany we see an example of creation; in the humorist, of transmission. Another excellent specimen of the modern zany is the curate, who apes the rector, who apes the bishop, who apes the archbishop, who apes the devil.

Zanzibari, *n.* An inhabitant of the Sultanate of Zanzibar, off the eastern coast of Africa. The Zanzibaris, a warlike people, are best known in this country through a threatening diplomatic incident that occurred a few years ago. The American consul at the capital occupied a dwelling that faced the sea, with a sandy beach between. Greatly to the scandal of this official's family, and against repeated remonstrances of the official himself, the people of the city persisted in using the beach for bathing. One day a woman came down to the edge of the water and was stooping to remove her attire (a pair of sandals) when the consul, incensed beyond restraint, fired a charge of bird-shot into the most conspicuous part of her person. Unfortunately for the existing *entente cordiale* between two great nations, she was the Sultana.

Zeal, *n.* A certain nervous disorder afflicting the young and inexperienced. A passion that goeth before a sprawl.

> When Zeal sought Gratitude for his reward
> He went away exclaiming: "O my Lord!"
> "What do you want?" the Lord asked, bending down.
> "An ointment for my cracked and bleeding crown."
> *Jum Coople.*

Zenith, *n.* The point in the heavens directly overhead to a standing man or a growing cabbage. A man in bed or a cabbage in the pot is not considered as having a zenith, though from this view of the matter there was once a considerable dissent among the learned, some holding that the posture of the body was immaterial. These were called Horizontalists, their opponents, Verticalists. The Horizontalist heresy was finally extinguished by Xanobus, the philosopher-king of Abara, a zealous Verticalist. Entering an assembly of philosophers who were debating the matter, he cast a severed human head at the feet of his opponents and asked them to determine its zenith, explaining that its body was hanging by the heels outside. Observing that it was the head of their leader, the Horizontalists hastened to profess themselves converted to whatever opinion the Crown might be pleased to hold, and Horizontalism took its place among *fides defuncti*.

Zeus, *n.* The chief of Grecian gods, adored by the Romans as Jupiter and by the modern Americans as God, Gold, Mob and Dog. Some explorers who have touched upon the shores of America, and one who professes to have penetrated a considerable distance to the interior, have thought that these four names stand for as many distinct deities, but in his monumental work on Surviving Faiths, Frumpp insists that the natives are monotheists, each having no other god than himself, whom he worships under many sacred names.

Zigzag, *v.t.* To move forward uncertainly, from side to side, as one carrying the white man's burden. (From *zed*, z, and *jag*, an Icelandic word of unknown meaning.)

> He zedjagged so uncomen wyde
> Thet non coude pas on eyder syde;
> So, to com saufly thruh, I been
> Constreynet for to doodge betwene.

> *Munwele.*

Zoölogy, *n.* The science and history of the animal kingdom, including its king, the House Fly (*Musca maledicta*). The father of Zoölogy was Aristotle, as is universally conceded, but the name of its mother has not come down to us. Two of the science's most illustrious expounders were Buffon and Oliver Goldsmith, from both of whom we learn (*L'Histoire générale des animaux* and *A History of Animated Nature*) that the domestic cow sheds its horns every two years.

A. SUPPLEMENTARY DEFINITIONS

The items in this section are from an envelope found among the Ambrose Bierce Papers at the Bancroft Library, University of California, Berkeley, labeled in Bierce's hand, "From which to select and prepare additions to 'The Devil's Dictionary' if needed." All the clippings except nine have names of definitions to which they might apply (Bierce supplied names to items not previously published originally as definitions). Because the intent of this edition of *The Devil's Dictionary* is to include all uncollected definitions, the clippings extracted from Bierce's "Devil's Dictionary" and "Cynic's Dictionary" columns are found in the text proper and are not reprinted below. They are Chase ~~Sport~~ (verses only in clipping from "The Devil's Dictionary"; in text with "Hunt" as originally published), Covet, Crest, Etiquette, Fly, Free-trade, Griffin, Grime, Horse, Incubate, Innocence, Insolvent, Inspiration, Logic (verses only in clipping from "The Cynic's Dictionary"), and Platter. Sources are identified in the Bibliography.

A1. Ambition.

David Alexander Hogshead has petitioned the Superior Court for a change of name to David Alexander Hodghead. — *Local Item.*

David Alexander Hogshead,
Once a discontented frog said:
"I will be a frog no more —
Call me a bird." But still in flying
He would light, despite his trying,
    Quite as quickly as before.
Still his toes were joined by leathers:
"I'm a duck," said he; but feathers,
        On his body,
        Cold and poddy,

Sprouted not to coat him o'er;
    And his head was still a frog's head,
    David Alexander Hogshead.

A2. Blasphemy.

Listen while the tale I tell
    Of a judgment and disaster
Which but recently befell
    One Lemay, who cursed his master.

In New Haven lived Lemay,
    And in divers other places,
And his name another way
    Frequently the story graces.

One short year ago 'twas Brown.
    In the previous December
He resided in the town
    Of Topeka, I remember.

But Lemay, as I explained,
    Met with a divine disaster;
For religion he disdained—
    Cared not for it one piastre.

For one hundred years or more
    He in sundry press dispatches
He's been scoffing, o'er and o'er—
    Incurring Heaven's slaps and scratches!

Sometimes (see above) by name
    One thing, sometimes quite another;
All depends upon the dame
    Who may chance to be his mother.

Fifty cities claim his birth—
    Or at least he has his dwelling
In them while upon the earth
    He's blaspheming and rebelling.

So, as I've already said,
    Tuesday last ('twas in New Haven)
This human chestnut reared his head,
    Croaking curses like a raven!

Blasphemies were on his tongue,
  Dreadful, horrible, unlawful;
And the way that sinner flung
  Insults at the Church was awful!

One would think he would have learned
  Long ago that nothing worse is
Than disaster that is earned
  By impenitential curses.

But he didn't, and the wire
  Tells again the same old story:
How his damnatory fire
  He flung round him *con amore;*

How his curses were like flames,
  As he hurled them at religion
And in all the devils' names
  Scorched it like a roasted pigeon.

Then, approaching as he spoke,
  Paralysis without resistance
Struck him a terrific stroke,
  Audible at quite a distance.

Never since, so runs the tale
  (All the versions here agreeing),
Has the man had speech to rail
  Like a normal human being.

But I'm told the wicked cuss
  Lately is engaged in writing
Books on books so blasphemous
  That they truly are affrighting!

A3. Broker.
  A lady, so the papers say—
They tell it, though, another way—
Was following her little feet
The other morning down the street,
Scanning the gilded figures o'er
Each honest broker's open door.
At last she found the web she sought,
Stretched hospitably broad and taut,

And flew against it—pardon: I
Forgot; a lady's not a fly.
I meant to say she did not shun
The place, but entered, saying to one
Who sat behind a sparkling pin:
"Good morning. Is the broker in?"
Suspending civilly his work
Upon his nails, that gorgeous clerk
(Indulge me, though, in the remark
That it is English to say clark)
Said "Nope," and pointed to a chair,
With the politeness of a bear.
Good manners ('tis a saying old
And wise) are worth their weight in gold.
The lady stood with absent mind
Against the counter, while behind
Her, all unheeded, passed the rout
Of clients, going in and out—
All kinds of persons: fat and lean,
Renowned, obscure, unthrifty, mean.
One was a Justice of the Peace,
And one was known to the police.
Ah! what a bitter cry arose!
The lady—see how pale she grows.
"O Lord!" she clamored in high C;
"I've lost my purse. O goodness me!
I had it in my hand when I
Came in. They've stolen it. O my!"
Then growing calmer by the flow
Of tears that dampened down her woe,
She ceased the shriek and smiled instead,
A bitter, bitter smile and said
To him behind the sparkling pin:
"You said the broker wasn't in!"

A4. Chaplain.

That recalls another anecdote. Soon after the close of the Civil War
the nameless commander of a regiment without a number was accosted
in New York by a sleek-looking person who introduced himself and shook
hands with effusion. "And have we met before?" the Colonel asked. "I
was Chaplain of the Eleventieth Pennsyltucky," was the reply; "we were

under fire together at Fishfield." "Ah, yes, I recollect the incident," said the other. "Thank you for setting me right. I have always believed you to be a rabbit."

A5. Co-defendant.

"Lo! the bad Prattler, with a mind malign,
All things attacking, human and divine!"
So cries good Pixley, proving the attack
By the false witness of his private back,
As an ass thinks, for trumpeting when bruised,
Musicians all are beaten and abused.

A6. Crossroad.

Professor Fred Bell has taken for the subject of his to-morrow evening's lecture at Metropolitan Temple "The Suicide of May Brookyn. From a Spiritualistic Standpoint." — *The Evening Post.*

The midnight gloom, the cross-roads tomb,
    The stake well hammered in,
Did once attest, Lord, thy behest
    Against the mortal sin.

Times change: to-day the dead we lay,
    Who by their own hands die,
In holy earth, and of their worth
    Thy servants, Father, lie. [. . .]

A7. Dialect.

When age benumbs him and his failing sense
Bewails his loss of power and renown—
Unable or to please or give offence;
When lifelong prodigality has wrecked
His purse and he is hooted of the town,
Which threatens him with charity as well,
And even prays for him; of self-respect
No vestige left, for God no reverence;
When senile cowardice and impotence
Of will and work forbid him to go drown;
When he's forgotten how to speak or spell—
Mumbling and chortling, all his bosom flecked
With drivel—what can a poor mortal do,
The wolf to baffle and the devil, too,
But, with a vain and tardy providence,
Write for the magazines in dialect?

A8. Duel.

THE MOUNTAIN IN LABOR.

The courage and chivalry of the ages, the romantic traditions of the field of honor, the history of the ordeal of combat—all the influences and suasions that spring from the duello and go broading through the thoughts and lives of men, to stir them to words of courtesy and deeds of daring in assertion of the right and its enforcement by feats of arms, centered their purposes and converged their powers and benign energies to the production of a champion who should restore the ancient and honorable régime. The World stood afar off, holding its breath, and Expectation fastened her eyes upon the luminous focus of those streams of spirit. And slowly thence evolving in visible genesis, lo, that son of thunder, Preskie Belknap!

A9. Eloquence (1).

[. . . San] Francisco is a suitable place to hold the next National convention. General Barnes, I believe, is the greatest living master of the art of putting the left arm under the coat tails and splitting the air straight downward with the edge of the right hand.

A10. Fallible.

On an isle of the Peaceful Sea,
Is the Fallible Filipee.
    The fellow infers
    (But he widely errs)
That he has the distinction to be.

He says: "The top entitee
Of the scale of being—that's me!"
    But his mind is linked
    To untruth. Extinct
In the land of his birth is he.

Now Otis comes over the sea,
Red handed, a great grandee!
    McArthur remains
    To efface the stains
Of the Fallible Filipee.

But something (O, what can it be?)
Disturbs the serenitee
    Of the men that mop
    The spot. They stop,
Remarking aloud: "Hully Gee!"

A11. Heresy.

A deal of nonsense is in process of utterance by sinners of the secular press, anent trials for "heresy," in the churches. To the untutored mind of the worldling the word "heresy" is loaded with awful suggestion, reminiscent of Fox's fat volume of "Christian Martyrs," wherein it is related that trials for heresy were commonly followed by the cooking of the accused, or his bisection with a saw, or the removal of his boweling to another place, himself unmoved. As he was always a most worthy man, and his judges were prelates of conspicuous malignity, instigated by the gory tyrant at Rome, the impression is given distinctly favorable to the conception of heresy as a glittering virtue, inviting to the tooth of persecution. Whereby the worthy worldling, problematically devout but indubitably Protestant, is sadly misled.

A trial for heresy, my fellow travelers of the broad road leading from the light, is not held with a view to determining unworth, but unfitness. Of the truth or falsity of the doctrines expounded by the accused it has nothing directly to say; it concerns itself only with their consistency with those which he professes and has undertaken to uphold. Your modern heretic is not a person striving for religious liberty, but one who is false to professions freely made and obligations voluntarily assumed. His offense is of the nature of a breach of trust, and his expulsion (if he is expelled) is not punishment, but assertion of a natural right by denial of a dishonest advantage to one who violates the letter and spirit of a contract. To the right of organization that of expulsion is as necessary as that of exclusion; without expulsion for heresy there would be no churches at all—in the contemplation of the which appalling possibility "I weeps extreme."

A12. History.

German critics are making much of Zola's inaccuracies and inveracities in his account of the battle at Sedan, and calling on the military authorities to put them down. This is ridiculous; it is of no importance what occurred at Sedan, but when such a man as Zola writes it is of capital importance that he say what he will. Students of history are not going to him for their profitless knowledge; they want the plain unvarnished tale of the mousing dullard. Does it matter that Waterloo was not fought in the way that Hugo imagined it? Would we willingly give up his sunken road of Ohain because it did not exist, or his Cambronne because the actual Cambronne was not a blackguard? It is not known that events at the siege of Troy by the cowards and savages of Agamemnon's following occurred as Homer relates them; it is not even known that there was a siege of Troy. Is the Iliad less precious for that? Suppose there was a siege of Troy and suppose a papyrus were discovered whereon a Trojan eye-witness had uttered the mind of him in austere reprobation of Homer's inaccuracies, pointing out that Diomed did not inflict a wound upon Venus, nor Achilles' horses have a word to say, that Æneas was not there, and that Hector footed it featly about the walls of the city only twice. Who but an historian would care for all that? Historical events are valuable only as suggestions to great writers and great artists. For anything else it does not matter who beat at Salamis or Lepanto, which side John Sobieski fought on at Vienna, nor how many Frenchmen laid down their legs at Sedan.

Anyhow, we can never know the truth about such matters; and in point of picturesqueness the falsehoods of fiction are far and away superior to those of history. In holding that Roman history was nine-tenths lying, Niebuhr was nine-tenths right; to have been wholly right he needed only to add that Roman history's remaining tenth was lying too. And that is what ails all history—which may be defined as a false account of crimes not worth telling.

A13. Horn ~~Punctuation~~.

The correspondent of a contemporary wants to know the meaning of an interrogation point parenthetically appended to certain statements in print, thus: (?). Dear man, have you not heard the phrase "in a horn?" For examples: Mr. Fitch is made in the image of his Maker—in a horn; Fleet Strother is a great statesman—in a horn, etc. In the early ages of printing it was customary to mark ironical statements with a point resembling a cow's horn, the sentence appearing to run into it. Many of the old printers being destitute of the point they substituted the note of interrogation as the one most nearly resembling it and this usage finally became universal. That great and good writer, Dr. Bartlett, of the *Bulletin,* and that bold, bad humorist, Peter (formerly *Pater,* Father) Robertson, of the *Chronicle,* habitually and wisely use this point to distinguish their irony from their folly. In oral discourse they substitute the nudge in the ribs, or that great convulsion of nature known as the sly wink.

By the way, punctuation has not always been what it is now. For a long time after the invention of printing there was no system at all; a pause was indicated by a straight stroke passing obliquely through the line, as in manuscript of the same period. A "Lactantius," printed in Italy in 1465, has only the colon, the note of interrogation and the full stop. In the first book printed in France, the *Liber Epistolarum,* the semicolon has greater force than the full point, which is sometimes used in the middle of a sentence, whereas the semicolon invariably closes a chapter. But I must ask pardon for being so infernally well informed; it is a vice that I got by contagion from Mr. Pickering of the *Call.* I will give you, from his weekly columns of "Notes and Queries," some examples of its awful ravages.

A14. Leader.

When John Sharp Williams died (great Scott,
    What grief had marked his birth!)
He journeyed to the gates of what
    He long had played on earth.

He rapped for entrance, Satan came
    And through the wicket peered,
Bearing a spirit, all aflame,
    That lately he had speared

Cried Satan: "Scat!" Said John: "I melt
    And faint and sink and slip!
I had no notion that you dwelt
    So far from Mississip.

"I'm lucky that you did, for my
    Constituents, I fear,
Had given me the glassy eye
    If you'd resided near.

"Now I'll be silent as a mouse
    If you will take me in
As Leader of the Lower House."
    Said Nick: "You've brought your chin!"

So he was coldly turned away
    And peace on Hades fell.
He went Above, they let him stay,
    And Heaven thenceforth was Hell.

A15. Liar.

If liars were not, what a desolate waste
    There'd be! Where great cities are flourishing
The wolf could indulge his unsociable taste
    His soul upon solitude nourishing.
The loon would repeat from the ends of the earth
The laughing hyena's irrational mirth.

A world without liars! Kind Fortune forbid
    That I should (I couldn't) reside in it.
'Twere dreary and dismal indeed if 'twere rid
    Of all who have cheerfully lied in it.
In such a vast solitude rather than dwell
I'd brave all the tongues of a country hotel.

A16. Libel.

> An editor in Omaha
> Is laid in limbo by the law,
> For something that he hotly said
> Displeasing to the sainted dead;
> Surviving relatives complained
> And had the libeler detained
> In prison to lament his prose
> And play at checkers with his nose.
>
> O men of every race and hue
> Beneath the sky's embracing blue,
> That fault in me pray overlook,
> And bring some other rogue to book.
> One luckless day, with mind attent
> Upon hereditary bent—
> How certain traits, from sire to son,
> Through ages undiminished run—
> My friends and foes alike I saw
> Were illustrations of the law;
> And tracing the polluted course
> Of folly to its ancient source,
> I seized my pen (O let it pass)
> And wrote that Adam was an ass.

A17. Penitence / Eloquence (2).

A pious poet seriously concerned for my immortal part concludes some rebuking verses thus:

> Cynic and friend, I implore you
> Kneel!—be like the Thief on the Cross.

There were two thieves on two crosses, but I infer that I should be like the penitent one. Why, as to that, I have never been like anybody else. The resemblance does not, I hope, go to character, but if any human being is chronically contrite it is I. I habitually confess as many of the sins of my enemies as I know, or even suspect; and there is hardly one of these erring persons whose existence I do not repent in sash-cloth and axes. I repent their prosperity, repent their pleasures—am sincerely sorry for every act of their lives that has brought them advantage or peace. Oh, I'm penitent enough for the Seventh Heaven, but as to kneeling, observe, good friend, how the wicked have transfixed my extremities with nails! Why, bless you, I can move neither hand nor foot! Unspike me, friend—withdraw the iron restraints of

the law and see how quickly I will kneel [upon the body of some one whom
I hate. It is the dream of my life!]

A18. Pension.

Jeff Davis sat sullenly nursing
    His hot and implacable hate,
His last bitter words rehearsing—
    He'd been feeling poorly of late.

An angel appeared to him, splendid
    With glittering pinion and plume.
"O Davis, let anger be ended
    And fair magnanimity bloom.

"Your victory ought to dispose you
    To pity. No longer display
Resentment and hatred to those you
    Have ruined forever and ay."

"What! victory? Sure you don't mean it!
    The war that I helped to provoke
Went—ah, but you cannot have seen it!—
    They licked us—they licked us like smoke!

"They'd three to our one." Then, divinely,
    In tones like the music of spheres,
The angel responded, benignly:
    "That's where your advantage appears.

"'Tis true you gave up, and your men did—
    Compelled by vast numbers to yield:
But the war was by no means ended,
    For Ingalls remained in the field.

"The land which the hosts of dissension
    Their failure to ruin deplored
Succumbs to its own, for the Pension
    Is mightier far than the Sword!"

A19. Polygamy.

They say that Brigham Young, who long has lain
    As dead as any door-nail—nay, as dead
As any coffin-screw—is up again
    And all prepared a second time to head
    The people who in former days he led.

If they won't follow I suppose he'll twig 'em
    Until they all have done as he has said,
Not as he does—rejuvenated Brigham
With his old widows hardly will polygam.

A20. Press.

The daily paper's lying at my door;
I pick it up and read it o'er and o'er,
Eager to learn what gladly I forget—
All's fish; e'en minnows that escape the net.
Devouring all, I chiefly relish what
I relished yesterday and then forgot.
For what occurred last week another way,
Or in another place, though news to-day,
Is vapid, tasteless, tedious and diffuse,
Through lack of appetite by long disuse.
Give me, then, nothing that is two days old;
Events and pancakes are not good when cold.
What matters it to me the world was here
Before MacCrellish ever spread his ear
Above its noises, like a sounding board,
To magnify the murmurs that it stored?
Of what importance that before De Young
Had got upon their scent and given tongue
Men had employed the vices they inherited,
And what they played had variously merited?
About events why should I care to know
That happened awkwardly so long ago
That even Mr. Pickering was not
As special correspondent on the spot,
Instead of Xenophon or others such,
Whose English was no better than their Dutch?
I care not what was crime (if anything)
Ere Fitch plucked out a goosequill from his wing
To make a note of it, or Colonel Jackson
Wrote of it more in sorrow than in Saxon.
As the small gossip in a country town
Talks up this neighbor and talks that one down;
Pricks up his ears to hear of ailing Ned,
But yawns when told the King of Spain is dead;
Within his small horizon finds repose
And cares for nothing, for he nothing knows;

So I, by living in the Present, find
My world has narrowed to my narrow mind.
Cloyed with my Yesterday, I know To-night
Will for To-day restore my appetite.
Concerning forty centuries of history
I nothing know but that it is a mystery.
If God had wished into the light to drag it
He had raised up in each decade a Baggett.
No; truly picturesque alone can be,
To me, the period including Me.

A21. Propitiation.

The workmen all were out in force—
    Their foreman was to leave them;
Loving that worthy man, of course
    The parting could but grieve them.

Long years his mild, benignant reign
    Their welfare had promoted:
To him they had a watch and chain
    Unanimously voted.

While these to tender was the aim
    And object of their massing,
Their foreman's young successor came,
    And sourly scowled in passing.

Then rose an aged workman who
    For baldness was respected,
And whom—for he was toothless, too—
    As spokesman they'd selected.

He said: "My mates, I've got a plan
    For to propoge—I think its
More wiser onto that young man
    For to confer them trinkets."

A22. Rake.

A fiercely sentimental contemporary, in whose columns once glowed the
luminous assertion that "Christian civilization has for its eternal basis the
purity of woman," has now gone and dug up the bones of poor Pope and
hoisted his yellow skull over the gates of the ancient city of Bosh because he
wrote the familiar couplet:

"Men, some to business, some to pleasure, take,
    But every woman is at heart a rake."

He must endure to be informed, the worthy champion of the unfair sex, that the word "rake" had not, in Pope's time, the meaning that it has now: it meant merely a person who cares too much for enjoyment and too little for affairs. It is in this sense that Pope always employs it, and in a letter to Congreve, in 1715, he makes, with the words "business" and "rake," the same obvious antithesis as in the luckless lines just discovered by our gallant contemporary. Relating that he sits up until 2 o'clock in the morning over burgundy and champagne, he adds:

"I am become so much of a rake that I shall be ashamed, in a short time, to be thought to do any sort of business."

If on the evidence of the famous couplet any blackguard has been cherishing the conviction that Pope thought as lightly of women as women think of blackguards, and blackguards of one another, let him dismiss the error with his blessing, and fill its place with some not very particular vice.

A23. Regret.

One of the last utterances of the late Dr. Richard Caulfield of Cork, says a contemporary, was: "I do not regret anything that I ever wrote."

May I, too, feel, when Death lets fall my curtain,
That satisfaction and in speech convey it.
And it may well be so—at least I'm certain
That Heaven will kill me if I ever say it.

A24. Stultus.

Stabat stultus dolorosus,
Exaltatus, lachrymosus,
Calcitratus, felisatus,
Per homunculum jocosum
Et verbosum,
Dicat: "Puer reprobatus!"

A25. Totality.

Alas that a tender American maid
Should rise from Obscurity's cover and shade,
To blink and to scorch in the light and the flame,
That forever envelop a noble name!
"Tackacs," "Festetics"—oh, maiden, beware:
False beacons are these, and the rocks are there
To shatter your bark. "De Kis Joka"—ah, me,
There's death in its music: flee, maiden, Oh, flee!
Far better just "Brown" and contentment therewith;
Just "Jones" and simplicity; virtue and "Smith."

A26. Trusts.

A CAREER.

He fought the Oil Trust. Wealth supplied
The means—the motive, sturdy pride.

He said: "I'm rich and I could stand
My losses by this robber band,

"But self-respect forbids. John D.
Will find the walking bad on Me!"

His millions so he lavished for
The prosecution of the war.

In all the courts the thunderous sound
Of battle shook the walls and ground!

The while, his countrymen's applause
Acclaimed him Champion of Laws.

And one said: "My applause has rose
Whenever Them has tackled Those."

("Them," were the Good—to whom with pride
He pointed—"Those" the Unsanctified.)

And so the Champion lived his life,
To entertain the Saints of Strife,

And when he died, untaught to yield,
Was laid to rest in Potter's Field.

[Unspecified.]

A27.

Some men there be who lie to gain an end,
And others for their natures that way tend.
And these be liars. Other men there be
Who tell a falsehood to oblige a friend.

A28.

"Rich but not vulgar, and though great yet clean,
Polite while cheating, mannerly when mean,
His birth a poem and his life a jig,
He lived and died an educated pig. [. . ."]

A29.

The Public are to be congratulated on the verdict which was rendered
yesterday in the Fitch–De Young libel suit.—*Fitch*.

The clown waysided long, his wench to meet,
Thinks nature brightens at her coming feet,
That simpering doxy, chucked beneath the chin,
Fancies on every face a happy grin.

A30.

Home Rule? I'm fur it till the law they make it,
And then, begorry, may the divil take it!

Parnell.

A31.

'Twas the song of the Poundkeeper man,
  As he fiddled his voluble chin:
"No capper am I for a confidence game,
  But I works, I says, with a similar aim,
    A-ropin' 'em—ropin' 'em in.
  I makes such a joke as I knows and can,
    And I says I'm a-ropin' 'em in."

'Tis the moan of the Poundkeeper man,
  As the grief runs off of his chin:
"I'm a caught galoot at my own pursoot;
  Impounded and fined, and sassed to boot—
    Oh, they've roped me—roped me in;
  For I hadn't no tag on my neck as I ran,
    And, by thunder, they've roped me in!"

A32.

"The vicious Oriental habit of lying." —*Bulletin.*

Observer thou with sense unblessed,
  Still dreaming dreams of youth.
Truth knows no north, south, east nor west,
  And none of them knows Truth.

A33.

DEPEW (SOLUS).
That's off my mind—I'll study up a speech.
Where's my J. Miller?—always out of reach.
Ah, here it is—dear volume that contains
The Sum of Things! My heart, my soul, my brains!
(SINGS.)
  The Joke, the Joke, I would I were it,
  With a body of breath and a soul of wit
    And the gift of eternal youth.
  I'd crack myself in humanity's ear,

And always I'd find a smile in the jeer;
          In the frown a leer,
          A grin in the tear
From the eyes of Sense and Truth.

From trammels of taste that hamper the sane
From my curst identity's chafing chain,
          Free me, O Fate, at a stroke.
Make me a fool with a fool's grimace,
Narrow my forehead and widen my face,
          The Joker has place
          In the ranks of Grace.
          But it's O, to be a Joke.

A34.

WHEN BOOKER WASHINGTON WAS LYNCHED IN BOSTON.

The lynching of Mr. Booker Washington, in Boston, was attended with few of the disagreeable incidents which have so frequently marred similar spectacles in the South. Regrettable as was the act itself, and inconvenient as it must have been to Mr. Washington, he who is most jealously devoted to the honor and good name of the old Bay State has little cause to blush for the method. The tragedy is necessarily painful to contemplate, but all was done in excellent and scholarly taste, the rope having been adjusted with extreme nicety to produce a maximum of effect with a minimum of physical dissent. When the victim was lifted from his feet (which promptly followed) and suspended in the air with his hands behind his back and his head inclined forward a careless attention might have thought him absorbed in some profound reflection on the future of his race. But that was an illusion; the man was really and truly engaged in surrendering the elective franchise into the hands of those who gave it. When the body was taken down and prepared for burial a white circle around the neck and an air of repose were all that served to distinguish it from its previous condition of pernicious activity. So perished in his pride the most notable contemporary protagonist of that ancient and outgrown faith, the doctrine that a negro is as good as a Boston man. Mr. Washington's passing away appears to have engendered few local animosities and caused little public excitement. He speaks of it himself with perfect composure.

A35.

So, Johann Hoch, they've changed the date
     Appointed for your hanging;
You'll have a little time to wait
     Before a harp you're twanging

In that Celestial State where joy
Burns brighter than in Illinois.

'Tis done that you may have a "show"
    To get some coin together
To pay for an appeal, and so
    Learn definitely whether
You're truly guilty; there's a doubt—
If you are able to "shell out."

But if you cannot get the gold
    Why, that's a hanging matter.
Don't think that Justice then will hold
    An even scale. Go at her
With coin, or lose the game. The hand
That wins is money, understand.

O Johann Hoch, if 'tis your lot
    To raise the cash to make you
A free man, here's my hand. If not,
    Death and the devil take you!
You knew the law, so just and wise:
"The penniless assassin dies!"

B. OTHER DEFINITIONS

The following satirical definitions by Bierce appeared within other writings, typically his weekly "Town-Crier" or "Prattle" columns, with the exception of item B3, which is a complete article. They are arranged chronologically.

B1.

Some astute philosopher with a *penchant* for definition describes man as "an animal which uses fire to prepare its food." Of cooking *in itself* he has not left a record of his valuable opinion; but of cooking as a distinguishing trait of the genus *Homo* —the one thing which elevates the race above the brute creation—he has expressed a decided appreciation. We may remark *en passant,* that if this profound interpretation of the culinary mission of mankind is correct, a good cook is the most nearly perfect type of humanity. Imbued with the same spirit which prompted this comprehensive description of man, if we were asked to define the term "San Francisco lady," we should unhesitatingly reply, "an animal which sells tickets." Other cities may boast of the beauty and intellect of their women—of their taste, their elegance, their wit—they may place to the credit of their ladies a thousand and one moral, social and intellectual sundries; we scorn to call in question their claims by the faintest protest. But with conscious pride, we boldly assert that an average specimen of the San Franciscaness can dispose of more tickets in a given time than any similar establishment in nature.

B2.

Beauty: noun, uncommon.—A thing kindly given by Providence to enable its possessor to swindle her admirers and other idiots.

B3.

WEBSTER REVISED.

Professor.—One who makes an avowal of his belief in Scripture: especially an officer in a college or university, whose business it is to instruct students in a particular branch of learning. [*Obsolete.*] A person who is skilled in breaking horses. One who is an adept in sleight-of-hand performances. A teacher of the art of self-defence. A teacher of the art of French cookery—example, Prof. Blot. In fine, the title may be applied to any jackass who has the boldness to assume it.

Doctor of Divinity.—A title conferred on a person of profound learning, who has written a work on theology, or by study and research has contributed largely to the fund of Bible knowledge. [Obsolete.] A title affixed to the name of a Christian minister having the same force as Reverend prefixed. One of the honorary degrees conferred indiscriminately by Colleges on ministers of the Gospel.

Honorable.—Formerly an epithet of respect or distinction given to a member of Congress or a State Senator. The term is now applied to any one elected to a public office, or to a person who distinguishes himself in prize-fighting, embezzling, gambling, etc.; also applied in any case where the word *dis*honorable would be more correctly used.

College.—Formerly a society of scholars incorporated for purposes of study of instruction; an educational institution with the powers of conferring degrees upon its graduates. Now, a school for the instruction of boys in book-keeping; a boarding school, where young ladies are taught music, drawing, etc.; any educational institution where, in addition to a primary and "common English" department, Latin and Greek are studied.

B4.

At a recent meeting of that cheerful society, the Dictionary Club of London, the principal topic was the definition of the word "Sacrilege." So far as it applies to language, it means talking hard sense in the wrong crowd.

B5.

Stealing may be defined as A. taking the property of B. from C.

B6.

Religion may be defined as the church member's ticket entitling him to a reserved seat in the dress circle of heaven, commanding a good view of the pit.

B7.

    Mr. Greeley—God bless her!—is opposed to the nomination of President Grant, because the latter is "encrusted with barnacles." This suggests a new definition, to which the literary executors of the late Noah Webster are very welcome: INELIGIBLE CANDIDATE.—A Man who is encrusted with barnacles when you wish to be encrusted yourself.

B8.

    In a lecture, the other evening, at the Royal Institute, Dr. Rutherford stated that the human muscles never act except when excited by exterior stimuli. EARTHLY PARADISE—a place where the muscles are protected by law from outside influence.

B9.

    BLASPHEMY, *n.* —Idle discourse concerning *my* Phemy.
Dr. Johnson.

B10.

    Fool.—Tell me, Hero, what is strategy?
    Soldier.—The art of laying two knives against one throat.
    F.—And what are tactics?
    S.—The art of driving them home.
    F.—Supermundane lexicographer!

B11.

    Mr. Dandrid has been convicted of receiving stolen goods—an offense that may be defined as concealing from A the property of B that C has taken from D.

B12.

    I copy the following from the dictionary in use at the offices of the various daily newspapers in this city. — *Dabster's Unabridged:* "PLUVIAL VISITATION, a rain." "AQUEOUS DISPENSATION, a rain." "VAPOROUS PRECIPITATION, a rain." Of these handy expressions the first is silly, the second idiotic, the third maniacal and each all three. Whereby all tastes are suited, and "elegant" writing is the result.

B13.

    The following definitions are from the *Idiot's Unabridged Dictionary,* in use at the office of the *Evening Post:* "CREDITOR, *n* —a miscreant who would be benefitted by resumption. DEBTOR, *n* —a worthy person, in whose interest the national finances should be so managed as to depreciate the national currency."

B14.

    Following are sample definitions from an unpublished dictionary for which (in behalf of the author) I am ready to receive subscriptions: "*Love,* the folly of thinking much of another before one knows anything of oneself."

"*Courtship,* the timid sipping of two thirsty souls from a goblet which both can easily drain but neither replenish." "*Marriage,* a feminine device for imposing silence, whereby one woman is made to guard the good name of a dozen others." "*Divorce,* a resumption of diplomatic relations and rectification of boundaries."

B15.

Most of these dismally indecent pictures, it is almost needless to say, are photographs of actresses. When one considers the multitude of photographs of naked, or half naked, actresses that are annually thrown upon the market; which meet the eye at every turn; which are found in the "collections" of young men, and even in the albums of otherwise respectable women, one is constrained to ask the lexicographers for a new definition of the word "actress" that shall take account of what appears to be an important part of her vocation: the display of her body—which is commonly hideous to a ghastly degree. If I were dictator I would have the shameless creatures who do this thing publicly whipped, and the virtuous dames and demoiselles who tolerate them publicly stripped.

B16.

Definition from *The Bulletin's Unabridged Dictionary of the Uptonese Language:* "BLOODCURDLINGHOLOCAUST, *n.* A smash-up on a railway."

B17.

Systematic Theology may be defined as holy nonsense reduced to rule.

B18.

Following is an extract from the *Chronicle's Unabridged Dictionary,* which will be published in book form as soon as the daily issues of the paper shall have sucked all the honey of its incomparable definitions:

STAB, *v.t.* To "open an avenue for the escape of the life fluid."

B19.

Mr. Walter Crane, the English delineator of impossible children in supernatural habiliments, bitterly complains that American publishers steal his pictures. "Steal," Walter is a harsh word: it pains. Let us see. You make certain marks upon a piece of paper. In order to encourage you to go on and make more, your Government thinks it expedient to forbid your fellow-subjects to copy them without your consent. It has no power to forbid any one else. But *this* Government, not caring whether you go on and make more marks or not, for it has no power to compel you to share your profit of mark-making with it, and you will not unless compelled, does not feel it owes you any encouragement. It permits its citizens to make marks like yours if they wish to. Some of them do so. This you have the civility to call "stealing." You demand that it be stopped. By virtue of what services or benefits of this country do you make this demand? Upon what scheme of reciprocal advantage is it based? In all the arguments for international copyright I do not remember to have seen this point made clear. One might almost think that it had been studiously kept out of sight. Walter, how do these definitions suit you and the gentlemen who think into the same teacup?

COPYRIGHT, *n.* A commercial advantage which Governments owe to non-resident aliens. STEAL, *v.* To take what you have a right to take.

B20.

[Gender] may be defined as the sex of words.

B21.

What is a technicality? One may be very sure that he knows, yet swift to blunder in the definition. Perhaps the word is best defined by example; and here is the neatest example that one may find in a month of Sundays. A suit against our excellent friends, Messrs. Fitch and Pickering, was dismissed the other day by Judge Lawler because it was brought by "Adolphe Flamant as guardian of the persons and estates of James Flamant and Adolphe Flamant Jr.," instead of by "James Flamant and Adolphe Flamant Jr., by Adolphe Flamant, guardian of their persons and estates." That is what is called a technicality. What? the dismissal? No. Either of the foregoing formulæ, or both? Clearly not. What, then, is the "technicality"? I really do not know—I think it is the Judge.

B22.

Conspicuous among the mottoes on the walls of the room in which the National Women's Christian Temperance Union is meeting in Chicago is a large inscription reading, "God's Curse Upon High License!" — *New York Tribune.*

If any irreverent wretch had secretly taken down that motto and substituted the words, "God Damn High License!" these Christian dames would have been severely shocked. Nevertheless the meaning would have been accurately the same.

SWEAR, *v.i.* To say something in a particular, and not too particular, way.

B23.

Following are sample definitions from *Henry George's Unabridged Dictionary:*

Progress, *n.* The act of going about the world making speeches.

Poverty, *n.* The thing that is avoided by going about the world making speeches.

B24.

The best definition of a crank is: "The man who holds opinions which we do not understand." Here is a man flippantly denouncing Miss

Kennedy as a crank because she held a theory which he does not understand, and is probably incapable of understanding.

B25.

The "San Francisco" is the first modern American war ship. — *The Daily Cockadoodledoo.*

Esteemed contemporary, you have enriched the dictionary with a new definition:

Antiquity, n. The period of time extending from the creation of the world to the creation of the "San Francisco."

B26.

When a Lexicographer who was writing a dictionary had got as far as the word "Commissioner" he paused in deep thought, unable to invent a satisfactory definition for the word. While he was racking his brain he looked out of his study window and saw passing along the street, in a gold carriage and clad in cloth-of-diamonds, a Person whom the King of that country had appointed to select a site for the royal postoffice. Inspired by the gorgeous pageant, the Lexicographer seized his pen and dashing at his manuscript, wrote, with inconceivable vivacity, as follows: —

"COMMISSIONER, *n.* One who gets a commission."

B27.

A pupil in one of the public schools opened his lips the other day, and from them fell like a falling star this glowing definition: "A hypocrite is a person who lives twice as long as we do."

B28.

The name of New York's distinguished investigator, Mr. Lexow, appears to have effected a permanent lodgment in the American language. Our newspapers are gravely demanding a "Lexow committee" for San Francisco, or apprising us that a "Lexow investigation" is to be set afoot; and one advanced sheet earnestly suggests that the police department be "Lexowed." Doubtless the philologist of the future will be angling his thinker in the endeavor to trace the history of the word, with a result that will be recorded in a twenty-first century dictionary somewhat as follows:

LEXOW, *v.t.* [Latin, *lex,* a law, and Old English, *owe,* to have, to possess.] To enforce the statutes against an offender; to "have the law on" one; to prosecute.

As to definitions, I have the happiness to present one from that standard work, *McEwen's Unabridged Dictionary of Objurgatory Reform.*

NARROW-SIGHTED, *adj.* Incapable of seeing behind Gunst Huntington; behind Buckley, Huntington; behind Flynn, Huntington; behind the Adversary of Souls, Huntington; behind bad weather, Huntington; behind pestilence and famine, Huntington; behind earthquake, Huntington—who once instigated an associate villain to insult Lexicography by putting the author of this dictionary off a train.

B29.

Burglary of a railway station may be defined as A snatching back from B the bread of C.

B30.

The House "resolutions of sympathy" introduced by Mr. Maguire are of the same sort: they are carefully charged with a blank cartridge for Turkey and the powers, and Greece is invited to be content with the noise of the discharge and the smell of the powder. That is called "moral support," which may be defined as encouragement without exertion. It never helped a good cause nor harmed a bad one. It has no value whatever—it is not support. The proofer of "moral support" is not a service meriting gratitude, but an impertinence deserving resentment. Naturally, as in this instance, it is commonly offered to the unworthy.

B31.

Mr. Andrew Carnegie (whose name be exalted!) disclaims the title "philanthropist." He says he understands it to mean "a man with more money than brains." If that is a good definition, the world is infested with philanthropists who never did a good deed in all their needless lives. "Philanthropist," I venture not to inform but to remind Mr. Carnegie, is the literal Greek equivalent of "one who loves his fellow man." Money has only this much to do with it: a man with money cannot afford to love his fellow men, and a man without soon tires of unreturned affection. Whether a man of brains can love his fellow men—oh, that depends; he may have been misinformed about them.

B32.

In his *Dictionary of Antiquities* the learned Pantin-Gwocx defines "pocket" as, first, "the main temple of the American deity;" second, "a small receptacle worn on the person." The latter definition is the one, doubtless, that concerns us if the two things are not the same.

B33.

The kindly, white-whiskered old veterans of the domino tables at the Family Club in San Francisco still tell amusing stories about the unprinted portions of his [Bierce's] "Devil's Dictionary," ending always with his definition of "Heaven": "Copulation without culmination."

Unless otherwise specified, all works cited in the notes are by AB. No distinction is made in the notes as to whether the item appeared under AB's byline or a pseudonym or was unsigned. Dates of first publication are provided when known (note that many of AB's "essays" in *CW* are composites made from material written over long periods of time). Page numbers in citations are exact page numbers for direct quotations, first page only for items not quoted. Obvious typographical errors in texts cited have been silently corrected. Minor variations in readings that sometimes occur between appearances in *Am* and *E* are not indicated. The misspellings in AB's Little Johnny sketches are intentional.

Preface, 2.5–11] The text here derives in part from the prospectus for *CW*. In *C*, for "*The Devil's* . . . slang" read:

> With reference to certain actual and possible questions of priority and originality, it may be explained that this Word Book was begun in the San Francisco "Wasp" in the year 1881, and has been continued, in a desultory way, in several journals and periodicals. As it was no part of the author's purpose to define all the words in the language, or even to make a complete alphabetical series, the stopping-place of the book was determined by considerations of bulk. In the event of this volume proving acceptable to that part of the reading public to which in humility it is addressed—enlightened souls who prefer dry wines to sweet, sense to sentiment, good English to slang, and wit to humor—there may possibly be another if the author be spared for the compiling.

2.14 plagiarism] See note on "Plagiarism," concerning charges leveled against AB.

2.18 wit] Cf. "Wit and Humor" (1903; *CW* 10.101): "Humor is tolerant, tender; its ridicule caresses. Wit stabs, begs pardon—and turns the weapon in the wound."

2.21 Gassalasca Jape, S.J.] *Jape* means to joke or quip; to make sport of. AB introduced Fr. Jape in "The Devil's Dictionary" for 2 Apr. 1881 as the priest-poet "Gassalaska Jape, S.B.T., of the Mission San Diablo." He mentioned Fr. Jape again the following week in "Prattle" (*W*, 9 Apr. 1881: 228), now spelling his first name "Gassalasca" (and publishing an unreprinted poem by Fr. Jape), and in "The Devil's Dictionary" for 28 Oct. Fr. Jape is not mentioned again until 1906 in the preface to *C*, now identified as a priest of the Society of Jesus, that is, a Jesuit. AB never again mentions the fictitious order "S.B.T." or the "Mission San Diablo." If AB did not know such proverbs as "Whenever two Jesuits come together, the devil always makes three" or "Don't trust a monk with your wife or a Jesuit with your money," he certainly knew that Jesuits are highly trained and well educated and was familiar with the stereotype of Jesuits as being deceitful and perfidious—the exact reason for associating Fr. Jape with them. Fr. Jape is credited with thirty-one poems in *D,* typically the most barbed, and pertaining mostly to religious matters.

Abacot] A spurious word, originating in a misprint of *bycocket* (see *OED*), an ornamental headdress worn by men and women.

Abada] I.e., the rhinoceros.

Abaddon] In Revelation 9 : 11, *Abaddon* is the name of "the angel of the bottomless pit."

Abandon] Chauncey Mitchell Depew (1834–1928) was a prominent Republican figure in the later nineteenth century. He served as president of the New York Central and Hudson River Railroad (1885–98) and was U.S. senator from New York (1899–1911) but declined several other prestigious posts, including secretary of state under Benjamin Harrison. AB was skewering Depew in the papers around the time this definition appeared in print.

Abasement] *Am* and *E* add the following verses:

> He prevented his displacement
> By the practice of *abasement;*
> But what made the wretch exempt
> From dismissal was contempt,
> For his master couldn't bring
> Himself to kick so base a thing.

Abatis] Cf. "Fool and Philosopher; or, Brief Seasons of Intellectual Dissipation" (1873; *Cobwebs from an Empty Skull* 100): "S[oldier].—What is an *abattis?* F[ool].—Rubbish placed in front of a fort to keep the rubbish outside from getting in the rubbish inside." See also "War Topics" (*E,* 5 June 1898: 18): "The front of the enemy's earthworks was protected by an intricate abatis of felled trees denuded of their foliage and twigs."

Abat-voix] From the French: a sounding board above a pulpit. Cf. 1 Corinthians 13 : 1: "Though I speak with the tongues of men and of angels, and have not charity, I am become as sounding brass, or a tinkling cymbal."

Abba] In the New Testament, Jesus' familiar name for God the Father; in Christian churches of Egypt, Syria, and Ethiopia, a title of honor for bishops and patriarchs. Note that, in both the secular and ecclesiastical sense, there are fathers who are not husbands.

Abbess] The superior of a convent (just as an abbot is the superior of a monastery; *abbé* in France).

Abderian] Democritus of Abdera (460?–370? BCE) came to be referred to in late antiquity as "The Laughing Philosopher," perhaps because of his ethical ideal of cheerfulness (*euthumie*). See "Prattle" (*W,* 13 Mar. 1886: 5): "A few years ago a 'chorus of indolent reviewers' was performing abderian ululations over Mr. Tilden's word 'usufruct.'"

Abdest] The Mohammedan rite of washing the hands before prayer, which also, as AB noted, involves inspiring water through the nose.

Abdication] Isabella II (1830–1904), queen of Spain (1833–68), died about the time of the publication of definition 1. After being ousted from the throne in 1868, she abdicated her rights in 1870 in favor of her son Alfonso XII. In definition 2, AB may be alluding to King Amadeo of Spain, who upon the restoration of the monarchy in 1871 ruled for less than two years, abdicating on 11 Feb. 1873 and returning to a life of obscurity in Italy, his birthplace. He died there in 1890.

Abdomen] See "Stomach."

Abelians] A small sect of ancient heretics in North Africa who, according to St. Augustine, lived in continence after marriage, supposedly after the example of Abel. In the second century, the Cainites were a heretical sect who professed reverence for Cain and other wicked scriptural characters.

Ablative] Relating to the grammatical case indicating separation, direction away from, sometimes manner or agency, and the object of certain verbs in Latin and some Indo-European languages. In Latin grammar, the ablative absolute is the "ablative case of a noun with a participle in concord, expressing the time, occasion, or circumstance of a fact stated, as . . . at, upon, or through the sun rising, darkness flees away" (*OED*). The adaptation of the ablative absolute in English, as used by AB, especially in his fables, had been good usage in the eighteenth century, but by his day it had come to be considered archaic, even ungrammatical. For an example, see "A Forfeited Right": "The Chief of the Weather Bureau having predicted a fine day, a Thrifty Person hastened to lay in a large stock of umbrellas . . ." (1892; *CW* 6.238). Cf. "The Maid of Podunk" (*J*, 10 Mar. 1901: 26; as "Ambrose Bierce's History of the Maid of Podunk," *E*, 19 Mar. 1901: 14): "It is not . . . within the province of the historian to utter dogmatic judgment in such matters, but this seems to be a pretty flagrant instance of ingenuity. I mention it only to show to what lengths the learned will sometimes go in explaining what is obviously a grammatical error (like the 'ablative absolute' in Latin). . . ."

Abracadabra] A magical incantation or charm (as below) having the power to ward off disease or other calamity; unintelligible talk. See also "Brahma" concerning the Abracadabranese. Jamrach Holobom, described as a professor at the University of Oshkosh (Wisconsin), is the "author" of *The Brass-Headed Whale,* of the sketch "His Waterloo" (*Oakland Daily Evening Tribune,* 16 Aug. 1890: 1), of two articles entitled "How Not to Eat" (n.d.), and of the poems "At the Close of the Canvass," "To the Grove Side," and "Election Day" (early verses by AB from *W* that he reprinted in "The Passing Show"), as well as four verse contributions, some epigrams, and a "translation" of the Dies Irae in *D*. AB developed Holobom more than he did Fr. Jape, who is mentioned but twice in the newspaper, all other attributions to Fr. Jape being in *C* or *D*.

```
A B R A C A D A B R A
  A B R A C A D A B R
    A B R A C A D A B
      A B R A C A D A
        A B R A C A D
          A B R A C A
            A B R A C
              A B R A
                A B R
                  A B
                    A
```

Abridge] The quotation is a parody of the opening of the Declaration of Independence. Its attribution to Cromwell (1599–1658) refers to his execution of King Charles I of England in 1649.

Abrupt] "[T]he thoughts, which to a reader of less skill seem thrown together by chance, are concatenated without any abruption." Samuel Johnson (1709–84), "Cowley," in *Lives of the English Poets* (1779–81; rpt. London: Oxford University Press, 1906), 1.34.

Abruption] Cf. "Concatenate."

Abscond] William Cowper (1731–1800), "Olney Hymns" (1774), 35.1: "God moves in a mysterious way." The definition in *Am* and *E* concludes: "An inelegant synonym for absquatulate."

Absence] Propertius, *Elegies* 2.33.43: "Absence makes the heart grow fonder" (*Semper in absentes felicior aestus amantes*). Cf. "The Passing Show" (*Fi*, 12 Nov. 1873: 10): "It is reported that the consort of Don Carlos has received an official intimation that her absence from France would make the French heart grow fonder of her."

Absent] See AB to Eleanor (Vore) Sickler, 19 Nov. 1910: "I have always found you interesting, despite my favorite dictum that 'a woman absent is a woman dead'" ("A Collection of Bierce Letters," ed. Carey McWilliams, *University of California Chronicle* 34 [Jan. 1932]: 43).

Absolute] Cf. "Letters from a Hdkhoite—No. 1" (*NL*, 4 Apr. 1868: 4): "The government of Hdkho is what you call an absolute monarchy; which I understand to mean, a state in which the king may do as he thinks fit, so long as his ministers and army think fit also." AB was a longtime foe of republican government; his most sustained attack on it is found in the satire "Ashes of the Beacon" (1888 [as "The Fall of the Republic"]; rpt. 1905, 1909; *CW* 1.17).

Abuse] Definition 2 applies to the common perception of AB's satire. See also "Vituperation."

Academe] Presumably the academy founded by Plato in 387 BCE. He and his pupils met in a garden outside Athens that was said to have belonged to the Trojan War hero Academos.

Accept] Cf. Hosea 8:7: "For they have sown the wind, and they shall reap the whirlwind. . . ."

Accident] The definition suggests AB's adherence to determinism. Cf. "One of the Missing" (1888): "But it was decreed from the beginning of time that Private Searing was not to murder anybody that bright summer morning, nor was the Confederate retreat to be announced by him. For countless ages events had been so matching themselves together in that wondrous mosaic to some parts of which, dimly discernible, we give the name of history, that the acts which he had in will would have barred the harmony of the pattern. . . . By the concurrence of an infinite number of favoring influences and their preponderance over an infinite number of opposing ones, this officer of artillery had been made to commit a breach of discipline and flee from his native country to avoid punishment" (*CW* 2.76–77).

Accomplice] AB treats the issue of lawyers defending clients they know to be guilty in "The Jury in Ancient America" (1905; rpt. 1909 as part of "Ashes of the Beacon") and "Some Features of the Law" (*CW* 11.99).

Accoucheur] One who assists in childbirth.

Accountability] The first name of "The Widower Turmore" (1891; *CW* 8.41) is Joram. In *Am* and *E*, for "caution" read "remorse and great first cause of penitence."

Aceldama] A potter's field near Jerusalem purchased with the reward Judas received for betraying Jesus and later returned (see Acts 1:17–19).

Acephalous] Headless. In *W*, for "absently pulled at his forelock" read "attempted to blow his nose with his fingers"; there is also an additional sentence at the end: "The final and permanent state of a modern sovereign who rules by right divine." Jean, Sire de Joinville (1224?–1317), a member of the Seventh Crusade, wrote a chronicle of the Crusades in his *Histoire de Saint Louis* (1304–09). The anecdote first published at "Head" and later at "Scimitar" expands on the quip made here.

Acerbity] AB often attacked George K. Fitch (1826–1906), deacon and also editor of the *San Francisco Bulletin*, as in "A Vision of Resurrection" (1889; *CW* 5.116).

Ache] See "Conscience" concerning the distress caused by the cucumber.

Acorn] Cf. "Prattle" (*W*, 23 Jan. 1886: 5): "It seems to be the prevailing opinion that if Germany holds on to the Samoan Islands an acorn should be planted at once to produce the keel of a first-class man-of-war."

Acquit] Cf. "My Favorite Murder" (1888; *CW* 8.147): "In charging the jury, the judge of the Court of Acquittal remarked that it was one of the most ghastly crimes that he had ever been called upon to explain away."

Acrobat] "*a*, priv." refers to the alpha privative, the prefix *a*- or *an*- used in Greek or words derived from Greek to express absence or negation. Thus the healthy acrobat is the opposite of "crow-bait," a corpse.

Acrostic] A poem in which certain letters (usually the first in each line) form a name or message when read in sequence. AB declared, "No acrostic is worth writing . . ." ("Prattle," *E*, 1 Dec. 1895: 6) but was himself guilty of at least one—the untitled poem beginning "Fate—whose edict oft hath wrung" (1864) on his pet name for his fiancée at the time, "Fatima" Wright (see Carey McWilliams, "Ambrose Bierce and His First Love: An Idyll of the Civil War," *Bookman* 75 [June–July 1932]: 257).

Actor] AB expressed frequent disdain at the supposed immorality of actors and actresses. Cf. "Small Contributions" (*Co*, Feb. 1909: 360): "it would be something of a shock to the actor folk to learn that we are not looking to them for instruction in the art of being good."

Actress] See also B15 in the Appendix.

Adage] AB wrote a series of fables entitled "Old Saws with New Teeth" (*CW* 6.363).

Adamant] *Solicitate* mimics *salycilate,* a salt or an ester of salicylic acid, which is a preservative and is used in making aspirin. To *solicit* can mean to approach someone with an offer of sexual services in return for payment.

Adder] AB makes a similar joke about the adder in "Kings of Beasts: The Snake" (1902; *CW* 12.44): "But the snake [addressing Adam in the Garden of Eden], it spoke up and sed, the snake did: 'If you please, sir, Ime willing to go 4th, but I cant multiply. Ime a adder.'"

Adipose] Cf. "Carmelite," line 6 of the verse: "Ragged and fat and as saucy as sin."

Adjutant] Adjutant officers appear in several of AB's Civil War stories (*CW* 2): "The Affair at Coulter's Notch" (1889; p. 105), "Parker Adderson, Philosopher" (1891; p. 133), "The Story of a Conscience" (1890; p. 165), and "One Kind of Officer" (1893; p. 178); also "A Major's Tale" (1890; *CW* 8.63).

Administration] Cf. "Corporation."

Admonition] *Judibras* fuses the names of *Judas* Iscariot and *Hudibras* (1663, 1674, 1680), the satiric epic by Samuel Butler (1613–80). The verses here (and most others attributed to Judibras) are *hudibrastic,* as is Butler's mock-heroic satirical poem, written in octo-syllabic couplets.

Adonis] A strikingly beautiful youth loved by both Persephone and Aphrodite (Venus), the latter of whom bore him a son and a daughter. After he was torn to pieces by a wild boar before Aphrodite's eyes (for his presumed unkindness), both goddesses claimed him. Zeus decreed that he spend half the year above ground with Aphrodite, the other half in the underworld with Persephone.

Affection] "An abnormal state of body; malady, disease" (*OED*).

Affliction] AB frequently used the phrase "another and bitter world" (i.e., hell) to mock the phrase "another and better world," a popular reference to paradise in the hereafter. In *W,* the definition reads:

The acclimatizing process whereby the soul is fitted for another and a warmer world. A method of breaking it to us gently.

> *Affliction* sore long time he bore,
> Physicians was in vain.
>
> *Ella Wheeler.*

Agrarian] Aeneas was the son of Anchises and Aphrodite. AB's allusion is to Vergil's *Aeneid* 2.804, where Aeneas carries Anchises on his back as they flee Troy.

Album] Just as Jesus was crucified between two thieves (Mark 15:27).

Alcohol] *Alcohol* originally referred to a fine metallic powder (usually antimony or stibnite) used to stain the eyelids, as in "On with the Dance!" (1880; *CW* 8.298); now the intoxicating element in fermented and distilled beverages.

Allah] The quatrain is patterned after that of the *Rubaiyat of Omar Khayyam,* and in *W* it is attributed to Khayyam.

Allegiance] *W* concludes: "The traditional bond of duty between the taxer and the taxee. It is not reversible."

Alligator] The reference to Herodotus is to *Histories* 4.45, where he notes that the Indus is the only river aside from the Nile where crocodiles are found. AB repeated the pun about the "sawrian" numerous times in his Little Johnny sketches.

Alone] In *W,* for *Booley Fito* read *Dr. Kalloch.* Isaac Smith Kalloch (1832–90) was both a Baptist minister and mayor of San Francisco (1879–82). During his stormy administration Kalloch was shot and wounded by Charles de Young, publisher of the *Chronicle.* In retaliation, Kalloch's son later shot and killed de Young but was acquitted of murder.

Amazon] A member of a nation of women warriors reputed to have lived in Scythia and to have removed the right breast for greater ease in using the bow; hence, any tall or aggressive or strong-willed woman. AB was much opposed to "women's rights and equality of the sexes." His admiration of Amazons and hatred of women's rights activists can be seen in "Prattle" (*W,* 11 Nov. 1881: 307): "A contemporary alludes to Mrs. Stow's disreputable following of malefactresses as 'Amazons.' I confess my inability to discern in what respect these withered harridans, with their cracked and disobedient voices and their abundant angles—feeble and foolish in mind, tough and tendinous in body—resemble the splendid creatures who battled with the Centaurs. The comparison is stupid. It is insulting. By Jove, it is flat blasphemy."

Ambition] In *W,* for "vilified . . . dead" read "abused by the newspapers during life, and have an epitaph by Hector A. Stuart after death." AB relentlessly attacked the poetry of local bard Hector A. Stuart, author of *A Vesper Bell* (1869) and *Ben Nebo: A Pilgrimage in the South Seas* (1871). See also A1 in the Appendix.

Animal] AB refers to the absurd belief that God thoughtfully provides for *all* His creatures, ignoring the fact that all creatures are sustained only by the loss of life of other creatures or plants. He tirelessly lampooned this notion in his Little Johnny sketches, for example, "Kings of Beasts: Domestical Hens": "Mister Jonnice . . . he says it was mighty thoughtful in the Creator to provide chickens for the hawks, but Uncle Ned he says it wasn't quite so thoughtful in him to provide hawks for the chickens" (*CW* 12.94). See "Air," "Bounty," and "Insectivora."

Animalism] Animals are the "beasts that perish," unlike human beings, who, in Christian belief, live on in the hereafter. Cf. Psalms 49:12: "Nevertheless man being in honour abideth not: he is like the beasts that perish."

Antiquity] The quotation is from Shakespeare, *Sonnets* 62.10.

Aphorism] The verses at "Diary" are also from *The Mad Philosopher* (presumably a fictitious verse drama or poem). AB mentions a mad philosopher at "Reality." In *W* and *C*, the definition reads: "A brief statement, bald in style and flat in sense."

Appetite] "For even when we were with you, this we commanded you, that if any would not work, neither should he eat" (2 Thessalonians 3 : 10).

Applause] The definition in *W* reads:

The echo of a platitude from the mouth of a fool.

There was a young reader who thundered
And lightened, and "rode the Six Hundred!"
But he got no *applause*
For his effort, because
His trowsers it sadly had sundered.

T-r-sa C-rl-tt.

AB alludes to San Francisco poet Theresa Corlett, whose work he frequently attacked.

Apron] The verses parody the last stanza of "Elegy Written in a Country Churchyard" (1751) by Thomas Gray (1716–71):

No farther seek his merits to disclose,
Or draw his frailties from their dread abode,
(There they alike in trembling hope repose)
The bosom of his Father and his God.

See "Elegy" for another parody of Gray's poem.

Arbitration] In "Prattle" (*E*, 12 May 1895: 6), AB described *arbitration* as "that first and last hope of the feeble freebooter. . . ."

Archbishop] AB penned a similar rhyme in "Prattle" (*E*, 9 Feb. 1890: 6), which he attributed to William Ingraham Kip (1811–93), first bishop of the Episcopal Church of California:

By help of my Assistant Bishop,
More souls from sin I hope to fish up,
And Nick with hotter sauce to dish up.

Architect] In *W* and *C*, the definition concludes: "who estimates the whole cost, and himself costs the whole estimate."

Ardor] AB refers to the *Amores* (love poems) of Ovid (43 BCE–18 CE). *W* adds the following verses:

He loved her with an *ardor* —
Such a hot one,
That her father had to guard her
With a shotgun.

Ovid.

Argonaut] *Ar* was a San Francisco newspaper for which AB wrote from 1877 to 1880. Its founder and editor, Frank M. Pixley (1824–95), was notoriously anti-Catholic. AB satirized that hatred in "The Subdued Editor" (1890; *CW* 5.134), addressed to Pixley.

Aristocracy] *W* adds: "Down wid *arishtocrats!* —D. *Kearney*." For Kearney, see "Sandlotter."

Arrayed] In *W*, for "as a rioter . . . lamp-post" read:

(Come to think of it, that definition describes with tolerable accuracy the condition of a rioter hung to a lamp-post.)
An Austrian army, awfully *arrayed*,
Boldly by battery besieged Belgrade.

Charles Warren Stoddard.

Charles Warren Stoddard (1843–1909) was an important literary figure in San Francisco for forty years, a coeditor of *Overland Monthly,* and a friend of AB. His works include *Poems* (1867), *South-Sea Idyls* (1873), and *The Lepers of Molokai* (1886).

Arrest] The King James Bible, the English translation from Hebrew and Greek published in 1611, was known as the "Authorized Version." One might expect that Satan would have a hand in an "Unauthorized Version." Cf. "Sabbath"; also "Kings of Beasts: Fish" (1878; *CW* 12.162): " . . . God made us all in 6 days and was arrested on the 7th."

Arsenic] A highly poisonous metallic element used in insecticides. Women once consumed arsenic in very small doses because it was believed to make the skin desirably pale.

Art] A *cate* is a delicacy.

Asbestos] Cf. "Prattle" (*Ar,* 25 Aug. 1877: 5): "Asbestos is now being woven into a fabric suitable for clothing, which is absolutely fire-proof. Good stuff for shrouds."

Ass] "Mr. Pixley . . . [u]nfortunately . . . cannot sing; like the Washoe canary (*Asinus Geigerii*) he has a good voice, but no ear" ("Prattle," *E,* 24 July 1887: 4). Ambrosius Theodosius Macrobius (fl. c. 400 CE) was an ancient philosopher and critic, best known for his *Saturnalia* (an academic symposium in seven books) and his commentary on Cicero's *Somnium Scipionis.* Ramasilus and Stantatus are fictitious. *W* concludes with two additional lines:

> To thine ears' length mayest thou enjoy life's span,
> In fathership with Mule and fellowship with Man!

See also "Griffin."

Avernus] The ancient name for Averno, a small crater lake of southern Italy near the Tyrrhenian Sea. Regarded by the ancient Romans as the entrance to the underworld because of its (formerly) gloomy aspect and intense sulfuric vapors. The expression *facilis descensus Averni* (the descent to Avernus [is] easy) is found in Vergil, *Aeneid* 6.126. Scrutator is fictitious. L. Caelius Firmianus Lactantius (240?–320?) was a Christian theologian and philosopher.

Baal] Baal was any of various fertility gods of the ancient Semitic people considered by the Hebrews to be false idols. Beelzebub is one of the many names for Satan. Berosus, or Berossus, was a Babylonian priest of the third century BCE. He wrote *Babyloniaca* to elucidate Babylonian creation myths to the Hellenistic Greeks. The work exists only in fragments, but Book II contains an account of a prehistoric flood analogous to that found in the Bible. See Stanley Mayer Burstein, *The Babyloniaca of Berossus* (Malibu, CA: Undena Publications, 1978). Berosus is also mentioned in "Prattle" (*W,* 19 Mar. 1881: 180). AB refers to the stomach as a god at "Abdomen," "Excess," and "Soul." A "Mr. Guttle" is one of two fictitious gastronomes mentioned in "A Sole Survivor" (1890; *CW* 1.401).

Babe or Baby] The story of Osiris also appears in "Replies to Correspondents" (*Fu,* 20 June 1874: 19).

Bacchus] *Jorace* is a parody of the Roman poet *Horace* (Quintus Horatius Flaccus [65–8 BCE]), referring specifically to the various tributes to Bacchus (and to drinking) found in his odes and epodes.

Back-slide] To *backslide* is, in religious practice, to revert to sin. Cf. "The Baptism of Dobsho" (1874; *CW* 8.98): "I fear we must let matters take the usual course, trusting to our later efforts to prevent the backsliding which may result."

Bait] *W* adds the following verses:

> Sweet Rosa Fenn,
> Adored of men,

By old Blazzay was married.
　　"You'd been," said he,
　　"As old as *me*,
Had you so long not tarried
　　In heaven." Said Rose:
　　"The good Lord knows
Impatiently I waited;
　　But ere they threw
　　Me down to you
I had to be well baited."

Beauty and the Beast.

Baptism] See also "The Baptism of Dobsho."

Barber] The root meaning of the Greek word *barbaros* is "non-Greek-speaking" (i.e., one whose speech was incomprehensible to the Greeks, sounding to them like "bar-bar-bar . . .").

Bark] The line "all writers quote" is presumably from "To Thomas Moore" (1817) by Lord Byron (1788–1824): "My boat is on the shore, / And my bark is on the sea . . ." See also note on "Bow-wow."

Basilisk] AB's earliest known published work is the poem "Basilica" (1867), addressed to the basilisk.

Bassinet] The word is in fact derived from the Old French *bacinet* (diminutive of *bacin*, basin). *Berceaunette* is AB's coined diminutive of *berceau* (cradle).

Bassoon] A *bassoon* is, of course, a woodwind instrument, not brass. AB makes a pun on *brazen* as meaning to have a loud, harsh, resonant sound. See also "Clarionet," "Calliope," and "Flute."

Basso-relievo] More commonly rendered in English as *bas-relief.*

Bastinado] Actually, to beat the soles of the feet with a stick or cudgel.

Bath] In *W,* there is an added sentence: "Its daily performance is attended with good results, but it is likely to be fatal when celebrated annually." A bath has indeterminate spiritual efficacy, unlike baptism, although they are outwardly similar.

Bear] An investor who sells securities or commodities in expectation of falling prices.

Beauty] See also B2 in the Appendix.

Bedlam] The quotation is from Shakespeare, *A Midsummer-Night's Dream* 5.1.8. Bedlam, now meaning a place of noisy uproar and confusion, once referred to an insane asylum, specifically, the contracted name of the Hospital of Saint Mary of Bethlehem for the mentally ill in London (see "Magdalene").

Beg] The verses here originally appeared in "Prattle" (*E,* 11 Apr. 1897: 6), although that appearance used the proper name "Monaghan" in place of "mendicant."

Beggary] The joke here was somewhat lost on readers of *W,* because the word *Beggar* had appeared in the previous week's installment of "The Devil's Dictionary."

Behavior] The Dies Irae is a medieval hymn describing Judgment Day, sung in some masses for the dead. AB claimed to have undertaken his own "translation" of the Dies Irae (printed in its entirety in *Shapes of Clay*) because of his disappointment with the translation by Gen. John A. Dix. Yet AB once stated in print that Dix "was the author of one of the noblest translations of the *Dies Iræ*" ("Prattle," *Ar,* 10 May 1879: 4). See AB to Herman Scheffauer (16 June 1903; transcript, Bancroft Library, University of California at Berkeley): "The 'Dies Iræ' is the most earnest and sincere of religious poems; my travesty of it is mere solemn fooling, which fact is 'given away' in the prose introduction, where I speak of my version being of possible service in the church! The travesty is not altogether unfair—it was inevitably suggested by the author's obvious inaccessibility to humor and logic—a peculiarity that is, however, observable in all religious literature, for it is a fundamental necessity to the religious mind. Without logic and a sense of the ludicrous a man is religious as certainly as without webbed feet a bird has the land habit." Cf. AB's reading of the second line of the stanza printed here: "Mine the playful hand that gave your . . ." (*CW* 4.323). A less irreverent reading of the entire stanza is: "Remember, merciful Jesus, / that I am the cause of your journey, / lest thou lose me in that day."

Belladonna] A poisonous Eurasian herb (*Atropa belladonna*), also known as *deadly nightshade*. An alkaloidal extract derived from the plant is used in medicine.

Benedictines] A Benedictine is a monk (not a friar) or nun belonging to the order founded c. 529 by St. Benedict of Nursia that stressed moderation rather than austerity. Black friars actually are members of the Dominican order, founded at the beginning of the thirteenth century by St. Dominic; the term refers to the color of their dress.

Benevolence] The definition is elaborated in the fable "The Dutiful Son" (1892; *CW* 6.298).

Berenice's Hair] A constellation in the northern sky near Boötes and Leo, containing the north pole of the Milky Way. Berenice was a queen of Egypt who promised her hair to Venus if her husband, Ptolemy III, returned safe from a campaign in Syria. When the hair was found to be missing from the temple where it had been dedicated, it was identified with the newly discovered constellation.

Bigamy] Cf. *WR* 19: "For lack of a suitable verb we just sometimes say committed this or that, as in the instance of bigamy, for the verb to bigam is a blessing that is still in store for us." Only in AB's Little Johnny tales is "bigam" used as a verb, and then for humorous effect; AB similarly used the word "polygam" as a verb (see also A19 in the Appendix).

Billingsgate] Foul, abusive language, named after a former fish market in London.

Blackguard] Cf. "Cynic."

Blank-verse] In *W*, the definition concludes with the sentence: "Of all English and American poets not a half-dozen have been able to write good blank-verse; and the six hundred Californian poets are not among them." AB himself eschewed blank verse—unrhymed lines in iambic pentameter. He considered himself a satirist, not a poet, and claimed that only three living poets could write it well. In correspondence with the poet George Sterling (1869–1926), AB wrote that blank verse "seems to me suitable (in serious verse) only to lofty, not lowly, themes. . . . I always expect something pretty high when I begin [to read] an unknown poem in blank" (AB to George Sterling, 28 Sept. 1906; ALS, NYPL).

Blubber] AB mentioned John B. Felton (1827–77), a member of the California Legislature and mayoral candidate in Oakland in 1869, in several "Town Crier" columns.

Blue-stocking] A *blue-stocking* is a woman with strong scholarly or literary interests, after the Blue Stocking Society, the nickname for a predominantly female literary club of eighteenth-century London.

Body-snatcher] The story "One Summer Night" (1906; *CW* 3.58) is about grave robbing for medical purposes. See also "Hyena" re body-snatchers.

Bologna-sausage] In his Little Johnny sketches, AB often suggested that the contents of sausage were best not known.

Bottle] Panurge is a character in *Gargantua et Pantagruel* (1532–34) by Rabelais (1494?–

1553?). AB refers to the lengthy episode, occupying the whole of books 4 and 5, in which Panurge seeks the advice of the Oracle of the Holy Bottle as to whether he should marry. "Crapuli" derives from *crapulent*, "suffering from excessive drinking, eating, etc." (*OED*). "Amphoristic" is a pun on *amphora*, a Greek two-handled jar with a narrow neck used to carry wine or oil.

Boundary] In *W*, the definition concludes: "Among the ancients the god of boundaries was Terminus, and it was customary to set up busts of him (*Termini*) as corner-stones. This is noted as an illustration of how the unconscious hoodlum and the gentle ignoramus come to talk the learned languages."

Bounty] Henry Ward Beecher (1813–87) was a clergyman, newspaper editor, and abolitionist whom AB frequently attacked. See "Animal."

Bow-wow] *Peruvian bark* refers to the dried bark of the cinchona, a tree or bush of the genus *Cinchona*, native to the Andes and cultivated for its bark, which yields quinine and quinidine, used to treat malaria. Also known as *Jesuit's bark*.

Brahma] In Hinduism, the creator god (not only of Hindus). AB makes a veiled allusion to the Holy Trinity of Christianity.

Brain] See also "Cartesian."

Brandy] "On Wednesday, Apr. 7[, 1779], I dined with him at Sir Joshua Reynolds's. . . . Johnson harangued upon the qualities of different liquors; . . . [he] said, 'Poor stuff! No, Sir, claret is the liquor for boys; port, for men; but he who aspires to be a hero (smiling,) must drink brandy'" (Boswell, *Life of Johnson* [1791; rpt. London: Oxford University Press, 1970], 1016). AB attributes the statement by Dr. Johnson to Emerson in *W*, to Carlyle in *C*.

Buddhism] Rev. Horatio Stebbins (1821–1902), minister of the First Unitarian Church in San Francisco from 1864 to 1902, about whom AB wrote favorably at first but later attacked in his columns. He conducted AB's marriage ceremony on 25 Dec. 1871.

Caaba] Usually *Kaaba*, a Muslim shrine in Mecca toward which the faithful turn to pray. It is a small building within the Great Mosque, built to enclose the Black Stone, the most venerated Muslim object. In *W*, the last sentence reads, "People who doubt are shown the stone."

Cabbage] The word *cabbage* derives from a Middle English word meaning head (probably from the Latin *caput*). Cabagius is fictitious. See "Prattle" (*Ar*, 21 July 1877: 5): "Mr. Owen is not much of an editor, but like a cabbage or a drum, he has an excellent head for business"; and "Tales of Two Kings" (*Am*, 14 Jan. 1906: 24; *E*, 21 Jan. 1906: 44): "The responchible hed of the cabinet is always a cabbidge." See also "Zenith."

Cackle] When AB compiled *D*, he omitted the definition for "Cackle" that had appeared in *C* and instead wrote the new definition "Vanity" (q.v.), where he used the verses formerly published here.

Cairn] A *cairn* is a mound of stones erected as a marker or memorial. It may be erected over a grave, but it does not itself contain a body. Dr. Berosus Huggyns is described as an Egyptologist at "Tomb." He is also a character (as "Huggins") in "Curried Cow" (1874; *CW* 8.76), although that story does not take place in the sixteenth century.

Calamity] In *W*, for "misfortune . . . others" read "private and national. The first consists of misfortune to ourselves, the second of good fortune to our enemies, the latter being the harder to endure."

Calliope] The Muse of epic poetry (pronounced kə-lī'ə-pē'); AB also refers to the musical instrument (in this case, often mispronounced kăl'-ē-ōp'). See "My Muse" (*Fu*, 28 Feb. 1874: 88): "A Calliope, I may explain, is simply a 'peal' of steam-whistles, with a key-board, and is operated in the manner of a piano. It is hardly a thing that the muse whose name it bears would have been proud of, but it makes a good deal of noise if the boiler is strong enough to generate sufficient steam, and under skilful fingers will hoot out a number of tunes." The story contains two examples in verse of the alternate pronunciations of *calliope:*

> . . . the next issues of the *Bullrush Bugle* and the *Hardbake Eagle* contained a poem each on the Calliope. This can be regarded only as a coincidence, for the initial couplets contain internal evidence that they are not the work of the same hand. The Bullrushian effusion begins thus: —

> Deceitful baffler of our hope,
> O evanescent Calliope!

> The Hardbackian bard begins less plaintively, but with a stronger indignation, thus: —

> The ruin thou'st wrought may it also seize thee,
> Thou fiendish, remorseless old Calliope!

Callous] Zeno of Citium (335?–263? BCE) was the founder of the Stoic school.

Calumnus] *Calumny* is the malicious utterance of a false statement to injure another's reputation. AB alludes to the play *A School for Scandal* (1777) by Richard Brinsley Sheridan (1751–1816) but more generally to the malicious gossip found throughout that play and, by implication, throughout upper-class society.

Calvary] Salmi Morse, editor of *W,* was publishing his "Wasp's Improved Webster" in *W* just before AB's "The Devil's Dictionary" began to appear there. Morse had written a "passion play," a dramatic representation of the Passion of Jesus. An unsigned squib in *W* (2 Dec. 1882: 755) about the play said: "They are to have the Passion Play in New York at last. Salmi Morse, the indefatigable maniac whose brain evolved its tangled and incomprehensible lines, has at last conceived a plan by which the courts and the newspapers can be appeased and the piece presented." O'Neill appears to have been an unfortunate actor performing in what was not a very good play. AB's "Prattle" (*Ar,* 19 Apr. 1879: 5) contains a mock "Passion Play."

Camel] AB's quasi-Latinate taxonomy means "splay-footed hump-back." The "improper" camel—the single-humped Arabian camel, or *dromedary* —is the kind most often exhibited in circuses, whereas the two-humped Bactrian camel of central Asia is not.

Candidate] The word derives from the Latin *candidatus,* originally meaning "clothed in white" (i.e., wearing a white toga). The writer Edward Townsend (1855–1942), author of *"Chimmie Fadden"; Major Max; and Other Stories* (1895), was a friend of AB.

Cane] See "Prattle" (*Ar,* 5 May 1877: 5): "Senor Herath, the Costa Rican Minister at Washington, had a diplomatic controversy with a hackman, whom, finally, he assured of his distinguished consideration by hitting him hard on the head with a cane." Concerning AB's final meeting with his erstwhile collaborator, Gustav Adolphe Danziger, George Sterling wrote: "Danziger was the person over whose head Bierce broke his cane to fragments" ("Introduction," *In the Midst of Life* [New York: Modern Library, 1927], x).

Cannibal] See "Heart" re *Delectatio Demonorum. W* and *C* contain the following additional paragraph: "The practice of cannibalism once was universal, as the smallest knowledge of philology will serve to show. 'Oblige us,' says the erudite author of the *Delectatio Demonorum,* 'by considering the derivation of the word "sarcophagus," and see if it be not suggestive of potted meats. Observe the significance of the phrase "sweet sixteen." What a world of meaning lurks in the expression "she is sweet as a peach," and how suggestive of luncheon are the words "tender youth"! A kiss is but a modified bite, and when a young girl insists on making a "strawberry mark" on the back of your hand she only gives way to an inherited instinct that she has not learned to control. The fond mother, when she rapturously avers that her babe is "almost good enough to eat," merely shows that she is herself only a trifle too good to eat it.'"

Canonicals] The dress prescribed by canon for officiating clergy.

Canonize] See also "Saint."

Capital] For AB's views on capital punishment, see "The Death Penalty" (*CW* 11.210).

Carmelite] As noted, an order of mendicant friars of Our Lady of Mount Carmel, founded c. 1154 by St. Berthold and reorganized as mendicant friars after the Crusades by St. Simon Stock; known as *white friars* (see "Friar"). In the sixteenth century, St. Teresa of Avila and St. John of the Cross undertook to reform their Carmelite orders.

Cartesian] Relating to the philosophy or methods of René Descartes (1596–1650). His famous dictum appears in *Discourse on Method* (1637). AB's Latin should have read *Cogito cogitare ergo cogito esse*.

Cat] In AB's Little Johnny sketches, Johnny's father frequently kicks Mose, the family cat, as in the situation described here. *Elevenson,* a play on Alfred, Lord Tennyson (1809–92), the Victorian poet, is a late change, the first attribution in *W* being to Sands W. Forman, one of many bad poets attacked by AB.

Catechism] A *catechism* is a book that briefly summarizes the basic principles of Christianity in question-and-answer form. AB's columns—especially in *W*—contain extracts from absurd "catechisms" on politics and other subjects. In *ND* under "Sacred Themes," he calls *The Calvary Catechism* "a book of riddles" (p. 113).

Cemetery] *W* adds the following verses:

> Though strate and narrow is the tomb,
> In heaven there is plenty romb.
> He suffered long and died phthisic,
> In spite of all the doctor's thphysic.

Cenotaph] AB repeats the verses here in "The Passing Show" (*Am* and *E*, 18 Feb. 1900: 26). A variant appears in "Prattle" (*Ar*, 29 June 1878: 9): "Here lies the bodies of our dear Tommy and Sally: / One resting here and the other in Grass Valley."

Censor] As noted, the *censor* was one of two officials in ancient Rome responsible not only for supervising public behavior and morals but also for taking the public census.

Centaur] A *centaur* had the head, arms, and trunk of a man and the body and legs of a horse. Chiron was a wise physician and prophet whose pupils included Achilles, Asclepius, Hercules, and Jason. When he suffered an incurable wound, he gave his immortality to Prometheus. Zeus turned Chiron into the constellation Sagittarius. Cf. Mark 6:25: "And she came in straightway with haste unto the king, and asked, saying, I will that thou give me by and by in a charger the head of John the Baptist." In this sense, a *charger* is a large, shallow dish, a platter. See also "Prattle" (*E*, 24 Nov. 1889: 6), where AB mocked a writer in another paper who had written of a military man, "He bestrode his horse like a centaur": "Nobody ever saw a regular soldier bestride his horse 'like a centaur.' A centaur on horseback would be a terrifying spectacle: it would make the shade of old Chiron shy worse than a tricksy colt. It is possible that the *Oregonian* man has forgotten just what a centaur was like—it is so long since there were any. The latest one of which we have any account was John the Baptist's head on a charger."

Chemise] A woman's loose, shirtlike undergarment or a loosely fitting dress or shift, sometimes worn with a belt. See "Hug" and "Kiss."

Chinaman] AB's lifelong defense of Chinese immigrants ("coolies") made him very unpopular in California.

Chiromancer] A palm-reader. AB continually railed against clairvoyants, palm-readers, astrologers, and other quacks but vilified their dupes equally. See "Clairvoyant."

Chivalry] See "Prattle" (*W*, 5 Aug. 1881: 83): "A *Bulletin* reporter is good enough to give us, as the latest joke on the street, that hoary pleasantry about the two wings of the Democracy being called the Chivalry and the Shovelry; and another forehanded writer in the same paper attempts to make it stick with an editorial builded for the purpose of lugging it in. Why, my dear fellows, the creature of that joke has turned up his toes, and in the top of the mighty tree that has grown up from his grave, 'the century-living crow' that was nestled in its branches is bleaching milk-white with age."

Christen] To baptize into a Christian church, and thus to give a name at baptism. AB felt that he had been inflicted as described in *D*. See AB to George Sterling (15 Feb. 1911; ALS, NYPL): "*My* name is Bierce, and I find, on reflection, that I like best those who call me just that. If my christen name were George I'd want to be called *that*; but 'Ambrose' is fit only for mouths of women — in which it sounds fairly well."

Christian] The verses here, added to *C* in 1906, originally appeared in "The Passing Show" (*E*, 26 Nov. 1899: 14; *J*, 3 Dec. 1899: 27). Cf. "Prattle" (*E*, 25 Dec. 1898: 12; *Am*, 1 Jan. 1899: 43): "I made no such 'statement' as that 'the Christian religion is a narrow religion'; so I am under no obligation to tell you 'what is wider.' Incidentally I may say that in the matter of width the gulf between Christianity and Christ is no floor-crack."

Christmas] See also the poems "An Unmerry Christmas" (1885; *CW* 4.155) and "The Yearly Lie" (1887; *CW* 4.317) and the essay "Christmas and the New Year" (*CW* 9.235) for AB's feelings about Christmas.

Clarionet] Now spelled *clarinet*.

Clergyman] *W* adds the following verses:

> The clergyman to Tom, one day,
> Said: "Work is worthy of its pay;
> You to your body did attend,
> But I your soul did ever mend."
> Said Tom: "I recognize the debt,
> And pay it thus." A coin he set
> Before the parson's eyes awhile,
> Then pocketed it with a smile,
> Remarking: "Since the thing you mend
> Is unsubstantial, pious friend,
> It clearly seems the fitting way
> In unsubstantial coin to pay."

Clinic] AB refers to the derivation of the word from the Greek *kline*, a bed.

Clio] Xenophon (430?–355? BCE) was a Greek soldier and writer, author of the *Anabasis*, an account of the expedition of the Greek mercenaries under Cyrus (401–399 BCE). Herodotus (fifth century BCE) was a Greek historian, known as the "Father of History," whose accounts of the Persian Wars are the earliest known examples of narrative history. Clio is also mentioned in the verses at "Prehistoric." In *W*, the definition concludes:

> . . . speakers, whose remarks elicited hearty and frequent applause, but with whom on all questions of fact we beg leave to differ.*
>
> *The illustrious author of this Dictionary seems to have made a long leap from ancient Grecian mythology to modern American politics. He was apparently "set off" by using the word "preside," with its associations of the "mass-meeting" and the "stump." —ED. WASP.

Clock] In *W,* the verses are attributed to AB's friend, the poet Jo[aquin] Miller, for whom, see "Heigh-ho."

Close-communion] Communion in the Lord's Supper restricted to the baptized members belonging to the same denomination or the same church, as opposed to open communion.

Close-corporation] A corporation in which the shares of stock are held by few persons and are not traded publicly.

Close-fisted] Samuel Johnson (1709–84) ridiculed the attempts of James Macpherson (1736–96) to pass off the poems of "Ossian" as the work of an ancient Gaelic bard.

Cœnobite] A *cenobite* (male or female) is a member of a convent or other religious community, as opposed to an *anchorite,* a religious person who lives in seclusion.

Clove] Cloves often were used to mask the odor of alcohol on the breath.

Colonel] AB continually vilified those who affected titles to which they had no right, "Colonel" being one such title. See "Prattle" (*E,* 27 Nov. 1887: 4): "We are simple republicans in America—we are not fond of titles—O, no! And every third man a 'General' or a 'Colonel,' and one of each two others a 'Judge.' The coarse good-will that bestows these titles with so abominable indiscrimination and the coarser vanity that accepts them are, apparently, proof against ridicule and inaccessible to shame."

Comet] Two weeks prior to the appearance of this definition in *W,* AB had written about comets in "Prattle" (*W,* 2 July 1881: 5): "I am a little warm on the subject of the comet because it can hardly be unknown to the world that despite the malevolent and interested falsehoods of my wicked contemporaries, I was the first man in San Francisco to discover it, as I came from dinner at three o'clock on last Wednesday morning. I had afterward the mortification to learn from the dispatches that it had previously been sighted by the Astronomer Royal of the Observatory at Omaha. This disposed, I admit, of my proprietary rights; but at least I am the manager and agent for the Pacific Coast."

Commit] See *WR* 30: "*Fully* for *Definitively,* or *Finally.* 'After many preliminary examinations he was fully committed for trial.' The adverb is meaningless: a defendant is never part committed for trial. This is a solecism to which lawyers are addicted. And sometimes they have been heard to be 'fullied.'"

Common-law] Based on custom and usage rather than on written law.

Compunction] AB alludes to the Greek proverbial expression "kick against the pricks" (sometimes "kick against the goad"), to feel or show pointless opposition to or resentment of an often necessary authority. See Acts 26 : 14: "And when we were all fallen to the earth, I heard a voice speaking unto me, and saying in the Hebrew tongue, Saul, Saul, why persecutest thou me? It is hard for thee to kick against the pricks." The verses from *W* are omitted because AB used them at "Symbolic" in *D.*

Concatenate] See "Abrupt." The verses were reprinted, slightly revised, as "A Mine for Reformers" (1881; *CW* 5.207).

Confession] *Confession* is not the place where the Sacrament of Reconciliation, as it is now known, occurs but the act by which penitents tell their sins to a confessor in order to receive absolution. The confessional was formerly a dark stall in the church in which penitent and confessor were separated by an opaque screen (as at "Jester"), but it is now commonly a less forbidding room where the penitent can face the confessor.

Congregation] See "Censor Literarum" (1892; *CW* 5.235), addressed to Parson (Horatio) Stebbins:

> What spreads
> The fame of your existence, once a week,

From the Pacific Mail dock to the Heads,
  Warning the people you're about to wreak
  Upon the human ear your Sunday freak? —
Whereat the most betake them to their beds,
Though some prefer to slumber in the pews
And not assent to your hypnotic views.

Conjugal] Cf. "Marriage."

Connoisseur] In *W*, the definition reads: "One who knows what is what, and is commonly content with that degree of knowledge."

Consolation] Cf. "Comfort."

Controversy] Dramer Brune is a character in "The Story of a Conscience" (1890; *CW* 2.165).

Cookery] Marion Harland was the pseudonym of Mary Virginia (Hawes) Terhune (1830–1922), author of many books on cookery, housekeeping, and similar subjects, as well as several novels.

Corned] A parody of William Congreve (1670–1729), *The Mourning Bride* (1697): "Heaven has no rage like love to hatred turned, / Nor hell a fury like a woman scorned" (iii.8). For Stuart, see "Ambition."

Coroner] See "A Bottomless Grave" (1888; *CW* 8.11): "'I must tell you, my children, that in a case of sudden and mysterious death the law requires the Coroner to come and cut the body into pieces and submit them to a number of men who, having inspected them, pronounce the person dead. For this the Coroner gets a large sum of money.'"

Corporal] *W* adds the following: "[Latin, *corpus*, a body. A corporal is so called because he isn't anybody.]"

Corporation] Cf. "Administration."

Corpse] AB calls the tomb (q.v.) the "House of Indifference." (He initially had defined it as "a habitation of the indifferent"; likewise, he initially defined "Impartial" as "Dead.")

Corsair] A pirate. *W* adds the following verses:
He was a cracking corsair
  And a bouncing buccaneer
But he got a rope of horse-hair,
  With the knot beneath his ear.

And when he felt that halter
  He repented all his crime,
And his life he swore to alter,
  But he didn't have the time.

But let sorrow not usurp us;
  Though he's cut all earthly joys,
Yet he serves a noble purpose
  In the story-books for boys.

Couple] William C. Bartlett (1818–1907) was an editorial writer for the *San Francisco Bulletin* frequently attacked by AB.

Court Fool] In *Am*, 22 Feb. 1906, AB defined "Plaintiff" as "*n*. See Court Fool." See "Jester."

Covet] The first major revision of the King James Bible was published in 1881 (New Testament) and 1885 (Old Testament), based on ancient manuscripts that had come to light since the publication of the "Authorized Version" in 1611. See "For a Revised Version"

(1879; *CW* 5.303), surely written with knowledge that the work was in progress. AB wrote a lengthy parody of public response to the Revised Version in "Prattle" (*W*, 3 June 1881: 357). Other distortions of the Ten Commandments appear at "Decalogue" and "Sabbath."

Cow] Apparently AB did not think the water from an artesian well was very good to drink. See "Prattle" (*E*, 26 June 1887: 4): "The long-disused artesian well at the New City Hall is to be cleaned out, and such of the statesmen thereabout as have the baneful habit of impairing the efficacy of their triple-distilled thunder-and-lightning with water will have to use the water of that well or go across the street—an unwonted exertion. This is a long step in the direction of reform, for the fluid will most consummately and irreparably efface them."

Coyness] "He who hesitates is lost" is a common misquotation of a line in Joseph Addison's *Cato* (1713): "The woman that deliberates is lost."

Crayfish] Or crawfish; a small, edible, freshwater crustacean resembling the lobster. Merivale is fictitious.

Creditor] See also B13 in the Appendix.

Cremona] The definition in *W* concludes:

> A genuine Connecticut Cremona is supposed to be mentioned in the following
> lines of Omar Khayyam:
>> Hey, diddle, diddle!
>> The cat got the fiddle,
>>> The cow jumped over the moon,
>> But the little dog stayed
>> To hear the thing played,
>>> And died of the very first tune.

These verses parody a well-known Mother Goose rhyme. Cremona is a city in northern Italy. In the seventeenth and eighteenth centuries it was reputed for its violin makers, including the Amati, Guernieri, and Stradivari families.

Crest] AB mocked heraldry as yet another "survival" in "Prattle" (*E*, 17 Apr. 1892: 6; rpt. in part as "Symbols and Fetishes," *CW* 9.185): "Heraldry dies hard. It is of purely savage origin, having its roots in the ancient necessity of tribal classification. . . . Among people where [heraldic devices] exist as 'survivals' their use is at least a tolerable stupidity; but in America, where they come by cold-blooded adoption essentially simian, they are offensive inexpressibly. Many of the devices upon the seals of our States are no less ridiculous than those used (and the use of any) by some of our 'genteel' families to hint at an illustrious descent. . . . [M]y notion of a suitable design for the national coat-of-arms is this: An illiterate voter, rampant, on a field gules. Motto: 'To Hell with Everything.'"

Critic] The verses here first appeared in "Prattle" (*E*, 29 Jan. 1893: 6). Cf. Isaac Watts (1674–1748), "Hymn 66":

> There is a land of pure delight,
> Where saints immortal reign;
> Infinite day excludes the night,
> And pleasures banish pain.

Cross] The verses here first appeared in "Prattle" (*E*, 21 Oct. 1895: 6).

Cui Bono?] A Latin phrase meaning "to whose advantage?" Thus, advantage or self-interest is considered a determinant of motivation or value.

Cunning] The definition in *W* concludes:

A different view of the matter, however, is taken in the following fable of the Rev.
Father Gassalasca Jape, of the Mission San Diablo:

> A Bear accosted once a Fox,
>   And the two stopped a Rabbit.
> Said Bruin: "I have found a box
>   Of honey; let us grab it!"
>
> The Fox said: "That is well enough
>   For you, but why should we fight?
> I like full well the pleasant stuff,
>   But do not love the bee-fight."
>
> Thus he, dissembling all his glee.
>   "Nay," said the Rabbit, feigning
> Assent; "as strong a force are we
>   As ever went campaigning.
>
> "All warlike virtues we unite,
>   Our character completing;
> Fox to manœuvre, Bear to fight,
>   And Rabbit for retreating.
>
> "The prizes of the war we'll share,
>   Like conquerors in story:
> Sweets to the Fox, stings to the Bear,
>   And I content with glory!"

Cupid] *W* adds the following verses:

> They slander thee, Venus
>   As mother of Cupid.
> Jove smite the vile *genus*
> That slander thee, Venus!
> For truly, between us,
>   The libel is stupid.
> They slander thee, Venus,
>   As mother of Cupid.
>
> If ever I catch him
>   About my heart prowling
> I'll bite him and scratch him,
>   If I can just catch him,
> Bald-headed I'll snatch him
>   And set him a-howling,
> If ever I catch him
>   About my heart prowling.

Cynic] Cf. "The Town Crier" (*NL*, 9 Mar. 1872: 9), where AB encapsulates his philosophy in his supposed parting column: "Be as decent as you can. Don't believe without
evidence. Treat things divine with marked respect—don't have anything to do with
them. Do not trust humanity without collateral security; it will play you some scurvy
trick. Remember that it hurts no one to be treated as an enemy entitled to respect until he shall prove himself a friend worthy of affection. Cultivate a taste for distasteful

truths. And, finally, most important of all, endeavor to see things as they are, not as they ought to be."

Dado] Actually the word has several specific meanings: (1) the section of a pedestal between the base and surbase; (2) the lower part of a wall of a room, decorated differently from the upper part; (3) a rectangular groove cut into a board into which a like piece may be fitted.

Damn] Paphlagonia was an ancient province in the Graeco-Roman world, situated in Turkey between Bithynia and Pontus. "Dolabelly" is a play on the ancient Roman name Dolabella. "Professor Groke" is a parody of George Grote (1794–1871), an English historian whose *History of Greece* (1846–56) was a landmark. Cf. "The Passing Show" (*E*, 2 Dec. 1900; *SS* 65–66): "At a recent meeting of a Congregational Club . . . Dr. Hubbell said: 'I bear personal testimony that if ever a man prays in his life it is in the midst of battle.' My personal testimony is the other way. I have been in a good many battles, and in my youth I used sometimes to pray—when in trouble. But I never prayed in battle. I was always too much preoccupied to think about it. Probably Dr. Hubbell was misled by hearing in battle the sacred Name spoken on all sides with great frequency and fervency. And probably he was too busy with his own devotions to observe, or, observing, did not understand the mystic word that commonly followed—which, as nearly as I can recollect, was 'dammit.'"

Dance] In the summer of 1877 a book entitled *The Dance of Death*, by "William Herman," scandalized San Francisco. Under the guise of condemning the growing practice of ballroom dancing as lewd and immoral, it portrayed the overheated emotions of the men and women who engaged in it in such frank terms as itself to be considered obscene. Only years later did AB admit that he had written it in conjunction with Thomas A. Harcourt (the book was financed by William Herman Rulofson). Although the work supposedly was a joke, it is likely AB did regard dancing as immoral.

Danger] Delaso is also the poet to whom the lines under "Tortoise" are attributed.

Datary] *Datum Romæ* means "dated at Rome."

Dead] *W* adds the following verses:

Ignoble end to all the strife!
To lie as ne'er we lay in life,
With legs uncomfortably straight
And rigid fixity of pate,
Pierced through and through by worms that live
To make, with needless skill, a sieve
Out of our skin, to sift our dust.
Vain labor! at the last they just
Bolt us unbolted till they bu'st!

Debt] See also B13 (Debtor) in the Appendix.

Decalogue] *W* for 9 Dec. 1881 contained the following comment (but note that the lines quoted correspond to the appearance in *W*): "In our Devil's Dictionary last week was given a metrical revised edition of the Ten Commandments, the fourth being as follows: 'Work not on Sabbath days at all, / Nor dare to read the *Sunday Call*.' True genius is always prophetic; while the writer was working at his idea a justice of the peace at Watsonville was convicting a local newsdealer of an infraction of the Sunday law in selling the *Sunday Call* on the day of publication. We could hardly have hoped that our revised Decalogue would so soon be adopted as the law of the land" (p. 370). See also "The New Decalogue" (1887; *CW* 5.233):

Have but one God: thy knees were sore
If bent in prayer to three or four.

Adore no images save those
The coinage of thy country shows.

Take not the Name in vain. Direct
Thy swearing unto some effect.

Thy hand from Sunday work be held—
Work not at all unless compelled.

Honor thy parents, and perchance
Their wills thy fortunes may advance.

Kill not—death liberates thy foe
From persecution's constant woe.

Kiss not thy neighbor's wife. Of course
There's no objection to divorce.

To steal were folly, for 'tis plain
In cheating there is greater gain.

Bear not false witness. Shake your head
And say that you have "heard it said."

Who stays to covet ne'er will catch
An opportunity to snatch.

AB's poem is itself suggested by "The Latest Decalogue" by Arthur Hugh Clough
(1819–61):

Thou shalt have one God only; who
Would be at the expense of two?
No graven images may be
Worshipped, except the currency:
Swear not at all; for, for thy curse
Thine enemy is none the worse:
At church on Sunday to attend
Will serve to keep the world thy friend:
Honour thy parents; that is, all
From whom advancement may befall:
Thou shalt not kill; but need'st not strive
Officiously to keep alive:
Do not adultery commit;
Advantage rarely comes of it:
Thou shalt not steal; an empty feat,
When it's so lucrative to cheat:
Bear not false witness; let the lie
Have time on its own wings to fly:
Thou shalt not covet, but tradition
Approves all forms of competition.

The sum of all is, thou shalt love,
If anybody, God above:
At any rate shall never labor
More than thyself to love thy neighbour.

In *The Poems of Arthur Hugh Clough,* ed. H. F. Lowry, A. L. P. Norrington, and F. L. Mulhauser (Oxford: Clarendon Press, 1951), 60–61. Robert G. Ingersoll (1833–99) was a renowned agnostic lecturer and writer whom AB defended in his columns.

Decide] See also the verses at "Free-will."

Deer] Cf. "Hare."

Degenerate] In the *Iliad,* Homer never says that the heroes could lift a stone that ten men could not lift; rather, he frequently asserts that the heroes lifted stones that would require two men of his day (see, e.g., *Iliad* 5.302–04). The line that AB quotes is from Pope's *Iliad:* "Such men as live in these degen'rate days" (5.372 = 12.540). The phrase in Homer (*Iliad* 5.304 = 12.449) is *hoioi nun brotoi eis.* AB alludes to this passage in "Is the Human Race Decreasing in Stature?" (*Am,* 4 Oct. 1903: 24; *E,* 25 Oct. 1903: 52 [as "The Long and Short of It"]).

Deinotherium] The word (sometimes spelled *dinotherium*) was a variant term for "deinosaur" or "dinosaur," derived from the Greek *deinos* and *therium,* or "terrifying wild beast."

Deiparous] Just as *viviparous* means to bring forth living young and *oviparous* means to produce eggs that hatch outside the body, *deiparous* means to give birth to gods and *stultiparous* means to give birth to fools. Nob Hill is an upper-class area of San Francisco.

Deist] A *deist* is one who believes, based solely on reason, that God created the universe and then abandoned it, exerting no influence or control over it.

Dejeuner] Actually, *déjeuner* means "lunch"; *petit déjeuner* is "breakfast."

Deluge] The story of the Deluge is told in Ezekiel 13 : 11–13. See also "Baal," "Flood," and "Inundation." In *W,* the definition concludes: "Since then it has been deemed advisable to let the sinners remain on their good behavior."

Demi-john] A large, narrow-necked bottle made of glass or earthenware, usually encased in wickerwork; in AB's sense, a wine bottle.

Demon] AB mocks the journalistic excesses of his time, as under "Deny," "Lacteal Fluid," and others.

Demonomania] AB's coined word is similar to *monomania,* a pathological obsession with one subject or idea.

Deny] The definition refers to the orotund speech of the politicians of AB's day.

Deputy] *W* adds the following lines between lines 10 and 11:

No time to lose—work with a will,
Nor further seek to prove your skill
In spitting at a mark; renounce
The joy of giving the grand bounce
To flies that settle on your crown
Or trace their courses up and down
The nose official. Spring to work!
No pains neglect, no labor shirk.

Deranged] The insanity defense is a frequent topic in AB's newspaper columns. In "An Execution in Batrugia" (1907), later incorporated into "The Land Beyond the Blow,"

AB addresses the insanity defense in the case of murder: "'Law . . . is for the good of the greatest number. Execution of an actual lunatic now and then is not an evil to the community, nor, when rightly considered, to the lunatic himself. He is better off when dead, and society is profited by his removal. We are spared the cost of exposing imposture, the humiliation of acquitting the guilty, the peril of their freedom, the contagion of their evil example'" (*CW* 1.166).

Descendant] AB loathed Oscar Wilde (1854–1900). This definition appeared in *W* just before Wilde's American tour of 1882 made its way to San Francisco (he arrived on 26 Mar. and remained in the area until 8 Apr.). In a "Prattle" written during Wilde's stay, AB excoriated Wilde at length (*W*, 31 Mar. 1882; *SS* 192). See also the note to "Eccentricity."

Descent] Charles Robert Darwin (1809–82), English naturalist, conceived the theory of evolution by natural selection. *The Descent of Man* (1871) is a supplement to his *Origin of Species* (1859).

Deshabille] Cf. "Presentable."

Desiccate] This is one of three verbs (the others are "Hug" and "Hunt") that AB designates as "*v.a.*," meaning "verb, active." It is erroneous to refer to verbs in English as such (they are typically designated either *v.i.* or *v.t.*), but AB jokingly alludes to the actions implied in the verbs.

Detective] See "The Circular Clew" (1893; *CW* 6.224):

> A Detective searching for the murderer of a dead man was accosted by a Clew.
> "Follow me," said the Clew, "and there's no knowing what you may discover."
> So the Detective followed the Clew a whole year through a thousand
> sinuosities and at last found himself in the office of the Morgue.
> "There!" said the Clew, pointing to the open register.
> The Detective eagerly scanned the page, and found an official statement that the deceased was dead. Thereupon he hastened to Police Headquarters to report progress. The Clew, meanwhile, sauntered among the busy haunts of men, arm in arm with an Ingenious Theory.

Devil] "Ella Wheeler" refers to Ella Wheeler Wilcox (1850–1919), a popular writer and poet whose later work often appeared adjacent to AB's in the Hearst papers. AB also twits Wilcox under the definitions "Leonine" (as "Bella Peeler Silcox") and "Lyre."

Dextrality] Brig. Gen. John McComb, later warden of the state penitentiary at San Quentin, was one of AB's favorite whipping boys.

Diary] When this definition appeared in *W* and *C*, AB's diarist was merely "Sam." AB changed the name to "Hearst" for *D*. William Randolph Hearst (1863–1951) was AB's employer from 1887 to 1909. Their relationship was amicable at first, but AB resigned from Hearst's employ following his growing displeasure with the way Hearst's editors handled his work.

Dictionary] In *W*, for "a most useful work" read "one of the most useful works that its author, Dr. John Satan, has ever produced. It is designed to be a compendium of everything that is known up to date of its completion, and will drive a screw, repair a red wagon or apply for a divorce. It is a good substitute for measels [*sic*], and will make rats come out of their holes to die. It is a dead shot for worms, and children cry for it." See also "Lexicographer."

Die] "The die is cast" (*iacta alea est*) was attributed to Julius Caesar by Suetonius (*Divus Julius* 32.3). AB plays upon the two meanings of "die" (*game piece* and *a device for form-*

ing) and "cast" (*tossed* and *molded*). For Senator Depew, see "Abandon." In *W*, attribution to Senator Depew is instead to "Mr. Charles Shinn, of the *Bulletin*."

Digestion] In *W*, the definition ends as follows:

> This brutal judgment is found in his pamphlet entitled *Why are Women Sickly* (John Camden Hotten: London, 1870), a work that has elicited well-merited execration in seventy languages.
>
> "Why are all our women sickly?"
>   Asks the famous Dr. Blenn.
> That is answered very quickly, —
>   "Our physicians are all men."
>
> There is not in this wide world a pleasure so sweet as the vindication of lovely woman against unjust aspersion.

John Camden Hotten (1832–73) published AB's first book, *The Fiend's Delight* (1873), "against [AB's] protest" (letter to James D. Blake, 22 Oct. 1907; ALS, San Francisco Public Library). AB characterized him as "not a nice publisher to deal with" (letter to C. W. Stoddard, 29 Dec. 1872; ALS, Huntington Library and Art Gallery).

Disenchant] Apparently AB objected to the wearing of pantaloons by women because they were a bit too clingy, as noted in his observation on summer fashions: "Pantaloons will probably hold their own" ("The Town Crier," *NL*, 8 May 1869: 9). For Mary Walker, see note on "Handkerchief." Mrs. Stow is probably the wife of William W. Stow (see note to "Epitaph"). See the poetic drama "Mrs. Stow's Pants" (*W*, 10 Feb. 1882: 83) and also "Prattle" (*W*, 9 June 1882: 357):

> Says Mrs. Stow: "I'd have you know
>   I heed not witless speeches,
> And I'll be dressed as suits me best,
>   And just as Nature teaches."
>
> So Mrs. Stow from top to toe
>   Will practice what she preaches —
> Divided shirt, divided skirt,
>   And corresponding breeches.

Dishonesty] The maxim "Honesty is the best policy" derives from Cervantes' *Don Quixote* (Book III, chap. 33). AB mentions the writings of Judas Iscariot in "The Town Crier" (*NL*, 18 Sept. 1869: 9) and a Church of St. Judas Iscariot in "The Town Crier" (*NL*, 21 Aug. 1869: 11) and "Prattle" (*E*, 22 Apr. 1888: 4), placing it in London in the earlier appearance.

Disobey] Israfel Brown is also the author of some short verses in "On with the Dance!" (1880; *CW* 8.332).

Dissyllable] See "Prattle" (*E*, 12 June 1887: 4): "I love a San Francisco poet—a good, downright, sentimental local songsmith. . . . This talented lyrist contributes to a presumably grateful contemporary a 'poem' on 'Enthusiasm,' and pronounces it in five syllables—enthusiazzum. I trust he will not think it sarcazzum if I urge him to favor us with an ode to Slippery Ellum."

Divination] *W* adds the following verses:

> There's a popular kind of divining
> That prospectors use in their mining.
>   'Tis done with a rod,

Carried over the sod,
One end to the ore vein inclining.

The mine thus discovered they docket,
And list it as soon as they stock it.
 A miner then delves,
 While they all help themselves
To the metal in stockholder's [*sic*] pockets.

I have never heard that the miner
Made business for any refiner,
 But the prospectors wink
 And (magnanimous) drink
The health of that blund'ring diviner.

Divine] As a noun, *divine* refers to a cleric. AB uses the phrase "bird of pray" in "Silhouettes of Orientals" (*CW* 4.76).

Divorce] See also B14 in the Appendix.

Doctor] Note that AB revised references to "doctor" in the appearances of "The Devil's Dictionary" to "physician" (q.v.) for inclusion in *D*. See "Prattle" (*E*, 15 Sept. 1889: 4): "'Doctor' means teacher, and most physicians not only do not teach but do all they can to keep the world in ignorance of their art."

Dog] Cf. Luke 12:27: "Consider the lilies how they grow; they toil not, they spin not; and yet I say unto you, that Solomon in all his glory was not arrayed like one of these." AB often described the dog as "an anachronism," as in this representative selection ("Prattle," *W,* 14 Apr. 1882; *SS* 195): "It must seem to the Dog that the substances, methods and functions of nature are arranged with special reference to his needs, his capacities, his future. He can hardly help thinking himself gifted with peculiar advantages and inheriting the earth. Yet the rascal is an anachronism who exhausted his mandate ages and ages ago, and now lags superfluous on the stage. He is a 'survival' who since the dawn of civilization has had no function and no meaning. Our love for him we have inherited along with many other instincts transmitted from our savage past. If there had never been a dog and one were created, we should fall foul of him with hard substances and a clamor of tongues. He would seem uglier than a reporter, and more hateful than a poet."

Domestic] Artemus Ward (pseudonym of Charles Farrar Browne [1834–67]) was an American humorist.

Dotage] Cf. "A Sole Survivor" (1890; *CW* 1.388): "Of reminiscences there is no end. I have a vast store of them laid up, wherewith to wile away the tedious years of my anecdotage—whenever it shall please Heaven to make me old." This pun is borrowed from Benjamin Disraeli's novel *Lothair* (1870): "When a man fell into his anecdotage, it was a sign for him to retire" (chap. 28).

Dragon] See also "Cockatrice."

Dragoon] A heavily armed trooper in European armies of the seventeenth and eighteenth centuries.

Drowsy] In *W,* this definition immediately followed "Dramatist."

Druids] The definition in *D* is fused together from two separate definitions from *W* from 12 Aug. and 23 Dec. 1882. The definition from 23 Dec. reads as follows:

 Druids, *n.pl.* The priests of an ancient Celtic religion which, originating in
 Britain, spread over Gaul, Germany and, according to Pliny, as far as Persia. The

Druids performed their religious rights in groves, and knew nothing of church mortgages and the season-ticket system of pew-rents. They were, in short, heathens and—as they were once complacently catalogued by a distinguished prelate of the Church of England—"Dissenters." The United Ancient Order of Druids, which has several "Groves" in San Francisco and one—Grove Johnson—in Sacramento, and whose mystic rites consist in tossing the startled initiate a blanket, claim a legitimate and unbroken succession from the ancient Celtic priesthood, but their pretensions are disposed of by the simple circumstance that the latter had no blankets. They tossed their initiates in a well.

Druids are mentioned sporadically throughout Pliny the Elder's *Natural History*. For Caesar on Druids, see *Gallic War* 6.13–16.

Drunk] See also "Corned," "Potable," and "Tope."

Duel] AB's sixteen-year-old son Day was killed in 1889 in a duel over a girl. See also A8 in the Appendix.

Dullard] Boeotia, a province in ancient Greece, became widely known for the stupidity of its inhabitants. The definition in *W* ends with the sentence: "And of the Californian Dullards we prefer Dr. Platt and Captain W. L. Merry."

Eat] The three functions are chewing, moistening, and swallowing. Anthelme Brillat-Savarin (1755–1826) was a French jurist and author of *Physiologie du goût* (1825), a classic work on gastronomy. Cf. "Prattle" (*E*, 29 June 1890: 6): "Brillat-Savarin protested against being disturbed 'while enjoying his dinner.' He had dined two hours before. This is accounted an instance of perfect digestion."

Eccentricity] See "Prattle" (*W*, 7 Apr. 1882; *SS* 194): "Let us admit that Mr. Wilde's eccentricities in hair and innovations in attire are not in themselves displeasing. It remains true and cogent against him that men of brains do not deem it worth while to differ from their fellow men in these particulars, but only in point of superior mental or moral excellence. They do not compete for honors easily won by clowns and cranks. It follows that Mr. Wilde is not a man of brains; why should I concern myself with his work? I have read it and been unpleasantly affected by it. That is enough."

Editor] The three judges of the underworld in Greek mythology. Minos, king of Crete, and Rhadamanthus were sons of Zeus and Europa; Aeacus was the son of Zeus and Aegina. An *obolus* was a silver coin used in ancient Greece, equivalent to one sixth of a drachma.

Effect] Cf. "Moxon's Master" (1899; *CW* 3.94–95): "'As Mill points out, we know nothing of cause except as an antecedent—nothing of effect except as a consequent. Of certain phenomena, one never occurs without another, which is dissimilar: the first in point of time we call cause, the second, effect. One who had many times seen a rabbit pursued by a dog, and had never seen rabbits and dogs otherwise, would think the rabbit the cause of the dog.'" AB repeats the illustration in "Concerning Terrestrial Lunarians" (*Am*, 15 May 1903: 14; *E*, 30 May 1903: 14).

Efferous . . .] *Efferous* means fierce or violent; *effigate*, to portray by painting or sculpture; *efflagitate*, to demand eagerly; *effodient*, accustomed to digging; and *effossion*, the act of digging out of the ground. All are rare or obsolete words.

Egotist] *Megaceph* means "large head."

Elector] AB directed much of his satire toward the folly of the electoral process. See, for example, "The Kingdom of Tortirra" (1888; later incorporated into "The Land Beyond the Blow," *CW* 1.180–81): "In Tortirran politics, as in Tamtonian, the population is always divided into two, and sometimes three or four 'parties,' each having a 'policy' and each conscientiously believing the policy of the other, or others, erroneous and destructive. In so far as these various and varying policies can be seen to have any relation whatever to practical affairs they can be seen also to be the result of purely selfish considerations. The self-deluded people flatter themselves that their elections are contests of principles, whereas they are only struggles of interests. They are very fond of the word *slagthrit*, 'principle'; and when they believe themselves acting from some high moral motive they are capable of almost any monstrous injustice or stupid folly. This insane devotion to principle is craftily fostered by their political leaders who invent captivating phrases intended to confirm them in it; and these deluding aphorisms are diligently repeated until all the people have them in memory, with no knowledge of the fallacies which they conceal. One of these phrases is 'Principles, not men.' In the last analysis this is seen to mean that it is better to be governed by scoundrels professing one set of principles than by good men holding another. That a scoundrel will govern badly, regardless of the principles which he is supposed somehow to 'represent,' is a truth which, however obvious to our own enlightened intelligence, has never penetrated the dark understandings of the Tortirrans. It is chiefly through the dominance of the heresy fostered by this popular phrase that the political leaders are able to put base men into office to serve their own nefarious ends." See also "Suffrage."

Electricity] The quotation about "Monsieur Franqulin" deliberately confuses Franklin's life with that of Capt. James Cook.

Elegy] The verses are a parody of the opening stanza of Gray's "Elegy Written in a Country Churchyard":

> The curfew tolls the knell of parting day,
>   The lowing herd wind slowly e'er the lea,
> The plowman homeward plods his weary way,
>   And leaves the world to darkness and to me.

See "Apron" for another parody of the poem.

Elephant] The elephant, along with the hippopotamus and rhinoceros, are frequently mentioned in AB's humorous sketches, particularly the Little Johnny tales. See also "Proboscis."

Eleusinian] The Eleusinian Mysteries, founded by Eumolpus, were the most famous religious mysteries of the ancient world, consisting of purification, fasts, rites, and dramas portraying the legend of Demeter (Ceres) and Persephone. They were believed to insure happiness in the future world and to forecast resurrection and immortality. The site of the Eleusinian Mysteries was Eleusis, a town fourteen miles west of Athens.

Eloquence] See also "White" and A9 and A17 in the Appendix.

Elysium] Also the Elysian Fields, Isles of the Blest, Heaven, Paradise. The home of the blessed in the afterlife, according to Greek mythology.

Embalm] See also "The Views of One" (*Am*, 20 Apr. 1905: 16; *E*, 28 Apr. 1905: 20): "The ancient custom of embalming the dead is what makes modern Egypt treeless: it locked up the gases needed by vegetation. There is an exact balance between the animal and the vegetable kingdoms; they feed on each other's decay, and neither can prosper if the other's dead is denied it. Embalm yourselves and make a desert—make a desert and your posterity will be sparse."

Ember Days] Days reserved for prayer and fasting by some Christian churches in the four seasons of the year. Observed on the Wednesday, Friday, and Saturday following the first Sunday of Lent, Whitsunday, 14 Sept. (Holy Cross Day), and 13 Dec. (St. Lucia's Day).

Emotion] *W* adds the following verses:
>She showed such strong emotion,
>>Leaning o'er the vessel's planks,
>That the man who owned the ocean
>>Said he'd have to raise its banks.

Loring Pickering.

Loring Pickering (1812–?), another of AB's favorite whipping boys, was co-owner of the *San Francisco Morning Call* and frequently wrote poetic obituaries for a fee; see AB's poem about him, "An Obituarian" (*CW* 5.23).

Encomiast] A eulogist; but also anyone who delivers warm, glowing praise.

Encumbrance] A legal usage. *OED* quotes the American lawyer Francis Wharton: "A claim, lien, liability attached to property, as a mortgage, a registered judgment, etc."

End] An *interlocutor* (q.v.) is a performer in whiteface in a minstrel show placed midway between the end men in blackface (Mr. Tambo, who played tambourine, and Mr. Bones) and who engages in banter with them. The attribution of the poem in *W* is to "Sir William Emerson." See "Prattle" (*W*, 12 Mar. 1881: 164): "a Washington journal affronts decency and outrages heaven by an 'interview' with Billy Emerson, the end-man of a nigger minstrel troupe. William split his face and agitated his tongue like the tail of a spring lamb, but to what purport and purpose I am unable to say; life, thank the good Lord, is too short to peruse the record of a nigger minstrel's mind."

Endear] Charles Crocker (1822–88) was one of the "Big Four" railroad tycoons of the later nineteenth century, acting as vice president of the Central Pacific Railroad. Maj. Benjamin Cummins Truman (1835–1916) was a widely published California journalist and historian. AB's references to him in print were not flattering. See "A Railroad Lackey" (1888; *CW* 5.100). AB applied the epithet "Rare" to Truman in "Prattle" (*W*, 15 May 1886: 5).

Enigma] AB refers to Loring Pickering (see note on "Emotion").

Enough] The attribution in *W* is to Leland Stanford (1824–93), governor of California (1861–63), U.S. senator from California (1885–93), president of the Central Pacific Railroad (1861–93), founder of Stanford University, and one of the builders of the first U.S. transcontinental railroad.

Entertainment] AB ironically applies the word "dejection" to various kinds of entertainment; see "Farce," "Gloom," "Jester," "Pastime," "Piano," "Pleasure," and "Recreation."

Enthusiasm] George Gordon, Lord Byron (b. 1788), the English poet, spent his last days in Missolonghi in Greece, where he had gone to assist in the Greek War of Independence, and died in 1824, not in battle but of a fever. In a letter dated 26 Apr. 1817, Byron wrote: "The Venus [de' Medici] is more for admiration than love; but there are sculpture and painting, which for the first time all gave me an idea of what people meant by their *cant,* and what Mr. [John] Braham calls 'entusimusy' (*i.e.,* enthusiasm) about those two most artificial of the arts" (quoted in Leslie A. Marchand, *Byron: A Biography,* 3 vols. [New York: Knopf, 1957], 2.690).

Eocene] The Eocene epoch (54 to 38 million years ago) was the second oldest epoch of the Tertiary period, which is part of the most recent era, the Cenozoic.

Epicure] Epicurus (341?–270 BCE) was the founder of the school of Epicureanism, a philosophy that considered pleasure (i.e., the avoidance of pain) to be the highest good. The pejorative use of the term "epicurean" was fostered by Epicurus' opponents, who claimed that he was advocating sensual pleasure. "Epicure" has a variety of meanings, for example, "one who gives himself up to sensual pleasure, *esp.* to eating" or "one who cultivates a refined taste for the pleasures of the table" (*OED*).

Epigram] The third epigram appeared in "Aphorisms of a Late Spring" (*Am,* 24 Apr. 1904: 25; *E,* 8 May 1904: 44). Most are collected in *CW* 8, slightly revised. Cf. the epigram at 2. to the following in "Epigrams" (*CW* 8.379):

When God had finished this terrestrial frame
And all things else, with or without a name,
The Nothing that remained within His hand
Said: "Make me into something fine and grand,
Thine angels to amuse and entertain."
God heard and made it into human brain.

The epigram at 3. appears in *CW* 5.203 as "An Epigrammatist." The following epigrams appeared in *C:*

Woman would be more charming if one could fall into her arms without falling into her hands.

Think not to atone for wealth by apology: you must make restitution by a loan to the accuser.

Study good women and ignore the rest,
For he best knows the sex who knows the best.

Before undergoing a surgical operation arrange your temporal affairs. You may live.

Intolerance is natural and logical, for in every dissenting opinion lies an assumption of superior wisdom.

"Who art thou?" said Saint Peter at the Gate.
"I am known as Memory."
"What presumption! — go back to Hell. And who, perspiring friend, art thou?"
"My name is Satan. I am looking for—"
"Take your penal apparatus and be off."
And Satan, laying hold of Memory, said: "Come along, you scoundrel; you make happiness wherever you are not."

Self-denial is the weak indulgence of a propensity to forego.

Men talk of selecting a wife; horses of selecting an owner.

You are not permitted to kill a woman that has injured you, but nothing forbids you to reflect that she is growing older every minute. You are avenged 1440 times a day.

A sweetheart is a bottle of wine. A wife is a wine bottle.

He gets on best with women who best knows how to get on without them.

"Who am I?" asked an awakened soul.
"That is the only knowledge that is denied to you here," answered a smiling angel. "This is Heaven."

Woman's courage is ignorance of danger; man's is hope of escape.

Women of genius commonly have masculine faces, figures and manners. In transplanting brains to an alien soil God leaves a little of the original earth clinging to the roots.

The heels of Detection are sore from the toes of Remorse.

Twice we see Paradise. In youth we name it Life; in age, Youth.

There are but ten Commandments, true,
But that's no hardship, friend, to you;
The unmentioned sins that tax your wit
You're not commanded to commit.

Fear of the darkness is more than an inherited superstition — it is at night, mostly, that the king thinks.

A chain is only as strong as its weakest link, but a multitude is as wise as its wisest member if it obeys him.

"Who art thou?" said Mercy.
"Revenge, the father of Justice."
"Thou wearest thy son's clothing."
"One must be clad."
"Farewell — I go to attend thy son."
"Thou wilt find him hiding in yonder jungle."

When God had finished this terrestrial frame
And all things else, with or without a name,
The Nothing that remained within His hand
Said: "Make me into something fine and grand,
Thine angels to amuse and entertain."
God heard and made it into human brain.

If you wish to slay your enemy make haste, O make haste, for already Nature's knife is at his throat and yours.

To most persons a sense of obligation is insupportable; beware upon whom you inflict it.

Bear me, good oceans, to some isle
    Where I may never fear
The snake alurk in woman's smile,
    The tiger in her tear.
Yet bear not with me her, O deeps,
Who never smiles and never weeps.

The ninety-and-nine who most loudly demand opportunity most bitterly revile the one who has made good use of it.

Life and Death threw dice for a child.
"I win!" cried Life.
"True," said Death, "but you need a nimbler tongue to proclaim your luck. The child is already dead of age."

How blind is he who, powerless to discern
The glories that about his pathway burn,

Walks unaware the avenues of Dream,
Nor sees the domes of Paradise agleam!
O Golden Age, to him more nobly planned
Thy light lies ever upon sea and land.
From sordid scenes he lifts his soul at will,
And sees a Grecian god on every hill!

In childhood we expect, in youth demand, in manhood hope and in age beseech.

Epitaph] AB wrote dozens of satirical epitaphs, many of which are collected in "On Stone" (*CW* 5.[371]) and "Some Ante-Mortem Epitaphs" (*CW* 4.[345]). AB incessantly poked fun at Loring Pickering, "the famous tomb-stone poet" of San Francisco. The four men mentioned here were all regular victims of AB's satire. Henry Vrooman (1844–89) was a state senator whom Bierce attacked in "Prattle" (*E*, 2 Sept. 1888: 4; rpt. as "A Californian Statesman," *CW* 12.407). William W. Stow (1824–95) was an official of the Central Pacific Railroad and later park commissioner of San Francisco who was accused of raiding public funds; see "Prattle" (*E*, 6 Oct. 1889: 4). For Crocker, see "Endear." Senator Cross is unidentified.

Equality] The following mot from "Prattle" (*W*, 16 Sept. 1882: 581) anticipates George Orwell's *Animal Farm* by sixty-three years: "All men are created equal. Some, it appears, are created a little more equal than others."

Erudition] AB's third book, published as by "Dod Grile," was entitled *Cobwebs from an Empty Skull* (1874).

Esoteric] Information that is *esoteric* is comprehensible to a small group, whereas that which is *exoteric* is popular, or comprehensible to the public.

Esquire] Frank M. Pixley became the object of AB's undying wrath when he failed to rehire AB to work at *Ar* upon AB's return from his Black Hills expedition of 1880–81.

Essential] *WR* contains another harangue about the misuse of *essential*. For Bartlett, see "Couple."

Estoppel] "A bar preventing one from making an allegation or a denial that contradicts what one has previously stated as the truth" (*AHD*). See use of the verb *estop* at "Righteousness."

Etiquette] Cf. "Abdication" (def. 1), line 4 of verse.

Eucalyptus] In AB's mock Latin, *nasocompressus* means "nose-squeezing"; *skunkatus* is a parodic past participle ("skunked"); *disgustifolium* means "foul-leaf." See "Prattle" (*E*, 18 Mar. 1888: 4): "I note with sunny satisfaction the decline and fall of the *Eucalyptus disgustus:* Alameda is cutting down hers and Oakland begins to think of taking action to procure an oak. A more abominable tree than the blue eucalyptus is, as an abstract idea, conceivable, but in the scheme of evolution the conception has never been practically realized. The best attempts at materializing it resulted in the poison-oak, the upas and the 'sticktight,' a Brazilian tree, covered all over with a transparent gum which captures and holds in decay everything that touches it, from the scratching hog to the drifted butterfly. The blue eucalyptus insults alike the eye and the nose—its odor is unhandsome and its color rank. In point of sanitary value—whereof Heaven has put it into the hearts of idiots to prate—it is a little more healing than smallpox and a little less than the sword." In the late nineteenth century eucalyptus trees from Australia were planted throughout California to exploit their oil and hardwood, but the plan failed.

Eucharist] The *Theophagi* are the "god-eaters." Christian sects disagree as to what the Eucharist is. Catholics maintain that Christ is physically present in the Eucharist, but other denominations maintain that he is present only symbolically. See "Close-communion." In *W*, the definition concludes: "Yet the viands are neither sausage or hash."

Euchre] Cf. "Cribbage."

Eulogy] See "Encomium."

Evanescence] To *evanesce* is to dissipate like a vapor.

Evangelist] The definition in *W* concludes: "The evangelists proper are Matthew, Mark, Luke and John; the evangelists improper are the parsons." *Evangelist* comes from a Greek word meaning "bringing good news."

Everlasting] The definition in *W* concludes: "If the illustrious author had not been an ingenious theologian he would doubtless have been an accomplished lawyer."

Exception] In *W*, instead of the last two sentences, the definition reads:

> They do not read *The Devil's Dictionary*, but the choice spirits who do may be reminded by this to inform them that they are victims of an imperfect quotation which, entire, reads thus: *"Exceptio probat regulam de rebus non exceptis"* — The exception proves the rule concerning the things not excepted; that is to say, if you admit that one thing is an exception you concede the existence of a rule to which the others conform. The malefactor who removed the rudder from this dictum and set it sailing upon the ocean of controversy (as Alcibiades cut off the tail of his dog in order to give the Athenians something beside himself to talk about) exercised an influence that appears to be immortal, and did more to darken counsel than the author of the most ingenious original fallacy could have hoped to do in his moment of wildest ambition.

Executive] See also "Lunarian."

Exile] See also "Consul." AB collected several humorous sea sketches, including "The Man Overboard" (1876), under the heading "The Ocean Wave" in *CW* 8.[217].

Experience] Two other Binks are credited with verse in *D*: Sir Abednego Bink ("Right") and Anonymus Bink ("Wall Street"). In *W*, the attribution is to William Sharon (1821–85), a wealthy bank manager and a senator from Nevada (1875–81). He and his executors were involved in a long-drawn-out lawsuit with Sarah Althea Hill, who claimed she had a valid marriage contract with Sharon and therefore a claim to his estate. Hill and his lawyers maintained that the contract was a forgery.

Fable] The definition is derived from the canonical definition of the fable as given by the rhetorician Theon in his *Progymnasmata: logos pseudēs eikonizōn alētheian* (A false [i.e., fictional] story picturing the truth). See Ben Edwin Perry, "Introduction," in *Babrius and Phaedrus* (Cambridge, MA: Harvard University Press; London: William Heine-mann, 1965), xx. AB composed nearly 850 fables, many of them parodies or modernized equivalents of fables such as Aesop's, most of which were first published in *Fu* and *E*. *CW* 6 contains his *Fantastic Fables*, first published in 1899.

Fairy] The definition in *W* concludes: "There have never been any fairies in America, the species most nearly allied to them being the Digger Indians of this state and the Democratic party of Nevada."

Faith] Cf. "Prattle" (*Ar*, 22 June 1878: 9): "faith . . . is nothing in the world but blind belief—belief not only without, but against evidence."

Farce] The definition reflects the ancient Greek practice of presenting a satyr play following tragedies by three competing playwrights during the festival of the Great Dionysia in Athens during the fifth century BCE.

Fashion] Cf. the essay "The Tyranny of Fashion" (*CW* 9.261).

Faun] In Latin, *fauna* as a feminine singular noun (plural *faunae*) does not occur. The proper noun *Fauna* denoted a rustic goddess.

Fear] James Graham, fifth earl and first marquis of Montrose (1612–50), was a Scottish general and poet. The poem quoted by AB can be found in Mark Napier, *The Life and Times of Montrose* (Edinburgh: Oliver and Boyd, 1840), 261. AB has altered the last two lines, which in the original read: "That puts it not unto the touch, / To win or lose it all."

Feast] The *Nemesia* or *Nemeseia* was a festival of Nemesis, also held in honor of the dead. Livy discusses the origin of the *novendiale* (a nine-day feast) in *Histories* 1.31 (trans. Aubrey de Selincourt): "before the very eyes of the investigators stones in large numbers fell from the sky and lay on the ground like drifted hail. At the same time a great voice seemed to issue from the grove on the top of the hill. . . . These strange events affected the Romans too: by the advice of their soothsayers—or perhaps even as a direct result of the mysterious voice from the hill-top—they decreed a nine-day public holiday for religious observance, and it was agreed that a similar festival should be held regularly in future should the phenomenon be repeated." The dates of "movable" feasts such as Easter change from year to year. In *W*, the definition concludes: "Of all the feast days of the various Christian churches none has any sanction in the Gospel. Men make gods of their bellies, and then these gods ordain festivals."

Female] AB perpetually referred to women as the "opposing" or "unfair" sex (punning on the genteel terms "opposite" and "fair"). See the poem "The Opposing Sex" (1895; *Shapes of Clay* [1903 ed. only], 291) and the essay of the same title (*CW* 11.270).

Fib] Epimenides the Cretan first posed this paradox when he declared, "All Cretans are liars."

Fiddle] Nero of course did not play a fiddle or violin during the burning of Rome in 64 CE; instead, he was said to have played on the lyre and sung—not in indifference to Rome's fate but as a kind of dirge for the city. See Tacitus, *Annals* 15.39; Suetonius, *Nero* 38.

Fiend] See "Demon." The phrase "form divine" is from Pope's *Odyssey* 10.278.

Fig-leaf] Irving M. Scott (1837–1903) was a shipbuilder long associated with the Union Iron Works in San Francisco, which built many warships for the U.S. Navy. The verses were reprinted in *CW* 5.203.

Flesh] The definition in *W* concludes:
the First and Third being the World and the Devil, respectively.

The World, the Flesh and the Devil
Once joined in a midnight revel.
The Devil he sunk
To the ground dead drunk—
Said the World: "There's a spirit level!"

Flood] See also "Deluge" and "Inundation."

Flop] A reference to St. Paul, called Saul before his conversion to Christianity (see Acts 9: 3–8). Cf. "Prattle" (*W*, 8 May 1886: 5): "It is really surprising what a number of valid objections to the anti-Chinese boycott our city dailies have found on a closer examination of—public opinion outside the Sandlot. . . . This quick and unpremeditated 'flop' resembles the one once executed by Saul of Tarsus. It may be described as conversion without conviction."

Fly] Beelzebub is the Lord of Flies, another name for Satan, one of the fallen angels in

Paradise Lost. The fly's attributes ("everywhere and always the same") are also God's. The housefly is designated *Musca domestica*, AB's mock taxonomical name meaning "cursed" fly. See also "Baal" and "Zoölogy." The poetic quotation is from the opening two lines of Samuel Johnson's *The Vanity of Human Wishes* (1749) ("extensive" for "comprehensive" and "Survey" for "Surveys" in Johnson). Adolphus Washington Greely (1844–1935) was a U.S. Army officer whose scientific expedition to the Arctic resulted in the exploration of a considerable amount of terrain on Ellesmere Island, Canada, and coastal Greenland; the mission, however, ended in tragedy. Greely commanded the U.S. station at Fort Conger on Ellesmere Island, beginning in Aug. 1881. When a relief ship failed to arrive in early Aug. 1883 his party abandoned Fort Conger and moved southward in small boats. Covering five hundred miles in 51 days, the men landed at Bedford Pym Island, north of Cape Sabine, in Smith Sound on 15 Oct. where they faced a 250-day winter, with rations for 40 days. Before the ordeal was over, they were reduced to eating their own leather clothing. Only Greely and six others survived. AB mentions the ill-fated expedition in several columns in *W* for 1884 and hints at cannibalism.

Fly-speck] In his fables AB referred frequently to the Fly-Speck Islands, his derisive name for Hawaii, which was annexed by the United States in 1893. The quotation is from Pope's "Essay on Criticism" (1711): "How the *Wit brightens!* How the *Style refines!*" (l. 420).

Fog] AB had to move out of San Francisco because the fog adversely affected his asthma. Cf. "Prattle" (*E*, 5 Jan. 1890: 6): "Then should our lungs, no longer full of dust, no longer have it made into fud (Fud is mud compounded of dust and fog—brumate of Park)." AB was writing of his having conceived of a combined fog-dispelling and climate-moderating device some twenty years earlier. Edmund Yates (1831–94) was an English novelist and journalist. *OED* states that the word *smog* was first used in 1905, but this definition suggests that it was in use at least twenty years earlier.

Fold] A "flock" is a group of animals that live, travel, or feed together—AB felt the word "herd" would have sufficed and would have reserved "flock" for discussion of birds only.

Folly] Cf. William Wordsworth (1770–1850), *The Excursion* (1814), 1.79: "the vision and the faculty divine." Desiderius Erasmus (1467?–1536) wrote a satirical work entitled *Encomium Moriae* (1511; trans. as *The Praise of Folly*). Richard Watson Gilder (1844–1909) was a poet and editor of *Scribner's Monthly* (1870–81) and *Century Magazine* (1881–1909). Of him AB wrote: "I have read much of Mr. Gilder's verse, but never found in it a line of poetry. As a poet he seems to be a fairly good editor of a magazine" (AB to Walter Neale, 19 Jan. 1906; ALS, Huntington Library and Art Gallery). AB twitted him also at "Incompossible" (*W* appearance only) and "Loss."

Footprints] The verses imitate the rhyme pattern of Longfellow's *Song of Hiawatha,* as do those at "Whangdepootanawah."

Foreman] See "Prattle" (*E*, 7 Apr. 1889: 4): "I am . . . a newspaperman; I certainly should not thank any vulgar idiot to call me a newspapergentleman. Nor do I believe that my fair critic would call her laundress a washerlady, nor the man who removes her slops a swillgentleman. He may or may not *be* a gentleman—in the best sense of the word— but why say anything about it when we know that he is a man? Shall we call an executioner a hanggentleman, or a headsgentleman, a sailor a seagentleman, a minister a clergygentleman, a cousin a kinsgentleman? Shall we say that a ship was well gentlemanned? Shall we say: 'His emotion ungentlemanned him'?"

Foreordination] Henry Codman Potter (1834–1908) was sixth Episcopal bishop of New

York. In preparing *C* and *D* for publication, AB revised all references to Bishop Kip (who had died in 1893) to say Bishop Potter. Likewise, he changed his reference in *W* to José Sadoc Alemany (1814–88), Spanish-born archbishop (Roman Catholic) of San Francisco (1853–84), to James, Cardinal Gibbons (1834–1921). See also "Frying-pan," "Homiletics," and especially "Predestination." Cf. "The Town Crier" (*NL,* 16 Dec. 1871: 9; rpt. under "Musings, Philosophical and Theological," *FD* 158): "The doctrine of foreknowledge does not imply the truth of foreordination. Foreordination is a cause antedating an event. Foreknowledge is an effect, not of something that is going to occur, which would be absurd, but the effect of its being going to occur."

Freebooter] One who pillages and plunders, especially a pirate.

Freedom] Thaddeus Kosciusko (1746–1817) was a Polish general who aided the American colonies during the American Revolution but failed to lead the Polish forces to victory against the Russians and the Prussians in 1794. As a result, Poland was partitioned among the victors. Between the second and third stanzas, *W* adds the following two:

> When judges mount the bench she howls,
> > And when the evening bell
> Rings *angelus* where monks in cowls
> > Their manhood quell,
>
> Her shrilling voice is heard, and where
> > The parsons, by the ell,
> Reel off the Word and all the prayer
> > They have to sell.

Freemasons] *W* adds the following verses:

> "Freemason, Freemason, pray what may be
> Your Order's exact antiquitee?"
>
> "'Twas founded by Adam, so far as we
> Are able to settle its pedigree."
>
> "Freemason, Freemason, O name to me
> Those who have taken the highest degree."
>
> "All renowned mortals on land and sea
> Grand Masters have been in our Mysteree."
>
> "Freemason, Freemason, give me the key
> To your records—the proofs I fain would see."
>
> "That will I not till you bend the knee
> And pay an initiation fee."
>
> O monstrous wag! in my ear a flea
> The meaning tells of Freemasonree:
> Ye build in this land, with a spirit free,
> A temple of stately mendacitee!

Free-school] Defined by Samuel Johnson as "a school in which learning is given without pay."

Freethinker] A freethinker is one who has rejected dogma, especially in religious thinking, in favor of rational inquiry, much like AB. Cf. Romans 12 : 19: "Dearly beloved, avenge not yourselves, but rather give place unto wrath: for it is written, Vengeance is mine; I will repay, saith the Lord."

Free-will] See "A Spread of Quick-Lunch Wisdom for Busy Readers" (*Am,* 24 Sept. 1903: 16; *E,* 30 Sept. 1903: 16):

> "There's no free will," says the philosopher;
> "To hang is most unjust."
> "There is no free will," assents the officer;
> "We hang because we must."

Freshman] Cf. Isaiah 53 : 3: "He [the suffering servant, or the messiah] is despised and rejected of men; a man of sorrows, and acquainted with grief: and we hid as it were our faces from him; he was despised, and we esteemed him not."

Friar] But see Black Friars under "Benedictines." Friar John of the Funnels is a lecherous monk in Rabelais's *Gargantua and Pantagruel.*

Friendship] The attribution in *W* is to "Sallie Sharon and Willie Neilson," two participants in the Hill-Sharon case (see note on "Experience").

Frog] The *Batrachomyomachia* (Battle of the frogs and mice) is a parody of epic poetry attributed by ancient critics to Homer but almost certainly not by him; it probably dates to the early fifth century BCE. The archaeologist Heinrich Schliemann (1822–90) began excavations at Hissarlik, now accepted as the site of Troy, in 1871; he also made notable discoveries at Mycenae (1876–78), Ithaca (1878), and Tiryns (1884–85). The biblical plague of frogs is found in Exodus 8 : 2–13. The reference to Aristophanes is to his play *The Frogs,* where the chorus of frogs cries, "brekekekèx koàx koàx." On the composer Richard Wagner (1813–83), see "Small Contributions" (*Co,* Feb. 1909: 360): "Wagner's music was said by the late Bill Nye to be 'better than it sounds.'" See also "Leviathan" re tadpoles.

Frontispiece] In architecture, an ornamental façade or a small ornamental pediment.

Frying-pan] John Calvin (1509–64), French-born Swiss Protestant whose tenets of theology are known as Presbyterianism. For Bishop Potter, see "Foreordination." Old Nick is Satan.

Functionary] James Buchanan (1791–1868) was fifteenth president of the United States (1857–61) when South Carolina seceded from the Union. Historians have attributed much of the army's unpreparedness before the Civil War to his inept and indecisive administration.

Funeral] AB sometimes used the pseudonym "Jex" in *W.*

Funny] For Dr. Bartlett, see "Couple." For Fitch, see "Acerbity."

Gallows] The definition in *W* concludes: "An appliance for the treatment of temporary insanity." For AB's views on the insanity defense, see "Deranged." *Miracle plays* were medieval dramas portraying events in the Bible or in the lives of saints and martyrs.

Garter] The Garter is "the badge of the highest order of English knighthood" (*OED*).

Gawby] Variant of *gaby,* a slang term referring to a silly or foolish person. For Hector A. Stuart, see "Ambition."

Gawk] As a noun, "an awkward person; a fool; a simpleton" (*OED*).

Geese] AB did not think much of those who advocated temperance.

Gender] AB lampoons "the sex of words" in "Prattle" (*E,* 1 Apr. 1888: 4). See *WR* 28 re "Feminine for Female."

Genesis] The prophet Moses, the first leader of the Israelites, was traditionally regarded as the author of the Pentateuch, known also as the Law of Moses. Modern scholarship indicates that the books have several sources dating from different periods and that the historicity of Moses is problematic.

Genius] Rory O'Donnell, first earl of Tyrconnel (1575–1608), delivered several rash speeches urging the independence of his tribe, leading to his abrupt departure from Ireland in 1607 in the so-called Flight of the Earls. The individuals referred to in *W* are all obscure or mediocre individuals who seem to have thought very highly of themselves. For Hector A. Stuart, see "Ambition"; for Loring Pickering, see "Emotion." Carl Albert Browne, "the illustrious inventor of the six-legged horse in art" ("Prattle," *W,* 27 Mar. 1887: 4), was an artist and illustrator in Los Angeles in the later nineteenth century. "Dr." H. D. Cogswell was a patent-medicine vendor in San Francisco who attempted to bestow fountains with statues of himself to many cities around the country, including New York City and Rochester, NY. Cogswell claimed that the fountain in Rochester was of bronze, but in fact it was made of sheet zinc. (See F. W. S., "That Offer of a Fountain" [letter to the editor], *New York Times,* 4 Feb. 1889: 8.) See [Editorial] (*W,* 10 Jan. 1885: 4): "Our Dr. Cogswell has presented one of his characteristic drinking-fountains to the city of Boston. . . . It is affirmed that the thing is in design so faultlessly hideous that women and children dare not approach it at night and avoid it as much as possible even on a cloudy day; so insultingly and exasperatingly ugly that in looking at it men forget their brotherhood, fall foul of one another with cries of rage and are gathered to their Pilgrim fathers; so diligently and industriously unhandsome that it frequently leaves its foundation and lies down on the grass to rest. An attempt was made to blow it up with gunpowder, but as soon as the head was knocked out of the keg and the powder saw the fountain it exploded with indignation and killed fifteen men. . . . Cheer up, sister: San Francisco has two of Dr. Cogswell's fountains, and has learned to prize them as her most precious possessions. By adding new terrors to existence they have robbed the grave of its victory." Swan is unidentified.

Gentlewoman] See "Lady."

Geology] The definition in *W* reads:

> GEOLOGY, *n.* The science that treats of the earth's crust—geologists sternly deny that it has anything to do with the earth's interior; they are specialists of the straitest sect. But just wait till somebody comes up out of a well and tells them what is inside that crust!
>
> The geological formations of the globe are thus divided. The *Primary,* or lower one, consists of rocks, bones of mired mules, gas and water pipes, coffins, miners' tools, corroded statues without noses, Spanish doubloons, corner-stones laid by Susan B. Anthony, dead clams, the American Navy and ex-passengers of the Pacific Mail Company's steamers. The *Secondary* is made up of water, earth, angle-worms, dead gophers and traces of moles. The *Tertiary* comprises railroad tracks, patent pavements, grass, snakes, mouldy boots, kitchen garbage, drunks, broken hoop-skirts, beer-bottles, sardine-boxes, decaying husbands whose domestic relations were of the happiest character, barrel-hoops, tomato-cans and dead cats.
>
> Geology is a noble study. In the words of Sir Charles Lyell, "it fascinates worse than a street-car off the track."

Sir Charles Lyell (1797–1875) was an English geologist. His research led him to divide the Tertiary period into the Eocene, Miocene, and Pliocene epochs. His *Principles of Geology* (1830–33, 3 vols.), went into twelve editions in his lifetime.

Ghost] Cf. "Prattle" (*Ar,* 2 Nov. 1878: 9), among others: "I remember Heine somewhere mentions a belief that when, in their dismal wanderings, ghosts meet human beings the dead are as much alarmed as the living. Lord knows why the poor devils should fear and avoid us; they carry no purses." Heinrich Heine (1797–1856) was a German poet and satirist much appreciated by AB. The last paragraph here addresses AB's continued vexation with ghost stories, as addressed at greater length in "The Clothing of Ghosts" (1900; *CW* 9.117). The quotation is from *Hamlet* 3.4.135. The definition in *W* concludes: "Still, I find no difficulty in believing that a spook of only the average intrepidity would be affected with a considerable apprehension if suddenly confronted in a lonely place by that prize beauty, Deacon Fitch, of the *Bulletin*."

Ghoul] AB's early sketch "The Discomfited Demon" (1870; *FD* 53) is about a demon encountering a ghoul in a cemetery. The definition in *W* concludes: "Against the testimony of such incidents as these, the declaration of the Musnud of Smaartellics (Prague, 1597) that 'ghouls are illusions of the devil' is without weight."

Gimlet] A small hand tool used for boring holes.

Glutton] See also "Epicure."

Gold] See "Prattle" (*Ar*, 11 May 1878: 9): "ever since the establishment of republican institutions on this continent the Old World nobility have been impoverished by the ever recurring necessity of sending over vast sums of gold ('British gold,' we call it, as it is all remitted by the Bank of England) to 'trample out popular liberty' in this country by 'controlling elections' and 'corrupting legislation.'"

Gold-bug] A *gold bug* was a supporter of the gold standard. AB alludes to the controversial doctrine of bimetallism—the use of a monetary standard consisting of two metals (gold and silver) in a fixed ratio of value. See "Bimetalism" (1885; *CW* 4.304) and "Monometallist" (q.v.).

Goose] *W* adds the following verses:

A critic who all day had railed
Against a poem which had failed
To please him, as the sun went down
Stopped cursing and forgot to frown.
A goose, which, sitting near, had heard
In silence each censorious word,
Now solemnly exclaimed: "My friend,
I've heard you calmly to the end,
Unwilling to disturb you, though
I smarted at each bitter blow."
"Pray what have my remarks to do,"
The critic cried, "with such as you?"
"With me, indeed! That serves to show
How little critics care to know
About the objects of their curses;
I grew the pen which wrote the verses!"

Gordian Knot] AB's account humorously intertwines ancient legend with modern history. King Gordius of Phrygia had tied a knot to fasten the yoke of his wagon that was so complex it could not be untied. An oracle stated that whoever undid the knot would rule Asia. Many attempted to untie the knot, but Alexander of Macedon simply cut it with his sword. AB alludes to Alexander Badlam of San Francisco, author of *The Wonders of Alaska* (1890). Charles George Gordon (1833–85), an English general, was governor-general of the Sudan in 1877–79. He returned to the area in 1884 to assist

Egyptian troops who were being harassed by the members of a local religious sect, the Mahdists. Gordon entered Khartoum on 18 Feb. 1884, and shortly thereafter the Mahdists besieged the city. Gordon heroically withstood the siege for ten months before finally being overwhelmed by the Mahdists. He died in Khartoum on 26 Jan. 1885.

Gorgon] Any of three sisters—Steheno, Euralye, and Medusa—who had snakes for hair and whose glance turned men to stone.

Graces] The three sister goddesses of Greek and Roman mythology who dispensed charm and beauty. Botticelli's *Spring* depicts them as described.

Grapeshot] A cluster of iron balls used as a cannon charge. AB was unrelentingly hostile to socialism and what he believed to be its inevitable corollary, anarchism.

Grass] Cf. Isaiah 40 : 6: "All flesh is grass, and all the goodliness thereof is as the flower of the field." The verses here were reprinted as "Famine in Prosperity" (*CW* 5.202).

Grasshopper] *Gryllus campestris* now denotes the field cricket. Although crickets and grasshoppers belong to the same order (Orthoptera, or straight-winged insects), crickets are now grouped in the suborder Grylloidea and grasshoppers in the suborders Tettigonioidea and Acridoidea. Carolus Linnaeus (Carl von Linné, 1707–78), Swedish botanist, was the founder of the modern classification system for plants and animals. Sarah Winnemucca Hopkins (1844?–91), a Paiute princess, was the author of *Life Among the Piutes; Their Wrongs and Claims* (1883) and had dedicated her life to improving the social conditions of her people. AB mentioned her father, the Indian chief Winnemucka, in "The Pi-Ute Indians of Nevada" (1868).

Great] The definition in *W* adds the following: "Distinguished by superior excellence among one's fellows, as Hector Stuart among Bards of the South Sea, Dr. Bartlett among the *Bulletin's* agricultural homilists, Peter Robertson among the writers of 'Undertones' in the *Chronicle* and Harrie McDowell among the fat boys of the *Ingleside*." In referring to Stuart, AB alludes to *Ben Nebo: A Pilgrimage in the South Seas, in Three Cantos* (1871). AB called Peter Robertson (1847–1911), whom he lampooned in "A Song in Praise" (1889; *CW* 5.85) and "A Crocodile" (*CW* 5.221), "that bold, bad humorist . . . of the *Chronicle*" ("Prattle," *E*, 24 July 1887: 4). Henry B. McDowell (here feminized as "Harrie") was editor of the *Ingleside*. AB wrote of George Sylvester Viereck (1884–1962), novelist, essayist, and editor, in "An Inspired Performance" (*CW* 4.375).

Griffin] *Quadrupavis amalgamata mirabilis* means "Marvelous compound four-footed creature." *Aquileo* is of AB's coinage, combining *Aquila* (eagle) and *Leo* (lion). The mule (q.v.) "owed nothing to the Creator" because it is the hybrid offspring of a male donkey and a female horse.

Grip] William H. Parks was speaker of the California assembly in 1881–83 and 1885–87. The verses from *W* are omitted because AB used them at "Tenacity" in *D*.

Guinea] AB parodies "For A' That and A' That" (1794) by Robert Burns (1759–96):

> For a' that, and a' that,
>> Our toils obscure, and a' that;
> The rank is but the guinea's stamp,
>> The man's the gowd for a' that.

Guinea-pig] *Cave canem* means "Beware of dog," found on an actual sign from ancient Rome.

Gunpowder] The reference to Milton is to a Latin epigram, "In Inventorum Bombardae" ("On the Inventor of Gunpowder"). James Wilson (1836–1920) was secretary of agriculture under McKinley, Roosevelt, and Taft (1897–1913). In *W,* Dr. Bartlett was the victim of the gunpowder demonstration. "Genius Overlooked" (*E*, 22 Nov. 1888: 4) contains another brief anecdote about Bartlett planting gunpowder in the ground with disastrous consequences. Cf. Exodus 13:21: "And the Lord went before them by day in a pillar of a cloud, to lead them the way; and by night in a pillar of fire, to give them light." In "A Leaf Blown in from Days to Be" (*Town Talk*, 17 Mar. 1910: 21), AB refers to the skunk as *Curio flabbergastor* (flabbergasting curiosity).

Gymnast] See "Prattle" (*Ar*, 27 Apr. 1878: 9):

> Advices from Japan state that Iwakuru is arranging to celebrate the 2538th anniversary of the death of Jimmu Tenno. Jim was the founder of the present dynasty, which is therefore officially known—to distinguish it from its immediate predecessors and prevent confusion in the State archives—as the Jim dynasty, a designation contracted, in popular speech, to Jimnasty. Hence our word gymnastics (which inferior philologists have professed to derive from the Greek), gymnastics being a sort of thing in which the Japs can beat a circus. From gymnastic we get the word gum-elastic, an indiarubber man, or contortionist, being an indispensable attraction at every show. It is a very useful and fascinating pursuit, this philology. . . . A daily paper suggests that at the next exhibition of the Olympic Club the performing members wear "trunks" over their "tights."
>
> Athletic men, 'twere hardly just
> Your charms to thus make shady;
> Shut up in trunks, you'll give, I trust,
> A key to every lady.

AB wrote disapprovingly on several occasions about the popularity of the Olympic Club exhibitions among young women.

Gymnodontes] Both the Malacopterygii (a group of soft-finned fishes) and the Plectognathi (including triggerfish, puffers, etc.) are suborders of the Teleosti. Gymnodontes are a subdivision of the Plectognathi but have no other relation to the Malacopterygii.

Gymnosophists] Members of an ancient sect of Hindu ascetics who wore little clothing (or none) and were devoted to contemplation. Adolph Spreckels was a member of a powerful California family that virtually controlled the manufacture and sale of refined sugar on the Pacific Coast. His brother Claus was called the "Sugar King."

Habeas Corpus] One of various writs that may be used to bring a person before a court or judge that allows for the person's release from unlawful restraint.

Hades] Cf. "Prattle" (*W*, 3 June 1881: 357): "In his opinion the substitution of 'hades' for 'hell' in the passage, 'The wicked shall be turned into hell,' is an unwarrantable and dangerous concession to the Democrats." Ironically, when AB was publishing his dictionary column in *Am* and *E* and when *C* was published, he was forced to substitute the words "Hades" and "cynic" for "hell" and "devil."

Hag] The phrase attributed to Drayton has not been found. *OED* does not corroborate AB's interpretation of the early use of this word, stating that it always referred to a witch or an ugly old woman. "Sweet wench" occurs several times in Shakespeare: *The Taming of the Shrew* 3.2.238; *I Henry IV* 1.2.40; *Titus Andronicus* 3.1.282.

Halcyon] Cf. "On a Mountain" (*CW* 1.228): "And, by the way, during those halcyon days (the halcyon was there, too, chattering above every creek, as he is all over the world) we fought another battle." Note that the author of the verses at "Weather" is Halcyon Jones.

Halo] See also "Hag."

Handkerchief] Dr. Mary Edwards Walker (1831–1919), a noted social reformer and suffragist and a nurse and physician during the Civil War, was awarded a medal from Congress. It has been argued that this was the Medal of Honor. She advocated the then-scandalous wearing of bloomers after the war and wore men's attire for most of her later life. See also "Disenchant."

Hangman] AB wrote several columns about execution by electrocution (a neologism that he despised, claiming the word was worse than the act). He seemed to think that it was a painless form of execution, intended to replace such barbaric practices as hanging.

Happiness] See also "Joy."

Harangue] AB dubbed several opponents "harangue-outangs" in his columns.

Hardware] See also "Adamant."

Hare] Baron Alexander von Humboldt (1769–1859) was a noted German traveler and naturalist who explored Central and South America from 1799 to 1804. AB's mock Latin means "Nevadan cat" and "Chismore's deer." (See the unsigned article "Another Breed of Cats," probably by AB [*E*, 27 May 1889: 4] re the Nevadan cat, which "rather resembles the tiger than the domestic cat.") AB relates a humorous story about a hunting trip by a Dr. George Chismore in "Prattle" (*E*, 12 Sept. 1897: 18).

Harmonists] Members of a communistic Protestant sect, founded by George Rapp of Würtemburg, Germany, who came to the United States in 1803 and founded the town of Harmony, Pennsylvania (whence their name).

Hash] Note that the part of speech identified here is *x*, the unknown.

Hatchet] Cf. "Sepulture" (1896; *CW* 4.376):

"Come, bury the hatchet," says Miller to Platt;
And Platt said to Miller: "I'll gladly do that."
On its grave, Warner Miller, the grasses grow not,
But the wind in your hair whistles over the spot.

Hautboy] An oboe.

Head] In revised form, the anecdote that originally appeared in *W* was used at "Scimitar" (q.v.).

Head-money] Besides being a poll tax, it can also be a bounty.

Heart] Presumably Henry J. Dam (d. 1906), briefly a co-owner of *W*. AB also refers to the French chemist Louis Pasteur (1822–95), specifically his germ theory of fermentation, propounded in *Mémoire sur la fermentation appelée lactique* (1857). *Delectatio Demonorum* (Delight of demons) was also mentioned in the original appearance of "Cannibal." M. E. Grenander, in her article "Ambrose Bierce, John Camden Hotten, *The Fiend's Delight*, and *Nuggets and Dust*," *Huntington Library Quarterly* 28, no. 4 (Aug. 1965), reprints the following statement from the *Nation* about AB (21 Nov. 1872: 336): "In consideration of a sum of money to him in hand paid, this enemy of man and worse enemy of woman has bound and obligated himself to gather together his compositions into a book—a sort of cynic's *vade mecum*, a *Delectatio Demonorum* and 'Fiends' [*sic*] Delight,' which Mr. Hotten will publish" (p. 359). Much of the text printed in *W* and *C* but not *D* is found in *FD* (p. 72; rpt. in "Did We Eat One Another" [*CW* 9.193]). The Thanksgiving anecdote told in *W* originated in the sketch "Thanksgiving" (1869; *FD* 91).

Heat] John Tyndall (1820–93), Irish-born British physicist, known for his work on the absorption of gases by radiant heat. He is referred to frequently in AB's writings. *Crede expertum* should read *crede experto* (believe one who has experienced it). The phrase is from Vergil, *Aeneid* 11.283.

Heathen] George Holmes Howison (1834–1917) was a professor of philosophy at the

University of California and author of numerous works on philosophy, religion, and other subjects. AB lampoons him in "Religious Progress" (1895; *CW* 5.50). The verses here originally appeared in longer form in "Prattle" (*E*, 16 May 1897: 18).

Heaven] In *Ambrose Bierce: A Biography*, Carey McWilliams published a definition of "Heaven" (B33 in the Appendix) that he claimed was one of several "Devil's Dictionary" definitions that had an oral history only (p. 253).

Hebrew] In *W*, the definition reads: "A male Jew, as distinguished as Shebrew. Among the Jews the word is not in use, but in speaking to them Christians usually employ it by way of avoiding what they consider the more offensive term of 'Jew'—a delicate and civil moderation which is imperfectly appreciated." AB later noted the word "Israelite" as another euphemism that gentiles used when referring to Jews.

Heigh-ho] Joaquin Miller (pseudonym of Cincinnatus Hiner Miller [1837–1913]), California poet and longtime friend of Bierce, attained spectacular fame in England upon the publication of his *Songs of the Sierras* (1871). Adair Welcker, the self-proclaimed "Sacramento Shakespeare" and author of numerous books such as *A Voyage with Death and Other Poems* (1878) and *The Snob Papers: A Humorous Novel* (c. 1885), was long a victim of AB's satire. See "Adair Welcker, Poet" (1888; *CW* 5.180).

Hell] See Introduction re Noah Webster and also "Mad."

Hemp] See also "Linen."

Hesitation] See note on "Coyness."

Hibernate] For Kip, see "Archbishop."

Historian] *Broad-gauge* means "the wider distance at which the rails are laid on some railways, involving a corresponding width of carriage" (*OED*).

History] Barthold Georg Niebuhr (1776–1831), German historian, noted for his three-volume history of Rome, *Römische Geschichte;* translated as *The History of Rome* (1828–42), which may be said to have inaugurated the modern scientific historical method. See also A12 in the Appendix.

Hog] John D. Rockefeller (1839–1937), the oil tycoon, was a victim of AB's later satire; the name originally used in *W* was Charles Crocker (as *Caroli Crocker*), for whom see note on "Endear."

Homœopathy] "A system for treating disease based on the administration of minute doses of a drug that in massive amounts produces symptoms in healthy individuals similar to those of the disease itself" (*AHD*). *Allopathy* is "a method of treating disease with remedies that produce effects different from those caused by the disease itself" (*AHD*). AB was decidedly hostile to homeopathy and Christian Science.

Homoiousian] "One who held the Father and the Son, in the Godhead, to be of like, but not the same, essence or substance; a Semi-Arian" (*OED*). *Arianism* is the heresy that denies Jesus was of the same substance as God, holding that he was only the highest of created beings.

Honorable] See B3 in the Appendix.

Hope] When AB returned from London to San Francisco in the fall of 1875, he took a job in the assay office of the U.S. Mint. These verses suggest that perhaps he was led to believe he might obtain a better position than the one he held, one that never materialized.

Horrid] AB parodies the well-known nursery rhyme:

There once was a girl, and she had a little curl
Right in the middle of her forehead;

> When she was good, she was very, very good,
>
> But when she was bad, she was horrid.

The poem was once attributed to Longfellow, but it probably originated in an anonymous broadside c. 1870. For text and commentary, see *The Oxford Dictionary of Nursery Rhymes,* ed. Iona and Peter Opie (Oxford: Clarendon Press, 1951), 187–89. AB also parodied the poem in "Prattle" (*Ar,* 24 May 1879: 1).

Hovel] In *W,* the following line appears between lines 6 and 7: "A phantasy as flashing as *aurora borealis!*"

Hug] See also "Kiss." AB coyly professes to be ignorant as to how or why either act is performed.

Humorist] AB parodies the poetic style of Alexander Pope (1688–1744). Cf. "An Essay on Man" (1733):

> Lo! the poor Indian, whose untutor'd mind
>
> Sees God in clouds, or hears him in the wind;
>
> His soul proud Science never taught to stray
>
> Far as the solar walk, or milky way; . . .
>
> But thinks, admitted to that equal sky,
>
> His faithful dog shall bear him company.

Epistle 1, lines 99–102, 111–12

Another parody of these lines is found at "Severalty."

Hybrid] For "pooled issue," cf. "Deiparous," line 7 of verse.

Hyena] See "Body-snatcher."

Hypochondriasis] In "Ashes of the Beacon" a "Bogul" is the author of "History of an Extinct Civilization."

Hypocrite] See B27 in the Appendix.

I] In *W,* instead of the last two sentences, the definition reads:

> The conception of two myselves is a singularly, or rather plurally, beautiful one. In literary composition the use of the word "I" is the severest test of ability. To use it frankly yet gracefully distinguishes a good writer from a bad. Perhaps the best examples are supplied by the *littérateurs* of the local press, who carry the big I with almost as gracious and modest a demeanor as we may suppose to have characterized the Impenitent Thief packing his cross up Calvary.

Ichor] The scene described in the poem—Diomedes wounding Aphrodite (Venus)—is found in Homer's *Iliad* 5.334f. Diomedes' soul is stained white because ichor was thought by some of the ancients to be white (although Homer appears to regard it as red).

Ichthyologist] Joseph D. Redding (1859–1932) was the subject of "A Fish Commissioner" (1889; *CW* 5.289) and also the mock epitaph "Here lies Joseph Redding, who gave us the catfish" (1889; *CW* 5.375).

Iconoclast] This definition corresponds with AB's own notion of a satirist. He frequently defended his satire against criticisms that he was tearing down beliefs without providing a substitute. Cf. "Prattle" (*Ar,* 21 Dec. 1878: 17): "No man of sane intelligence will plead for religion on the ground that it is better than nothing. It is not better than nothing if it is not true. Truth is better than anything or all things; the next best thing to truth is absence of error. When you are in the dark, stand still; when you do not know what to do, do nothing. To say 'don't take away my faith unless you can give me another' is to beg the question—to assume the very point in dispute for the taker-away denies that you need a faith. If you think you do that is your affair."

Ignis Fatuus] A phosphorescent light that flits over swampy ground at night, possibly caused by the combustion of gases emitted by rotting organic matter. Also known as "will-o-the-wisp." Thus, anything that misleads or deludes.

Ignoramus] AB's attribution may allude to Giovanni Alfonso Borelli (1608–1679), Italian physiologist and physicist, the first to explain muscular movement and other body functions according to the laws of statics and dynamics.

Illuminati] *Cunctationes* means "delays" rather than "weights."

Immaculate] AB puns on *immaculate* meaning "spotless" and the verb *to spot* meaning "to detect."

Immodest] Ispahan (or Isfāhān, or Esfāhān) was a city in ancient Persia founded by the Seljuk Turks in the eleventh century. AB mentions it in "The Cynic's Bequest" (1874; *CW* 4.169) and one of his "Fables of Zambri, the Parsee." Sukker Uffro is the poet also cited at "Perseverance."

Immoral] In *W*, for "all . . . mind" read "the inspired writer who evolves this dictionary from an understanding illuminated from Below has been basely misled by the Personage whose title it bears."

Immortality] See also "On Death and Immortality" (*FD* 64) and "Immortality" (1901; *CW* 11.246).

Impale] AB's "The Chair of Little Ease" (1891, 1892; *CW* 11.363–67) concerns the torture of impalement. Wolecraft and Ludwig Salzmann are fictitious.

Improvidence] The definition in *W* reads: "The vice of enjoying to-day what we may not have to-morrow."

Inauspicious] In "The Wisconsin Mines" (*E*, 22 Jan. 1888: 4), AB uses a similar construction: "all reports about rich strikes—rock 'lousy with free' . . . —should be received with infinite caution." *English as She Is Spoke; or, A Jest in Sober Earnest* (1883) by José da Fonseca was a translation of a book of unintentionally grotesque instances of conversational English designed for Portuguese speakers. The book was the object of derision throughout the English-speaking world.

Incense] Cf. "Joss-sticks."

Incivism] Lack of good citizenship; interpreted by AB specifically as the practice of not voting. See "Prattle" (*E*, 28 Oct. 1888: 4): "This eternal harping upon the sin of 'incivism' is incivility. . . . What a man really means when he accuses another of not voting is not that it is a sin to abstain from voting, but that it is a sin not to vote as *he* votes. If A does not vote at all, and B votes one way and C another, B is logically bound to consider A less mischievous than C is, while C is logically bound to think him a better citizen than B is. And, in point of fact, we never complain of incivism in the other party, but do all we can to encourage it. It is easy to say: 'I like a man who votes according to his light, right or wrong.' As to that, I beg leave to say that this is not a question of who is the more lovable man. And if it were it should be submitted for decision to a woman, upon the competent, relevant and material evidence of personal acquaintance." The poem "Incivism" (1885) in *CW* 5.202 is the same as that published here.

Income] Sir Sycophas Chrysolater is AB's mock-Greek coinage, meaning "Sycophantic Gold-worshiper."

Incompossible] In *W*, for "Walt Whitman's poetry" read "the pictures at the Mechanics' Fair"; in *C*, "the poet Gilder." See "Small Contributions" (*Co*, June 1907: 219): "If 'What Walt Whitman Did for Poetry' is not to be a work of fiction it should be at least a short story—the shortest short story in the world." For Gilder, see note on "Folly."

Incomprehensibility] For Adair Welcker, see "Heigh-ho."

Inconsolable] Cf. AB's fable "The Inconsolable Widow" (1907; *CW* 6.311).

Incorporation] See "The Reign of the Ring" (1892; *CW* 9.132): "The attribution of magical and medicinal virtues to rings pervades all ancient and mediæval history. Gyges, King of Lydia, had a ring by which the wearer could become invisible—a result accomplishable, though sometimes too tardily, by our modern plan of going away." The anecdote about Gyges is found in Herodotus, *Histories* 1.8–12.

Incubus] The source of the anecdote has not been traced, but presumably it refers to the period in the 1850s when Hugo, in exile on the island of Jersey (one of the Channel Islands), conducted a celebrated series of séances with his family and with local inhabitants.

Indecision] Maj. Gen. (USV) Ulysses Simpson Grant (1822–85), a native of Ohio, West Point graduate, and Mexican War veteran, was commander of the Army of the Tennessee and the Middle Tennessee Department at Shiloh. Maj. Gen. (USV) Gordon Granger (1822–76) of New York, a West Point graduate, was a lieutenant in the Regular Army when the war began and commander of the Reserve Corps of the Army of the Cumberland at Chickamauga. If this incident happened, it would have been occasioned by the sudden assault up Missionary Ridge (outside Chattanooga, TN) by IV Corps on 25 Nov. 1863. At that time, Grant was commanding the entire Western Department and on the verge of becoming the senior officer in the army, and Granger was commanding IV Corps.

Indifferent] "Apuleius" refers to the satirical writer Lucius Apuleius (2nd century CE), author of the *Metamorphoses* or *The Golden Ass*.

Inexpedient] In *W,* the definition concludes: "interest—as asking a lady whom you are trying to marry how much she is worth."

Infallible] *Ex cathartica* is a play on the Latin expression *ex cathedra* (from the [teacher's] chair, or speaking with authority and thus with thought). Since a *cathartic* is an agent for purging the bowels, AB's phrase means something like "from a purging" and thus something expelled quickly, perhaps without much thought.

Infancy] The Wordsworth quotation is from "Ode: Intimations of Immortality from Recollections of Early Childhood" (1807), line 66.

Infidel] A *giaour* is (in Islam) a nonbeliever.

Influence] AB puns on the Latin expression *quid pro quo,* meaning an equal exchange (this for that), and the British word *quid,* or one pound sterling.

Infralapsarian] (= sublapsarian) "A term applied in the 17th c. to Calvinists holding the view that God's election of some to everlasting life was consequent to his prescience of the Fall of man, or that it contemplated man as already fallen, and was thus a remedial measure," as opposed to *supralapsarian,* "a name applied to those Calvinists who held the view that, in the divine decrees, the predestination of some to eternal life and of others to eternal death was antecedent to the creation and the fall" (*OED*).

Ink] In *W,* the definition concludes:

> Some journalists, to their lasting credit be it said, keep only the one kind of bath— a sanitarium for affluent fools, soiled doves and people in no particular kind of social health.
>
> > There is a fountain filled with ink
> > > Drawn from a flatterer's brains,
> > And sinners in that pool who sink
> > > Lose all their guilty stains.

In'ards] "Dr. Gunsaulus" presumably is Frank W. Gunsaulus (1856–1921), a prolific writer on religion, education, and other subjects. Garrett P. Serviss (1851–1929), journalist and writer, entered journalism after studying science and then law. His specialty was astronomy, and he wrote several science fiction novels. Like AB, he was a regular contributor to the Hearst papers.

Innate] *W* adds the following sentence: "Locke was smarter than a whip, but when he undertook to show that the brief period between the cradle and the gibbet sufficed for the giant development of these notions from no germ he bit off more than he could chew." British philosopher John Locke (1632–1704) refuted the notion of innate ideas in Book I of *An Essay Concerning Human Understanding* (1690).

Insanity] The "poet" quoted is AB himself, lifting lines 29–47 from "The Cynic's Bequest" (1874; *CW* 4.170).

Inscription] In *W,* for "tombstones" read:
>   tombstones in Laurel Hill cemetery in this city:
>   "Here lies a man who never flinched,
>   But with the devil battled.
>   'Twas very seldom he was cinched,
>   Though sometimes badly rattled."

See "Prattle" (*Ar,* 29 June 1878: 9): "In answer to 'Inquirer,' I would say that I was not aware that Mr. Swinburne had made a claim to the authorship of the lines beginning
>   'Affliction sore long time he bore,
>   Physicians was in vain.'

There is a tooth-and-nail dispute as to who wrote them first, and the question is complicated with a new element of uncertainty almost daily by their appearance under the *Call's* deaths [*sic*] head with fresh initials appended. Public opinion had at one time settled upon Mr. Pickering as their author, but I can not say if for any better reason than his habit of putting a great deal of himself into his work—as also into his boots—and the circumstance that the final words of each of the two lines quoted seem to hint at some of his distinguishing literary peculiarities. The opinion may, not improbably, have been partly founded on the dazzling merit of the grammar." AB used the couplet in several Little Johnny sketches. See also note on "Affliction."

Insectivora] *W* adds the following definition: "Historians. As they derive their subsistence from chronicles of the deeds of the great, they may justly be said to live on insects." Cf. "Animal."

Insurance] See "Insurance in Ancient America: Translated from the Work of the Future Historian" (1906; in "Ashes of the Beacon," *CW* 1.17).

Intelligent] The Chautauqua Movement of the late nineteenth century, centered at Lake Chautauqua, NY, was devoted to adult education.

Intention] *W* adds the following paragraph: "When figured out and accurately apprehended this will be found one of the most penetrating and far-reaching definitions in this whole dictionary. It has taken the first premium at three county fairs and is prescribed by all respectable physicians as a dead shot for worms. It increased the corn yield of Illinois one million bushels in a single season, discovered the source of the Nile and saved the day at Shiloh."

Interlocutor] See also "End."

Intimacy] Seidlitz powder (after Seidlitz, a village in northwestern Czechoslovakia, the site of large mineral springs) is a mild cathartic, a mixture of tartaric acid, sodium bicarbonate, and potassium sodium tartrate, that is dissolved in water and drunk.

Intoxication] Cf. Proverbs 16:18: "Pride goeth before destruction, and an haughty spirit before a fall."

Introduction] "Abridge" has another parody of the Declaration of Independence. See "A Social Nuisance" (1902; as "Disintroductions" [*CW* 9.257]) and "Prattle" (*W,* 28 Apr. 1882: 261): "Why should we not adopt a social custom of disintroduction? What embarrassment we should be spared—what a waste of time and temper would be prevented. I cannot speak for others, but I no sooner am introduced to a person whom there is no particular reason why I know (and ninety-nine in every one hundred of my acquaintances are of that sort) than straightway I fall to devise a plan to unknow him. How I should welcome an opportunity to be disintroduced!"

Inundation] AB mentions the Assyrian expeditions of George Smith (1840–76) several times in his *Fi* columns of 1873–74. See also "Deluge" and "Flood."

Inventor] AB clearly did not equate technological advances with civilization. Cf. "Prattle" (*Ar,* 31 May 1879: 9): "it is of the nature of the Philistine to consider civilization very largely a matter of railroads and telegraphs—not altogether, for it is partly, also, a thing of steamboats and coal gas; and it was an example of noble moderation in the *Bulletin* man to leave them out. Was it from charitable and magnanimous consideration for the memory of Shakspeare, Bacon, Spenser, Raleigh and Drake that he contented himself with dimly sketching the overshadowing figures of Stephenson and Whatshisname (the telegraph person), forbearing to even outline the stupendous images of the other two immortals, Robert Fulton and the illustrious inventor of the gas bill?"

Isthmus] A canal through Central America had been debated since at least the 1840s. President Grant established a United States Interoceanic Canal Commission, which in 1876 recommended construction in Nicaragua, but no action was taken. The French undertook a canal in Panama in the 1880s, but the effort collapsed in 1889 from bad planning and lack of funds. President McKinley's Isthmian Canal Commission, appointed in 1899, determined that a Panamanian canal would cost considerably less than a Nicaraguan canal, but the money France demanded for release of its rights to the region made the cost of the Panamanian canal prohibitive. In 1901 the United States negotiated the Hay-Pauncefote Treaty, granting it control of any isthmian canal in the Western Hemisphere. (AB himself generally favored the Nicaragua site.) France drastically reduced its demand for its rights in Panama, and so Panama ultimately was selected as the canal site. After ten years of construction, the Panama Canal opened in Aug. 1914. AB observed the construction in May 1910 on his way to California.

Itch] See "King's Evil."

Jacob's-ladder] Cf. Genesis 28:12: "And he [Jacob] dreamed, and behold a ladder set up on the earth, and the top of it reached to heaven: and behold the angels of God ascending and descending on it."

Jews-harp] In *W,* the definition concludes: "So called from the impossibility of a Jew playing it without a new deal in noses."

Joss-sticks] Sticks of incense (q.v.) as burned before a Chinese idol.

Jove] Actually, Jove, or Jupiter, is the supreme God in Roman mythology, corresponding to Zeus (q.v.) of Greek myth.

Joy] The emotion AB describes here corresponds exactly to the German word *Schadenfreude* (joy at another person's misfortune).

Judge] Chris Buckley was an unscrupulous Democratic political "boss" in late-nineteenth-century San Francisco who was finally driven out of town by state senator Jeremiah Lynch.

Jury] AB's low opinion of the jury system is exhibited in the satire "The Jury in Ancient America: An Historical Sketch Written in the Year of Grace 3687" (1905; rpt. in "Ashes of the Beacon," *CW* 1.17).

Kangaroo] AB's description of the most well known feature of the most well known of marsupials is somewhat exaggerated. The pouch of the female contains the mammary glands and is where the young (at an almost embryonic stage) develops after leaving the uterus. Cf. "Kings of Beasts: Kangaroons" (1902; *CW* 12.76–77): "The kangs tail is the biggest in the world and is highly respected for soup."

King's Evil] "Scrofula, which in England and France was formerly supposed to be curable by the king's (or queen's) touch" (*OED*). Edward the Confessor (1042–66) is referred to as "most pious Edward" in *Macbeth* 3.6.27. The three other quotations from *Macbeth* are as follows: "a crowd of wretched souls": 4.3.141–45 ("crew" for "crowd"); "'tis spoken": 4.3.154–56; "strangely visited people": 4.3.150–52.

Kiss] See also "Hug."

Kleptomaniac] A kleptomaniac, as hinted, steals because of an obsessive impulse to steal, not because of need.

Koran] (or Quran) The sacred text of Islam, containing the revelations of God to Mohammed.

Krishna] The eighth and principal avatar of Vishnu, depicted as a handsome young man. (See also "Brahma.")

Lace] For *D*, AB placed the verses that initially appeared here at "Seine."

Lady] See also "Gentleman."

Land] See "Insurance in Ancient America: Translated from the Work of the Future Historian" (*Co*, Sept. 1906: 555): "To those unlearned in the economical institutions of antiquity it is necessary to explain that in ancient America, long prior to the Japanese conquest, individual ownership of property prevailed; every person was permitted to get as much as he was able, and to hold it as his own without regard to his needs, or whether he made any good use of it or not. By some plan of distribution not now understood even the habitable surface of the earth, with the minerals beneath, was parceled out among the favored few, and there was really no place except at sea where children of the others could lawfully be born."

Laocoön] In Greek mythology, a Trojan priest of Apollo, killed along with his two sons by two sea serpents for having warned his people of the Trojan horse. By extension, the statue dating to the first century BCE attributed to Agesander, Athenodorus, and Polydorus of Rhodes, as described and lampooned by AB.

Lap] AB first put forth this notion in "Laps" (*NL*, 5 June 1869: 2).

Lapidate] St. Stephen is the first martyr of the Christian faith (see Acts 7:59). As noted, he was stoned to death.

Last] In *W*, the definition concludes: "It has been calculated that the sum of misery suffered by the accident of this thing's name, equals that resulting from seven long wars and a general pestilence; and the punsters are still unsated." A *last* is a block or form shaped like the human foot used to make and repair shoes.

Latitudinarian] Holding or expressing broad or tolerant views, especially with respect to religion.

Laughter] Cf. the description of laughter in the verses at "Whangdepootenawah." AB's mock Latin phrase means "spattering convulsion." In *W*, for "answered . . . holds" read "determined by experiment, but valuable work in that direction may be looked for soon, the Austro-Hungarian Government having appropriated a large sum for the purpose. It is held by the learned and ingenious Dr. Trahigh, sometime physician in ordinary to the late Ahkoond of Swat." For "*Convulsio spargens*" read "*Twisteriasis broadcasta.*" By "Dr. Meir Witchell," AB refers to Dr. S[ilas] Weir Mitchell (1829–1914), a prolific American novelist, short story writer, and poet who also wrote on scientific and medical topics. One of his most important medical volumes was *Fat and Blood: An Essay on the Treatment of Certain Forms of Neurasthenia and Hysteria* (1877; 8th ed. 1905).

Laureate] Robert Southey (1774–1843) was named poet laureate of England in 1813. In *W,* the definition concludes: "Our Californian Poet Laureate is Mr. Adair Welcker, the Shakespeare of Rabel's Tannery, a literary artist of such consummate skill that he can express a whole emotionette on the disk of a single millstone—and a Sacramento gentleman who, with a suicidal intention, was wearing one on his neck had the forethought to get him to do it."

Lawyer] C concludes with the following (the verses are from "Prattle," *E,* 6 Nov. 1887: 4):
One of the chief duties of the modern lawyer is defense of eminent rogues by vituperation of "anonymous scribblers" of the press—an employment which drew from that "scurril jester," Editor Fum, of "The Daily Livercomplaint," the hortatory words here following:

> Take notice, lawyers all. For many a year
> Your cheerful tribe (I mean to stint your cheer)
> When hired to cheat the gallows of its prey
> Or turn the law-gods' noses all astray
> From a thief's track, and take of what he stole
> The lion's share—that is to say, the whole—
> Have deemed it right his grievance to redress
> With fine philipics on the brutal press
> That persecutes a blameless soul—alas,
> How angels suffer from the felon class!
> Now mark ye, lawless lawyers, if ye still
> Shall think it well to serve a client ill,
> Accept his money on the false pretense
> That slander of accusers is defense,
> Deal out damnation to sustain his hope
> And handle without gloves all things but soap,
> I'm for retaliation. Hear me swear,
> With head uncovered and with hand in air,
> By that sole deity whom lawyers hold
> In pious reverence, Almighty Gold
> (Whose name, with deep hypocrisy, they spell,
> Pronounce and take in vain without the l)
> My scourging weapon shall remain unstirred,
> Gracing the pinion of its parent bird.
> I'll let you struggle for the blackguard's wreath
> And tear your tongues to rags upon your teeth!

Lead] *Chirurgeon* is an archaic form of *surgeon.*

Legacy] In *W,* for "this vale of tears" read "the world, or has one leg in the grave. The question whether, with a due regard to derivation, the disability of a one-legged soldier can properly be called a legacy of the war has been much debated. The editor of the 'Query Column' in the *Sunday Call* is of the opinion that it can."

Leonine] AB again lampoons Ella Wheeler Wilcox, although in *W* he originally attributed these verses to "Mr. T-m Gr-g-ry" (i.e., Tom Gregory), whose poetry appeared in *W.*

Leptocephalidans] Literally *slender-headed ones,* by which AB probably meant "stupid people."

Lethe] By the Third Commandment AB means the admonition not to use the Lord's name in vain. The joke is that the water of the Spring Valley Water Company is so bad that it causes drinkers to curse. Note that for a time *W* was owned by the Spring Valley Water Company.

Leviathan] In Job 41, Yahweh does not merely mention Leviathan but describes the fearsome and uncontrollable beast at length (along with Behemoth in chap. 40). Whereas Behemoth represents the realm of natural power beyond man's, Leviathan represents the realm of supernatural, mythic power beyond creation. "Dr. Jordan" is David Starr Jordan (1851–1931), who taught biology at various universities before serving as president of Stanford University (1891–1913). The English novelist Jane Porter (1776–1850) wrote a popular historical novel, *Thaddeus of Warsaw* (1803), about Thaddeus Kosciusko (see "Freedom").

Lexicographer] See Matthew 7:28–29, the conclusion of the Sermon on the Mount: "when Jesus had ended these sayings, the people were astonished at his doctrine: For he taught them as one having authority, and not as the scribes." In Jesus' time, the scribes merely recorded and interpreted the law, but Jesus, coming from the Father, was the one who revealed the Father's will. "The first lexicographer" was Samuel Johnson.

Liar] See A15 in the Appendix.

Libelous] See A16 in the Appendix.

Liberty] See "War Topics" (*E,* 26 June 1898: 22): "When asked if I am not an advocate of liberty I ask in my turn: 'Whose liberty to do what?'"

Lickspittle] The definition in *W* concludes:

> To both forms of exaction the rich are peculiarly exposed.
>
> A PICTURE.
>
> A spotless honor and a fair renown;
> > Two disconcerted fiends, grown sick and sicker:
> Detraction throwing all his tar-sticks down
> > And Sycophancy scabbarding his licker.

Life] Cf. "A Paradox" (1885; *CW* 4.364):

> "If life were not worth living," said the preacher,
> "'Twould have in suicide one pleasant feature."
> "An error," said the pessimist, "you're making:
> What's not worth having cannot be worth taking."

Also the following lines from "Prattle" (*E,* 27 Oct. 1889: 6):

> "Is life worth living?" some fools are crying,
> And others are "Yes" and "No" replying.
> Go to!—you live it with ne'er a trying,
> So the question is, "Is death worth dying?"

And finally "Taking Oneself Off" (1900; *CW* 11.338): "The notion that we have not the right to take our own lives comes of our consciousness that we have not the courage. It is the plea of the coward—his excuse for continuing to live when he has nothing to live for—or his provision against such a time in the future. If he were not egotist as well as coward he would need no excuse. To one who does not regard himself as the center of creation and his sorrows as the throes of the universe, life, if not worth living, is also not worth leaving. The ancient philosopher who was asked why he did not die if, as he taught, life was no better than death, replied: 'Because death is no better than life.' We do not quite know that either proposition is true, but the matter is not worth bothering about, for both states are supportable—life despite its pleasures and death despite its repose." See also note on "Preference."

Limb] The "censorious stone" refers to Christ's charge to those who wished to stone the adulterous woman, "He that is without sin among you, let him first cast a stone at her" (John 8:7).

Literally] One of AB's most frequent grammatical complaints.

Literature] Hubert Howe Bancroft (1832–1918) was "author" of a history of the Pacific states that AB attacked in "Prattle" (E, 14 Aug. 1887: 4; 4 Sept. 1887: 4). The thrust of AB's criticism was that Bancroft's histories were not his own work but rather were written by an array of uncredited and poorly paid assistants. The Bancroft Library in Berkeley, CA, to which he donated many books, is named after him.

Liver] George Gascoigne (1534?–77), British soldier and poet.

LL.D.] In E the definition reads as follows:

LL.D. Letters indicating the degree *Legumptionis Doctor,* one learned in the laws, gifted with legal gumption. Some suspicion is cast upon this derivation by the fact that the title was formerly written *££, d.,* and conferred only upon gentlemen distinguished for their wealth. The Regents of the University at Berkeley are considering a proposal to set up a degree to be conferred on clergymen, in place of the old D. D. — *Damnator Diaboli.* The new honor will be known as *Sanctorum Custos* and written *$$, c.* The name of the Rev. John Satan has already been suggested as a suitable recipient by a lover of consistency, who pertinently points out that the Rev. W. C. Bartlett of the *Bulletin* has long enjoyed a degree, and that it constitutes the difference between him and the other person.

LL.D. actually means Legum Doctor (Doctor of Laws). *Sanctorum custos* means "custodian of the sacred [places]." Harry Thurston Peck (1856–1914) was a professor of Latin at Columbia University, literary critic, and editor of the *Bookman* (1895–1902) for whom AB did not have much respect.

Lodger] See "Prattle" (E, 19 Feb. 1888: 4): "*Roomer,* for *Lodger.* This is one of the most abominable words in the language of illiteracy. How it came I cannot imagine. I have myself, by way of experiment, and perhaps revenge, tried to give it company, having 'invented and gone round advising' the words *bedder* and *mealer,* constructed on the same lines, but they lack some mysterious vital quality and will not 'stick.'" AB made a similar complaint in "Prattle" (W, 2 Dec. 1881: 358).

Logic] E adds the following verses:

Logic, fair daughter of the gods divine,
My steps be ever guided by thy light:
Teach thou my feeble feet, through reason's night,
To shun all other bogs and walk in thine.
Still ever on my pathway dance and shine,
And when I deviate to left or right
Be still obligingly before my sight,
Consenting always to the chosen line.
And if into some hole that I abhor
I plump, or bramble-bound, like Abram's ram,

See neither hope of extrication, nor
    Can feel contentment in the place I am,
My prayer direct and my last words supply,
And let me syllogistically die!

Logomachy] Either a dispute about words or a battle of words. See "To a Word-Warrior" (1885; *CW* 5.180). Claudius Salmasius (1588–1653) was a French classical scholar of great influence. During the English Civil Wars (1642–51) he was regarded as an ally by Presbyterians. On their behalf he wrote *Defensio regia pro Carolo I* (Defense of the reign of Charles I), published anonymously in November 1649, a defense of absolute monarchy and condemnation of parliamentary government in England. John Milton (1608–74), then secretary for foreign languages to the Commonwealth, wrote a scathing reply in 1651 entitled *Pro Populo Anglicano Defensio* (A defense of the people of England), which was reprinted in 1692.

Loke] Or Loki. The Norse god who created discord, especially among his fellow gods.

Longanimity] Long-suffering; forbearance or patience, as under provocation.

Lord] In *E*, for "Being; . . . reverence" read "Being, considered, in the fervency of adoration, as an Englishman; but this is thought to be rather a desecration of the word, like calling a pugilist 'Professor.'" See "The American Sycophant" (*CW* 11.296) for AB's scorn of Americans' reverence for foreign nobility.

Lore] S[abine] Baring-Gould (1834–1924), *Curious Myths of the Middle Ages* (1866). "Grizzly Papers: No. V" (*OM*, June 1871: 565) contains a discussion of Baring-Gould and folk legends. The real titles of the fables in question are "Jack the Giant Killer," "The Sleeping Beauty," "Little Red Riding Hood," "Beauty and the Beast," "The Seven Sleepers of Ephesus," and "Rip Van Winkle." Teddy refers to Theodore Roosevelt. John Sharp Williams was a U.S. representative from Mississippi. Arthur Brisbane (1864–1936) was one of Hearst's leading editors and writers.

Loss] For Gilder, see "Folly." Collis P. Huntington (1821–1900) was one of the "Big Four" railroad tycoons. AB attacked him mercilessly during the first half of 1896 when AB was in Washington, D.C., reporting on a funding bill that Huntington was attempting to convince Congress to pass in order to give him a long extension in repaying government loans given to him for the building of the Southern Pacific Railroad.

Love] Cf. "Epigrams" (*CW* 8.348): "Of two kinds of temporary insanity, one ends in suicide, the other in marriage"; and the heading of section I of "The Eyes of the Panther" (1897; *CW* 3.385): "One does not always marry when insane." See also B14 in the Appendix. *Caries* is decay of the bones or teeth.

Lunarian] Lucian of Samosata, a Greek satirist who flourished in the second century CE, is considered by science fiction historians to be a precursor of science fiction. His *True History* features a trip to the moon. Richard Adams Locke (1800–71), American journalist and editor, is usually regarded as the author of a famous hoax published in 1835 in the *New York Sun*. He described the inhabitants of the moon as observed through a new high-powered telescope by Sir John Herschel. The book version of the story, *Great Astronomical Discoveries Lately Made by Sir John Herschel at the Cape of Good Hope* (1835), appeared under various titles and was widely translated. Simon Newcomb (1835–1909), Canadian-born professor of mathematics at the U.S. Naval Observatory, was a prolific writer on astronomy.

Lyre] AB updated the initial reference to Fred Emerson Brooks in *E* to read "Ella Wheeler Wilcox" but then unaccountably affixed to the verses the attribution "Farquharson Harris."

Macrobian] "Old Parr" was Thomas Parr, who died in November 1635 at the alleged age of 152 years. For Senator Depew, see note on "Abandon." The editor of the *American* was Sam Chamberlain, with whom he had frequent disagreements about the publication of his work. (In *Am* and *E* "the *American*" reads "a certain daily.") The president referred to is Theodore Roosevelt (1858–1919), twenty-sixth president (1901–09).

Magdalene] Mary of Magdala was one of Jesus' female disciples. The unnamed penitent woman mentioned in Luke 7:37–50 is popularly (but incorrectly) identified with Mary of Magdala.

Magnetism] Similar skepticism is displayed at "Gravitation."

Magnitude] Cf. "A Spread of Quick-Lunch Wisdom for Busy Readers" (*Am*, 30 Sept. 1903: 16; *E*, 15 Oct. 1903: 18): "Magnitude being relative, to augment the size of everything in the universe would be to do nothing. Similarly to double the intelligence and education of every human being would leave the scholar still a scholar, the peasant still a peasant, the savage still a savage." See also "My Favorite Murder" (1888; *CW* 8.147–48), in which a similar notion of relativity is broached: "'crimes are ghastly or agreeable only by comparison. If you were familiar with the details of my client's previous murder of his uncle you would discern in his later offense (if offense it may be called) something in the nature of tender forbearance and filial consideration for the feelings of the victim. The appalling ferocity of the former assassination was indeed inconsistent with any hypothesis but that of guilt; and had it not been for the fact that the honorable judge before whom he was tried was the president of a life insurance company that took risks on hanging, and in which my client held a policy, it is hard to see how he could decently have been acquitted.'"

Majesty] See "The Town Crier" (*NL*, 25 Sept. 1969: 9): "'Among the delegates to the Grand Lodge of Odd Fellows are Joshua Maris, of Delaware, and Hugh Latham, of Virginia. Both these gentlemen are Past Great Incohonees of the Improved Order of Red Men, the highest official position known to that order. Both are talented and eloquent speakers.' —*Bulletin*. There must be some mistake here; Incohonees are among the most intelligent of the brute creation, and are remarkably imitative in their habits, but we have never learned that they had been taught to articulate words. Buffon expressly states that the ingenuity of man has been completely baffled in the vain attempt to confer speech upon the lower quadrumans."

Malthusian] Thomas Robert Malthus (1766–1834) was a British economist. In his *Essay on the Principle of Population* (1798), he argued that population tends to increase faster than the food supply unless checked by war, famine, and disease or by certain moral restraints. When the astrologers told King Herod of Judea that they had come seeking Jesus, the newborn king of the Jews, he became fearful about losing his throne and ordered that all male children in Bethlehem under the age of two be slain to eliminate potential competitors for his throne (see Matthew 2:16–17). Cf. "Little Johnny on the Domestic Hen" (*Am*, 22 Oct. 1901: 16; 27 Oct. 1901: 30): "Then Uncle Ned . . . said . . . 'There never has been only but jest one man in the werld wich did kno [what to do with children], and that was Herod.'"

Mammon] Riches and worldly gain, personified as a false god in the New Testament, as in Luke 16:13: "No servant can serve two masters: for he will hate the one, and love the other; or else he will hold to one, and despise the other. You cannot serve God and mammon."

Man] The verses here are similar in form to those at "Macrobian."

Manes] See also "Inferiæ."

Manicheism] The religious philosophy taught by the Persian prophet Manes (216?–276? CE).

Manna] God miraculously provided the Israelites with manna to eat on their flight from Egypt (Exodus 16:15). Cf. "Aborigines."

Marriage] See B14 in the Appendix.

Mayonnaise] See "Sauce."

Me] The three cases being one and the same mirrors the doctrine of the Trinity, which AB persistently mocked.

Meander] *Am* and *E* add the following verses:

Goosey, goosey gander,
Where do you meander?

Susan B. Anthony.

For Susan B. Anthony, see note on "Woman."

Meerschaum] Cf. "The Passing Show" (*Fi*, 29 Oct. 1873: 9): "We are reminded of the young man who shut himself up in a country house, and went in for coloring a meerschaum. After several months his friends broke in, and found him holding the still milk-white pipe between his teeth, but stone dead, and of a rich beautiful brown from head to foot."

Mendacious] In *Am* and *E* the definition reads: "Having a mannerism which consists in addition to the rhetorical figure known as the lie."

Mesmerism] A form of hypnotism promulgated by Friedrich Anton Mesmer (1733–1815).

Mind] Understanding (q.v.), too, is "secreted by the brain." *Mens [sibi] conscia recti* (Vergil, *Aeneid* 1.604) means "A mind conscious of the right." AB made a similar quip on this phrase at "Lettuce" (*W* appearance only).

Misericorde] *Misericordia* is mercy. The weapon described by AB was used to deliver the death stroke to a seriously wounded knight.

Miss] Cf. "Prattle" (*W*, 15 July 1881: 38): "Those horrible words 'Mr.,' 'Mrs.' and 'Miss' will have to 'go,' too, some day. The first is a detestable corruption of 'Master' and the second of 'Mistress.' The last is, I think, the special creation and gift of a Providence bent upon testing human stupidity. It may therefore be called the divine element in our language and should be resented accordingly, as an unwarrantable interference with the laws of growth and evolution. Who's bossing this language, I should like to know?"

Molecule] Ernst Heinrich Haeckel (1834–1919), German philosopher and naturalist.

Monad] Gottfried Wilhelm von Leibnitz (1646–1716), German philosopher and mathematician. AB discusses the recent discovery of the electron and the discovery that the atom is not the smallest unit of matter in "An Infant Crying for the Light" (*E*, 22 Sept. 1903: [14]). This definition and the one previous appeared in separate columns rather than the same one, obscuring AB's joke.

Monarchical Government] AB felt that a democracy, where people "govern themselves," is no government at all.

Monday] Cf. the lines at "Decalogue": "Work not on Sabbath days at all, / But go to see the teams play ball."

Money] Cf. "Commercial Retaliation" (*E*, 12 Feb. 1898: 6): "Money is not wealth. It is good for nothing but to spend or to base credits on—which means to pledge it for expenditure later. A with one thousand dollars in his pocket and B with nothing are equally wealthy, and they so continue until A begins to get rid of his money. When he has got rid of one hundred dollars judiciously he is one hundred dollars wealthier than B—is wealthier by that amount than himself was when all the money lay in his pocket."

Monogenist] Monogenism is the theory that all races of human beings are descended from a common ancestry or a single pair of ancestors.

Monometallist] The reference is to a shift in policy by the Democratic presidential candidates for the years in question, William Jennings Bryan advocating bimetallism in 1896 and Judge Aldon B. Parker declaring himself a monometallist in 1904. Both lost their respective elections.

Monosyllabic] AB railed against Joaquin Miller's admonition that poets use only Saxon words: "Our words of one syllable are commonly Saxon words, that is to say, the words of a primitive people without a wide range of thought, feeling and sentiment. One can express in them only what their inventors had to express; the richer thoughts and higher emotions must clothe themselves in the words of peoples to whom they were known—in the ductile derivatives of the Norman-French, the Greek and the incomparable Latin. It is to the unlearned only that our brief bald Saxon words seem the only natural, graphic and sufficient ones" ("Joaquin Miller on Joaquin Miller," *E*, 30 Jan. 1898: 7 [magazine section]). He reasserted this opinion in "Small Contributions" under the article "Milk for Babes" (*Co*, Apr. 1907: 692).

Monument] *Am* and *E* add the following verses:

"For memory of work or worth we go
  To other records than the stone can show.
These lacking, naught survives. To fame
  The stone is needless, for the world will know."

These lines appeared as part of a longer, untitled poem in "Prattle" (*E*, 24 July 1887: 4) and also in "A Word to the Unwise" (1883; *CW* 5.173). Cf. "A Bivouac of the Dead" (1903; *CW* 11.396): "True, more than a half of the green graves in the Grafton cemetery are marked 'Unknown,' and sometimes it occurs that one thinks of the contradiction involved in 'honoring the memory' of him of whom no memory remains to honor; but the attempt seems to do no great harm to the living, even to the logical."

Morganatic] Cf. "Another Aspirant" (1900; *CW* 5.102): "See how she served McKinley! All his life / He wooed her for his morganatic wife."

Mormon] Just as AB defended the persecuted Chinese, he continually defended the Mormons against unjust persecution (see "Prattle" [*W*, 26 Mar. 1881; *SS* 180). He did not, however, have any compunction about ribbing them for the illogic of some facets of their faith.

Motion] The Milton quotation is from *Comus,* line 476.

Mouse] In "Oil of Dog" (1890; *CW* 8.170), Boffer Bings flees to "the famous city of Otumwee." Otumwee appears to be a play on Ottumwa, Iowa.

Mousquetaire] Cf. "Prattle" (*W*, 27 Dec. 1884: 5):

Last summer a letter from Stockton
  The carrier left at my door,
And my heart, ah, how loudly it knocked on
  My ribs!—for *her* writing it bore.

"Please send me, my darling, a pair of
  These new-fangled things, real quick:

> The hands *you* love *I* must take care of—
> And skeeters are awfully thick!"

> Enclosed, an advertisement, blotted
> In the way that a woman loves.
> And I learned, from the words she had dotted,
> She wanted some "mousquetaire gloves."

Mugwump] A Republican who left the party in 1884, refusing to support presidential candidate James G. Blaine. Thus, a person who acts independently or remains neutral. AB declared that he himself was a Mugwump in 1884 ("Prattle," *E,* 7 July 1888; *SS* 219).

Mule] The sterile offspring of a male donkey and a female horse.

Multitude] Cf. "Ashes of the Beacon" (*CW* 1.61–62): "An inherent weakness in republican government was that it assumed the honesty and intelligence of the majority, 'the masses,' who were neither honest nor intelligent. It would doubtless have been an excellent government for a people so good and wise as to need none. In a country having such a system the leaders, the politicians, must necessarily all be demagogues, for they can attain to place and power by no other method than flattery of the people and subserviency to the will of the majority. In all the ancient American political literature we look in vain for a single utterance of truth and reason regarding these matters. In none of it is a hint that the multitude was ignorant and vicious, as we know it to have been, and as it must necessarily be in any country, to whatever high average of intelligence and morality the people attain; for 'intelligence' and 'morality' are comparative terms, the standard of comparison being the intelligence and morality of the wisest and best, who must always be the few. . . . That a body of men can be wiser than its wisest member seems to the modern understanding so obvious and puerile an error that it is inconceivable that any people, even the most primitive, could ever have entertained it; yet we know that in America it was a fixed and steadfast political faith." See also "Certain Fool Epigrams for Certain Foolish People" (*Am,* 10 Aug. 1903: 14): "A chain is only as strong as its weakest link, but a multitude can be as wise as its wisest member. It has only to obey him."

Mummy] See "The Views of One" (*Am,* 20 Apr. 1905: 16; *E,* 28 Apr. 1905: 20): "admirers of the great Ramses can see him, looking pretty well, in the Boulak Museum. He looks as if, rightly distilled, he would yield several ounces of good mummy—a medicament in high favor with our grandfathers—or serve to fervor the furnace of a locomotive engine." See also "Embalm." Powdered mummy was indeed once used for medicinal purposes. Dramer Brune is the protagonist of "The Story of a Conscience" (1890; *CW* 2.165). Disrespect for the dead (by means of plundering tombs) is also mentioned at "Cairn" and "Tomb."

Myrmidon] The Myrmidons were a warlike race in Thessaly whom Achilles led to the siege of Troy. See Homer, *Iliad* 2.681f.

Nectar] *Am* and *E* add the following lines:
> When she wakes what will she do?
> Join the W.C.T.U.

W.C.T.U. stands for Woman's Christian Temperance Union, founded in 1874. See also "Wine."

Newtonian] Cf. "Prattle" (*W,* 12 Apr. 1884: 5): "the great publicist might be as profoundly moved as Newton was when he discovered that an apple parted from the tree would fall to the ground if there was nothing to hinder it." See also "Gravity."

Nihilist] AB defines the word not in the philosophical sense ("negative doctrines in religion or morals; total rejection of current religious beliefs or moral principles" [*OED*]) but in the political sense, as referring to a Russian revolutionary party loosely affiliated with the socialists. Leo Tolstoi of course had nothing to do with them.

Nobleman] See "Lord."

Non-combatant] During the Civil War, many Quakers served as nurses in the hospitals on both sides, but most refused to serve as soldiers, some even being imprisoned for the offense. There were cases of drafted Quakers who also refused to buy a substitute and were prosecuted. However, more than one Quaker farm was defended by its owner, a fact that did not pass unnoticed by the soldiers. AB suggests that a live Quaker is still a potential combatant. Only a dead one would truly be a noncombatant.

Nose] Cf. the "nursery rhyme" about a nose from "Prattle" (*W*, 12 Aug. 1881: 101):

> There's a man with a nose
> And wherever he goes
> The men and the women all shout:
> "What a wonderful nose!
> We will watch till he blows
> That very remarkable snout."
>
> But the man with a nose
> Is so shy that he goes
> In a calico tent to begin.
> And a placard he shows:
> "At 8 : 30 she blows —
> It will cost you ten cents to get in."

Noumenon] George Henry Lewes (1817–78) was a historian and critic and the common-law husband of George Eliot. The quotation has not been identified but probably derives from *A Biographical History of Philosophy* (1845–46) or *The History of Philosophy from Thales to Comte* (1867). It is also found in "Grizzly Papers: No. II" (*OM*, Feb. 1871: 181) and "Moxon's Master."

Novel] The views expressed here are echoed throughout AB's writings on literature, especially in "The Novel" (*CW* 10.17) and "The Short Story" (*CW* 10.234). The notion that the novel is "too long to be read at a sitting" is a clear parallel to Edgar Allan Poe's condemnation of the long poem as found in "The Philosophy of Composition" (1846) and "The Poetic Principle" (1849).

Oblivion] Cf. AB's wry couplet entitled "The Discoverers" (*CW* 4.366): "My! how my fame rings out in every zone — / A thousand critics shouting: 'He's unknown!'"

Obsessed] In Gadara, Jesus healed a man possessed with demons by expelling them into a herd of swine, which then hurled themselves into a lake and drowned (Luke 8 : 26–33).

Obsolete] Cf. "Lexicographer."

Ocean] The definition is one of AB's many attacks on the religious conception of the "argument from design," that is, that everything in the world is created for the benefit of human beings.

Old] Cf. "Prattle" (*E*, 10 Apr. 1892: 6): "G is for Goby, a fowl of no use."

Oleaginous] The source of the Disraeli anecdote is unknown. AB refers to Samuel Wilberforce (1805–73), successively bishop of Oxford and of Winchester and a leading Anglican theologian of his day. He initiated the revision of the King James Bible (see "Covet").

Omnipresent] Cf. "Ubiquity." Sir Boyle Roche (1743–1807) was an Irish politician known for the flamboyance of his speeches. The expression about a man being in two places at once is given, unattributed, in "Bierce on the Funding Bill" (*E*, 1 Feb. 1896: 1).

Opera] AB's mock Latin taxonomic names mean "the audible ape" and "loud ape-man." Ernst Haeckel coined the word *Pithecanthropos* to denote the putative link between apes and human beings.

Opposition] Ghargaroo was a mythical island used throughout AB's fiction and fables as a setting for his political or moral satires. In the latter half of the last sentence, AB parodies Abraham Lincoln's Gettysburg Address.

Optimist] Cf. "The Views of One" (*Am*, 13 Mar. 1905: 14; *E*, 20 Mar. 1905: 14): "The Rev. Dr. Newman has been lecturing here on Browning, whom he describes as 'an incurable optimist.' I think he was cured—he died." See also "White."

Orthodox] Cf. "Prattle" (*E*, 28 Apr. 1895: 6): "The Seventh-Day Adventists recently imprisoned in Tennessee must possess their souls with patience until heaven shall inspire the Orthodox heart to explain. They may have to wait a good while for the inspiration to get in; for the Orthodox heart is the toughest ox heart in the world."

Orthography] See "Our Sacrosanct Orthography" (*Co*, Mar. 1907: 581).

Outcome] *Am* and *E* add the following verses:

"You acted unwisely," I cried, "as you see,
   By the outcome." He calmly eyed me.
"When choosing the course of my action," said he,
"I had not the outcome to guide me."

Shapes of Clay.

The verses were published as "A Lacking Factor" under "Brevigraphs" (*W*, 20 Mar. 1886: 6) and were reprinted in *Shapes of Clay* (1903; *CW* 4.360).

Out-of-doors] The verses here were first published as "Communing with Nature" (*W*, 25 Nov. 1881: 342).

Ovation] Cf. "Prattle" (*Ar*, 9 June 1877: 5): "The newspapers are full of accounts of the 'ovations' Gen. Grant is receiving in England, and one of my personal correspondents wishes to know what an 'ovation' is. I do not accurately know; it is certainly not what an *ovatio* was amongst the Romans. I am inclined to think—with all deference to the superior judgment of our native lexicographers and philologists—that we have made the word anew from either *ovis*, a sheep, or *ovum*, an egg. If so, it may mean either 'a great cry and little wool,' as the vulgar proverb has it, or a pelting with the over-ripe fruit of the domestic hen." See also "Prattle" (*E*, 4 Mar. 1888: 4) concerning misuse of the word ("*Ovation* for *honors*, or *applause*. An 'ovation,' among the Romans, was a formal ceremony in honor of a person whose deeds were not thought quite worthy of a 'triumph'") and *WR* 48.

Pain] See also "Compunction."

Painting] AB published several parodic catalogs of paintings in *E*.

Palm] AB's mock taxonomic name means "the human palm." Cf. "Prattle" (*E*, 26 Oct. 1890: 6): "The editor of the *Bulletin* is himself not without some claim to the title of benefactor, I understand. He is an ardent and enthusiastic arboriculturist, and introduced into California the *Palma Fitchii* —the well known itching palm"; in this case the palm of George K. Fitch. An itching palm wants to be relieved by money, as in the verses at "Inauspiciously."

Palmistry] See also "Phrenology" and "Physiognomy." An unsigned article by a palm-reader, "The Hands of Our Prominent People and What Their Markings Mean" (*E*, 28 Apr. 1895: 22–23), contains the following analysis of AB's personality based on examination of his hand, a drawing of which accompanied the article: "This man has strong mental ability and is a professional. The indications are that he is an author and leads a literary life. He is calculating—strongly so, mathematical and more or less artistic. He has large scientific qualities. Uses wisdom and is thoughtful in what he does. He is rather pugnacious, but not domineering. His nature is in no way brutal, neither is he selfish. He has a critical mind and is a man to say sharp things about people. His criticisms are keen and to the point. Naturally he is sympathetic and is well endowed with imagination. His will power is of the stubborn kind. He is philosophical, but disposed to be pessimistic and take a gloomy view of life. He thinks well, the scope of his intellectual and emotional development being large. This man belongs to the professional type, his hand indicating professional qualities to be stronger than business qualities. He has pretty good governing ability. He has not had many love experiences" (p. 23).

Pandemonium] In *Paradise Lost,* Pandæmonium is the capital of Hell.

Pantaloons] The abbreviation of "pantaloons" to "pants" was considered vulgar. Oliver Wendell Holmes said it was "a word not made for gentlemen, but 'gents,'" a sentiment (and distinction) that would have appealed to AB.

Pantheism] AB lampooned many of the seemingly pointless debates about theological and other minutiae, much like the dispute in Jonathan Swift's *Gulliver's Travels* (1726) between the Big Endians and Small Endians (itself a satire of hairsplitting arguments concerning theological matters), for example, foreordination vs. predestination, infralapsarianism vs. supralapsarianism, omnipresence vs. ubiquity, homoiousianism vs. arianism, horizontalism vs. verticalism (under "Zenith"), and Trinitarianism vs. Unitarianism.

Parricide] AB wrote several stories of parricide, most notably "My Favorite Murder" (1888), one of four collected under the title "The Parenticide Club" (*CW* 8).

Passport] Cf. "The Passing Show" (*Fi,* 7 Feb. 1874: 1): "The passport system between France and Switzerland is to suffer extinction. The passport system being a heritage of barbarism, and an anachronism, might be advantageously 'squelched' throughout Europe."

Patriot] The definition in *Am* and *E* concludes: "A person whose zeal for the defense of his country's altars and fires is not inconsistent with a fierce desire to cross the border to overturn the altars and extinguish the fires of another land."

Patriotism] Johnson's actual comment is: "Patriotism is the last refuge of a scoundrel." It derives not from his dictionary but from Boswell's *Life of Johnson* (under the date 7 Apr. 1775). Cf. "Prattle" (*Ar,* 9 Feb. 1878: 9) ("Patriotism is fierce as a fever, pitiless as the grave, blind as a stone, and irrational as a headless hen") and "Prattle" (*E,* 27 Nov. 1898: 12; *J,* 4 Dec. 1898: 32), where it is defined as "love of country, as distinguished from love of mankind."

Peace] See "The Passing Show" (*Am,* 3 Jan. 1904: 32; *E,* 17 Jan. 1904: 44): "One of the most hideous of the many hideous 'memorials' in Washington is that at the foot of Capitol Hill, popularly known as the Peace Monument. Considering it studiously one day last week was an old gentleman, obviously not of this world—probably from Kansas. Former Congressman Charles F. Joy came along and the old gentleman said to him: 'Mister, can you tell me what all that means?' 'Certainly, my friend,' said Mr. Joy, with the solemnity that serves to distinguish him from a funeral. 'That represents the horrors of Peace.'"

Penitence] See A17 in the Appendix.

Perfection] AB refers to the Victorian poet and critic Matthew Arnold (1822–88).

Pericardium] The membranous sac filled with serous fluid enclosing the heart and roots of the aorta and other large blood vessels. Cf. the following lines (dating to 1885) from "Epigrams" (*CW* 8.354):

> Artistically set to grace
> The wall of a dissecting-place,
> A human pericardium
> Was fastened with a bit of gum,
> While, simply underrunning it,
> The one word, "Charity," was writ
> To show the student band that hovered
> About it what it once had covered.

Peripatetic] Aristotle and his pupils were called Peripatetics because they conducted their discussions while walking about in a *peripatos,* or place for walking, in the Lyceum at Athens.

Persuasion] Cf. "Prattle" (*E,* 19 July 1896: 6): "I have long been convinced that personal persuasion is a matter of animal magnetism—what in its more obvious manifestation we now call hypnotism. At the back of the words and the postures, and independent of them, is that secret, mysterious power, addressing, not the ear, not the eye, nor, through them, the understanding, but through its matching quality in the auditor, captivating the will and enslaving it. That is how persuasion is effected; the spoken words merely supply a pretext for surrender. They enable us to yield without loss of our self-esteem, in the delusion that we are conceding to reason what is really extorted by charm. The words are necessary, too, to point out what the orator wishes us to think, if we are not already apprised of it. When the nature of his power is better understood and frankly recognized, he can spare himself the toil of talking. The parliamentary debate of the future will probably be conducted in silence, and with only such gestures as go by the name of 'passes.'"

Pettifogger] Specifically, a petty, unscrupulous lawyer.

Philanthropist] See B31 in the Appendix.

Philosophy] AB to Jean Hazen, 16 Mar. 1898: "Don't imagine that this disciple of Epictetus [i.e., AB] worries, nor for a moment forgets his brief philosophy—his before Zeno stole it from him—that 'nothing matters'" ("'Putting You in the Papers': Ambrose Bierce's Letters to Edwin Markham," ed. Joseph W. Slade, *Prospects* 1 [1975]: 350).

Phœnix] A mythical bird that lived for 500 years and then consumed itself by fire, to rise renewed from its ashes.

Phonograph] See "The Views of One" (*Am,* 21 Feb. 1906: 16; *E,* 27 Feb. 1906: 20): "In the instance of the Chicago woman who by means of a phonograph sang a hymn at her own funeral, it was observed that death makes the human voice a trifle brassy." See also "A Benign Invention" (1889; *CW* 9.161) concerning the phonograph.

Photograph] See "A Bit of Science" (1887; *CW* 4.261) concerning the supposed impossibility of color photography.

Phrenology] The study of the shape and protuberances of the skull in the belief that it revealed character and mental capacity. See "Prattle" (*E,* 5 May 1895: 6): "If the female men and silly women of the phrenology fad choose to be duped by him, well and good; it is for the betterment of their poor understandinglets."

Physiognomy] See "Prattle" (*Am,* 2 Aug. 1896: 6): "It is pleasing to note that Colonel Ingersoll is 'down upon' the 'physiognomy' fakirs, who pretend to 'read the mind's construction in the face,' to do which, saith Shakespeare, 'there is no art.' Every physiognomist, from Lavater down, takes his own face as the highest type and judges the mental and moral excellence of other persons by that convenient standard. I once knew a bullet-headed chap who, in the same spirit, described a well-known author as having 'a weak overgrowth of the head.' Colonel Ingersoll, an acute and analytic observer, could hardly fail to discern the folly and imposture of a science founded upon that almost universal vanity which serves to distinguish man from the beasts that perish to supply his table." The quotation from Shakespeare (*Macbeth* 1.4.11–12) reads: "There's no art / To find the mind's construction in the face." Johann Caspar Lavater (1741–1801), German theologian and author of *Physiognomische Fragmente* (1775–78; trans. as *Essays on Physiognomy*, 1793–94), was the inventor of "physiognomy" as here described.

Piano] The definition in *Am* concludes: "The word is a deaf person's abbreviation of 'Pianoforte.'"

Pianoforte] The quotation, which AB repeated frequently in his columns, is from the novel *Devereux* (1829) by Edward Bulwer-Lytton (1803–73). It comes from the end of chapter 13, where Sir William Devereux states: "I love to see the dear creatures amuse themselves; for, to tell you the truth . . . the best thing to keep them from playing the devil is to encourage them in playing the fool!"

Pickaninny] AB's mock Greek and Latin translate to "pre-dog-man" (presumably the most primitive of all prehominids) and "dominant American."

Picture] Cf. "Painting."

Pie] Cf. "Prattle" (*E*, 22 Dec. 1895: 6): "John Camden Hotten, the publisher, who had given me a check, died of a pork pie in order to beat me out of the money."

Pig] AB's mock Latin means "omnivorous pig." In a similar vein, see "The Town Crier" (*NL*, 30 Dec. 1871: 9; rev. slightly in "Epigrams" [*CW* 8.357]): "If a jackass were to describe the Deity he would represent Him with long ears and a tail. Man's idea is the higher and truer one; he pictures Him as somewhat resembling a man."

Pigmy] AB makes a similar joke about pigmies and hogmies in "The Passing Show" (*Am*, 6 Mar. 1904: 24; *E*, 20 Mar. 1904: 45).

Pilgrim] See "Prattle" (*Ar*, 12 Oct. 1878: 9): "the lawless traditions of 1620 still impart a bloody tinge to the social system of our Eastern brethren, and human life is but little safer now than in the days of the adventurous Puritans drawn thither by the golden dream of a universal psalm-singing through the nose. There is still the same reckless impatience of the forms of law, the same alacrity to resort to the crude, hasty justice of the mob, that marked the jurisprudence of the New England colonies and Dutch settlements in the times of Cotton Mather and Deidrich Knickerbocker. This ugly legacy of the old evil days—the wild life of the potato-placers—discourages immigration, frightens away Western capital and retards the development of the country. It is time, high time, that these turbulent tendencies were abated and those who exhibit them haled out of their houses and summarily hanged."

Plagiarize] AB once defended himself against accusations that "The Damned Thing" (1893; *CW* 3.280) was borrowed from "What Was It?" by Fitz-James O'Brien (1828–62). See "Prattle" (*E*, 27 May 1894; *SS* 254).

Plague] *Am* adds the following verses:
    "No diet gives freedom from Plague,"
        Said the noted physician, Montague,
        "But attend to your victual

And you'll have very lictual
To fear from the Fever-and-Ague."

Jacko Mepple.

AB alludes to the story of the ten plagues of Egypt (Exodus 7–12) and how Pharaoh's people but not Pharaoh succumbed to them.

Platter] This definition is from an unpublished proof found in an envelope containing material potentially to be added to *D* (see Appendix A). Cf. "Husband" and "Satiety."

Plebeian] In chemistry, a saturated solution is one that contains all the solute that can normally be dissolved at a given temperature.

Plenipotentiary] Cf. the reference to the Simurgh at "Rabble."

Pleonasm] The use of more words than necessary to express a thought.

Plunder] *Am* (6 Mar. 1906) and *E* (12 Mar. 1906) add the following verses:

He's a great financial wonder,
Always deprecating plunder
    As a game
With advantages accruing
To the player for undoing
The man who keeps the table;
    For the same
Is frequently unable
To prevent the player's flight,
With his property, by night.
But the game of financiering
Can prevent his interfering
    With the play
By cornering the darkness and the day.

See also "Morganatic."

Pocket] See B32 in the Appendix.

Polecat] "From Virginia to Paris" (1889; *CW* 4.157) is about the polecat.

Politics] In *Am* and *E* the definition concludes: "The game of graft, as named by the players."

Polygamy] See also "Bigamy" and A19 in the Appendix.

Populist] Populism was a reform movement among farmers and others who worried about excessive industrialization and concentration of money in the hands of a few wealthy financiers. The movement began in Kansas in the 1890s. "Morse" may be J. C. Morse, a candidate for the Kansas railroad commission, nominated in Mar. 1904. Whitney is unknown.

Portable] "Carrie Slupsky" (a thin parody of Carry Nation) is a character in "The Maid of Podunk" (*J*, 10 Mar. 1901: 26; as "Ambrose Bierce's History of the Maid of Podunk," *E*, 19 Mar. 1901: 14).

Portion] See "Prattle" (*E*, 5 Nov. 1893: 6): "No word in the language is more misused than 'portion' for 'part.' It means part and more—an allotted part. In speaking of the leg of Fijian missionary as a 'portion' of him you would be within measurable distance of good usage."

Positivism] "The system of Auguste Comte designed to supersede theology and metaphysics and depending on a hierarchy of the sciences beginning with mathematics and culminating in sociology" (*AHD*). Comte was friendly with both John Stuart Mill (who wrote *Auguste Comte and Positivism* [1865]) and Herbert Spencer, although neither could genuinely be regarded as Comte's followers.

Potable] Cf. "The Nations That Drink Too Much" (*E*, 6 Nov. 1902: 16; *Am*, 13 Nov. 1902: 6): "All peoples in all ages have used intoxicants, even those whose religions forbade. Probably there is no one thing upon which so much human ingenuity has been expended as invention of alcoholic substitutes for water, which we are told is our 'natural' drink. We never drink water because we like it, as we do wine, coffee, and half a score of other beverages. We take it only as a handy medicine for the recurrent disorder known as thirst. When thirsty we like it, as we like almost anything that is wet; and it is cheap, accessible and abundant." See also "Tope."

Practically] See *WR* 52.

Pre-Adamite] Cain's wife (not named) is mentioned at Genesis 4:17; she bore a son, Enoch. The "controversy" alluded to refers to the debate over whether the Pre-Adamite race was sprung from the same source as Adam (see "Monogenism"). See "Prattle" (*E*, 16 Apr. 1893: 6): "The motto of my ancestral coat-of-arms (bestowed by one of the Pre-Adamite Kings upon Cain Bierce, the founder of my family) is: 'To none another's, each to his own.'"

Precedent] See the dialogue at "Executive" and also "The Kingdom of Tortirra" (1888; included in "The Land Beyond the Blow," *CW* 1.186) re the notion of legal precedent.

Predestination] See also "Foreordination."

Preference] The "ancient philosopher" was Thales. The anecdote can be found in Diogenes Laertius, *Lives of the Eminent Philosophers* 1.9. See also note on "Life."

Prehistoric] Orpheus Bowen (Nallo Gampus in *Am* and *E*) is also the author of the verses at "Preside."

Present] Cf. "Past."

Presentable] See also "Deshabille."

Presentiment] The verse is a parody of "Lochiel's Warning" by Thomas Campbell (1777–1844): "'Tis the sunset of life gives me mystical lore, / And coming events cast their shadows before."

Preside] Another of AB's grammatical bugbears. See *WR* 52–53: "'Professor Swackenhauer presided at the piano.' 'The deviled crab table was presided over by Mrs. Dooley.' How would this sound? 'The ginger pop stand was under the administration of President Woolwit, and Professor Sooffle presided at the flute.'"

President] See "Prattle" (*E*, 3 Nov. 1889: 6): "'I do not wish my husband to be President again.' — *Mrs. Harrison*. Wishes, madam, do not appear to count for much in this matter. With a single exception, your husband is the only man in the United States of whom it is certainly known that several millions of his fellow citizens did not wish him to be President this time."

Prevaricator] A *prevaricator* is one who equivocates or avoids making a direct statement but is nevertheless a liar.

Prison] The quotation "Stone walls do not a prison make" is from Richard Lovelace (1618–58), "To Althea: From Prison," stanza 4.

Private] See also "Cadet."

Proboscis] Edward Bok (1863–1930), editor and essayist who took over editorship of the *Ladies' Home Journal* in 1899, is satirized in "Insurance in Ancient America" and "The Evolution of a Story" (1874, rev. 1911; *CW* 12.398). Jo. Miller refers to Joaquin Miller.

Pyrrhonism] A philosophy propounded by the Greek philosopher Pyrrho of Elis (c. 300 BCE) expressing a broad skepticism about the possibility of obtaining certain knowledge about phenomena.

Quill] See also "Goose."

Quixotic] The couplet parodies Thomas Gray's "Ode on a Distant Prospect of Eton College" (1742), lines 99–100: "where ignorance is bliss, / 'Tis folly to be wise."

Quorum] In *Am*, the Chairman is referred to as "Mr. Aldrich," that is, Nelson Wilmarth Aldrich (1841–1915), U.S. senator from Rhode Island (1881–1911) and a leading Republican politician of his day. Cf. "The Views of One" (*Am*, 5 Mar. 1906: 16; *E*, 10 Mar. 1906: 18): "'God and I are a majority,' said a famous European statesman. The devil and Senator McCumber are a quorum."

Rabble] Cf. "The Novel" (*CW* 10.22): "He [the romance writer] is lord of two worlds and may select his characters from both. In the altitudes where his imagination waves her joyous wing there are no bars for her to beat her breast against; the universe is hers, and unlike the sacred bird Simurgh, which is omnipotent on condition of never exerting its power, she may do as she will."

Radium] Marie and Pierre Curie discovered radium in 1898. The element gives off radioactivity, not heat. It initially was baffling to scientists and was thought by some to upset the entire understanding of classical physics, because, in giving off radioactivity and thereby reducing its mass, it seemed to defy the thesis that matter could not be spontaneously created or destroyed.

Ramshackle] The Doric order is the oldest and simplest of the three orders of classical Greek architecture. Theodoric the Great (454?–526) was king of the Ostrogoths. Theodore Roosevelt had new West Wing offices constructed in the White House during his first term as president (1901–05). AB equates these additions with the barbarism of the Dark Ages.

Rarebit] Welsh rarebit (rabbit) is a dish of melted, seasoned cheese served hot over toast. Toad-in-a-hole is a sausage or other meat baked in a batter. Feuillete de ris-de-veau à la financière is the thymus gland (sweetbreads) of a young calf baked with morels or truffles in a pastry shell and served with a sauce made of Madeira. AB makes a play on the French word *ris* (laughter).

Rascal] See "Prattle" (*E*, 29 Jan. 1899: 12; *J*, 5 Feb. 1899: 23): "a rascal is merely a fool in activity."

Rattlesnake] AB's coined Latin means "man who walks on his belly."

Reach] See "Honorable."

Reading] One of AB's greatest bêtes noires was the Indiana poet James Whitcomb Riley (1849–1916), some of whose poems are in dialect. AB's hostility toward the use of slang in literature was unrelenting; however, he regarded the fractured English of his four hundred "Little Johnny" stories as "not 'phonetic spelling' humor at all; the spelling is done for *vraisemblance* and is intended to represent the actual spelling of such a kid" (AB to Myles Walsh, 6 June 1905; ALS, University of Cincinnati), and in any event AB used it for satiric purposes. The name "Jupiter Muke" resembles that of the protagonist of "Jupiter Doke, Brigadier-General" (1885; *CW* 8.23).

Reality] *The Mad Philosopher* is the source of the verses at "Aphorism" and "Diary." Cf. "Small Contributions" (*Co*, June 1908: 110): "Subject a novel to the fire assay and what remains at the bottom of the cupel—the precious metal with the worthless stuff burned out of it—is a short story." A *cupel* is a porous cup used in assaying to remove precious metals from base elements.

Reason] AB's coined word *propensitate*, much like *solicitate* at "Adamant," seems to be a kind of chemical extract (analogous to precipitate), ironically suggesting that an irrational judgment can somehow be reduced to an emotionless chemical compound. See also "Understanding."

Rector] See also "Zany."

Redemption] The verses here initially appeared in "Prattle" (*E*, 13 Jan. 1889: 4). See "The Town Crier" (*NL*, 15 Apr. 1871: 9): "We have likewise ascertained . . . that the mystery of redemption is sublime but unintelligible."

Redundant] Roosevelt's purported remark is in regard to Eugene V. Debs (1855–1926), labor leader, socialist candidate for president, and a constant thorn in Roosevelt's side during both his vice-presidency (1897–1901) and presidency (1901–09).

Refuge] AB alludes to Joshua 20:2–9. The cities of refuge were "appointed for all the children of Israel, and for the stranger that sojourneth among them, that whosoever killeth any person at unawares might flee thither, and not die by the hand of the avenger of blood, until he stood before the congregation."

Regalia] Cf. AB's "Sons of the Fair Star" (1888) to "Sons of the South Star." "My Credentials" (1886; *CW* 12.360–61) and "Some of Our Societies" (*W*, 1 May 1886: 3) contain listings of still more humorously named organizations. See also "Auspiciously."

Religion] The marquis de Rochebriant is also mentioned under "Eat." See also B6 in the Appendix.

Reliquary] *Gesta Sanctorum* is AB's fictitious parallel to *Gesta Romanorum*, the famous medieval collection of Latin stories, each with a moral.

Renown] The verses here originally appeared in slightly different form (and attributed to Adair Welcker) in "Prattle" (*E*, 15 Dec. 1889: 6).

Repartee] Cf. "Little Johnny on Politics" (*J*, 16 Aug. 1896: 6; *E*, 23 Aug. 1896: 6): "Repertee is the art of insultin a feller in sech a way that he cant resent it."

Repentance] The verses here initially appeared in an unsigned editorial (*W*, 21 Aug. 1886: 5). Charles Stewart Parnell (1846–91) was a celebrated Irish politician whose career was ruined in late 1890 when he was proven to be an adulterer.

Replica] AB continuously mocked the notion that a painting by a famous artist is more valuable (hence more beautiful) than one by an obscure artist.

Report] This definition appeared in Dx but was omitted from *D*. Cf. "Prattle" (*E*, 2 Aug. 1891: 6): "Strange that a gun's absurd report / Should win belief!" Lt. Gen. (CSA) Richard Stoddert Ewell (1817–72) fought at Gettysburg, Kelly's Ford, and Spotsylvania. Ewell had returned to the army from convalescent leave just in time for Gettysburg as a new corps commander, inheriting half of T. J. Jackson's corps. His corps was the first to contact Buford's cavalry screen and Reynolds's I Corps at Gettysburg on 1 July, and his divisions deployed slowly, arguably allowing the Army of the Potomac the advantage of the high ground for the battle. The debate on Ewell's slowly moving subordinates and the reasons for it continues to this day.

Reporter] The verses here originally appeared in "The Passing Show" (*E*, 13 Aug. 1899: 12).

Republic] See "Monarchical Government" for AB's terse commentary on what constituted real government.

Resign] One of the most distinguished soldiers of his time, Gen. Leonard Wood (1860–1927) fought in the Spanish-American War and was military governor of Cuba from 1899 to 1902. AB, along with many in the army, objected to Wood's promotion to brigadier general in 1901 because he had been promoted over many other officers with greater seniority.

Resolute] See also "Obstinate."

Respectability] See "Prattle" (*E*, 3 Nov. 1892: 6): "With the hair the case is different. It goes, not merely because its mandate is exhausted, but because it is really detrimental to us in the struggle for existence. Its departure is an instance, pure and simple, of the survival of the fittest. But little reflection is required to show the superior fitness of the man who is bald. Baldness is respectability, baldness is piety, rectitude and general worth. Persons holding responsible and well-salaried positions are commonly bald — bank cashiers especially. The prosperous merchant is usually of shiny pate; the head of most of the great corporations are thinly haired. Of two otherwise equal applicants for a position of trust and profit who would not instinctively choose the bald one, or, both being bald, the balder? Having, therefore, a considerable advantage in the struggle for existence, the bald person naturally lives longer than his less gifted competitor (any one can observe that he is usually the older) and leaves a more numerous progeny, inheriting the paternal endowment of precarious hair. In a few generations more those varieties of our species known as the Mophead and the Curled Darling will doubt-less have become extinct, and the barber (*Homo loquax*) will have followed them into oblivion."

Respite] In Dx, the following line is canceled: "A break in the continuity of the disagree-able." The verses here appeared initially in "Prattle" (*W*, 17 Oct. 1885: 5) addressed to Gen. George Stoneman (1822–94), who served as governor of California (1883–87). John Peter Altgeld (1847–1902) was governor of Illinois (1891–97). He gained notori-ety when, in 1893, he pardoned a group of anarchists accused of murder during the Chicago Haymarket riot of 4 May 1886. AB had earlier criticized Stoneman for what he believed to be undue leniency toward criminals. See the short play "Metempsycho-sis" (1895; *CW* 5.231).

Respond] Herbert Spencer (1820–1903), British philosopher. Cf. "Moxon's Master" (1899; *CW* 3.94):

> Do you happen to recall Herbert Spencer's definition of "Life"? I read it thirty years ago. He may have altered it afterward, for anything I know, but in all that time I have been unable to think of a single word that could profitably be changed or added or removed. It seems to me not only the best definition, but the only possible one.
>
> "Life," he says, "is a definite combination of heterogeneous changes, both simultaneous and successive, in correspondence with external coexistences and sequences."

The passage quoted in "Moxon's Master" was first propounded in rudimentary form in *The Principles of Psychology* (1855) and in definitive form in *The Principles of Biology* (1864–67), Part 1, chaps. 4–5. It was first quoted by AB in "The Fables of Zambri, the Parsee" (*Fu*, 27 July 1872: 37): First Series, No. 12.

Responsibility] The verses here initially appeared within an unsigned editorial (*W*, 9 Oct. 1886: 5). See "Prattle" (*E*, 15 Jan. 1899: 12; *J*, 22 Jan. 1899: 28): "in England a man able but unwilling to work is called a 'sturdy beggar.'"

Restitution] Leland Stanford endowed Stanford University, and Andrew Carnegie en-dowed many public libraries. AB implies that these philanthropic acts were restitution for the criminality of their prior business actions.

Retaliation] The eye-for-an-eye law of the Old Testament seemed "natural," whereas Jesus' admonition to forgive one's neighbor, to turn the other cheek, struck people as unnatu-ral and illogical.

Retribution] Dom Pedro II (1825–91) was emperor of Brazil from 1840 to 1889, when he was deposed by the army and the leaders of a growing republican movement. He fled to Portugal, then to France, where he died. He is addressed in AB's "A False Prophecy" (1888; *CW* 4.311). Lines 9–16 were canceled in Dx:

> Why, man, this is not an auspicious time
>> For Liberators: Lincoln's brain was scattered;
> Big Alexander in the sooty grime
>> Of dynamite with his own blood was spattered;
>> And you, with your imperial purple tattered—
> You came off well, considering your crime.
> But don't go back—that were to be a gander:
> They'll send you to join Abe and Alexander.

Reveille] The second sentence of the definition alludes to the army's mispronunciation of the French word.

Revelation] Revelation is the final book of the New Testament. Cf. "Prattle" (*E*, 22 Aug. 1897: 18): "there is not a man in the world that denies the authority of revelation—not even the wickedest atheist. What some deny is revelation. What may have been revelation to the good Saint John (for example) is not revelation to me, but an assertion requiring evidence to support it. I may or may not deem the evidence sufficient, but at least nothing has been revealed to me, not even that something was revealed to him. Revelation is such to the person to whom it is made; to all others it is hearsay."

Rhadomancer] More properly "Rhabdomancer": one who practices rhabdomancy ("divination by means of a rod or wand; *spec.* the art of discovering ores, springs of water, etc., in the earth by means of a divining rod" [*OED*]).

Ribroaster] A ribroasting is a cudgeling or a beating.

Rice-water] A liquid prepared from rice boiled in water, often used for medicinal purposes (especially for children). AB suggests that "popular novelists and poets" produce bland, tepid products; the pseudo-chemical terms "obtundite" (= obtuseness) and "lethargine" (= lethargy) enhance the idea.

Riches] Cf. Mark 1:11: "And there came a voice from heaven, saying, Thou art my beloved Son, in whom I am well pleased." Rockefeller and Morgan thought that their riches were deserved; Debs (a socialist) did not.

Ridicule] The statement that AB attributes to Anthony Ashley Cooper, third earl of Shaftesbury (1671–1713), was actually attributed to him by Philip Dormer Stanhope, earl of Chesterfield (1694–1773), in his *Letters to His Son* (1774): "It is commonly said, and more particularly by Lord Shaftesbury, that ridicule is the best test of truth" (letter dated 6 Feb. 1752). This exact utterance is not found in Shaftesbury, but close approximations of it can be; cf., for example, *A Letter Concerning Enthusiasm* (1708): "How comes it to pass, then, that we appear such cowards in reasoning, and are so afraid to stand the test of ridicule?" See "Le Diable Est aux Vaches" (*FD* 74).

Right] The verses originally appeared in "Prattle" (*E*, 10 June 1888: 4). *In partibus infidelium* means "in the realms of the infidels." In Dx AB originally named the poet "Abednego Shadrach Bink," alluding to Shadrach, Meshach, and Abednego, who emerged unharmed from the fiery furnace (Daniel 3:26).

Righteousness] Bishop Rowley is fictitious.

Rime] See AB to S. O. Howes, 21 Dec. 1909 (ALS, Huntington Library and Art Gallery): "That chap is right about 'rime'—the present spelling (sacred to the guardians of our noble tongue) is a recent innovation and without sense."

Rimer] In Dx the following definition is canceled: "Rimester, *n.*, A poet that is held in disesteem."

R.I.P.] AB's mock Latin means "reduced to dust."

Robber] AB also related this anecdote in "Prattle" (*W*, 22 Nov. 1884: 5) and "Fables and Anecdotes" (*E*, 11 Feb. 1893: 6).

Romance] The distinction between the novel and the romance is the topic of the essay "The Novel" (*CW* 10.17). The quotation "drags at each remove a lengthening chain" is from Oliver Goldsmith, *The Traveller*, line 10. For "laid waste their powers," see Samuel Taylor Coleridge, "The World Is Too Much with Us": "The world is too much with us; late and soon, / Getting and spending, we lay waste our powers" (ll. 1–2).

Rope] See "Prattle" (*E*, 29 July 1888: 4): "It is a fact having a cheerful significance that a brace of New York murderers sentenced to die by hanging, under the old law, have asked to be permitted to die by electricity, under the new. This appears to show that the reform is favored by the class to be reformed. Philanthropists and assassins having agreed upon a suitable punishment for the latter, it only remains to apply it to the former."

Roundhead] AB refers to the civil war in England between the Parliamentarians and the Royalists from 1642 to 1649.

Rubbish] *Boreaplas* means "regions south of the North Pole," that is, *all* regions.

Rumor] A General Buxter appears in "Jupiter Doke, Brigadier-General" (*CW* 8.23).

Russian] AB puns on *tarter emetic*, a poisonous crystalline compound used in medicine as an expectorant.

Sabbath] See note on "Arrested." Cf. (among others) "Prattle" (*E*, 3 Mar. 1889: 4): "The holy folk who find in the Decalogue the commandment, 'Remember the Sabbath day to make your neighbor keep it wholly,' are petitioning Congress for a Sunday law with the old, immemorial hope." Also "Prattle" (*E*, 23 Sept. 1894: 6):

> God, I think, did never say:
> "Remember thou the Sabbath day
> To make your neighbor keep it wholly."
> "*Keep* it holy" —that is solely
> What He said and meant to say.

"Holystoning the deck" of a wooden ship required backbreaking work with large pumice stones and, often, days spent on hands and knees. The verses are from Richard Henry Dana (1815–82), *Two Years Before the Mast* (1840), chap. 3: "Six days shalt thou labour and do all thou art able; / And on the seventh, holystone the decks and scrape the cable."

Sacerdotalist] Actually, one who asserts "the existence in the Christian church of a sacerdotal order or priesthood having sacrificial functions and invested with supernatural powers" (*OED*).

Sacrament] A sacrament is not a ceremony but an outward sign, instituted by Jesus Christ, to communicate grace to the soul. The two common to Roman Catholics and Protestants are baptism and holy communion.

Sacred] AB mentions the "Mufti of Moosh" in several late columns.

Safety-clutch] The verses here originally appeared in "Prattle" (*E*, 23 Sept. 1888: 4).

Saint] Dx contains a clipping of the paragraph beginning "The Duchess . . ." in which St. Francis de Sales is named, but the source of that clipping has not been identified. A similar rendering is found in "Prattle" (*E*, 31 July 1892: 6).

Salamander] In ancient Greek folklore, the salamander bred in fire but quenched it by the coldness of its body. Christians adapted this belief to make the salamander a symbol for the desires of the flesh.

Sandlotter] Denis Kearney (1847–1907) was the rabble-rousing leader of the Workingmen's Party and was known for his rabid anti-Chinese stance. A *sans-culotte* was a radical extremist during the French Revolution and thus refers to any revolutionary extremist.

Sarcophagus] A coffin made of limestone, often inscribed or decorated with sculpture, that was thought to consume the flesh of corpses laid within it. An *obsequiographer* is one who writes about funerary matters. AB jokes about writers who use the term *sarcophagus* to refer to a coffin made of wood. See "Cannibal" and also "Prattle" (*E*, 8 Jan. 1888: 4): "I venture, not to inform but to remind this honorable court that cremation, now a revival, was once a *survival*, and originally no rite, but a culinary process; and that burial of the dead is but a modification by time and circumstance of the custom of hiding them away as potted meats to await the need of the ancestral unready tooth, as squirrels bury nuts. Witness the derivation of the word sarcophagus—meaning, not meat-eater, as the unlearned have assumed, but eat-meater, a receptacle for eat-meats, meats intended to be eaten—as we say to-day 'larder,' a place for lard, and 'pitcher,' a vessel to contain—er—'m—as I was saying, may it please the court, this prisoner has much to answer for."

Satan] The fable here first appeared in "Prattle" (*E*, 6 Nov. 1887: 4).

Satiety] This definition appeared initially as "Aversion." See also "Enough."

Satire] Cf. the Timorous Reporter sketch, "The Passing of Satire" (1909; *CW* 10.283–84): "'Satire,' said the Melancholy Author, 'is punishment. As such it has fallen into public disfavor through disbelief in its justice and efficacy. So the rascals go unlashed. Instead of ridicule we have solemn reprobation; for wit we have "humor"—with a slang word in the first line, two in the second and three in the third. Why, sir, the American reading public hardly knows that there ever was a distinctive kind of writing known, technically, as satire—that it was once not only a glory to literature but, incidentally, a terror to all manner of civic and personal unworth. If we had to-day an Aristophanes, a Jonathan Swift or an Alexander Pope, he would indubitably be put into a comfortable prison with all sanitary advantages, fed upon yellow-legged pullets and ensainted by the Little Brothers of the Bad. For they would think him a thief. In the same error, the churches would pray for him and the women compete for his hand in marriage.'" Herman Scheffauer (1878–1927), one of AB's protégés, wrote an article entitled "The Death of Satire" (*Fortnightly Review* 99, no. 6 [June 1913]: 1188–99) in which AB figures prominently. The phrase "endowed by their Creator" is from the Declaration of Independence.

Satyr] Leviticus 17:7: "And they shall no more offer their sacrifices unto devils [satyrs], after whom they have gone a whoring. This shall be a statute for ever unto them throughout their generations." See also Isaiah 34:14: "The wild beasts of the desert shall also meet the wild beasts of the island, and the satyr shall cry to his fellow; the screech owl also shall rest there, and find for herself a place of rest."

Sauce] See also "Mayonnaise."

Saw] These saws and others appeared in "Prattle" (*E*, 22 Jan. 1888: 4). See also "Adage."

Scarabæus] A tumble-bug, more properly a tumble-dung, is "a scarabaeid beetle which rolls up balls of dung, in which it deposits its eggs and in which the larvae go through their transformations; a dung-beetle" (*OED*).

Scarabee] The verses originally appeared in "Prattle" (*W*, 26 Dec. 1885: 11).

Scarification] For the phrase "The founding of a library or endowment of a university," see "Restitution."

Scepter] See "Mace."

Scimitar] The anecdote in this definition appeared in somewhat different form in *W* under "Head."

Scrap-book] The verses here originally appeared as "To Fr-nk M. P-xl-y" (*W*, 1 Aug. 1885: 6). AB was not above keeping scrapbooks of clippings of his writings, but his purpose was purely practical. Philip Melanchthon (1497–1560) was a German theologian, initially a follower of Martin Luther, whose *Loci Communes* (1521) was the first systematic presentation of the principles of the Reformation.

Seal] The Pribilof Islands off southwestern Alaska in the Bering Sea are noted as a breeding ground for seals; hence AB's pun. The United States took over the islands as a term of the Treaty of Portsmouth that ended the Russo-Japanese War of 1904–05 and began a long-term commitment to international resource management restrictions by the United States. The administration of the islands has been the responsibility of the United States ever since (they are now considered part of Alaska). At the time, there was great controversy regarding the islands and what should become of them. The *OED* states, in regard to the etymology of "sincere": "There is no probability in the old explanation from *sine cera* 'without wax.'" (AB's "cero" is an error.) AB makes a similar joke about *locum sigilis* (place of the seal) in "Little Johnny's Notions" (*E*, 7 Feb. 1897: 6). This definition, not in Dx, appeared previously as "Great Seal":

> GREAT SEAL, *n*. A mark impressed upon state papers to attest their authoritative character. It is a survival of the ancient custom of inscribing upon important documents certain cabalistic words or signs to give them a magical efficacy independent of human authority. In the British museum are preserved many papers—mostly of a sacerdotal character—validated by necromantic pentagrams and other devices, bearing, usually, the initial letters of words to conjure with; and it is significant that these are attached, in many instances, in the same way as seals are appended now. As nearly every reasonless and apparently meaningless custom, rite or observance of modern times has had its origin in some remote utility, it is pleasing to note an example of an ancient nonsense evolving, in the process of the ages, something really useful. By the way, our word "sincere" is from *sine cero*, without wax—open, as a letter which all may read; at least that is the interpretation most scholars have put upon it. But may it not mean "unsealed," in the other sense?—impressed with no occult or magical charm and power, but frankly reliant on the goodwill and understanding of the person addressed. The question is submitted with respectful deference to that great philological and archæological authority who illuminates the whole world of learning by his answers to "Letters from the People" in the *Morning Call*.

Seine] The verses here had initially appeared under "Lace."

Serial] The anecdote about James F. Bowman (d. 1882) is from "Books and Book-Folk" under AB's column "Small Contributions" (*Co*, June 1907: 218). Bowman was the author of *The Island Home; or, The Young Castaways* (1852) and a contributor to *Ar*. AB wrote a sonnet on Bowman entitled "J. F. B." (1882; *CW* 4.129).

Severalty] Not in Dx. The verses here, which first appeared in "Prattle" (*E*, 6 Mar. 1892: 16), are another parody of Pope's "Essay on Man." See "Humorist."

Sheriff] J. Milton Sloluck purportedly compiled *ND* (1873), AB's early volume of humorous sketches.

Siren] The following verses were canceled in Dx:

> Debs, Debs for President! O siren Fate,
> Must his ambition still be lured and wrecked?—
> The men that can elect won't nominate;
> The men that nominate cannot elect.

Two sleeping fowls the fox approaches—lo!
One roosting out of reach, and one a crow!

These verses originally appeared in "Prattle" (*E*, 12 Aug. 1888: 4) addressed to Frank Pixley. For Debs, see "Redundant." Note AB's group of stories about the sea, "The Ocean Wave" (*CW* 8.[217]).

Slang] AB displayed a longstanding hostility toward the use of slang and dialect in literature. See also the fable "Two Parrots" (1907; *CW* 6.306) and "Word Changes and Slang" (*CW* 10.103).

Smithareen] The verses here first appeared in "Prattle" (*E*, 12 July 1896: 6) and were prefaced by the following paragraph: "Miss Charlotte Smith, the President of the Woman's Rescue League, says that bicycle riding by women is 'leading them headlong to the devil' and proposes to have it stopped by an act of Congress." In the late nineteenth century, bicycle riding by women was in fact regarded as unhealthy.

Sophistry] The verses here first appeared in "Prattle" (*E*, 16 Sept. 1888: 4). The pejorative connotation of the word derives from Plato's disapproval of the Sophists.

Sorcery] The anecdote about Augustin Nicolas appeared first in "Confessions of a Weak-Minded Man: No. 3" (*NL*, 21 Mar. 1868: 2). The text here is taken nearly verbatim from "Grizzly Papers: No. III" (*OM*, Mar. 1871: 283; rpt. *ND* 83).

Soul] The anecdote about the soul appeared first in "Confessions of a Weak-Minded Man: No. 2" (*NL*, 14 Mar. 1868: 9). The text here is taken nearly verbatim from "Grizzly Papers: No. II" (*OM*, Feb. 1871: 184; rpt. *ND* 81). Cf. Philippians 3:19: "Whose end is destruction, whose God is their belly, and whose glory is in their shame, who mind earthly things." AB discusses this notion at length in "Prattle" (24 Nov. 1889: 6).

Spooker] AB refers to William Dean Howells (1837–1920), *Between the Dark and the Daylight* (New York: Harper and Brothers, 1907). Howells also wrote an earlier collection of ghost stories, *Questionable Shapes* (New York: Harper and Brothers, 1903), and co-edited (with Henry Mills Alden) the anthology *Shapes That Haunt the Dusk* (New York: Harper and Brothers, 1907). AB of course contributed to the form with his classic collection *Can Such Things Be?* (1893). Cf. "Small Contributions" (*Co*, June 1908: 109): "Mr. Howells has 'gone in' for the supernatural. His book, 'Between the Dark and the Daylight,' introduces the reader to as respectable and mannerly ghosts as one could wish to meet, or does meet. To the terror that invests the chairman of a village school board the Howells ghost adds something of the mystery enveloping the farmer from another township."

Story] Not in Dx. Rudolph Block (1870–1940) was a journalist and short story writer who also wrote under the pseudonym Bruno Lessing. His work frequently appeared in *Co* during the period of AB's tenure with the magazine (1905–09). In fact, AB complained to Hearst in 1907 that the editor at *Co* gladly published a Block story every month but felt he could not publish AB's own fiction so frequently. *CW* 4 contains AB's verses "Rudolph Block" (p. 373). Percival Pollard (1869–1911) was a fiction writer, critic, and good friend of AB. He discussed AB in a chapter of his treatise *Their Day in Court* (1909). See AB to Pollard (19 June 1911; ALS, Yale): "In VII you'll find yourself the hero of an apocryphal anecdote, under the word 'Story', in 'The Devil's Dictionary'. Hope you won't mind." The anecdote about Block and Pollard initially appeared in different form in "Unauthenticated Tales" (*W*, 11 Apr. 1891: 14), with Dr. William Bartlett instead of Block and Dan O'Connell instead of Pollard.

The fiction writer W. C. Morrow (1854–1923) was another of AB's friends. AB highly praised his volume of weird tales, *The Ape, the Idiot and Other People* (1897).

"Prattle" (*Ar,* 27 Oct. 1877: 5) contains AB's verses about J. J. Owen and the ghost of Vasquez. J. J. Owen (1827–95) was the author of a column for *Better Times,* a religious magazine in San Jose, and such books as *Our Sunday Talks; or, Gleanings in Various Fields of Thought* (1880) and *Spiritual Fragments* (1890). The anecdote about Morrow and Owen initially appeared in "Unauthenticated Tales" (*W,* 24 Jan. 1891: 3).

Adm. Winfield Scott Schley (1839–1911) engaged in a controversial maneuver at the Battle of Santiago, Cuba (3 July 1898), in which it appeared that he was leaving the blockading line, when in fact he seems to have been swinging his flagship, the *Brooklyn,* to a position for a fight on a parallel line. The furor over the incident lasted for years; the public largely took Schley's side, but the navy generally regarded Adm. William Thomas Sampson (1840–1902) as the true victor of the battle. AB, with his many friends at the Army and Navy Club in Washington, clearly approved of Sampson and wrote many articles condemning Schley.

Charles Frederick Joy was a U.S. representative from Missouri (1893–94, 1895–1903). See note on "Peace." Champ Clark was a U.S. representative from Missouri (1893–95, 1897–1905). The anecdote about Clark first appeared in "Unauthenticated Tales" (*W,* 3 Jan. 1891: 7), although with different characters.

Brig. Gen. Harold Herbert Wotherspoon (1855–1940), president of the Army War College at Carlisle Barracks, PA, originally brought the General Staff System to the United States. AB corresponded with him briefly in 1908. Edmund Chaffee Barry (1854–1915) suceeded Wotherspoon at the War College. The anecdote about the rib-nosed baboon first appeared in "Unauthenticated Tales" (*W,* 3 Jan. 1891: 7), with Edward M. Greenway instead of Wotherspoon and Frank Carolan instead of Barry. Gen. Nelson Appleton Miles (1839–1925) was a distinguished soldier who led the force that pacified Puerto Rico following the Spanish-American War.

Success] Col. John Alexander Joyce (1842–1915) was a poet who also wrote biographies of Shakespeare, Poe, and other poets. AB wrote unfavorably of his verse in a letter to Walter Neale (3 Feb. 1913; ALS, Huntington Library and Art Gallery). The verses here first appeared in "The Passing Show" (*Am,* 21 Feb. 1904: 24; 6 Mar. 1904: 45).

Suffrage] Cf. "Prattle" (17 Jan. 1892: 6): "Imposture is of no sex and entitled to no immunity when it wears a petticoat. Women who are ambitious to get out of that garment to have 'an equal chance with men' are quick to get back into it when threatened with an equal switching for the same misdeeds." AB wrote often that women who committed murder deserved the same punishment accorded men for the same crime, in response to public outcry against such punishment.

Sycophant] The verses here first appeared in "Prattle" (*W,* 6 Jan. 1882: 6). "Gelasma" is a Greek word meaning "smile" (hence, here, a laughable person). William Frederick Havemeyer (1804–74) was a businessman who attained great wealth in sugar refinery, coal, railroads, and banking. He also served several terms as mayor of New York.

Symbol] AB wrote often about various "survivals" — actions committed primarily out of habit, long after the original reasons for them had been forgotten. Funereal urns are discussed in "Fetishism" (1902; *CW* 10.323).

Symbolic] The verses here first appeared under "Compunction." *Line 6:* The Greek word *splangchnidzomai* (to feel pity or compassion) derives from the word *splangchnon* (viscera), where the emotion was believed to originate.

Table d'Hôte] A full-course meal offering a limited number of choices and served at a fixed price in a hotel or restaurant. The verses here first appeared in "Prattle" (*W,* 16 Apr. 1881: 244). AB makes a pun similar to "table d'hotage" at "Dotage."

Tail] James Burnett, Lord Monboddo (1714–99) gained notoriety and ridicule when, in the first volume of his *On the Origin and Progress of Language* (1773–92), he reported the story of a Swedish sailor named Koeping that there were men with tails living in the Nicobar Islands.

Tariff] The verses here originally appeared in "Prattle" (*E*, 8 July 1888: 4). Edam (Adamn in Dx) Smith is a pun on Adam Smith (1723–90), the Scottish political economist and philosopher whose *Wealth of Nations* (1776) laid the foundations of classical free-market economic theory.

Technicality] This definition appears in Dx as a handwritten entry on a separate leaf, numbered page 321½. See also B21 in the Appendix.

Tedium] *Tedium* derives from the Latin verb *taedere*, to weary. The Te Deum is a hymn of praise to God, sung as part of a liturgy. See also "Congregation" about liturgical tedium.

Telephone] In 1876 Alexander Graham Bell appropriated the word *telephone* for his invention, the word having appeared as early as 1844 in English (1830 in French). See AB to Blanche Partington, 3 Aug. 1913 (ALS, Bancroft Library, University of California): "I am indeed pleased to know that you are comfortable and happy—albeit afflicted with that devil's device, a telephone. *I* have sworn off the telephone, ordered my name out of the telephone directory . . . and forbidden a telephone message to be sent to my apartment."

Telescope] AB actually desired to have a larger telescope than the "toy" telescope that he enjoyed using.

Tenacity] The verses here originally appeared at "Grip."

Theosophy] The beliefs of the Theosophical Society, a religious sect incorporating aspects of Buddhism and Brahmanism, founded in 1875 by Madame Helena Petrovna Hahn Blavatsky (1831–91). Cf. "Prattle" (*E*, 11 Oct. 1891: 6): "As a reincarnationary Mr. Judge gives satisfaction to the most exacting. His beliefs have all the reasonableness of religion and all the grace of science. He thinks that we live a great number of times on this earth, in as many several bodies, *because* one life is not long enough for our complete spiritual development; that is, we cannot become as wise and good as we choose to wish to be. To be absolutely wise and absolutely good—that is perfection; and Mr. Judge has so keen an eye as to have observed that in this world everything capable of improvement eventually becomes perfect, though I am myself inclined to except cats, which seem to me neither wiser nor better than they were last year." Cf. also the fable "The Ashes of Madame Blavatsky" (*CW* 6.198) and the article "Blathering Blavatskians" (*E*, 28 Nov. 1897), incorporated into "The Death Penalty" (*CW* 11.210).

Tights] Lillian Russell (1861–1922) was an American entertainer known for her roles in comic operas. The text of this definition originates in "Miss Russell's No Tights" (*E*, 22 Feb. 1889: 4). "A Question of Tights" (*E*, 26 June 1892: 6), unsigned but probably by AB, further treats the issue of Ms. Russell and modesty. Pauline Hall (1860–1919) was a popular American prima donna.

Tomb] A definition written to take the place of the omitted definition "Cairn" (q.v.) in order to fill out the back of *D*. See also "Worm's-meat" and the essay "The Late Lamented" (1889; *CW* 9.341).

Tope] Much of the text here originated in "The Nations That Drink Too Much" (*E*, 6 Nov. 1902: 16; *Am*, 13 Nov. 1902: 16). See also "Potable."

Tortoise] The verses here first appeared as "To My Pet Tortoise" (*Am*, 15 July 1901: 12; *E*, 18 July 1901: 14). AB did in fact have a pet tortoise. Ambat Delaso is also the author of the verses at "Danger."

Tree] AB also pretends to quote from Morryster's *Marvells of Science* in "The Man and the Snake." Judge Lynch is an imaginary judge whose decisions were thought to have instituted the practice of lynching. Some have believed that the term derived from Charles Lynch, a justice of the peace in Virginia who in 1780 illegally fined and imprisoned some Tories; but there is no evidence that Lynch instituted or encouraged the sort of extra-legal executions that later constituted the act of lynching.

Trial] Not in Dx. *In contumaciam* refers to contemptuous resistance to authority; see "In Contumaciam" (1887; *CW* 4.292).

Trichinosis] Moses Mendelssohn (1729–86) was a celebrated German Jewish philosopher and theologian. AB wrote of the perils of trichinosis in "Prattle" (*E*, 9 Dec. 1888: 4).

Trinity] AB noted that the Irish called the devil the fourth person of the Trinity (see "Introduction"). There are four other trinities in *D* — "Flesh" (secular), "Lodger" (newspaper), "Rector" (parochial), and "Usage" (literary) — as well as implied trinities at "Brahma" and "Me." Cf. "The Town Crier" (*NL*, 3 Feb. 1872; *SS* 93): "These are the things that we believe: A Trinity — three Gods united by a rope at the waist; that being about the only method of *Tria Juncta in Uno* that our humble intelligence can accurately comprehend. This triple Deity is flesh and blood, for spirit, if it is anything, is breath; and in this case the question, Whose breath? would be utterly answerable." AB makes frequent suggestion that the safe solution to deciding which of two (usually contradictory) notions to believe in is to believe in both.

Troglodyte] Troglodytes were a fabulous race of people who lived in caves; thus, any persons who are reclusive or brutish. See 1 Samuel 22:1–2.

Trust] AB frequently defended trusts or monopolies. See "In the Infancy of 'Trusts'" (*CW* 9.91), "Trustland: The Tale of a Traveler" (1899; later incorporated into "The Land Beyond the Blow" as "The Jumjum of Gokeetle-Guk"), and A26 in the Appendix.

Truth] See A32 in the Appendix.

Turkey] Cf. "The Annual Gobble" (*NL*, 20 Nov. 1869: 8): "Thanksgiving Day. Yah! there be those of us whose memories, though vexed with an oyster-rake would not yield matter for gratitude, and whose piety though strained through a sieve would leave no trace of an object upon which to lavish thanks."

Tzetze] The African tsetse fly, by transmitting either of two trypanosomes (*Trypanosma rhodesiense* or *T. gambiense*), infects human beings and animals with "sleeping sickness" (encephalitis lethargica), an often fatal disease characterized by fever, severe headache, and swelling of the lymph nodes and in later stages by extreme weakness, sleepiness, and deep coma. AB's mock taxonomical name *Mendax interminabilis* means "interminable liar." *Glossina morsitans* is an actual species of tsetse fly.

Ubiquity] See also "Omnipresent."

Ugliness] According to biographers, AB called his secretary Carrie Christiansen his "ugly duckling."

Ultimatum] AB lifted the text for this definition nearly verbatim from "The Passing Show" (*Am*, 29 Nov. 1903: 24; *E*, 13 Dec. 1903: 68). The definition here describes what AB liked to call an "antepenultimatum." In prosody, the last syllable (or foot) in a line of verse is the *ultima*; thus, the next to last is the *penult*, the third to last the *antepenult*. An antepenultimatum would be several steps away from delivering the ultimatum, just as *CW* 11, subtitled *Antepenultimata*, was meant to be a collection of essays that do not profess to be "the last word." See the fable "Diplomacy" (1905; *CW* 6.300):

"If you do not submit my claim to arbitration," wrote the President of Omohu to the President of Modugy, "I shall take immediate steps to collect it in my own way!"

"Sir," replied the President of Modugy, "you may go to the devil with your threat of war."

"My great and good friend," wrote the other, "you mistake the character of my communication. It is an antepenultimatum."

Unction] See also "Anoint."

Understanding] AB refers to the *Essay Concerning Human Understanding* (1690) by John Locke (1632–1704) and the *Critique of Pure Reason* (1781) by Immanuel Kant (1724–1804).

Universalist] An adherent of Unitarian Universalism, "a religious association derived from Christianity that considers God to be unipersonal, salvation to be granted to the entire human race, and reason and conscience to be the criteria for belief and practice" (*AHD*).

Urbanity] The verses here first appeared in "Prattle" (*W,* 12 Mar. 1881: 164). AB makes a similar joke in the following verses from "Prattle" (*W,* 9 Jan. 1886: 5):

"Two dozen Chinamen *went,*" said A,
　"When Kearney's great skull exploded."
Said B: "I'm surprised by what you say—
　I didn't know it was loaded."

Usage] *WR* was AB's "little blacklist of literary faults."

Uxoriousness] Excessive submission or devotion to one's wife.

Valor] Cf. "Prattle" (*E,* 17 Jan. 1892: 6):

Indianapolis has an Assistant Superintendent of Police in whom it ought to exult, as the ripest and rarest product of popular government. Required to protect a street-railway company in its right to run cars despite the dissent of the employees and other ruffians, he permitted his officers to be whacked awhile by the crowd, and then telegraphed to the headquarters of the company that if he persisted in moving the cars there would be bloodshed!

"Why have you halted?" roared a brigade commander who at the battle of Perryville had ordered a charge of his whole line. "Move forward at once, sir, do you hear?—at once!"

"General," replied Colonel J. P. Jackson, solemnly saluting, "I am persuaded that I cannot advance further without coming into contact with the enemy."

As a veteran of the Civil War who fought at the Battle of Chickamauga on 19–20 Sept. 1863, AB had little patience for the romantic notion of the display of valor on the "field of glory." See his short story "Chickamauga" (1889; *CW* 2.46) and memoir "A Little of Chickamauga" (1898; *CW* 1.270).

Vanity] The verses here originally appeared at "Cackle."

Vituperation] See also "Wit."

W] The word *epichoriambikon* refers to a type of Greek poetic meter. The quoted lines are from Poe's "To Helen" (1831), lines 9–10. Note that the sixth letter of the Hebrew alphabet, *vav* (or *waw*), has the sound of *w*.

Wall Street] AB also takes steel magnate Andrew Carnegie to task in the poem "An Impostor" (1888; *CW* 4.308) and the essay "Poverty, Crime and Vice" (*CW* 9.100); see also "Restitution." He is also the subject of the fable "The Farmer's Friend" (1890; *CW* 6.209) and several uncollected fables. The verses here originally appeared in "The Views of One" (*Am,* 3 Apr. 1905: 16).

War] The text of this definition, following the first sentence, is from "The Views of One" (*Am,* 28 Apr. 1905: 16; *E,* 4 May 1905: 16). The quoted lines are from Coleridge's "Kubla Khan" (c. 1797–98), lines 2, 29–30.

Washingtonian] AB himself lived on the banks of the Potomac during his residence in Washington, D.C. The idea behind this definition is that the citizens of the city of Washington (and the District of Columbia) could not elect offices to the city government until 1974, could not vote in presidential elections until 1961, and had no representatives in Congress until 1970. To AB, the term *self-government* was an oxymoron.

Weakness] Not in Dx.

Weather] The poem "An Offer of Marriage" (1894; *CW* 4.54) begins with virtually the same first line as the verses here. The verses parody lines from Tennyson's "Locksley Hall" (1842): "For I dipped into the future, far as human eye could see, / Saw the Vision of the world, and all the wonder that would be" (lines 119–20). "Halcyon Jones" was selected as the author of the poem because *halcyon* (q.v.) as an adjective refers to calm, clear skies.

Whangdepootenawah] Not in Dx. The word is AB's coinage. The Ojibwa were a large tribe who occupied the Upper Midwest and eastern and central Canada. The verses originally appeared in "Prattle" (*E*, 1 May 1892: 6). The meter imitates that of *The Song of Hiawatha* (1855) by Henry Wadsworth Longfellow (1807–82), itself modeled on the Finnish national epic poem, *Kalevala*, used also in AB's untitled verses starting "Should you ask me whence this fable" in "Prattle" (*W*, 7 Mar. 1885: 5). William Jennings Bryan (1860–1925) was a member of the U.S. House of Representatives. He lost the presidential elections in 1896 and 1900 to Willam McKinley and in 1908 to William H. Taft. From 1913 to 1915 he was Woodrow Wilson's secretary of state. An advocate of religious fundamentalism, he appeared for the prosecution in the 1925 Scopes trial.

Wheat] Cf. "Prattle" (*E*, 17 June 1894: 6): "A thoughtless contemporary manifests surprise that statistics of wheat consumption show that the French eat more wheat *per capita* than any other people. There is nothing remarkable in that: they are the only people who know how to make the stuff good to eat."

White] See "Optimist" and also AB to George Sterling (2 May 1909; ALS, NYPL): "I have long despaired of convincing poets and artists of anything, even that white is not black."

Widow] Jesus told several parables in which widows were treated with more compassion than the rich and powerful; see Luke 18:1–9, 21:1–4; Mark 17:40–43; Matthew 23: 14. Jesus also brought a widow's dead son back to life (Luke 7:12–14). Widows are a frequent subject of AB's fables.

Wine] The name "Women's Christian Union" should actually be "Woman's Christian Temperance Union." See "Nectar."

Wit] See the essay "Wit and Humor" (*CW* 10.98), "Epigrams" ("wit is a serious matter. To laugh at it is to confess that you do not understand"; *CW* 8.346), and AB's "Preface" to *D*.

Woman] AB refers to Susan B. Anthony (1820–1906), American feminist and suffragist. This definition has an air of being composed in a far future time, like AB's "future histories." AB's mock taxonomy means "fighting cat."

Worms'-meat] AB relentlessly mocked those who erected elaborate mausoleums (see "Mausoleum") for themselves. Cf. Luke 21:33: "Heaven and earth shall pass away; but my words shall not pass away." By "Grantarium" AB means Grant's Tomb in New York, dedicated in 1897.

Wrath] In Homer's *Iliad*, Chryses was a priest of Apollo who offered a ransom for the return of his captured daughter, Chryseis, which Agamemnon, her captor, rejected;

angered, Chryses appealed to Apollo, who sent a plague upon the Greeks (*Iliad* 1.11f.). See 1 Chronicles 27:24: "Joab the son of Zeruiah began to number, but he finished not, because there fell wrath for it against Israel; neither was the number put in the account of the chronicles of king David." See "Behavior" re AB's mock translation of the Dies Irae.

X] The cross on which Jesus was traditionally said to be crucified more nearly resembled the letter T than the letter X.

Yankee] Cf. "The Matter of Manner" (1906; *CW* 10.63): "As it is, they are in much the same state of darkness as that of the Southern young woman before she went North and learned, to her astonishment, that the term 'damned Yankee' was two words—she had never heard either without the other."

Yesterday] A collection of AB's journalism was published under the title *The Shadow on the Dial* (1909). Compare the following untitled verses from "Prattle" (*W*, 9 Dec. 1882: 773):

> "What men most wish in youth," the sage
> Explains, "they will possess in age."
> What! Is it so? Then I indeed am blest,
>   Standing high-pinnacled upon the peak
>   Of middle life and looking down the bleak
> And unfamiliar foreslope to the West,
> Where solemn shadows all the land invest,
>   And bodiless voices babble in the reek
>   Of moving mists, and vagrant meteors freak
> The darkness in the Valley of Unrest.
> In youth I cherished this supreme desire—
>   To stay the shadow on the dial plate
> At manhood's noonmark, and be all exempt
> From vile decay. So now my vital fire
>   Shall burn undimmed: in man's mature estate
> I'll live—or die (of age) in the attempt.

Yoke] See also "Conjugal."

Youth] Archimedes (287?–212 BCE), the Greek mathematician, claimed that with a big enough fulcrum he could move the world. In Greek mythology, Cassandra, daughter of Priam of Troy, had the gift of prophecy but was fated never to be believed. Seven Greek cities were reputed to have boasted of being the birthplace of Homer, but they did so only after his death.

Zany] Not in Dx.

Zanzibari] Not in Dx. Like some African tribeswomen, the Sultana was steatopygous.

Zeal] See note to "Intoxication." In Dx the definition reads: "A fatiguing activity rewarded by a long rest on the stool of repentance."

Zigzag] The *white man's burden* (from Rudyard Kipling's poem "The White Man's Burden" [1899]) was his supposed responsibility to govern and impart his culture to non-white peoples.

Zoölogy] The reference is to *L'Histoire générale des animaux* (1788–1804), begun by the French naturalist Georges-Louis Leclerc, comte de Buffon (1707–88), and completed by E. de Lacépède, and *An History of the Earth and Animated Nature* (1774) by English poet, essayist, and playwright Oliver Goldsmith (1730?–74), an eight-volume work derived from Buffon, Linnaeus, and other sources. Goldsmith's *History* is mentioned in

"A Wingless Insect" (*FD* 78). See also "Fly," where AB also declares it to be the king of beasts. AB, writing as Little Johnny, named numerous animals the "King of Beasts," a title traditionally reserved only for the African lion. He mentions "that pius natcherlist, Ollifer Gold Smith" in "In the Beginning" (*Am,* 29 Oct. 1905: 22; *E,* 10 Dec. 1905: 48).

SUPPLEMENTARY DEFINITIONS

A5.] AB clipped only lines 1–6 of twelve lines of verse.

A6.] AB clipped only lines 1–8 of twelve lines of verse. Fred Bell was another of the many charlatans AB rebuked in his columns, as in "Prattle" (*E,* 5 May 1895: 6).

A8. Duel] A young man named Prescott Belknap had written a letter to *Ar* (published in the issue for 13 Oct. 1890) attacking AB and accusing him of cowardice because he failed to follow up on a whimsical offer to fight a duel with anyone conscientiously opposed to duelling. Later Belknap (apparently a minor) threatened to horsewhip AB. See "Prattle" (*E,* 19 Oct., 2 Nov., and 23 Nov. 1890; all appearances on p. 6).

A9. Eloquence] The column from which this clipping was taken also contained a mock epitaph on Gen. W. H. L. Barnes, a prominent attorney and Republican politician in San Francisco (*CW* 5.378). See also "W. H. L. Barnes" (1888; *CW* 5.196).

A10. Fallible] Maj. Gen. Elwell Stephen Otis (1838–1909) went to the Philippines in July 1898 as commander of the Eighth Army Corps. His task was to replace the ousted Spanish government with an American government, a task he accomplished successfully, although it involved the suppression of the Filipino resistance movement led by Emilio Aguinaldo. On 5 May 1900, Otis was replaced by Gen. Arthur MacArthur (1845–1912), who remained in the Philippines until 1901.

A11. Heresy] John Foxe (1516–87) was the author of *Acts and Monuments of Matters Happening in the Church* (1554; rev. 1563), commonly known as "Foxe's Book of Martyrs." It is a history of Christian persecution, focusing on the martyrdom of Protestants at the hands of Queen Mary.

A12. History] Sedan is a small town in northeastern France where, on 1 Sept. 1870, the French army suffered a disastrous defeat in the Franco-Prussian War. French novelist Emile Zola (1840–1902) wrote of it in his novel *La Débâcle* (serialized in *La Vie Populaire,* 21 Feb.–21 July 1892; in book form in 1892).

A13. Horn] The volume by Lactantius is his *Opera* (Rome: Conrad Sweyheim and Arnold Pannartz, 1465). The other item is possibly the *Liber Epistolarum* of Aurelius Augustinus (1493), but its place of publication is unknown.

A14. Leader] For John Sharp Williams, see note to "Lore."

A18. Pension] See "Prattle" (*E,* 18 Mar. 1888: 4): "'General' Salomon is as candid a robber as Senator Ingalls: he believes that 'every man who fought for the Union should receive a pension.'" Ironically, Jefferson Davis (1808–89), the president of the Confederacy, died the year after AB wrote the verses mocking him. AB speculated satirically about Davis's last words in "Prattle" (*E,* 8 Dec. 1889: 6). John James Ingalls (1883–1900) was a United States senator from Kansas (1873–91) and a vigorous supporter of the Grand Army of the Republic.

A19. Polygamy] Brigham Young (1801–77) took over leadership of the Mormons after their founder, Joseph Smith, was murdered in 1844. He had twenty-seven wives.

A20. Press] Frederick MacCrellish was a writer for the *Alta California.* See "The Town-Crier" (*NL,* 13 Mar. 1869: 9): "We find the following lexicographical wisdom in an unpublished edition of Webster: 'MacCrellish, *a.* Like a mackerel; fishy.'"

A22. Rake] The lines of verse come from Pope's *Moral Essays* (1733–34), Epistle 2, lines

215–16. The quotation from the letter is in fact from a letter jointly written by Pope and John Gay to John Caryll (c. Apr. 1715) but included in earlier editions of Pope's letters as a letter to William Congreve (7 Apr. 1715). AB probably saw it in *The Works of Alexander Pope,* ed. Whitwell Elwin (London: John Murray, 1871), 6.415. The section quoted was indeed written by Pope, not Gay.

A24. Stultus] Fool. AB parodies the well-known sequence Stabat Mater, which opens with the lines "Stabat mater dolorosa / iuxta Crucem lacrimosa, / dum pendebat Filius." (At the Cross her station keeping, / stood the mournful Mother, weeping, / close to Jesus at the last.) A rough translation of AB's lines would be: "The stupid, sad person stands, / Exalted, weeping, / Kicked, crying like a panther, / By the little man jesting, / And wordy, / Says: 'Condemned boy!'"

A27.] AB clipped only lines 5–8 of eight lines of verse.

A28.] AB clipped only lines 1–4 of ten lines of verse.

A34.] Booker T. Washington (1856–1915) was a noted African-American leader and educator. He was in Boston for much of Nov. and Dec. 1904; from there he visited the White House on 19 Nov. and 21 Dec. after the election of Theodore Roosevelt, whom he supported. He had been invited to dine at the White House by Roosevelt on 16 Oct. 1901—the first African-American to do so.

OTHER DEFINITIONS

B7.] Horace Greeley (1811–72), journalist who founded and edited the *New-York Tribune* from 1841 to his death. An influential voice in Republican politics, Greeley had unsuccessfully sought to secure the nomination of Salmon P. Chase over Ulysses S. Grant in 1868. In 1872, his opposition to Grant still intense, he himself accepted the presidential nomination of the Liberal Republicans and Democrats but lost badly to Grant and died a few weeks after the election.

B14.] For "Marriage," see "Prattle" (*E,* 2 Mar. 1890: 6): "They were telling (under the breath) of a clever thing which Mrs. X—— said the other day. 'My dear,' said an old schoolgirl friend whom she had not met since her marriage, 'how could you venture to marry Mr. X——, with that awful scandal hanging over you?' 'The most natural thing in the world,' was the piscid reply. 'People were beginning to talk, and I married X—— at once to keep him from hearing about it.'"

B19.] Walter Crane (1845–1915), British artist and illustrator.

B23.] Henry George (1839–97), journalist, lecturer, and author of the economic treatise *Progress and Poverty* (1879), which advocated the "single tax."

B28.] AB tangled frequently with Arthur McEwen, another editorial writer for *E,* particularly in May and June 1895, when McEwen claimed that he had given Bierce a "caning"; see "Bierce and McEwen" (*E,* 11 Nov. 1895: 6).

B30.] James G. Maguire (1853–1920) was a judge in the California supreme court before becoming a U.S. representative from California (1893–99).

WORD	DATE ———————————			C/DX	D
A	NL	11 De 75	—	—	—	—
Abacot	NL	11 De 75	—	—	—	—
Abactor	NL	11 De 75	—	—	—	—
Abacus	NL	11 De 75	—	—	—	—
Abada	NL	11 De 75	—	—	—	—
Abaddon	NL	11 De 75	—	—	—	—
Abaddon	Am	26 Jn 04	E	10 Jy 04	—	—
Abandon	NL	11 De 75	—	—	—	—
Abandon	Am	26 Jn 04	E	10 Jy 04	—	—
Abasement	Am	26 Jn 04	E	10 Jy 04	*	*
Abatis	NL	11 De 75	—	—	—	—
Abatis	Am	26 Jn 04	E	10 Jy 04	*	*
Abattoir	NL	11 De 75	—	—	—	—
Abat-voix	NL	11 De 75	—	—	—	—
Abba	NL	11 De 75	—	—	—	—
Abbess	NL	11 De 75	—	—	—	—
Abderian	NL	11 De 75	—	—	—	—
Abdest	NL	11 De 75	—	—	—	—
Abdication	NL	11 De 75	—	—	—	—
Abdication	Am	26 Jn 04	E	10 Jy 04	*	*
Abdomen	NL	11 De 75	—	—	—	—
Abdomen	Am	26 Jn 04	E	10 Jy 04	*	*
Abduction	NL	11 De 75	—	—	—	—
Abduction	Am	26 Jn 04	E	10 Jy 04	—	—
Abeliens	NL	11 De 75	—	—	—	—
Aberration	NL	11 De 75	—	—	—	—
Abet	NL	11 De 75	—	—	—	—
Abhorrence	NL	11 De 75	—	—	—	—
Abide	NL	11 De 75	—	—	—	—
Ability	NL	11 De 75	—	—	—	—
Ability	Am	26 Jn 04	E	10 Jy 04	*	*
Abject	NL	11 De 75	—	—	—	—
Abjectly	NL	11 De 75	—	—	—	—
Abjure	NL	11 De 75	—	—	—	—
Ablative	NL	11 De 75	—	—	—	—
Abnegation	NL	11 De 75	—	—	—	—
Abnormal	Am	26 Jn 04	E	10 Jy 04	*	*

WORD	DATE			C/DX	D
Abominable	NL	11 De 75	—	—	—	—
Aborigines	NL	11 De 75	—	—	—	—
Aborigines	Am	26 Jn 04	E	10 Jy 04	*	*
Abracadabra	Am	26 Jn 04	E	10 Jy 04	*	*
Abridge	Am	9 Jy 04	E	17 Jy 04	*	*
Abridgement	NL	11 De 75	—	—	—	—
Abroad	NL	11 De 75	—	—	—	—
Abrupt	Am	9 Jy 04	E	17 Jy 04	*	*
Abruption	NL	11 De 75	—	—	—	—
Abscond	NL	11 De 75	—	—	—	—
Abscond	Am	9 Jy 04	E	17 Jy 04	*	*
Absence	NL	11 De 75	—	—	—	—
Absent	NL	11 De 75	—	—	—	—
Absent	Am	9 Jy 04	E	17 Jy 04	*	*
Absentee	Am	9 Jy 04	E	17 Jy 04	*	*
Absolute	NL	11 De 75	—	—	—	—
Absolute	Am	9 Jy 04	E	17 Jy 04	*	*
Abstainer	Am	9 Jy 04	E	17 Jy 04	*	*
Abstemious	NL	11 De 75	—	—	—	—
Abstruseness	NL	11 De 75	—	—	—	—
Absurdity	NL	11 De 75	—	—	—	—
Absurdity	Am	9 Jy 04	E	17 Jy 04	*	*
Abundance	NL	11 De 75	—	—	—	—
Abuse	NL	11 De 75	—	—	—	—
Abuse	Am	9 Jy 04	E	17 Jy 04	—	—
Academe	Am	9 Jy 04	E	17 Jy 04	*	*
Academy	NL	11 De 75	—	—	—	—
Academy	Am	9 Jy 04	E	17 Jy 04	*	*
Accept	NL	11 De 75	—	—	—	—
Accident	Am	9 Jy 04	E	17 Jy 04	*	*
Acclimated	NL	11 De 75	—	—	—	—
Accommodate	NL	11 De 75	—	—	—	—
Accomplice	NL	11 De 75	—	—	—	—
Accomplice	Am	9 Jy 04	E	17 Jy 04	*	*
Accord	Am	9 Jy 04	E	17 Jy 04	*	*
Accordion	Am	9 Jy 04	E	17 Jy 04	*	*
Accoucheur	NL	11 De 75	—	—	—	—
Accountability	Am	9 Jy 04	E	17 Jy 04	*	*
Accountable	Am	9 Jy 04	E	17 Jy 04	—	—
Accuracy	W	5 Ma 81	—	—	—	—
Accuse	Am	9 Jy 04	E	17 Jy 04	*	*
Accuser	W	5 Ma 81	—	—	—	—
Ace	W	5 Ma 81	—	—	—	—
Aceldama	W	5 Ma 81	—	—	—	—
Acephalous	W	5 Ma 81	—	—	*	*
Acerbity	W	5 Ma 81	—	—	—	—
Ache	W	5 Ma 81	—	—	—	—
Achievement	W	5 Ma 81	—	—	*	*
Acknowledge	W	5 Ma 81	—	—	*	*
Acorn	W	5 Ma 81	—	—	—	—
Acquaintance	W	5 Ma 81	—	—	*	*
Acquit	W	5 Ma 81	—	—	—	—

WORD	DATE			C/DX	D
Acrobat	W	5 Ma 81	—	—	—	—
Acrostic	W	5 Ma 81	—	—	—	—
Actor	W	5 Ma 81	—	—	—	—
Actress	W	5 Ma 81	—	—	—	—
Actually	W	5 Ma 81	—	—	*	*
Adage	W	5 Ma 81	—	—	—	—
Adage	—	—	—	—	*	*
Adamant	W	5 Ma 81	—	—	*	*
Adam's Apple	W	5 Ma 81	—	—	—	—
Adder	W	5 Ma 81	—	—	*	*
Address	W	5 Ma 81	—	—	—	—
Adherent	W	5 Ma 81	—	—	*	*
Adipose	W	5 Ma 81	—	—	—	—
Adjutant	W	12 Ma 81	—	—	—	—
Administration	W	12 Ma 81	—	—	*	*
Admirability	W	12 Ma 81	—	—	*	—
Admiral	W	12 Ma 81	—	—	*	*
Admiration	W	12 Ma 81	—	—	*	*
Admonition	W	12 Ma 81	—	—	*	*
Adolescent	W	12 Ma 81	—	—	—	—
Adonis	W	12 Ma 81	—	—	—	—
Adore	W	12 Ma 81	—	—	*	*
Advice	W	12 Ma 81	—	—	*	*
Æsthetics	W	12 Ma 81	—	—	—	—
Affection	W	12 Ma 81	—	—	—	—
Affectionate	W	12 Ma 81	—	—	—	—
Affianced	W	12 Ma 81	—	—	*	*
Affirm	W	12 Ma 81	—	—	—	—
Affliction	W	12 Ma 81	—	—	*	*
Afraid	W	12 Ma 81	—	—	—	—
African	W	12 Ma 81	—	—	*	*
Age	W	12 Ma 81	—	—	*	*
Agitator	W	12 Ma 81	—	—	*	*
Agony	W	12 Ma 81	—	—	—	—
Agrarian	W	12 Ma 81	—	—	—	—
Aim	W	12 Ma 81	—	—	*	*
Air	W	19 Ma 81	—	—	*	*
Album	W	19 Ma 81	—	—	—	—
Alcohol	W	19 Ma 81	—	—	—	—
Alderman	W	19 Ma 81	—	—	*	*
Alien	W	19 Ma 81	—	—	*	*
All	W	19 Ma 81	—	—	—	—
Allah	W	19 Ma 81	—	—	*	*
Allegiance	W	19 Ma 81	—	—	*	*
Allegory	W	19 Ma 81	—	—	—	—
Alliance	W	19 Ma 81	—	—	*	*
Alligator	W	19 Ma 81	—	—	*	*
Alone	W	19 Ma 81	—	—	*	*
Altar	W	9 Ap 81	—	—	*	*
Amateur	W	19 Ma 81	—	—	—	—
Amatory	W	19 Ma 81	—	—	—	—
Amazon	W	19 Ma 81	—	—	—	—

WORD	DATE			C/DX	D
Ambidextrous	W	19 Ma 81	— —	*	*
Ambition	W	19 Ma 81	— —	*	*
Ambrosia	W	19 Ma 81	— —	—	—
A Mensa et Thoro	W	19 Ma 81	— —	—	—
Amnesty	W	19 Ma 81	— —	*	*
Animal	W	26 Ma 81	— —	—	—
Animalism	W	26 Ma 81	— —	—	—
Anoint	W	26 Ma 81	— —	*	*
Antagonist	W	26 Ma 81	— —	—	—
Ante-chamber	W	26 Ma 81	— —	—	—
Antipathy	W	26 Ma 81	— —	*	*
Antiquity	W	26 Ma 81	— —	—	—
Apathetic	W	26 Ma 81	— —	—	—
Aphorism	W	26 Ma 81	— —	*	*
Apologize	W	26 Ma 81	— —	*	*
Apostate	W	26 Ma 81	— —	*	*
Apothecary	W	26 Ma 81	— —	*	*
Appeal	W	26 Ma 81	— —	*	*
Appetite	W	26 Ma 81	— —	*	*
Applause	W	26 Ma 81	— —	*	*
Apple	W	26 Ma 81	— —	—	—
April Fool	W	26 Ma 81	— —	*	*
Apron	W	26 Ma 81	— —	—	—
Arab	W	26 Ma 81	— —	—	—
Arbitration	W	26 Ma 81	— —	—	—
Arbitration	—	—	— —	*	—
Archbishop	W	2 Ap 81	— —	*	*
Architect	W	2 Ap 81	— —	*	*
Ardor	W	2 Ap 81	— —	*	*
Arena	W	2 Ap 81	— —	*	*
Argonaut	W	2 Ap 81	— —	—	—
Argue	W	2 Ap 81	— —	—	—
Aristocracy	W	2 Ap 81	— —	*	*
Armor	W	2 Ap 81	— —	*	*
Army	W	2 Ap 81	— —	—	—
Arrayed	W	2 Ap 81	— —	*	*
Arrears	W	2 Ap 81	— —	—	—
Arrest	—	—	— —	*	*
Arrested	W	2 Ap 81	— —	—	—
Arsenic	W	2 Ap 81	— —	*	*
Art	W	2 Ap 81	— —	*	*
Artlessness	W	2 Ap 81	— —	*	*
Asbestos	W	9 Ap 81	— —	—	—
Asperse	W	9 Ap 81	— —	*	*
Ass	W	9 Ap 81	— —	*	*
Astrology	W	9 Ap 81	— —	—	—
Attorney	W	9 Ap 81	— —	—	—
Attraction	W	9 Ap 81	— —	—	—
Auctioneer	W	9 Ap 81	— —	*	*
Auricle	W	16 Ap 81	— —	—	—
Austere	W	9 Ap 81	— —	—	—
Australia	W	16 Ap 81	— —	*	*

WORD	DATE			C/DX	D
Authentic	W	9 Ap 81	—	—	—	—
Autocrat	W	16 Ap 81	—	—	—	—
Avaunt	W	16 Ap 81	—	—	—	—
Avenge	W	16 Ap 81	—	—	—	—
Avernus	W	16 Ap 81	—	—	*	*
Aversion [Satiety]	W	16 Ap 81	—	—	*	—
Awkward	W	16 Ap 81	—	—	—	—
Baal	W	16 Ap 81	—	—	*	*
Babe	W	16 Ap 81	—	—	*	*
Bacchus	W	23 Ap 81	—	—	*	*
Bachelor	W	23 Ap 81	—	—	—	—
Back	W	23 Ap 81	—	—	*	*
Backbite	W	23 Ap 81	—	—	*	*
Back-slide	W	23 Ap 81	—	—	—	—
Bacon	W	23 Ap 81	—	—	—	—
Bait	W	23 Ap 81	—	—	*	*
Bald	W	23 Ap 81	—	—	—	—
Balloon	W	23 Ap 81	—	—	—	—
Ballot	W	23 Ap 81	—	—	—	—
Bandit	W	23 Ap 81	—	—	—	—
Bang	W	23 Ap 81	—	—	—	—
Bang	W	23 Ap 81	—	—	—	—
Baptism	W	23 Ap 81	—	—	*	*
Barber	W	23 Ap 81	—	—	—	—
Bard	W	30 Ap 81	—	—	—	—
Bark	W	30 Ap 81	—	—	—	—
Barometer	W	30 Ap 81	—	—	*	*
Barrack	W	30 Ap 81	—	—	*	*
Barrister	W	30 Ap 81	—	—	—	—
Base	W	30 Ap 81	—	—	—	—
Basilisk	W	30 Ap 81	—	—	*	*
Bassinet	W	30 Ap 81	—	—	—	—
Bassoon	W	30 Ap 81	—	—	—	—
Basso-relievo	W	30 Ap 81	—	—	—	—
Bastinado	W	30 Ap 81	—	—	*	*
Bath	W	30 Ap 81	—	—	*	*
Battle	W	30 Ap 81	—	—	*	*
Bayonet	W	30 Ap 81	—	—	—	—
Bear	W	30 Ap 81	—	—	—	—
Beard	W	30 Ap 81	—	—	*	*
Beauty	W	30 Ap 81	—	—	*	*
Bed	W	30 Ap 81	—	—	—	—
Bedlam	W	30 Ap 81	—	—	—	—
Bed-quilt	W	30 Ap 81	—	—	—	—
Befriend	W	30 Ap 81	—	—	*	*
Beg	W	30 Ap 81	—	—	*	*
Beggar	W	30 Ap 81	—	—	—	—
Beggar	—	—	—	—	*	*
Beggary	W	7 My 81	—	—	—	—
Behavior	W	7 My 81	—	—	*	*
Belladonna	W	7 My 81	—	—	*	*
Benedictines	W	7 My 81	—	—	*	*

WORD	DATE			C/DX	D
Benefactor	W	7 My 81	—	—	*	*
Benevolence	W	7 My 81	—	—	—	—
Bequeath	W	7 My 81	—	—	—	—
Berenice's Hair	W	7 My 81	—	—	*	*
Betray	W	7 My 81	—	—	—	—
Betrothed	W	7 My 81	—	—	—	—
Biddy	W	7 My 81	—	—	—	—
Bigamy	W	7 My 81	—	—	*	*
Bigot	W	7 My 81	—	—	*	*
Billet-doux	W	7 My 81	—	—	—	—
Billingsgate	W	7 My 81	—	—	*	*
Biography	W	7 My 81	—	—	—	—
Birth	W	7 My 81	—	—	*	*
Blackguard	W	14 My 81	—	—	*	*
Blank-verse	W	14 My 81	—	—	*	*
Bloodthirsty	W	14 My 81	—	—	—	—
Blubber	W	14 My 81	—	—	—	—
Blue-stocking	W	14 My 81	—	—	—	—
Blushing	W	14 My 81	—	—	—	—
Body-snatcher	W	14 My 81	—	—	*	*
Bologna-sausage	W	14 My 81	—	—	—	—
Bomb	W	14 My 81	—	—	—	—
Bondsman	W	14 My 81	—	—	*	*
Book-learning	W	14 My 81	—	—	—	—
Bore	W	14 My 81	—	—	*	*
Botany	W	14 My 81	—	—	*	*
Bottle	W	21 My 81	—	—	—	—
Bottle-nosed	W	21 My 81	—	—	*	*
Boundary	W	21 My 81	—	—	*	*
Bounty	W	21 My 81	—	—	*	*
Bow-wow	W	21 My 81	—	—	—	—
Brahma	W	21 My 81	—	—	*	*
Brain	W	21 My 81	—	—	*	*
Brain	W	21 My 81	—	—	—	—
Brandy	W	21 My 81	—	—	*	*
Bribe	W	21 My 81	—	—	—	—
Bride	W	21 My 81	—	—	*	*
Brute	W	21 My 81	—	—	*	*
Buddhism	W	21 My 81	—	—	—	—
Caaba	W	4 Jn 81	—	—	*	*
Cab	W	4 Jn 81	—	—	—	—
Cabbage	W	4 Jn 81	—	—	*	*
Cabinet	W	4 Jn 81	—	—	—	—
Cackle [Vanity]	W	4 Jn 81	—	—	*	
Cadet	W	4 Jn 81	—	—	—	—
Cairn	W	4 Jn 81	—	—	—	—
Calamity	W	4 Jn 81	—	—	*	*
Calliope	W	4 Jn 81	—	—	—	—
Callous	W	4 Jn 81	—	—	*	*
Calumnus	W	4 Jn 81	—	—	*	*
Calvary	W	4 Jn 81	—	—	—	—
Camel	W	11 Jn 81	—	—	*	*

WORD	DATE			C/DX	D
Candidate	W	11 Jn 81	—	—	—	—
Candy	W	11 Jn 81	—	—	—	—
Cane	W	11 Jn 81	—	—	—	—
Cannibal	W	11 Jn 81	—	—	*	*
Cannon	W	11 Jn 81	—	—	*	*
Canonicals	W	11 Jn 81	—	—	*	*
Canonize	W	11 Jn 81	—	—	—	—
Capital	W	11 Jn 81	—	—	*	*
Carmelite	W	11 Jn 81	—	—	*	*
Carnivorous	W	18 Jn 81	—	—	*	*
Carouse	W	18 Jn 81	—	—	—	—
Cartesian	W	18 Jn 81	—	—	*	*
Cat	W	18 Jn 81	—	—	*	*
Catechism	W	18 Jn 81	—	—	—	—
Caterpillar	W	18 Jn 81	—	—	—	—
Caviler	W	18 Jn 81	—	—	*	*
Cemetery	W	18 Jn 81	—	—	*	*
Cenotaph	W	18 Jn 81	—	—	—	—
Censor	W	18 Jn 81	—	—	—	—
Centaur	W	1 Jy 81	—	—	*	*
Cerberus	W	18 Jn 81	—	—	*	*
Charity	W	18 Jn 81	—	—	—	—
Chemise	W	18 Jn 81	—	—	—	—
Child	W	1 Jy 81	—	—	— .	—
Childhood	W	1 Jy 81	—	—	*	*
Chimpanzee	W	1 Jy 81	—	—	—	—
Chinaman	W	1 Jy 81	—	—	—	—
Chiromancer	W	1 Jy 81	—	—	—	—
Chivalry	W	1 Jy 81	—	—	—	—
Chop	W	1 Jy 81	—	—	—	—
Chorus	W	1 Jy 81	—	—	—	—
Christen	W	1 Jy 81	—	—	—	—
Christian	—	—	—	—	*	*
Christmas	W	1 Jy 81	—	—	—	—
Church	W	1 Jy 81	—	—	—	—
Circumlocution	W	15 Jy 81	—	—	—	—
Circus	W	1 Jy 81	—	—	*	*
Clairvoyant	W	15 Jy 81	—	—	*	*
Clarionet	W	15 Jy 81	—	—	*	*
Clergyman	W	1 Jy 81	—	—	*	*
Client	W	15 Jy 81	—	—	—	—
Clinic	W	15 Jy 81	—	—	—	—
Clio	W	15 Jy 81	—	—	*	*
Clock	W	15 Jy 81	—	—	*	*
Close-communion	W	15 Jy 81	—	—	—	—
Close-corporation	W	15 Jy 81	—	—	—	—
Close-fisted	W	15 Jy 81	—	—	*	*
Clove	W	15 Jy 81	—	—	—	—
Club	W	15 Jy 81	—	—	—	—
Cœnobite	W	5 Au 81	—	—	*	*
Colonel	W	5 Au 81	—	—	—	—
Comedy	W	15 Jy 81	—	—	—	—

WORD	DATE			C/DX	D
Comet	W	15 Jy 81	— —	—	—
Comfort	W	5 Au 81	— —	*	*
Commendation	W	5 Au 81	— —	*	*
Commerce	W	5 Au 81	— —	*	*
Commit	W	5 Au 81	— —	—	—
Common-law	W	5 Au 81	— —	—	—
Commonwealth	—	—	— —	*	*
Competitor	W	5 Au 81	— —	—	—
Compliment	W	5 Au 81	— —	—	—
Compromise	W	12 Au 81	— —	*	*
Compulsion	W	12 Au 81	— —	*	*
Compunction [Symbolic]	W	5 Au 81	— —	—	—
Concatenate	W	5 Au 81	— —	—	—
Conceit	W	12 Au 81	— —	—	—
Concert	W	12 Au 81	— —	—	—
Concession	W	12 Au 81	— —	—	—
Conciliation	W	12 Au 81	— —	—	—
Conclusive	W	12 Au 81	— —	—	—
Condole	W	12 Au 81	— —	*	*
Condone	W	12 Au 81	— —	—	—
Conductor	W	12 Au 81	— —	—	—
Confession	W	12 Au 81	— —	—	—
Confidant	W	12 Au 81	— —	*	*
Congratulation	W	12 Au 81	— —	*	*
Congregation	W	12 Au 81	— —	—	—
Congress	W	12 Au 81	— —	*	*
Conjugal	W	12 Au 81	— —	—	—
Connoisseur	W	12 Au 81	— —	*	*
Conscience	W	12 Au 81	— —	—	—
Conservative	W	12 Au 81	— —	*	*
Consolation	W	26 Au 81	— —	*	*
Consul	W	26 Au 81	— —	*	*
Consult	W	26 Au 81	— —	*	*
Contempt	W	26 Au 81	— —	*	*
Contributor	W	26 Au 81	— —	—	—
Controversy	W	26 Au 81	— —	*	*
Convent	W	26 Au 81	— —	*	*
Coquette	W	26 Au 81	— —	—	—
Cordiality	W	26 Au 81	— —	—	—
Corkscrew	W	26 Au 81	— —	—	—
Conversation	W	26 Au 81	— —	*	*
Cookery	W	26 Au 81	— —	—	—
Corned	W	26 Au 81	— —	—	—
Coronation	W	26 Au 81	— —	*	*
Coroner	W	7 Oc 81	— —	—	—
Corporal	W	7 Oc 81	— —	*	*
Corporation	W	7 Oc 81	— —	*	*
Corpse	W	7 Oc 81	— —	—	—
Corrupt	W	7 Oc 81	— —	—	—
Corsair	W	7 Oc 81	— —	*	*
Counterfeit	W	7 Oc 81	— —	—	—

WORD	DATE			C/DX	D
Country	W	7 Oc 81	—	—	—	—
Couple	W	7 Oc 81	—	—	—	—
Court Fool [Plaintiff]	W	7 Oc 81	—	—	*	*
Covet	W	7 Oc 81	—	—	—	—
Cow	W	21 Oc 81	—	—	—	—
Coward	W	21 Oc 81	—	—	*	*
Cowlick	W	21 Oc 81	—	—	—	—
Coyness	W	21 Oc 81	—	—	—	—
Cradle	W	21 Oc 81	—	—	—	—
Craft	W	21 Oc 81	—	—	*	*
Crapulent	W	21 Oc 81	—	—	—	—
Crayfish	W	21 Oc 81	—	—	*	*
Creditor	W	21 Oc 81	—	—	*	*
Cremation	W	21 Oc 81	—	—	—	—
Cremona	W	21 Oc 81	—	—	*	*
Crescent	W	21 Oc 81	—	—	—	—
Crest	W	21 Oc 81	—	—	—	—
Cribbage	W	28 Oc 81	—	—	—	—
Critic	W	28 Oc 81	—	—	*	*
Cross	—	—	—	—	*	*
Cudgel	W	28 Oc 81	—	—	—	—
Cui Bono?	W	28 Oc 81	—	—	*	*
Culprit	W	28 Oc 81	—	—	—	—
Cunning	W	28 Oc 81	—	—	*	*
Cupid	W	28 Oc 81	—	—	*	*
Cur	W	28 Oc 81	—	—	—	—
Curiosity	W	28 Oc 81	—	—	*	*
Curse	W	11 No 81	—	—	*	*
Custard	W	11 No 81	—	—	—	—
Cynic	W	28 Oc 81	—	—	*	*
Dad	W	11 No 81	—	—	—	—
Dado	W	11 No 81	—	—	—	—
Damn	W	11 No 81	—	—	*	*
Dance	W	11 No 81	—	—	*	*
Dandle	W	11 No 81	—	—	—	—
Dandy	W	11 No 81	—	—	—	—
Danger	W	11 No 81	—	—	*	*
Daring	W	11 No 81	—	—	*	*
Darling	W	11 No 81	—	—	—	—
Datary	W	11 No 81	—	—	*	*
Dawn	W	2 De 81	—	—	*	*
Day	W	11 No 81	—	—	*	*
Dead	W	2 De 81	—	—	*	*
Debauchee	W	2 De 81	—	—	*	*
Debt	W	2 De 81	—	—	*	*
Decalogue	W	2 De 81	—	—	*	*
Decanter	W	2 De 81	—	—	—	—
Decide	W	2 De 81	—	—	*	*
Deer	W	20 Ja 82	—	—	—	—
Defame	W	20 Ja 82	—	—	*	*
Defraud	W	20 Ja 82	—	—	—	—
Degenerate	W	20 Ja 82	—	—	*	*

WORD	DATE				C/DX	D
Degradation	W	20 Ja 82	—	—	*	*
Deinotherium	W	20 Ja 82	—	—	*	*
Defaulter	W	20 Ja 82	—	—	—	—
Defenceless	W	20 Ja 82	—	—	*	*
Defendant	W	20 Ja 82	—	—	—	—
Deiparous	W	20 Ja 82	—	—	—	—
Deist	W	20 Ja 82	—	—	—	—
Dejeuner	W	20 Ja 82	—	—	*	*
Delegation	W	20 Ja 82	—	—	*	*
Deliberation	W	20 Ja 82	—	—	*	*
Deluge	W	20 Ja 82	—	—	*	*
Delusion	W	20 Ja 82	—	—	*	*
Demagogue	W	20 Ja 82	—	—	—	—
Demented	W	20 Ja 82	—	—	—	—
Demi-john	W	20 Ja 82	—	—	—	—
Demise	W	20 Ja 82	—	—	—	—
Demon	W	17 Fe 82	—	—	—	—
Demonomania	W	17 Fe 82	—	—	—	—
Demure	W	17 Fe 82	—	—	—	—
Dentist	W	17 Fe 82	—	—	*	*
Deny	W	17 Fe 82	—	—	—	—
Dependent	W	17 Fe 82	—	—	*	*
Depilatory	W	17 Fe 82	—	—	—	—
Deportment	W	17 Fe 82	—	—	—	—
Deposit	W	17 Fe 82	—	—	—	—
Depraved	W	17 Fe 82	—	—	—	—
Depression	W	17 Fe 82	—	—	—	—
Deputy	W	17 Fe 82	—	—	*	*
Deranged	W	3 Ma 82	—	—	—	—
Derision	W	17 Fe 82	—	—	—	—
Descendant	W	3 Ma 82	—	—	—	—
Descent	W	3 Ma 82	—	—	—	—
Desert	W	3 Ma 82	—	—	—	—
Desertion	W	3 Ma 82	—	—	—	—
Deserve	W	3 Ma 82	—	—	—	—
Deshabille	W	3 Ma 82	—	—	—	—
Desiccate	W	3 Ma 82	—	—	—	—
Despatches	W	3 Ma 82	—	—	—	—
Destiny	W	3 Ma 82	—	—	—	—
Destiny	—	—	—	—	*	*
Detective	W	3 Ma 82	—	—	—	—
Devil	W	3 Ma 82	—	—	—	—
Devotion	W	3 Ma 82	—	—	—	—
Dew	W	3 Ma 82	—	—	—	—
Dextrality	W	3 Ma 82	—	—	—	—
Diagnosis	W	24 Ma 82	—	—	*	*
Diamond	W	24 Ma 82	—	—	—	—
Diaphragm	W	24 Ma 82	—	—	*	*
Diary	W	24 Ma 82	—	—	*	*
Dice	W	24 Ma 82	—	—	—	—
Dictator	W	24 Ma 82	—	—	*	*
Dictionary	W	24 Ma 82	—	—	*	*

WORD	DATE			C/DX	D
Die	W	24 Ma 82	—	—	*	*
Digestion	W	24 Ma 82	—	—	*	*
Dine	W	24 Ma 82	—	—	—	—
Diplomacy	W	24 Ma 82	—	—	*	*
Director	W	24 Ma 82	—	—	—	—
Disabuse	W	2 Ap 82	—	—	*	*
Disannul	W	2 Ap 82	—	—	—	—
Discreditable	W	2 Ap 82	—	—	—	—
Discriminate	W	2 Ap 82	—	—	*	*
Discussion	W	2 Ap 82	—	—	*	*
Disease	W	2 Ap 82	—	—	—	—
Disobedience	W	2 Ap 82	—	—	*	*
Disobey	W	2 Ap 82	—	—	*	*
Disrepute	W	2 Ap 82	—	—	—	—
Dissemble	W	2 Ap 82	—	—	*	*
Disenchant	W	2 Ap 82	—	—	—	—
Dishonesty	W	2 Ap 82	—	—	—	—
Disincorporation	W	2 Ap 82	—	—	—	—
Dissyllable	W	2 Ap 82	—	—	—	—
Distance	W	2 Ap 82	—	—	*	*
Distillery	W	2 Ap 82	—	—	—	—
Distress	W	2 Ap 82	—	—	*	*
Divination	W	2 Ap 82	—	—	*	*
Divine	W	22 Jy 82	—	—	—	—
Divorce	W	22 Jy 82	—	—	—	—
Doctor	W	22 Jy 82	—	—	—	—
Doctrinaire	W	22 Jy 82	—	—	—	—
Dog	W	22 Jy 82	—	—	*	*
Domestic	W	22 Jy 82	—	—	—	—
Dotage	W	22 Jy 82	—	—	—	—
Dowry	W	22 Jy 82	—	—	—	—
Dragon	W	22 Jy 82	—	—	—	—
Dragoon	W	23 De 82	—	—	*	*
Dramatist	W	12 Au 82	—	—	*	*
Dropsy	W	23 De 82	—	—	—	—
Drowsy	W	12 Au 82	—	—	—	—
Druids	W	12 Au 82	—	—	*	*
Druids	W	23 De 82	—	—	*	*
Drunk	W	12 Au 82	—	—	—	—
Duck-bill	W	12 Au 82	—	—	*	*
Duel	W	12 Au 82	—	—	*	*
Dullard	W	12 Au 82	—	—	*	*
Duty	W	23 De 82	—	—	*	*
Eat	W	23 De 82	—	—	*	*
Eavesdrop	W	23 De 82	—	—	*	*
Eccentricity	W	23 De 82	—	—	*	*
Economy	W	23 De 82	—	—	*	*
Edible	W	23 De 82	—	—	*	*
Editor	W	23 De 82	—	—	*	*
Education	W	23 De 82	—	—	*	*
Effect	W	23 De 82	—	—	*	*
Efferous, etc.	W	23 De 82	—	—	—	—

WORD	DATE				C/DX	D
Ego	W	17 My 84	—	—	—	—
Egotist	W	17 My 84	—	—	*	*
Ejection	W	17 Fe 83	—	—	*	*
Elected	W	17 Fe 83	—	—	—	—
Electioneer	W	17 Fe 83	—	—	—	—
Elector	W	17 Fe 83	—	—	*	*
Electricity	W	17 Fe 83	—	—	*	*
Elegy	W	17 Fe 83	—	—	*	*
Elephant	W	17 Fe 83	—	—	—	—
Eleusinian	W	17 Fe 83	—	—	—	—
Elope	W	17 My 84	—	—	—	—
Eloquence	W	17 Fe 83	—	—	*	*
Eloquence	W	17 My 84	—	—	—	—
Elysium	W	17 Fe 83	—	—	*	*
Elysium	W	17 My 84	—	—	—	—
Emancipation	W	17 Fe 83	—	—	*	*
Embalm	W	17 Fe 83	—	—	*	*
Embalm	W	17 My 84	—	—	—	—
Embassador	W	17 My 84	—	—	—	—
Ember Days	W	17 My 84	—	—	—	—
Embezzle	W	10 Ma 83	—	—	—	—
Emergency	W	10 Ma 83	—	—	—	—
Emetic	W	10 Ma 83	—	—	—	—
Emotion	W	10 Ma 83	—	—	*	*
Encomium	W	10 Ma 83	—	—	—	—
Encore	W	10 Ma 83	—	—	—	—
Encourage	W	10 Ma 83	—	—	—	—
Encumbrance	W	10 Ma 83	—	—	—	—
Emperor	W	17 My 84	—	—	—	—
Empyrean	W	10 Ma 83	—	—	—	—
Encomiast	W	10 Ma 83	—	—	*	*
End	W	10 Ma 83	—	—	*	*
Endear	W	10 Ma 83	—	—	—	—
Enemy	W	10 Ma 83	—	—	—	—
English	W	10 Ma 83	—	—	—	—
Enigma	W	10 Ma 83	—	—	—	—
Enough	W	10 Ma 83	—	—	*	*
Entertainment	W	10 Ma 83	—	—	*	*
Enthusiasm	W	10 Ma 83	—	—	*	*
Entr'acte	W	28 Ap 83	—	—	—	—
Envelope	W	10 Ma 83	—	—	*	*
Envy	W	28 Ap 83	—	—	—	—
Envy	W	17 My 84	—	—	*	*
Eocene	W	28 Ap 83	—	—	—	—
Epaulet	W	28 Ap 83	—	—	*	*
Epicure	W	28 Ap 83	—	—	*	*
Epicure	W	17 My 84	—	—	—	—
Epidemic	W	28 Ap 83	—	—	—	—
Epidermis	W	28 Ap 83	—	—	—	—
Epigram	W	28 Ap 83	—	—	—	—
Epigram	W	17 My 84	—	—	—	—
Epigram	—	—	—	—	*	*

WORD	DATE			C/DX	D
Epitaph	W	28 Ap 83	—	—	*	*
Epitaph	W	17 My 84	—	—	—	—
Equal	W	24 My 84	—	—	—	—
Equality	W	24 My 84	—	—	—	—
Erin	W	24 My 84	—	—	—	—
Ermine	W	28 Ap 83	—	—	—	—
Err	W	24 My 84	—	—	—	—
Erudition	W	24 My 84	—	—	*	*
Esophagus	W	24 My 84	—	—	*	—
Esoteric	W	28 Ap 83	—	—	*	*
Esquire	W	28 Ap 83	—	—	—	—
Essential	W	28 Ap 83	—	—	*	—
Esteem	W	28 Ap 83	—	—	—	—
Esteem	W	24 My 84	—	—	—	—
Estoppel	W	24 My 84	—	—	—	—
Ethnology	W	6 Oc 83	—	—	*	*
Ethnology	W	24 My 84	—	—	—	—
Etiquette	W	6 Oc 83	—	—	—	—
Eucalyptus	W	6 Oc 83	—	—	—	—
Eucalyptus	W	24 My 84	—	—	—	—
Eucharist	W	6 Oc 83	—	—	*	*
Euchre	W	6 Oc 83	—	—	—	—
Eulogy	W	6 Oc 83	—	—	*	*
Euphemism	W	6 Oc 83	—	—	—	—
Euphemism	W	24 My 84	—	—	—	—
Evanescence	W	24 My 84	—	—	—	—
Evangelist	W	24 My 84	—	—	*	*
Everlasting	W	6 Oc 83	—	—	*	*
Evolution	W	6 Oc 83	—	—	—	—
Exception	W	24 My 84	—	—	*	*
Excess	W	24 My 84	—	—	*	*
Excommunication	W	6 Oc 83	—	—	*	*
Excommunication	W	7 Jn 84	—	—	—	—
Excursion	W	6 Oc 83	—	—	—	—
Executioner	W	7 Jn 84	—	—	—	—
Expectation	W	7 Jn 84	—	—	—	—
Expediency	W	7 Jn 84	—	—	—	—
Experience	W	7 Jn 84	—	—	*	*
Expostulation	W	7 Jn 84	—	—	*	*
Extinction	W	7 Jn 84	—	—	*	*
Fable	W	7 Jn 84	—	—	—	—
Executive	W	6 Oc 83	—	—	*	*
Exhort	W	7 Jn 84	—	—	*	*
Exile	W	7 Jn 84	—	—	*	*
Existence	W	7 Jn 84	—	—	*	*
Exonerate	W	7 Jn 84	—	—	—	—
Fairy	W	7 Jn 84	—	—	*	*
Faith	W	7 Jn 84	—	—	*	*
Falsehood	W	7 Jn 84	—	—	—	—
Family	W	7 Jn 84	—	—	—	—
Famous	W	28 Jn 84	—	—	*	*
Fanatic	W	28 Jn 84	—	—	—	—

WORD	DATE				C/DX	D
Farce	W	28 Jn 84	—	—	—	—
Fashion	W	28 Jn 84	—	—	*	*
Father	W	28 Jn 84	—	—	—	—
Fatigue	W	2 Au 84	—	—	—	—
Fault	W	2 Au 84	—	—	—	—
Faun	W	2 Au 84	—	—	—	—
Fauna	W	2 Au 84	—	—	—	—
Fear	W	2 Au 84	—	—	—	—
Feast	W	2 Au 84	—	—	*	*
Felon	W	2 Au 84	—	—	*	*
Female	W	2 Au 84	—	—	*	*
Ferule	W	27 Se 84	—	—	—	—
Fib	W	27 Se 84	—	—	*	*
Fickleness	W	27 Se 84	—	—	*	*
Fiddle	W	27 Se 84	—	—	*	*
Fidelity	W	27 Se 84	—	—	*	*
Fiend	W	27 Se 84	—	—	—	—
Fig-leaf	W	27 Se 84	—	—	—	—
Filial	W	27 Se 84	—	—	—	—
Finance	W	27 Se 84	—	—	*	*
Flag	W	27 Se 84	—	—	*	*
Flatter	W	27 Se 84	—	—	—	—
Flesh	W	29 No 84	—	—	*	*
Flint	W	29 No 84	—	—	—	—
Flirtation	W	29 No 84	—	—	—	—
Flood	W	29 No 84	—	—	—	—
Flop	W	29 No 84	—	—	*	*
Flunkey	W	29 No 84	—	—	—	—
Flute	W	29 No 84	—	—	—	—
Fly	W	29 No 84	—	—	—	—
Fly-speck	W	6 De 84	—	—	*	*
Foe	W	6 De 84	—	—	—	—
Fog	W	6 De 84	—	—	—	—
Fold	W	6 De 84	—	—	—	—
Folly	W	6 De 84	—	—	*	*
Fool	W	13 De 84	—	—	*	*
Foolhardy	W	13 De 84	—	—	—	—
Footprints	W	13 De 84	—	—	—	—
Forbidden	W	13 De 84	—	—	—	—
Force	W	13 De 84	—	—	*	*
Forefinger	W	13 De 84	—	—	*	*
Foreign	W	13 De 84	—	—	—	—
Foreigner	W	13 De 84	—	—	—	—
Foreman	W	13 De 84	—	—	—	—
Forenoon	W	13 De 84	—	—	—	—
Foreordination	W	13 De 84	—	—	*	*
Foresight	W	13 De 84	—	—	—	—
Forgetfulness	W	13 De 84	—	—	*	*
Fragment	W	10 Ja 85	—	—	—	—
Frail	W	10 Ja 85	—	—	—	—
Frankalmoigne	W	10 Ja 85	—	—	*	*
Fratricide	W	10 Ja 85	—	—	—	—

WORD	DATE			C/DX	D
German	W	28 Fe 85	—	—	—	—
Ghost	W	28 Fe 85	—	—	*	*
Ghoul	W	28 Fe 85	—	—	*	*
Gimlet	W	28 Fe 85	—	—	—	—
Gipsy	W	7 Ma 85	—	—	—	—
Giraffe	W	7 Ma 85	—	—	—	—
Gloom	W	7 Ma 85	—	—	—	—
Glutton	W	7 Ma 85	—	—	*	*
Gnome	W	7 Ma 85	—	—	*	*
Goose	W	7 Ma 85	—	—	*	*
Gordian Knot	W	14 Ma 85	—	—	—	—
Gorgon	W	14 Ma 85	—	—	*	*
Gout	W	14 Ma 85	—	—	*	*
Government	W	14 Ma 85	—	—	—	—
Governor	W	14 Ma 85	—	—	—	—
Gnostics	W	7 Ma 85	—	—	*	*
Gnu	W	7 Ma 85	—	—	*	*
Gold	W	7 Ma 85	—	—	—	—
Gold-bug	W	7 Ma 85	—	—	—	—
Good	W	7 Ma 85	—	—	*	*
Graces	W	14 Ma 85	—	—	*	*
Grammar	W	14 Ma 85	—	—	*	*
Grape	W	14 Ma 85	—	—	*	*
Grapeshot	W	14 Ma 85	—	—	*	*
Grass	W	14 Ma 85	—	—	—	—
Grasshopper	W	28 Ma 85	—	—	—	—
Gratitude	W	28 Ma 85	—	—	—	—
Grave	W	28 Ma 85	—	—	*	*
Gravitation	W	28 Ma 85	—	—	*	*
Great	W	28 Ma 85	—	—	*	*
Great Seal [Seal]	W	28 Ma 85	—	—	—	—
Griffin	W	28 Ma 85	—	—	—	—
Grime	W	28 Ma 85	—	—	—	—
Grip [Tenacity]	W	28 Ma 85	—	—	—	—
Groan	W	28 Ma 85	—	—	—	—
Guardian	W	28 Ma 85	—	—	—	—
Guillotine	W	4 Ap 85	—	—	*	*
Guilt	W	4 Ap 85	—	—	—	—
Guinea	W	4 Ap 85	—	—	—	—
Guinea-pig	W	4 Ap 85	—	—	—	—
Gull	W	4 Ap 85	—	—	—	—
Gum	W	4 Ap 85	—	—	—	—
Gunpowder	W	4 Ap 85	—	—	*	*
Gymnast	W	4 Ap 85	—	—	—	—
Gymnodontes	W	4 Ap 85	—	—	—	—
Gymnosophists	W	4 Ap 85	—	—	—	—
Habeas Corpus	W	11 Ap 85	—	—	*	*
Habit	W	11 Ap 85	—	—	*	*
Hades	W	11 Ap 85	—	—	*	*
Hag	W	11 Ap 85	—	—	*	*
Halcyon (Alcedo)	W	11 Ap 85	—	—	—	—
Half	W	11 Ap 85	—	—	*	*

WORD	DATE			C/DX	D
Halo	W	11 Ap 85	—	—	*	*
Hammer	W	11 Ap 85	—	—	—	—
Hand	W	11 Ap 85	—	—	*	*
Handkerchief	W	11 Ap 85	—	—	*	*
Hangman	W	25 Ap 85	—	—	—	—
Hangman	—	—	—	—	*	*
Happiness	W	25 Ap 85	—	—	*	*
Harangue	W	25 Ap 85	—	—	*	*
Harbor	W	25 Ap 85	—	—	*	*
Hardware	W	25 Ap 85	—	—	—	—
Hare	W	25 Ap 85	—	—	—	—
Harmonists	W	25 Ap 85	—	—	*	*
Hash	W	25 Ap 85	—	—	*	*
Hatchet	W	25 Ap 85	—	—	*	*
Hatred	W	25 Ap 85	—	—	*	*
Haughty	W	25 Ap 85	—	—	—	—
Hautboy	W	25 Ap 85	—	—	—	—
Head [Scimitar]	W	25 Ap 85	—	—	—	—
Head-money	W	16 My 85	—	—	*	*
Hearer	W	16 My 85	—	—	—	—
Hearse	W	16 My 85	—	—	*	*
Heart	W	16 My 85	—	—	*	*
Heigh-ho	W	23 My 85	—	—	—	—
Hell	W	23 My 85	—	—	—	—
Helpmate	W	23 My 85	—	—	*	*
Hemp	W	23 My 85	—	—	*	*
Hermit	W	23 My 85	—	—	*	*
Hers	W	23 My 85	—	—	*	*
Heat	W	16 My 85	—	—	*	*
Heathen	W	16 My 85	—	—	*	*
Heaven	W	23 My 85	—	—	*	*
Hebrew	W	23 My 85	—	—	*	*
Hedgehog	W	23 My 85	—	—	—	—
Hesitation	W	23 My 85	—	—	—	—
Hibernate	W	23 My 85	—	—	*	*
Hippogriff	W	23 My 85	—	—	*	*
Hireling	W	23 My 85	—	—	—	—
Historian	W	23 My 85	—	—	*	*
History	W	23 My 85	—	—	*	*
Hog	W	23 My 85	—	—	*	*
Home	W	18 Jy 85	—	—	—	—
Homesick	W	18 Jy 85	—	—	—	—
Homicide	W	18 Jy 85	—	—	*	*
Homiletics	W	18 Jy 85	—	—	*	*
Homœopathist	—	—	—	—	*	*
Homœopathy	W	18 Jy 85	—	—	—	—
Homœopathy	—	—	—	—	*	*
Homoiousian	W	18 Jy 85	—	—	—	—
Honest	W	18 Jy 85	—	—	—	—
Honorable	W	18 Jy 85	—	—	—	—
Honorable	—	—	—	—	*	*
Hope	W	18 Jy 85	—	—	*	*

WORD	DATE			C/DX	D
Hornet	W	18 Jy 85	—	—	—	—
Horrid	W	8 Au 85	—	—	—	—
Horse	W	8 Au 85	—	—	—	—
Hospital	W	8 Au 85	—	—	—	—
Hospitality	W	8 Au 85	—	—	*	*
Host	W	8 Au 85	—	—	—	—
Hostility	W	8 Au 85	—	—	*	*
Houri	W	8 Au 85	—	—	*	*
House	W	8 Au 85	—	—	*	*
Houseless	W	8 Au 85	—	—	*	*
Hovel	W	8 Au 85	—	—	*	*
Hug	W	8 Au 85	—	—	—	—
Humanitarian	W	8 Au 85	—	—	—	—
Humanity	W	8 Au 85	—	—	*	*
Humorist	W	8 Au 85	—	—	*	*
Hun	W	22 Au 85	—	—	—	—
Hunger	W	22 Au 85	—	—	—	—
Hunt	W	22 Au 85	—	—	—	—
Hurricane	W	22 Au 85	—	—	*	*
Hurry	W	22 Au 85	—	—	*	*
Husband	W	22 Au 85	—	—	*	*
Hybrid	W	22 Au 85	—	—	*	*
Hydra	W	22 Au 85	—	—	*	*
Hyena	W	22 Au 85	—	—	*	*
Hygeia	W	22 Au 85	—	—	—	—
Hypochondriasis	W	22 Au 85	—	—	*	*
Hypocrite	W	22 Au 85	—	—	*	*
I	W	22 Au 85	—	—	*	*
Ichor	W	22 Au 85	—	—	*	*
Ichthyologist	W	22 Au 85	—	—	—	—
Iconoclast	W	22 Au 85	—	—	*	*
Idiot	W	29 Au 85	—	—	*	*
Idleness [Idler]	W	29 Au 85	—	—	*	*
Idol	W	29 Au 85	—	—	—	—
Idolator	W	29 Au 85	—	—	—	—
Imbecility	W	29 Au 85	—	—	*	*
Immaculate	W	29 Au 85	—	—	—	—
Immigrant	W	29 Au 85	—	—	*	*
Immodest	W	29 Au 85	—	—	*	*
Immolation	W	12 Se 85	—	—	—	—
Immoral	W	12 Se 85	—	—	*	*
Ignis Fatuus	W	29 Au 85	—	—	—	—
Ignoramus	W	29 Au 85	—	—	*	*
Illuminati	W	29 Au 85	—	—	*	*
Illustrious	W	29 Au 85	—	—	*	*
Imagination	W	29 Au 85	—	—	*	*
Immortality	W	12 Se 85	—	—	*	*
Impale	W	12 Se 85	—	—	*	*
Impartial	W	12 Se 85	—	—	*	*
Impeccable	W	12 Se 85	—	—	—	—
Impenitence	W	12 Se 85	—	—	*	*
Imperialist	W	12 Se 85	—	—	—	—

WORD	DATE				C/DX	D
Impiety	W	12 Se 85	—	—	*	*
Implacable	W	12 Se 85	—	—	—	—
Importer	W	12 Se 85	—	—	—	—
Imposition	W	12 Se 85	—	—	*	*
Impostor	W	12 Se 85	—	—	*	*
Improbability	W	12 Se 85	—	—	*	*
Impromptu	W	12 Se 85	—	—	—	—
Impropriety	W	19 Se 85	—	—	—	—
Improvidence	W	19 Se 85	—	—	*	*
Improvisator	W	19 Se 85	—	—	—	—
Imprudence	W	19 Se 85	—	—	—	—
Impudence	W	19 Se 85	—	—	—	—
Impunity	W	19 Se 85	—	—	*	*
Inadmissible	W	19 Se 85	—	—	*	*
Inalterable	W	19 Se 85	—	—	—	—
Inappropriateness	W	19 Se 85	—	—	—	—
Inauspicious	W	19 Se 85	—	—	—	—
Inauspiciously	W	19 Se 85	—	—	*	*
Incatenation	W	26 Se 85	—	—	—	—
Incense	W	26 Se 85	—	—	—	—
Incivism	W	26 Se 85	—	—	—	—
Income	W	26 Se 85	—	—	*	*
Incompatibility	W	26 Se 85	—	—	*	*
Incompossible	W	26 Se 85	—	—	*	*
Incomprehensibility	W	26 Se 85	—	—	—	—
Inconsiderate	W	26 Se 85	—	—	—	—
Inconsolable	W	26 Se 85	—	—	—	—
Inconstancy	W	26 Se 85	—	—	—	—
Inconstant	W	26 Se 85	—	—	—	—
Incorporation	W	3 Oc 85	—	—	—	—
Incubate	W	3 Oc 85	—	—	—	—
Incubus	W	3 Oc 85	—	—	*	*
Incumbent	W	3 Oc 85	—	—	*	*
Indecision	W	3 Oc 85	—	—	*	*
Indian	W	3 Oc 85	—	—	—	—
Indifferent	W	3 Oc 85	—	—	*	*
Indigestion	W	10 Oc 85	—	—	*	*
Indiscretion	W	10 Oc 85	—	—	*	*
Inexpedient	W	10 Oc 85	—	—	*	*
Infallible	W	10 Oc 85	—	—	—	—
Infancy	W	10 Oc 85	—	—	*	*
Inferiæ	W	10 Oc 85	—	—	*	*
Infidel	W	10 Oc 85	—	—	*	*
Influence	W	10 Oc 85	—	—	*	*
Infalapsarian	W	10 Oc 85	—	—	*	*
Ingrate	W	17 Oc 85	—	—	*	*
Ingratitude	W	17 Oc 85	—	—	—	—
Innocence	W	24 Oc 85	—	—	—	—
Inquisition	W	24 Oc 85	—	—	—	—
Insane	W	24 Oc 85	—	—	—	—
Insanity	W	24 Oc 85	—	—	—	—
Inscription	W	24 Oc 85	—	—	*	*

WORD	DATE			C/DX	D
Insectivora	W	7 No 85	—	—	*	*
Insolvent	W	7 No 85	—	—	—	—
Inhumanity	W	17 Oc 85	—	—	—	—
Injury	W	17 Oc 85	—	—	*	*
Injustice	W	17 Oc 85	—	—	*	*
Ink	W	17 Oc 85	—	—	*	*
In'ards	W	17 Oc 85	—	—	*	*
Innate	W	17 Oc 85	—	—	*	*
Inspiration	W	7 No 85	—	—	—	—
Insurance	W	7 No 85	—	—	*	*
Insurrection	W	7 No 85	—	—	*	*
Intellectual	W	7 No 85	—	—	—	—
Intelligent	W	7 No 85	—	—	—	—
Intemperance	W	21 No 85	—	—	—	—
Intention	W	21 No 85	—	—	*	*
Interim	W	21 No 85	—	—	—	—
Interlocutor	W	21 No 85	—	—	—	—
Interpreter	W	21 No 85	—	—	*	*
Interregnum	W	21 No 85	—	—	*	*
Interview	W	21 No 85	—	—	—	—
Intimacy	W	21 No 85	—	—	*	*
Intoxication	W	21 No 85	—	—	—	—
Intractable	W	21 No 85	—	—	—	—
Introduction	W	21 No 85	—	—	*	*
Intruder	W	21 No 85	—	—	—	—
Inundation	W	21 No 85	—	—	—	—
Invasion	W	19 De 85	—	—	—	—
Inventor	W	19 De 85	—	—	*	*
Irreligion	W	19 De 85	—	—	*	*
Isthmus	W	19 De 85	—	—	—	—
Itch	W	19 De 85	—	—	*	*
Ivory	W	19 De 85	—	—	—	—
J	W	19 De 85	—	—	*	*
Jacob's-ladder	W	19 De 85	—	—	—	—
Jealous	W	19 De 85	—	—	*	*
Jealousy	W	19 De 85	—	—	—	—
Jester	W	19 De 85	—	—	*	*
Jews-harp	W	9 Ja 86	—	—	*	*
Jockey	W	9 Ja 86	—	—	—	—
Joss-sticks	W	9 Ja 86	—	—	*	*
Jove	W	9 Ja 86	—	—	—	—
Joy	W	9 Ja 86	—	—	—	—
Judge	W	9 Ja 86	—	—	—	—
Jurisprudence	W	9 Ja 86	—	—	—	—
Jury	W	9 Ja 86	—	—	—	—
Justice	W	9 Ja 86	—	—	*	*
Jute	W	9 Ja 86	—	—	—	—
K	W	9 Ja 86	—	—	*	*
Kangaroo	W	9 Ja 86	—	—	—	—
Keep	W	9 Ja 86	—	—	*	*
Kill	W	13 Fe 86	—	—	*	*
Kilt	W	13 Fe 86	—	—	*	*

WORD	DATE				C/DX	D
Kindness	W	13 Fe 86	—	—	*	*
Kine	W	13 Fe 86	—	—	—	—
King	W	13 Fe 86	—	—	*	*
King's evil	W	13 Fe 86	—	—	*	*
Kiss	W	13 Fe 86	—	—	*	*
Kleptomaniac	W	13 Fe 86	—	—	*	*
Knight	W	13 Fe 86	—	—	*	*
Koran	W	13 Fe 86	—	—	*	*
Language	W	6 Ma 86	—	—	*	*
Laocoön	W	6 Ma 86	—	—	*	*
Lap	W	6 Ma 86	—	—	*	*
Lapidate	W	6 Ma 86	—	—	—	—
Last	W	1 My 86	—	—	*	*
Latitudinarian	W	1 My 86	—	—	—	—
Laughter	W	1 My 86	—	—	*	*
Krishna	W	13 Fe 86	—	—	—	—
Labor	W	6 Ma 86	—	—	*	*
Lace [Seine]	W	6 Ma 86	—	—	*	—
Lacteal Fluid	W	6 Ma 86	—	—	—	—
Lady	W	6 Ma 86	—	—	—	—
Land	W	6 Ma 86	—	—	*	*
Laureate	W	1 My 86	—	—	*	*
Laurel	W	1 My 86	—	—	*	*
Law	W	1 My 86	—	—	*	*
Lawful	—	—	—	—	*	*
Lawyer	E	6 No 87	—	—	*	*
Lay-figure	W	19 Jn 86	—	—	—	—
Laziness	W	19 Jn 86	—	—	*	*
Lead	W	19 Jn 86	—	—	*	*
League	W	19 Jn 86	—	—	—	—
Learning	W	19 Jn 86	—	—	—	—
Learning	—	—	—	—	*	*
Leatherhead	W	14 Au 86	—	—	—	—
Lecturer	W	14 Au 86	—	—	*	*
Legacy	W	14 Au 86	—	—	*	*
Legislator	W	19 Jn 86	—	—	—	—
Leisure	W	19 Jn 86	—	—	—	—
Leonine	W	19 Jn 86	—	—	*	*
Leptocephalidans	W	19 Jn 86	—	—	—	—
Lethe	W	19 Jn 86	—	—	—	—
Lettuce	W	19 Jn 86	—	—	*	*
Leveler	W	14 Au 86	—	—	—	—
Leviathan	W	14 Au 86	—	—	*	*
Levite	W	14 Au 86	—	—	—	—
Lexicographer	W	14 Au 86	—	—	*	*
Liar	W	14 Au 86	—	—	*	*
Libelous	W	14 Au 86	—	—	—	—
Libertarian	W	14 Au 86	—	—	—	—
Libertine	W	14 Au 86	—	—	—	—
Liberty	W	14 Au 86	—	—	*	*
Lickspittle	W	14 Au 86	—	—	*	*
Life	E	4 Se 87	—	—	*	*

WORD	DATE				C/DX	D
Manicheism	Am	13 Au 04	E	15 No 04	*	*
Manna	Am	13 Au 04	E	15 No 04	*	*
March	Am	13 Au 04	E	15 No 04	—	—
Marriage	Am	13 Au 04	E	15 No 04	*	*
Martyr	Am	13 Au 04	E	15 No 04	—	—
Martyr	—	—	—	—	*	*
Marvellous	Am	13 Au 04	E	15 No 04	—	—
Material	Am	13 Au 04	E	15 No 04	*	*
Mausoleum	Am	13 Au 04	E	15 No 04	*	*
Mayonnaise	Am	26 Au 04	E	13 Oc 04	*	*
Me	Am	26 Au 04	E	13 Oc 04	*	*
Meander	Am	26 Au 04	E	13 Oc 04	*	*
Medal	Am	26 Au 04	E	13 Oc 04	*	*
Mediate	Am	26 Au 04	E	13 Oc 04	—	—
Medicine	Am	26 Au 04	E	13 Oc 04	*	*
Meekness	Am	26 Au 04	E	13 Oc 04	*	*
Meerschaum	Am	26 Au 04	E	13 Oc 04	*	*
Mendacious	Am	26 Au 04	E	13 Oc 04	*	*
Merchant	Am	30 Au 04	—	—	*	*
Mercy	Am	30 Au 04	—	—	*	*
Mesmerism	Am	30 Au 04	—	—	*	*
Metropolis	Am	30 Au 04	—	—	*	*
Millennium	Am	30 Au 04	—	—	*	*
Mind	Am	30 Au 04	—	—	*	*
Mine	Am	30 Au 04	—	—	*	*
Minister	Am	30 Au 04	—	—	*	*
Minor	Am	30 Au 04	—	—	*	*
Minstrel	Am	30 Au 04	—	—	*	*
Miracle	Am	30 Au 04	—	—	*	*
Miscreant	Am	30 Au 04	—	—	*	*
Misdemeanor	Am	30 Au 04	—	—	*	*
Misericorde	Am	30 Au 04	—	—	*	*
Misfortune	Am	30 Au 04	—	—	*	*
Money	Am	3 Se 04	E	9 Se 04	*	*
Monkey	Am	3 Se 04	E	9 Se 04	*	*
Monogenist	Am	3 Se 04	E	9 Se 04	—	—
Monologue	Am	3 Se 04	E	9 Se 04	—	—
Monometallist	Am	3 Se 04	E	9 Se 04	—	—
Monosyllabic	Am	3 Se 04	E	9 Se 04	*	*
Monsignor	Am	3 Se 04	E	9 Se 04	*	*
Monument	Am	3 Se 04	E	9 Se 04	*	*
Miss	Am	30 Au 04	—	—	*	*
Molecule	Am	30 Au 04	—	—	*	*
Monad	Am	3 Se 04	E	9 Se 04	*	*
Monarch	Am	3 Se 04	E	9 Se 04	*	*
Monarchical Government	Am	3 Se 04	E	9 Se 04	*	*
Monday	Am	3 Se 04	E	9 Se 04	*	*
Moral	Am	3 Se 04	E	9 Se 04	*	*
More	Am	3 Se 04	E	9 Se 04	*	*
Morganatic	Am	13 Se 04	E	8 No 04	—	—
Mormon	Am	13 Se 04	E	8 No 04	—	—

WORD	DATE					C/DX	D
Morning	Am	13 Se 04	E	8 No 04		—	—
Morrow	Am	13 Se 04	E	8 No 04		—	—
Mortality	Am	13 Se 04	E	8 No 04		—	—
Mosaic	Am	13 Se 04	E	8 No 04		—	—
Mosquito	Am	13 Se 04	E	8 No 04		—	—
Motion	Am	13 Se 04	E	8 No 04		—	—
Motive	Am	13 Se 04	E	8 No 04		—	—
Mouse	Am	22 Se 04	E	30 Se 04		*	*
Mousquetaire	Am	22 Se 04	E	30 Se 04		*	*
Mouth	Am	22 Se 04	E	30 Se 04		*	*
Mugwump	Am	22 Se 04	E	30 Se 04		*	*
Mulatto	Am	22 Se 04	E	30 Se 04		*	*
Mule	Am	22 Se 04	E	30 Se 04		—	—
Multitude	Am	22 Se 04	E	30 Se 04		*	*
Mummy	Am	22 Se 04	E	30 Se 04		*	*
Mustang	Am	22 Se 04	E	30 Se 04		*	*
Myrmidon	Am	22 Se 04	E	30 Se 04		*	*
Mythology	Am	22 Se 04	E	30 Se 04		*	*
Namby-pamby	Am	22 Se 04	E	30 Se 04		—	—
Nectar	Am	22 Se 04	E	30 Se 04		*	*
Negro	Am	23 Se 04	E	4 Oc 04		*	*
Neighbor	Am	23 Se 04	E	4 Oc 04		*	*
Nepotism	Am	23 Se 04	E	4 Oc 04		*	*
Newtonian	Am	23 Se 04	E	4 Oc 04		*	*
Nihilist	Am	23 Se 04	E	4 Oc 04		*	*
Nirvana	Am	23 Se 04	E	4 Oc 04		*	*
Nobleman	Am	23 Se 04	E	4 Oc 04		*	*
Noise	Am	23 Se 04	E	4 Oc 04		*	*
Nominate	Am	23 Se 04	E	4 Oc 04		*	*
Nominee	Am	23 Se 04	E	4 Oc 04		*	*
Non-combatant	Am	23 Se 04	E	4 Oc 04		*	*
Nonsense	Am	23 Se 04	E	4 Oc 04		*	*
Nose	Am	26 Se 04	E	6 Oc 04		*	*
Notoriety	Am	26 Se 04	E	6 Oc 04		*	*
Noumenon	Am	26 Se 04	E	6 Oc 04		*	*
Novel	Am	26 Se 04	E	6 Oc 04		*	*
November	Am	26 Se 04	E	6 Oc 04		*	*
Nudity	Am	26 Se 04	E	6 Oc 04		—	—
Oath	Am	27 Se 04	E	28 Oc 04		*	*
Oblivion	Am	27 Se 04	E	28 Oc 04		*	*
Observatory	Am	27 Se 04	E	28 Oc 04		*	*
Obsessed	Am	27 Se 04	E	28 Oc 04		*	*
Obsolete	Am	5 Oc 04	E	31 Oc 04		*	*
Obstinacy	Am	5 Oc 04	E	31 Oc 04		—	—
Obstinate	Am	5 Oc 04	E	31 Oc 04		*	*
Occasional	Am	6 Oc 04	E	31 Oc 04		*	*
Omen	Am	17 Oc 04	E	24 Oc 04		*	*
Omnipresent	Am	17 Oc 04	E	24 Oc 04		+	—
Once	Am	17 Oc 04	E	24 Oc 04		*	*
Opera	Am	17 Oc 04	E	24 Oc 04		*	*
Opiate	Am	17 Oc 04	E	24 Oc 04		*	*
Opportunity	Am	17 Oc 04	E	24 Oc 04		*	*

WORD	DATE				C/DX	D
Oppose	Am	17 Oc 04	E	24 Oc 04	*	*
Opposition	Am	17 Oc 04	E	24 Oc 04	*	*
Occident	Am	6 Oc 04	E	31 Oc 04	*	*
Occult	Am	6 Oc 04	E	31 Oc 04	—	—
Ocean	Am	6 Oc 04	E	31 Oc 04	*	*
Offensive	Am	6 Oc 04	E	31 Oc 04	*	*
Old	Am	6 Oc 04	E	31 Oc 04	*	*
Oleaginous	Am	22 No 04	E	2 De 04	*	*
Olympian	Am	17 Oc 04	E	24 Oc 04	*	*
Optimism	Am	5 No 04	E	12 No 04	*	*
Optimist	Am	5 No 04	E	12 No 04	*	*
Oratory	Am	5 No 04	E	12 No 04	*	*
Ordinary	Am	5 No 04	E	12 No 04	—	—
Orphan	Am	5 No 04	E	12 No 04	*	*
Orthodox	Am	5 No 04	E	12 No 04	*	*
Orthography	Am	5 No 04	E	12 No 04	*	*
Ostrich	Am	5 No 04	E	12 No 04	*	*
Otherwise	Am	5 No 04	E	12 No 04	*	*
Outcome	Am	5 No 04	E	12 No 04	*	*
Outdo	Am	5 No 04	E	12 No 04	*	*
Out-of-doors	—	—	—	—	*	*
Outrage	Am	19 No 04	E	28 No 04	—	—
Outsider	Am	19 No 04	E	28 No 04	—	—
Ovation	Am	19 No 04	E	28 No 04	*	*
Overcharge	Am	19 No 04	E	28 No 04	—	—
Overdose	Am	19 No 04	E	28 No 04	—	—
Overeat	Am	19 No 04	E	28 No 04	*	*
Overwork	Am	22 No 04	E	2 De 04	*	*
Owe	Am	22 No 04	E	2 De 04	*	*
Oyster	Am	22 No 04	E	2 De 04	*	*
Pagan	Am	1 De 04	E	8 De 04	—	—
Pain	Am	1 De 04	E	8 De 04	*	*
Painting	Am	1 De 04	E	8 De 04	*	*
Palace	Am	1 De 04	E	8 De 04	*	*
Palm	Am	1 De 04	E	8 De 04	*	*
Palmistry	Am	1 De 04	E	8 De 04	*	*
Pandemonium	Am	1 De 04	E	8 De 04	*	*
Pantaloons	Am	26 De 04	E	3 Ja 05	*	*
Pantheism	Am	26 De 04	E	3 Ja 05	*	*
Pantomime	Am	26 De 04	E	3 Ja 05	*	*
Pardon	Am	26 De 04	E	3 Ja 05	*	*
Parricide	Am	26 De 04	E	3 Ja 05	—	—
Partisan	Am	26 De 04	E	3 Ja 05	—	—
Passport	Am	26 De 04	E	3 Ja 05	*	*
Past	Am	26 De 04	E	3 Ja 05	*	*
Pastime	Am	26 De 04	E	3 Ja 05	*	*
Patience	Am	26 De 04	E	3 Ja 05	*	*
Patriot	Am	26 De 04	E	3 Ja 05	*	*
Patriotism	Am	26 De 04	E	3 Ja 05	*	*
Peace	Am	26 De 04	E	3 Ja 05	*	*
Pedestrian	Am	7 Ja 05	E	14 Ja 05	*	*
Pedigree	Am	7 Ja 05	E	14 Ja 05	*	*

WORD	DATE				C/DX	D
Penitent	Am	7 Ja 05	E	14 Ja 05	*	*
Perdition	Am	7 Ja 05	E	14 Ja 05	*	—
Perfection	Am	7 Ja 05	E	14 Ja 05	*	*
Pericardium	Am	7 Ja 05	E	14 Ja 05	—	—
Peripatetic	Am	7 Ja 05	E	14 Ja 05	*	*
Peroration	Am	7 Ja 05	E	14 Ja 05	*	*
Perseverance	Am	7 Ja 05	E	14 Ja 05	*	*
Phonograph	Am	11 Ja 05	E	18 Ma 05	*	*
Photograph	Am	11 Ja 05	E	18 Ma 05	*	*
Phrenology	Am	11 Ja 05	E	18 Ma 05	*	*
Physician	Am	11 Ja 05	E	18 Ma 05	*	*
Physiognomy	Am	11 Ja 05	E	18 Ma 05	*	*
Piano	Am	22 Fe 06	—	—	*	*
Pianoforte	Am	27 Ja 05	E	11 Fe 05	—	—
Pickaback	Am	22 Fe 06	—	—	—	—
Persuasion	Am	7 Ja 05	E	14 Ja 05	—	—
Pessimism	Am	7 Ja 05	E	14 Ja 05	*	*
Pettifogger	Am	11 Ja 05	E	18 Ma 05	—	—
Philanthropist	Am	11 Ja 05	E	18 Ma 05	*	*
Philistine	Am	11 Ja 05	E	18 Ma 05	*	*
Philosophy	Am	11 Ja 05	E	18 Ma 05	*	*
Phœnix	Am	11 Ja 05	E	18 Ma 05	*	*
Pickaninny	Am	22 Fe 06	—	—	*	*
Picture	Am	22 Fe 06	—	—	*	*
Pie	Am	22 Fe 06	—	—	*	*
Piety	Am	27 Ja 05	E	11 Fe 05	*	*
Pig	Am	22 Fe 06	—	—	*	*
Pigmy	Am	22 Fe 06	—	—	*	*
Pilgrim	Am	22 Fe 06	—	—	*	*
Pillage	Am	22 Fe 06	—	—	—	—
Pillory	Am	22 Fe 06	—	—	*	*
Piracy	Am	22 Fe 06	—	—	*	*
Pitiful	Am	22 Fe 06	—	—	*	*
Pity	Am	22 Fe 06	—	—	*	*
Plagiarism	Am	22 Fe 06	—	—	*	*
Plagiarize	Am	22 Fe 06	—	—	*	*
Plaintiff [Court Fool]	Am	22 Fe 06	—	—	—	—
Plague	Am	22 Fe 06	—	—	*	*
Plan	Am	22 Fe 06	—	—	*	*
Platitude	Am	22 Fe 06	—	—	*	*
Platonic	—	—	—	—	*	*
Platter	—	—	—	—	—	—
Plaudits	Am	6 Ma 06	E	12 Ma 06	*	*
Please	Am	6 Ma 06	E	12 Ma 06	*	*
Pleasure	Am	6 Ma 06	E	12 Ma 06	—	—
Pleasure	Am	27 Ja 05	E	11 Fe 05	*	*
Plebeian	Am	6 Ma 06	E	12 Ma 06	*	*
Plebiscite	Am	6 Ma 06	E	12 Ma 06	*	*
Plenipotentiary	Am	27 Ja 05	E	11 Fe 05	*	*
Pleonasm	Am	6 Ma 06	E	12 Ma 06	*	*
Plow	Am	6 Ma 06	E	12 Ma 06	*	*
Plunder	Am	6 Ma 06	E	12 Ma 06	*	*

WORD	DATE				C/DX	D
Plunder	Am	27 Ja 05	E	11 Fe 05	*	*
Plutarchy	Am	6 Ma 06	E	12 Ma 06	—	—
Plutocracy	Am	27 Ja 05	E	11 Fe 05	—	—
Pocket	Am	6 Ma 06	E	12 Ma 06	*	*
Poetry	Am	6 Ma 06	E	12 Ma 06	*	*
Poker	Am	6 Ma 06	E	12 Ma 06	*	*
Polecat	Am	16 Ma 06	E	21 Ma 06	—	—
Police	Am	16 Ma 06	E	21 Ma 06	*	*
Polite	Am	16 Ma 06	E	21 Ma 06	—	—
Politeness	Am	16 Ma 06	E	21 Ma 06	*	*
Politics	Am	16 Ma 06	E	21 Ma 06	*	*
Politician	Am	16 Ma 06	E	21 Ma 06	*	*
Polygamy	Am	16 Ma 06	E	21 Ma 06	*	*
Populist	Am	16 Ma 06	E	21 Ma 06	—	—
Port	Am	16 Ma 06	E	21 Ma 06	—	—
Portable	Am	16 Ma 06	E	21 Ma 06	*	*
Portion	Am	16 Ma 06	E	21 Ma 06	*	—
Portuguese	Am	6 Ap 06	E	11 Ap 06	*	*
Positive	Am	16 Ma 06	E	21 Ma 06	*	*
Precedent	Am	6 Ap 06	E	11 Ap 06	*	*
Precipitate	Am	6 Ap 06	E	11 Ap 06	*	*
Predestination	Am	6 Ap 06	E	11 Ap 06	*	*
Predicament	Am	30 My 06	E	20 Jn 06	*	*
Predict	Am	30 My 06	E	20 Jn 06	+	—
Predilection	Am	30 My 06	E	20 Jn 06	*	*
Pre-existence	Am	30 My 06	E	20 Jn 06	*	*
Preference	Am	30 My 06	E	20 Jn 06	*	*
Prehistoric	Am	30 My 06	E	20 Jn 06	*	*
Positivism	Am	16 Ma 06	E	21 Ma 06	*	*
Possession	Am	16 Ma 06	E	21 Ma 06	—	—
Posterity	Am	6 Ap 06	E	11 Ap 06	*	*
Potable	Am	6 Ap 06	E	11 Ap 06	*	*
Poverty	Am	6 Ap 06	E	11 Ap 06	*	*
Practically	Am	6 Ap 06	E	11 Ap 06	—	—
Pray	Am	6 Ap 06	E	11 Ap 06	*	*
Pre-Adamite	Am	6 Ap 06	E	11 Ap 06	*	*
Prejudice	Am	30 My 06	E	20 Jn 06	*	*
Prelate	Am	30 My 06	E	20 Jn 06	*	*
Prerogative	Am	30 My 06	E	20 Jn 06	*	*
Presbyterian	Am	30 My 06	E	20 Jn 06	*	*
Prescription	Am	30 My 06	E	20 Jn 06	*	*
Present	Am	30 My 06	E	20 Jn 06	*	*
Present	Am	30 My 06	E	21 Jn 06	—	—
Presentable	Am	30 My 06	E	20 Jn 06	*	*
Presentiment	Am	30 My 06	E	20 Jn 06	—	—
Preside	Am	30 My 06	E	20 Jn 06	*	*
Presidency	Am	14 Jn 06	—	—	*	*
President	Am	14 Jn 06	—	—	*	*
Pretty	Am	14 Jn 06	—	—	—	—
Prevaricator	Am	14 Jn 06	—	—	*	*
Price	Am	14 Jn 06	—	—	*	*
Primate	Am	14 Jn 06	—	—	*	*

WORD	DATE ────────────────				C/DX	D
Prison	Am	14 Jn 06	—	—	*	*
Private	Am	14 Jn 06	—	—	*	*
Proboscis	Am	14 Jn 06	—	—	*	*
Projectile	Am	14 Jn 06	—	—	*	*
Promise	Am	27 Jn 06	—	—	—	—
Promote	Am	27 Jn 06	—	—	—	—
Proof	Am	27 Jn 06	—	—	*	*
Proof-reader	Am	27 Jn 06	—	—	*	*
Property	Am	27 Jn 06	—	—	*	*
Prophecy	Am	27 Jn 06	—	—	*	*
Prospect	Am	27 Jn 06	—	—	*	*
Providential	Am	28 Jn 06	E	4 Jy 06	*	*
Prude	Am	28 Jn 06	E	4 Jy 06	*	*
Public	Am	28 Jn 06	E	4 Jy 06	—	—
Publish	Am	28 Jn 06	E	4 Jy 06	*	*
Push	Am	28 Jn 06	E	4 Jy 06	*	*
Pyrrhonism	Am	28 Jn 06	E	4 Jy 06	*	*
Queen	Am	28 Jn 06	E	4 Jy 06	*	*
Quill	Am	28 Jn 06	E	4 Jy 06	*	*
Quiver	Am	28 Jn 06	E	4 Jy 06	*	*
Quixotic	Am	28 Jn 06	E	4 Jy 06	*	*
Quorum	Am	29 Jn 06	—	—	*	*
Quotation	Am	29 Jn 06	—	—	*	*
Quotient	Am	29 Jn 06	—	—	*	*
Rabble	Am	29 Jn 06	—	—	*	*
Rack	Am	29 Jn 06	—	—	*	*
Radical	Am	29 Jn 06	—	—	—	—
Radicalism	Am	29 Jn 06	—	—	*	*
Radium	Am	29 Jn 06	—	—	*	*
Rags	Am	30 Jn 06	—	—	+	—
Railroad	Am	30 Jn 06	—	—	*	*
Ramshackle	Am	30 Jn 06	—	—	*	*
Rank	—	—	E	A	*	*
Ransom	—	—	E	A	*	*
Rapacity	—	—	E	A	*	*
Rarebit	—	—	E	A	*	*
Rascal	—	—	E	A	*	*
Rascality	—	—	E	A	*	*
Rash	—	—	E	A	*	*
Rational	—	—	E	A	*	*
Rattlesnake	—	—	E	A	*	*
Razor	—	—	E	A	*	*
Reach	—	—	E	A	*	*
Read	—	—	E	A	*	—
Reading	—	—	E	A	*	*
Realism	—	—	E	B	*	*
Reality	—	—	E	B	*	*
Really	—	—	E	B	*	*
Rear	—	—	E	B	*	*
Reason	—	—	E	B	*	*
Reason	—	—	E	B	*	*
Reasonable	—	—	E	B	*	*

WORD	DATE				C/DX	D
Rebel	—	—	E	B	*	*
Recollect	—	—	E	B	*	*
Reconciliation	—	—	E	B	*	*
Reconsider	—	—	—	—	*	*
Recount	—	—	—	—	*	*
Recreation	—	—	—	—	*	*
Recruit	—	—	—	—	*	*
Rector	—	—	—	—	*	*
Redemption	—	—	—	—	*	*
Redress	—	—	—	—	*	*
Red-skin	—	—	—	—	*	*
Redundant	—	—	—	—	*	*
Referendum	—	—	—	—	*	*
Reflection	—	—	—	—	*	*
Reform	—	—	—	—	*	*
Refuge	—	—	—	—	*	*
Refusal	—	—	—	—	*	*
Regalia	—	—	—	—	*	*
Religion	—	—	—	—	*	*
Reliquary	—	—	—	—	*	*
Renown	—	—	—	—	*	*
Reparation	—	—	—	—	*	*
Repartee	—	—	—	—	*	*
Repentance	—	—	—	—	*	*
Replica	—	—	—	—	*	*
Report	—	—	—	—	*	—
Reporter	—	—	—	—	*	*
Repose	—	—	—	—	*	*
Representative	—	—	—	—	*	*
Reprobation	—	—	—	—	*	*
Republic	—	—	—	—	*	*
Requiem	—	—	—	—	*	*
Resident	—	—	—	—	*	*
Resign	—	—	—	—	*	*
Resolute	—	—	—	—	*	*
Respectability	—	—	—	—	*	*
Respirator	—	—	—	—	*	*
Respite	—	—	—	—	*	*
Resplendent	—	—	—	—	*	*
Respond	—	—	—	—	*	*
Responsibility	—	—	—	—	*	*
Restitution	—	—	—	—	*	*
Restitutor	—	—	—	—	*	*
Retaliation	—	—	—	—	*	*
Retribution	—	—	—	—	*	*
Rice-water	—	—	—	—	*	*
Rich	—	—	—	—	*	*
Riches	—	—	—	—	*	*
Ridicule	—	—	—	—	*	*
Right	—	—	—	—	*	*
Righteousness	—	—	—	—	*	*
Rime	—	—	—	—	*	*

WORD	DATE				C/DX	D
Rimer [Rimester]	—	—	—	—	*	*
Riot	—	—	—	—	*	*
Reveille	—	—	—	—	*	*
Revelation	—	—	—	—	*	*
Reverence	—	—	—	—	*	*
Review	—	—	—	—	*	*
Revolution	—	—	—	—	*	*
Rhadomancer	—	—	—	—	*	*
Ribaldry	—	—	—	—	*	*
Ribroaster	—	—	—	—	*	*
R. I. P	—	—	—	—	*	*
Rite	—	—	—	—	*	*
Ritualism	—	—	—	—	*	*
Road	—	—	—	—	*	*
Robber	—	—	—	—	*	*
Romance	—	—	—	—	*	*
Rope	—	—	—	—	*	*
Rostrum	—	—	—	—	*	*
Roundhead	—	—	—	—	*	*
Rubbish	—	—	—	—	*	*
Ruin	—	—	—	—	*	*
Rum	—	—	—	—	*	*
Rumor	—	—	—	—	*	*
Russian	—	—	—	—	*	*
Sabbath	—	—	—	—	*	*
Sacerdotalist	—	—	—	—	*	*
Sacrament	—	—	—	—	*	*
Sacred	—	—	—	—	*	*
Safety-clutch	—	—	—	—	*	*
Saint	—	—	—	—	*	*
Salacity	—	—	—	—	*	*
Salamander	—	—	—	—	*	*
Sandlotter	—	—	—	—	*	*
Sarcophagus	—	—	—	—	*	*
Satan	—	—	—	—	*	*
Satiety [Aversion]	—	—	—	—	*	*
Satire	—	—	—	—	*	*
Satyr	—	—	—	—	*	*
Sauce	—	—	—	—	*	*
Saw	—	—	—	—	*	*
Scarabæus	—	—	—	—	*	*
Scarabee	—	—	—	—	*	*
Scarification	—	—	—	—	*	*
Scepter	—	—	—	—	*	*
Scimitar [Head]	—	—	—	—	*	*
Scrap-book	—	—	—	—	*	*
Scribbler	—	—	—	—	*	*
Scriptures	—	—	—	—	*	*
Seal [Great Seal]	—	—	—	—	—	*
Seine [Lace]	—	—	—	—	*	*
Self-esteem	—	—	—	—	*	*

WORD	DATE				C/DX	D
Self-evident	—	—	—	—	*	*
Selfish	—	—	—	—	*	*
Senate	—	—	—	—	*	*
Serial	—	—	—	—	*	*
Severalty	—	—	—	—	—	*
Sheriff	—	—	—	—	*	*
Siren	—	—	—	—	*	*
Slang	—	—	—	—	*	*
Smithareen	—	—	—	—	*	*
Sophistry	—	—	—	—	*	*
Sorcery	—	—	—	—	*	*
Soul	—	—	—	—	*	*
Spooker	—	—	—	—	*	*
Story	—	—	—	—	—	*
Success	—	—	—	—	*	*
Suffrage	—	—	—	—	*	*
Sycophant	—	—	—	—	*	*
Syllogism	—	—	—	—	*	*
Sylph	—	—	—	—	*	*
Symbol	—	—	—	—	*	*
Symbolic [Compunction]	—	—	—	—	*	*
T	—	—	—	—	*	*
Table d'hote	—	—	—	—	*	*
Tail	—	—	—	—	*	*
Take	—	—	—	—	*	*
Talk	—	—	—	—	*	*
Tariff	—	—	—	—	*	*
Technicality	—	—	—	—	*	*
Tedium	—	—	—	—	*	*
Teetotaler	—	—	—	—	*	*
Telephone	—	—	—	—	*	*
Telescope	—	—	—	—	*	*
Tenacity [Grip]	—	—	—	—	*	*
Theosophy	—	—	—	—	*	*
Tights	—	—	—	—	*	*
Tomb	—	—	—	—	*	*
Tope	—	—	—	—	*	*
Tortoise	—	—	—	—	*	*
Tree	—	—	—	—	*	*
Trial	—	—	—	—	—	*
Trichinosis	—	—	—	—	*	*
Trinity	—	—	—	—	*	*
Troglodyte	—	—	—	—	*	*
Truce	—	—	—	—	*	*
Truth	—	—	—	—	*	*
Truthful	—	—	—	—	*	*
Trust	—	—	—	—	*	*
Turkey	—	—	—	—	*	*
Twice	—	—	—	—	*	*
Type	—	—	—	—	*	*

WORD	DATE				C/DX	D
Tzetze Fly	—	—	—	—	*	*
Ubiquity	—	—	—	—	*	*
Ugliness	—	—	—	—	*	*
Ultimatum	—	—	—	—	*	*
Un-American	—	—	—	—	*	*
Unction	—	—	—	—	*	*
Understanding	—	—	—	—	*	*
Unitarian	—	—	—	—	*	*
Universalist	—	—	—	—	*	*
Urbanity	—	—	—	—	*	*
Usage	—	—	—	—	*	*
Uxoriousness	—	—	—	—	*	*
Valor	—	—	—	—	*	*
Vanity [Cackle]	—	—	—	—	*	*
Virtues	—	—	—	—	*	*
Vituperation	—	—	—	—	*	*
Vote	—	—	—	—	*	*
W	—	—	—	—	*	*
Wall Street	—	—	—	—	*	*
War	—	—	—	—	*	*
Washingtonian	—	—	—	—	*	*
Weaknesses	—	—	—	—	—	*
Weather	—	—	—	—	*	*
Wedding	—	—	—	—	*	*
Werewolf	—	—	—	—	*	*
Whangdepootenawah	—	—	—	—	—	*
Wheat	—	—	—	—	*	*
White	—	—	—	—	*	*
Widow	—	—	—	—	*	*
Wine	—	—	—	—	*	*
Wit	—	—	—	—	*	*
Witch	—	—	—	—	*	*
Witch	—	—	—	—	*	*
Witticism	—	—	—	—	*	*
Woman	—	—	—	—	*	*
Worms'-meat	—	—	—	—	*	*
Worship	—	—	—	—	*	*
Wrath	—	—	—	—	*	*
X	—	—	—	—	*	*
Yankee	—	—	—	—	*	*
Year	—	—	—	—	*	*
Yesterday	—	—	—	—	*	*
Yoke	—	—	—	—	*	*
Youth	—	—	—	—	*	*
Zany	—	—	—	—	—	*
Zanzibari	—	—	—	—	—	*
Zeal	—	—	—	—	*	*
Zenith	—	—	—	—	*	*
Zeus	—	—	—	—	*	*
Zigzag	—	—	—	—	*	*
Zoölogy	—	—	—	—	*	*

Am   *New York American*
C   *The Cynic's Word Book* (1906)
D   *The Devil's Dictionary* (1911)
Dx   Typesetting copy of *The Devil's Dictionary*
E   *San Francisco Examiner*
NL   *San Francisco News Letter and California Advertiser*
W   *Wasp*
*   Indicated item was contained in these volumes. Note that the last published word in C
    was "Lord." Subsequent items in the column C/Dx, beginning with "Lore," consist of
    clippings or new handwritten or typed definitions.
+   Canceled in Dx
A   Unidentified clipping in Dx
B   Unidentified clipping in Dx

Bracketed items indicate a previous or subsequent appearance of the basic definition.

BIBLIOGRAPHY

The Devil's Dictionary

A. FIRST APPEARANCES

"The Demon's Dictionary," *NL*, 25, no. 46 (11 Dec. 1875): 13. 48 definitions. Unsigned.

"The Devil's Dictionary," *W.* 79 columns:
  No. 240 (5 Mar. 1881): 149. 24 definitions. Unsigned.
  No. 241 (12 Mar. 1881): 165. 23 definitions. Unsigned.
  No. 242 (19 Mar. 1881): 182. 20 definitions. Unsigned.
  No. 243 (26 Mar. 1881): 198. 20 definitions Unsigned.
  No. 244 (2 Apr. 1881): 214 [misnumbered 212]. 15 definitions. As by B.
  No. 245 (9 Apr. 1881): 227. 10 definitions. Unsigned.
  No. 246 (16 Apr. 1881): 243. 10 definitions. Unsigned.
  No. 247 (23 Apr. 1881): 259. 15 definitions. As by B.
  No. 248 (30 Apr. 1881): 275. 23 definitions. As by B.
  No. 249 (7 May 1881): 291. 17 definitions. As by B.
  No. 250 (14 May 1881): 307. 13 definitions. As by B.
  No. 251 (21 May 1881): 323. 13 definitions. As by B.
  No. 253 (4 June 1881): 355. 12 definitions. Unsigned.
  No. 254 (11 June 1881): 374. 10 definitions. As by B.
  No. 255 (18 June 1881): 390. 13 definitions. As by B.
  No. 257 (2 July 1881): 6. 14 definitions. Unsigned.
  No. 259 (15 July 1881): 37. 14 definitions. Unsigned.
  No. 262 (5 Aug. 1881; dateline San Francisco, 2 Aug. 1881): 82. 11 definitions. Unsigned.
  No. 263 (12 Aug. 1881): 103. 19 definitions. Unsigned.
  No. 265 (26 Aug. 1881): 130. 14 definitions. Unsigned.
  No. 271 (7 Oct. 1881; dateline San Francisco, 3 Oct. 1881): 227. 11 definitions. As by B.
  No. 273 (21 Oct. 1881; dateline San Francisco, 15 Oct. 1881): 259. 13 definitions. As by B.
  No. 274 (28 Oct. 1881): 285. 10 definitions. As by B.
  No. 276 (11 Nov. 1881): 318. 13 definitions. Unsigned.
  No. 279 (2 Dec. 1881): 366. 7 definitions. As by B.
  No. 286 (20 Jan. 1882): 38. 20 definitions. As by B.
  No. 290 (17 Feb. 1882): 102. 13 definitions. As by B.
  No. 292 (3 Mar. 1882): 134. 15 definitions. Unsigned.
  No. 295 (24 Mar. 1882): 179. 12 definitions. Unsigned.
  No. 297 (7 Apr. 1882): 211. 18 definitions. As by B.
  No. 312 (22 July 1882): 459. 9 definitions. Unsigned.
  No. 315 (12 Aug. 1882): 501. 7 definitions. Unsigned.
  No. 334 (23 Dec. 1882): 834. 13 definitions. As by B.
  No. 342 (17 Feb. 1883): 11. 12 definitions. As by B.

No. 345 (10 Mar. 1883): 3. 19 definitions. Unsigned.
No. 352 (28 Apr. 1883): 5. 14 definitions. Unsigned.
No. 375 (6 Oct. 1883): 11. 12 definitions. Unsigned.
No. 407 (17 May 1884): 6. 13 definitions. Unsigned.
No. 408 (24 May 1884): 3. 15 definitions. Unsigned.
No. 410 (7 June 1884): 3. 16 definitions. Unsigned.
No. 413 (28 June 1884): 6. 5 definitions. Unsigned.
No. 418 (2 Aug. 1884): 6. 8 definitions. Unsigned.
No. 425 (20 Sept. 1884): 6. 11 definitions. Unsigned.
No. 435 (29 Nov. 1884): 6. 8 definitions. Unsigned.
No. 436 (6 Dec. 1884): 3. 5 definitions. Unsigned.
No. 437 (13 Dec. 1884): 6. 13 definitions. Unsigned.
No. 441 (10 Jan. 1885): 3. 13 definitions. Unsigned.
No. 442 (17 Jan. 1885): 6. 4 definitions. Unsigned. (No definitions reprinted in *D*.)
No. 443 (24 Jan. 1885): 6. 10 definitions. Unsigned.
No. 447 (21 Feb. 1885): 6. 18 definitions. Unsigned.
No. 448 (28 Feb. 1885): 3. 14 definitions. Unsigned.
No. 449 (7 Mar. 1885): 3. 11 definitions. Unsigned.
No. 450 (14 Mar. 1885): 3. 10 definitions. Unsigned.
No. 452 (28 Mar. 1885): 3. 11 definitions. Unsigned.
No. 453 (4 Apr. 1885): 3. 10 definitions. Unsigned.
No. 454 (11 Apr. 1885): 3. 10 definitions. Unsigned.
No. 456 (25 Apr. 1885): 6. 13 definitions. Unsigned.
No. 459 (16 May 1885): 6. 6 definitions. Unsigned.
No. 460 (23 May 1885): 6. 16 definitions. Unsigned.
No. 468 (18 July 1885): 5. 10 definitions. Unsigned.
No. 471 (8 Aug. 1885): 3. 14 definitions. Unsigned.
No. 473 (22 Aug. 1885): 2. 16 definitions. Unsigned.
No. 474 (29 Aug. 1885): 3. 13 definitions. Unsigned.
No. 476 (12 Sept. 1885): 3. 15 definitions. Unsigned.
No. 477 (19 Sept. 1885): 6. 11 definitions. Unsigned.
No. 478 (26 Sept. 1885): 3. 11 definitions. Unsigned.
No. 479 (3 Oct. 1885): 6. 7 definitions. Unsigned.
No. 480 (10 Oct. 1885): 3. 9 definitions. Unsigned.
No. 481 (17 Oct. 1885): 6. 8 definitions. Unsigned.
No. 482 (24 Oct. 1885): 6. 5 definitions. Unsigned.
No. 484 (7 Nov. 1885): 6. 7 definitions. Unsigned.
No. 486 (21 Nov. 1885): 3. 13 definitions. Unsigned.
No. 490 (19 Dec. 1885): 6. 11 definitions. Unsigned.
No. 493 (9 Jan. 1886): 3. 13 definitions. Unsigned.
No. 498 (13 Feb. 1886): 7. 11 definitions. Unsigned.
No. 501 (6 Mar. 1886): 6. 9 definitions. Unsigned.
No. 509 (1 May 1886): 2. 6 definitions. Unsigned.
No. 516 (19 June 1886): 3. 14 definitions. Unsigned.
No. 524 (14 Aug. 1886): 6. 10 definitions. Unsigned.

"The Cynic's Dictionary." All signed by Ambrose Bierce, except as noted. 35 in *Am* columns; 30 in *E*.

E, 4 Sept. 1887: 4. 14 definitions. As by B.
E, 29 Apr. 1888: 4. 15 definitions. As by B.

Am, 26 June 1904: [22]; *E*, 10 July 1904: [44]. 11 definitions.
Am, 9 July 1904: [14]; *E*, 17 July 1904: [44]. 18 definitions.

Am, 23 July 1904: [12]; *E,* 2 Aug. 1904: [16]. 4 definitions.
Am, 3 Aug. 1904: [12]; *E,* 13 Aug. 1904: [14]. 9 definitions.
Am, 6 Aug. 1904: [12]; *E,* 19 Aug. 1904: [16]. 8 definitions.
Am, 13 Aug. 1904: [12]; *E,* 15 Nov. 1904: [16]. 11 definitions.
Am, 26 Aug. 1904: [12]; *E,* 13 Oct. 1904: [16]. 9 definitions.
Am, 30 Aug. 1904: [12]; no appearance found in *E.* 17 definitions.
Am, 3 Sept. 1904: [12]; *E,* 9 Sept. 1904: [14]. 14 definitions.
Am, 13 Sept. 1904: [12]; *E,* 8 Nov. 1904: [16]. 9 definitions. (No definitions reprinted
   in *D.*)
Am, 22 Sept. 1904: [12]; *E,* 30 Sept. 1904: [16]. 13 definitions.
Am, 23 Sept. 1904: [12]; *E,* 14 Oct. 1904: [16]. 12 definitions.
Am, 26 Sept. 1904: [12]; *E,* 6 Oct. 1904: [16]. 6 definitions.
Am, 27 Sept. 1904: [12]; *E,* 28 Oct. 1904: [16]. 4 definitions.
Am, 5 Oct. 1904: [12]. 3 definitions.
Am, 6 Oct. 1904: [14]. 6 definitions.
E, 31 Oct. 1904: [14] (combines *Am* of 5 and 6 Oct. 1904). 9 definitions.
Am, 17 Oct. 1904: [14]; *E,* 24 Oct. 1904: [16]. 9 definitions.
Am, 5 Nov. 1904: [16]; *E,* 12 Nov. 1904: [16]. 11 definitions.
Am, 19 Nov. 1904: [14]; *E,* 28 Nov. 1904: [14]. 6 definitions.
Am, 22 Nov. 1904: [16]; *E,* 2 Dec. 1904: [16]. 4 definitions.
Am, 1 Dec. 1904: [14]; *E,* 8 Dec. 1904: [16]. 7 definitions.
Am, 26 Dec. 1904: [12]; *E,* 3 Jan. 1905: [20]. 13 definitions.
Am, 7 Jan. 1905: [14]; *E,* 14 Jan. 1905: [16]. 11 definitions.
Am, 11 Jan. 1905: [14]; *E,* 18 Mar. 1905: [16]. 10 definitions.
Am, 27 Jan. 1905: [16]; *E,* 11 Feb. 1905: [16]. 6 definitions.
Am, 22 Feb. 1906: [16]; no appearance found in *E.* 20 definitions.
Unpublished proof, c. Feb.–Mar. 1906. Platter.
Am, 6 Mar. 1906: [16]; *E,* 12 Mar. 1906: [16]. 12 definitions.
Am, 16 Mar. 1906: [16]; *E,* 21 Mar. 1906: [20]. 14 definitions.
Am, 6 Apr. 1906: [16]; *E,* 11 Apr. 1906: [22]. 10 definitions.

"The Cynic's Word Book."
   Am, 30 May 1906: [16]; *E,* 20 June 1906: [14]. 15 definitions.
   Am, 14 June 1906: [18]; *Los Angeles Examiner,* 28 July 1906: [20]; no appearance found in *E.*
      10 definitions.
   Am, 27 June 1906: 18; no appearance found in *E.* 7 definitions.
   Am, 28 June 1906: 18; *E,* 4 July 1906: 14. 10 definitions; *Los Angeles Examiner,* 17 July 1906:
      [22]. (Combines *Am* of 27 and 28 June 1906.) 17 definitions.
   Am, 29 June 1906: 18; *Los Angeles Examiner,* 17 July 1906: [22]; no appearance found in *E.* 8
      definitions.
   Am, 11 July 1906: [16]; *Los Angeles Examiner,* 28 June 1906: [20]; no appearance found in *E.*
      3 definitions.
   Two clippings present in typesetting copy, but no appearance found in *Am* or *E:* one
      contains 13 definitions, the other 10 definitions.

The Cynic's Word Book. 1906. 17 previously unpublished definitions.
The Devil's Dictionary. 1911. 197 previously unpublished definitions; another 6 published under
   new names.

B. APPEARANCES OF VERSE PRIOR TO INCLUSION IN *THE DEVIL'S DICTIONARY*

All initial appearances of verse are untitled except as noted.
Beg. From "Prattle" (*E,* 11 Apr. 1897: 6).

Christian. From "The Passing Show" (*E*, 26 Nov. 1899: 14; *J*, 3 Dec. 1899: 26).

Critic. From "Prattle" (*E*, 29 Jan. 1893: 6).

Cross. From "Prattle" (*E*, 21 Oct. 1895: 6).

Heathen. From "Prattle" (*E*, 16 May 1897: 18).

Lawyer [verses in *C* only]. From "Prattle" (*E*, 6 Nov. 1887: 4).

Outcome. From "Brevigraphs" (*W*, 10 Mar. 1886: 6), as "A Lacking Factor."

Out-of-doors. As "Communing with Nature" (*W*, 25 Nov. 1881: 342). As by "B."

Redemption. From "Prattle" (*E*, 13 Jan. 1889: 4).

Renown. From "Prattle" (*E*, 15 Dec. 1889: 6).

Repentance. From [Editorial] (*W*, 21 Aug. 1886: 5). Unsigned.

Reporter. From "The Passing Show" (*E*, 13 Aug. 1899: 12).

Respite. From "Prattle" (*W*, 17 Oct. 1885: 5).

Responsibility. From [Editorial] (*W*, 9 Oct. 1886: 5). Unsigned.

Retribution. From "Prattle" (*E*, 2 Mar. 1890: 6).

Right. From "Prattle" (*E*, 10 June 1888: 4).

Safety-clutch. From "Prattle" (*E*, 23 Sept. 1888: 4).

Scarabee. From "Prattle" (*W*, 26 Dec. 1885: 11).

Scrap-book. As "To Fr-nk M. P-xl-y" (*W*, 1 Aug. 1885: 6).

Seine [Lace]. From "The Devil's Dictionary" (*W*, 6 Mar. 1886: 6).

Severalty. From "Prattle" (*E*, 4 Sept. 1892: 6).

Siren [as in Dx]. From "Prattle" (*E*, 12 Aug. 1888: 4).

Smithareen. From "Prattle" (*J*, 5 July 1896 [not seen]; *E*, 12 July 1896: 6).

Sophistry. From "Prattle" (*E*, 16 Sept. 1888: 4).

Success. From "The Passing Show" (*Am*, 21 Feb. 1904: 24; 6 Mar. 1904: 45).

Sycophant. From "Prattle" (*W*, 6 Jan. 1882: 6).

Symbolic [Compunction]. From "The Devil's Dictionary" (*W*, 5 Aug. 1881: 82).

Table d'Hôte. From "Prattle" (*W*, 16 Apr. 1881: 244).

Tariff. From "Prattle" (*E*, 8 July 1888: 4).

Tenacity [Grip]. From "The Devil's Dictionary" (*W*, 28 Mar. 1885: 5).

Tortoise. As "To My Pet Tortoise" (*Am*, 15 July 1901: 12; *E*, 18 July 1901: 14).

Urbanity. From "Prattle" (*W*, 12 Mar. 1881: 164).

Vanity [Cackle]. From "The Devil's Dictionary" (*W*, 4 June 1881: 355).

Wall Street. From "The Views of One," (*Am*, 3 Apr. 1905: 16).

Weather. From "Prattle" (*E*, 10 June 1894: 6).

Whangdepootanowah. From "Prattle" (*E*, 1 May 1892: 6).

Yesterday. From "Prattle" (*W*, 9 Dec. 1882: 773).

C. SUPPLEMENTARY DEFINITIONS

A1. From "Prattle" (*E*, 15 Sept. 1889: 4).

A2. From "Prattle" (*E*, 15 Mar. 1891: 6).

A3. From "Prattle" (*E*, 23 Dec. 1888: 4).

A4. From "The Passing Show" (*E*, 19 Nov. 1899: 14).

A5. From "Prattle" (*E*, 4 Nov. 1888: 4).

A6. From "Prattle" (*E*, 4 Mar. 1894: 6).

A7. From "A Spread of Quick-Lunch Wisdom for Busy Readers" (*Am*, 2 Oct. 1903: 14; *E*, 17 Oct. 1903: 16).

A8. From "Æsop's Fables, Applied" (*E*, 19 Feb. 1891: 6).

A9. From "Prattle" (*E*, 22 Nov. 1891: 6).

A10. From "The Passing Show" (*Am* and *E*, 13 May 1900: 26).

A11. From "Prattle" (*E*, 20 Nov. 1892: 6).

A12. From "Prattle" (*E*, 18 Sept. 1892: 6).

A13. From "Prattle" (*E*, 24 July 1887: 4).
A14. From "The Views of One" (*Am*, 21 Dec. 1905: 16; *E*, 1 Jan. 1906: 16).
A15. From "Prattle" (*E*, 25 Nov. 1888: 4).
A16. From "Prattle" (*E*, 24 July 1887: 4).
A17. From "Prattle" (*E*, 27 Aug. 1893: 6).
A18. From "Prattle" (*E*, 11 Mar. 1888: 4).
A19. Source unknown.
A20. From "Prattle" (*W*, 30 Dec. 1881: 438).
A21. From "Prattle" (*W*, 16 Aug. 1884: 5).
A22. From "Prattle" (*E*, 22 Jan. 1888: 4).
A23. From "Prattle" (*E*, 3 Apr. 1887: 4).
A24. From "Prattle" (*E*, 7 Aug. 1887: 4).
A25. From "The Views of One" (*Am*, 29 Mar. 1905: 16; *E*, 6 Apr. 1905: 16).
A26. From "The Views of One" (*Am*, 17 Apr. 1905: 16; *E*, 26 Apr. 1905: 16).
A27. From "A Whopper" (*W*, 28 Oct. 1881: 278). Unsigned.
A28. From "The Lone Epitapher of Laurel Hill" (*W*, 22 Sept. 1883: 6). Unsigned.
A29. From "Prattle" (*E*, 22 May 1887: 4).
A30. From "Prattle" (*E*, 24 July 1887: 4).
A31. Source unknown.
A32. Source unknown.
A33. From "Three in a Box–A Drametta." Exists as a clipping with title in AB's scrapbooks at the University of Virginia. Identified as being from the *New York Morning Telegraph* (4 July 1901).
A34. From "The Views of One" (*Am*, 17 Jan. 1905: 16).
A35. From "The Views of One" (*Am*, 1 July 1905: 16; *E*, 7 July 1905: 16).

D. OTHER DEFINITIONS

B1. From "Concerning Tickets" (*Californian* 7, no. 32 [28 Dec. 1867]: 8). As by A. Gwinnett.
B2. From "The Town Crier" (*NL*, 26 Dec. 1868: 9). Unsigned.
B3. "Webster Revised" (*NL*, 30 Jan. 1869: 3). Unsigned.
B4. From "The Town Crier" (*NL*, 3 July 1869: 11). Unsigned.
B5. From "'News Letter Aphorisms'–By Our Special Philosopher" (*NL*, 24 July 1869: 4).
B6. From "The Town Crier" (*NL*, 14 Aug. 1869: 11). Unsigned.
B7. From "The Town Crier" (*NL*, 9 Mar. 1872: 9). Unsigned.
B8. From "The Town Crier" (*Fi*, 15 Feb. 1873: 10). Unsigned.
B9. From "Sacred Themes" (*ND*, 1873: 100).
B10. From "Brief Seasons of Intellectual Dissipation" (*Fu*, 5 July 1873: 7); rpt. in *Cobwebs from an Empty Skull* (p. 99).
B'1. From "The Prattler" (*Ar*, 1 Apr. 1877: 5).
B12. From "The Prattler" (*Ar*, 2 June 1877: 5).
B13. From "Prattle" (*Ar*, 17 Nov. 1877: 1). Unsigned.
B14. From "Prattle" (*Ar*, 14 Sept. 1878: 9). As by B.
B15. From "Prattle" (*W*, 4 Nov. 1881: 293). As by B.
B16. From "Prattle" (*W*, 27 Jan. 1883: 5).
B17. From "Prattle" (*W*, 20 Feb. 1886: 5). Unsigned.
B18. From [Editorial] (*W*, 18 Sept. 1886: 5). Unsigned.
B19. From "Prattle" (*E*, 29 July 1888: 4).
B20. From "Prattle" (*E*, 14 Apr. 1889: 4).
B21. From "Prattle" (*E*, 22 Sept. 1889: 4).
B22. From "Prattle" (*E*, 1 Dec. 1889: 6).
B23. From "Prattle" (*E*, 9 Feb. 1890: 6).

B24. From "Prattle" (*E*, 6 Apr. 1890: 18).

B25. From "Prattle" (*E*, 31 Aug. 1890: 6).

B26. From "Fables and Anecdotes" (*E*, 24 Oct. 1891: 6).

B27. From "Prattle" (*E*, 18 Feb. 1894: 6).

B28. From "Prattle" (*E*, 20 Jan. 1895: 6).

B29. From "Prattle" (*E*, 28 July 1895: 6).

B30. From "Prattle" (*E*, 2 May 1897: 18; *J*, 16 May 1897: 50 [as "Ambrose Bierce's Peculiar View of the Turk"]).

B31. From "The Views of One" (*Am*, 7 Apr. 1905: 16; *E*, 13 Apr. 1905: 16).

B32. "The Future Historian: The Dispersal" (*Co*, Mar. 1909: 472; rpt. as "The Reversion to Barbarism" [*CW* 12.344]).

B33. n.d. Reported in Carey McWilliams, *Ambrose Bierce: A Biography* (New York: Albert and Charles Boni, 1929), 257.

E. VERSES REPRINTED IN *BLACK BEETLES IN AMBER* (*CW* 4 [1911])

Epigram. From "The Devil's Dictionary" (*W*, 17 May 1884: 6); as "An Epigrammatist" (*CW* 5.203).

Grass. From "The Devil's Dictionary" (*W*, 14 Mar. 1885: 3); as "Famine in Prosperity" (*CW* 5.202).

Fig-Leaf. From "The Devil's Dictionary" (*W*, 20 Sept. 1884: 6); as "Fig Leaf" (*CW* 5.203).

Concatenate. From "The Devil's Dictionary" (*W*, 5 Aug. 1881: 82); as "A Mine for Reformers" (*CW* 5.207).

PRIMARY BIBLIOGRAPHY

Black Beetles in Amber. San Francisco and New York: Western Authors Publishing Co., 1892; rpt. Upper Saddle River, NJ: Literature House, 1970.

"[Clippings] From which to select and prepare additions to *The Devil's Dictionary* if needed." Ms. Bancroft Library, Berkeley, CA. Fifty items. Sources listed under "Supplementary Definitions."

Cobwebs from an Empty Skull (as by "Dod Grile"). London and New York: George Routledge and Sons, 1874.

The Collected Works of Ambrose Bierce. New York and Washington, D.C.: Neale Publishing Co. (dates as indicated); New York: Gordian Press, 1966: I. *Ashes of the Beacon; The Land Beyond the Blow; For the Ahkoond; John Smith, Liberator;* and *Bits of Autobiography* (1909); II. *In the Midst of Life (Tales of Soldiers and Civilians)* (1909); III. *Can Such Things Be?* (1910); IV. *Shapes of Clay* (1910); V. *Black Beetles in Amber* (1911); VI. *The Monk and the Hangman's Daughter;* and *Fantastic Fables* (1911); VII. *The Devil's Dictionary* (1911); VIII. *Negligible Tales; On with the Dance;* and *Epigrams* (1911); IX. *Tangential Views* (1911); X. *The Opinionator* (1911); XI. *Antepenultimata* (1912); XII. *In Motley: Kings of Beasts; Two Administrations;* and *Miscellaneous* (1912).

The Cynic's Word Book. New York: Doubleday, Page and Co.; London: Arthur F. Bird, 1906.

The Devil's Dictionary. Typesetting copy (MS., Huntington Library and Art Gallery, San Marino, CA).

The Fiend's Delight (as by "Dod Grile"). London: John Camden Hotten, [July 1873]; New York: A. L. Luyster, 1873.

Nuggets and Dust Panned Out in California (as by "Dod Grile"; "Collected and Loosely Arranged by J. Milton Sloluck"). London: Chatto and Windus, [1873].

Shapes of Clay. San Francisco: W. E. Wood, 1903.

A Sole Survivor: Bits of Autobiography. Ed. S. T. Joshi and David E. Schultz. Knoxville: University of Tennessee Press, 1998.

Write It Right: A Little Blacklist of Literary Faults. New York and Washington, D.C.: Neale Publishing Co., [Oct.] 1909.

SECONDARY BIBLIOGRAPHY

Bierce, Ambrose. *The Enlarged Devil's Dictionary.* Ed. Ernest J. Hopkins. Garden City, NY: Doubleday, 1967.

Davidson, Cathy N., ed. *Critical Essays on Ambrose Bierce.* Boston: G. K. Hall, 1982.

Fatout, Paul. *Ambrose Bierce: The Devil's Lexicographer.* Norman: University of Oklahoma Press, 1951.

Grenander, M. E. *Ambrose Bierce.* New York: Twayne, 1971.

Highsmith, James M. "The Forms of Burlesque in *The Devil's Dictionary.*" *Satire Newsletter* 7 (1970): 115–27.

Joshi, S. T., and David E. Schultz. *Ambrose Bierce: An Annotated Bibliography of Primary Sources.* Westport, CT: Greenwood Press, 1999.

McWilliams, Carey. *Ambrose Bierce: A Biography.* New York: A. and C. Boni, 1929.

———. "Introduction." *The Devil's Dictionary.* New York: Sagamore Press, 1957.

Morris, Roy, Jr. *Ambrose Bierce: Alone in Bad Company.* New York: Crown, 1995.

[Neale, Walter.] [Prospectus to] *The Collected Works of Ambrose Bierce: Ten Octavo Volumes.* New York and Washington, D.C.: Neale Publishing Co., [1908].

O'Connor, Richard. *Ambrose Bierce: A Biography.* Boston: Little, Brown, 1967.

[Unsigned.] "A Cynic's Word Book: Some New Definitions." *T. P.'s Weekly* (12 July 1907): 51.

[Unsigned.] [Review of *The Collected Works,* Vols. VII–X.] *Athenæum* (16 Sept. 1911): 322–23.

Scheffauer, Herman. "The Death of Satire." *Fortnightly Review* 99, no. 6 (whole number 558) (June 1913): 1188–99.

Smith, H. Greenbough. "Bierce's Devil Dictionary." *Biblio* 4 (July 1924): 678–80.

INDEX

Hubbell, Dr., 289
Huck, Joel, 17, 239
Huckle, Gat, 73
Hudibras (Butler), 275
Huggyns, Berosus, 30, 226, 281
Hugo, Victor, 126, 135, 253, 314
Humboldt, Alexander von, 106, 310
Hungarians, 114
Hunsiker, Hannibal, 234
Huntington, Collis P., 155, 269–70, 321

Idiot's Unabridged Dictionary, 266
Iliad (Homer), 253–54, 291, 312, 325, 345–46
"Immortality," 313
"Impostor, An," 344
"In Contumaciam," 343
"In Inventorum Bombardae" (Milton), 308
"In the Beginning," 347
"In the Infancy of 'Trusts,'" 343
"Incivism," 313
"Inconsolable Widow, The," 314
Indians of North America, 106, 128, 181, 195, 197, 213–14, 237–38, 301, 345
"Infant Crying for the Light, An," 323
Ingalls, John James, 257, 347
Ingersoll, Robert G., 50, 291, 329–30
Ingleside, 308
"Inspired Performance, An," 308
"Insurance in Ancient America," 315, 317, 332
"Is the Human Race Declining in Stature?," 291
Isabella II (Queen of Spain), 6, 272
Iscariot, Judas, 11, 57, 72, 274, 275, 293
Islam, 6, 14, 113, 272, 281, 314, 317. *See also* Muslims
Israelites. *See* Jews
Italian language, 23, 35, 121
Itama, Shusi, 210

J., G. *See* Jape, Gassalasca, S.J.
"J. F. B.," 339
Jackson, John P., 258, 344
Jackson, T. J., 334
Jacob, 138, 170, 316
Jakak-Zotp, 167
Jape, Gassalasca, S.J., 3, 6, 10, 13, 14, 16, 17, 18, 23, 26, 33, 35, 46, 50, 51, 61, 65, 79, 86, 94, 108, 113, 119, 130, 147, 155, 193, 200, 220, 222, 225, 271–72, 273, 288
Jefferson, Thomas, xviii
Jesuits, 271–72
Jesus Christ, xii–xiii, xxvii (n. 11), 35, 128,

231, 238, 241, 274, 276, 280, 282, 284, 301, 319, 320, 326, 337, 345, 348
Jews, 14, 91, 108–9, 110, 205, 278, 311, 316; as Israelites, 162, 311
Jex, 305
Jhones, Bettel K., 27
Jijiji Ri, 210
Joab, 346
"Joaquin Miller on Joaquin Miller," 324
Job, 149
Jocordy, Jebel, 13
John, Friar, 90, 305
John, St., 336
John of the Cross, St., 283
John the Baptist, 34, 283
John the Divine, St., 200
Johnes, Squatol, 49
Johnson, Samuel, 9, 29, 37, 39, 179, 266, 273, 281, 285, 303, 304, 319, 328
Johnson, Thompson, 194
Joinville, Jean, Sire de, 11, 274
Jones, Halcyon, 237, 309, 345
Jones, Opaline, 160
Joop, Averil, 174
Jorace, 22, 278
Jordan, David Starr, 149, 319
Joshua, 195
Jove. *See* Jupiter
Joy, Charles F., 218, 328, 341
Joyce, John Alexander, 220, 341
Judibras, 12, 15, 166, 182, 186
Jukes, Aramis, 193
Juno, 123
Jupiter (or Jove), 16, 23, 39, 245, 316
"Jupiter Doke, Brigadier-General," 333, 337
"Jury in Ancient America, The," 274, 317

K., R. S., 157
Kalevala, 345
Kalloch, Isaac Smith, 276
Kant, Immanuel, 232, 344
Kearney, Denis, 207, 277, 337–38, 344
Kennedy, Miss, 268
Khan, Kubla, 236
Khayyam, Omar, 99, 276
"Kingdom of Tortirra, The," 295–96, 332
"Kings of Beasts" ("Little Johnny" sketches), 275, 278, 317
Kip, William Ingraham, 110, 277, 304, 311
Kipling, Rudyard, 346
Knickerbocker, Deidrich, 330
Kosciusko, Thaddeus, 87, 304, 319
"Kubla Khan" (Coleridge), 236, 344

CPSIA information can be obtained
at www.ICGtesting.com
Printed in the USA
LVHW04s0303290918
591728LV00004B/5/P